D1232129

THE TWO NATIONS

THE TWO NATIONS

Aspects of the Development of Race Relations
in the Rhodesias and Nyasaland

RICHARD GRAY

Issued under the auspices of the
Institute of Race Relations
OXFORD UNIVERSITY PRESS
LONDON NEW YORK TORONTO
1960

Oxford University Press, Amen House, London E.C.4

GLASGOW NEW YORK TORONTO MELBOURNE WELLINGTON
BOMBAY CALCUTTA MADRAS KARACHI KUALA LUMPUR
CAPE TOWN IBADAN NAIROBI ACCRA

PRINTED IN GREAT BRITAIN

CONTENTS

MAPS

Grateful acknowledgement is made to the International African Institute for permission to use the material quoted from T. Cullen Young's article in *Africa*, vol. xi, p. 68.

FOREWORD

'I was told that the Privileged and the People formed Two Nations.' These words are to be found in Disraeli's novel *Sybil or The Two Nations* and they were written of England just over a hundred years ago. They illustrate very clearly the theme which emerges as outstanding from the mass of detail—sayings, thoughts, Blue Books, Acts of Parliament—which Richard Gray has collected about Rhodesia, and that is why *The Two Nations* has been borrowed as the title of this book.

It was surely inevitable that to begin with there should be very little understanding between peoples so utterly different in their background as the Bantu tribes of Rhodesia and the British and Afrikaners who made the bulk of the first settlers. At the end of the great Victorian period, the differences were taken for granted and there was no question that the two could have much to say to each other. It was only after the First World War that it became necessary to express as a conscious opinion what before had been a matter of course. Legal barriers were then built and a deliberate policy of segregation and separation was adopted. This was the Two-Pyramid policy; it was expounded in Parliament and the Press and on the whole most people regarded it as wise and enlightened. In philosophy it was very like what in the Union of South Africa today is called separate development, though less rigid and less formulated. After the Second World War this policy was abandoned and a beginning made of an alternative and opposed ideal of bringing the two nations together in partnership. But it is much easier to sow suspicion than to get rid of it; by any reckoning the story has an element of tragedy. Looked at today, what the African wanted in the thirties seems pathetically moderate, but by the time the privileged—with a goodwill and an effort of imagination that must not be under-rated—were ready to meet their wishes, waiting had made the people bitter and they wanted more. 'Partnership', which would have been welcomed as a generous offer a few years earlier, was by now too often regarded as a trap. Today there are sharply divided opinions about Rhodesia's future, but everyone, surely, who has looked at the country's problem with any honesty must agree that there are two nations, black and white, which speak to each other infrequently and between which lie wide areas of misunderstanding.

This has a lamentable consequence in the United Kingdom. Visitors to Rhodesia are almost always visitors to one of the two nations and not to the other. There is one stream of inquirers who stay with leading figures in the Federation, with Governors, Ministers, the managers of mines and businesses—all people who are working with vigour and courage to make the Federation a success and who very naturally show their guests every sign of co-operation and understanding they can find. Ten years ago such visitors would hardly have spoken to any African but a servant; today they do meet Africans of another class, but each meeting is apt to be an occasion. It is arranged; there is a constraint. The sentiments expressed will not be those which either side would put with unbuttoned ease across the table in his own home; sometimes they will deliberately be meant to please and reassure. The visitor who forms part of this stream will hardly establish very intimate terms with any African who would stand much chance of being chosen as their representative by any large body of Africans. Nor —unless he has a good deal of time to spare and makes a considerable effort—is he very likely to see much of the European artisan: the man whose work may be done by an African in Nyasaland but not in Southern Rhodesia, a compositor, for instance, or a bricklayer, the man whose job is threatened by African advancement. Such a visitor is likely to come back to England convinced that in spite of many difficulties the idea of partnership is making headway, that things are moving as fast as it is wise to let them, and that there are grounds for moderate optimism. This was what he hoped to find.

There is another and smaller stream of visitors whose experience and reactions are very different. It is composed of people who are in general suspicious of the good intentions of governments and managers, particularly in a colonial situation, and at the same time generously concerned to do justice to the poor and downtrodden. Visitors of this stream frequently stay with people who share the generous concern, if not the suspicion. They do see the kind of African who is ready to voice the grievances of his people without restraint. They are likely to hear many stories of what is felt as an intolerable wrong—stories to which there is sometimes, perhaps always, another side, but a side which will not have been heard or understood by the African who tells the story. These visitors, like the first, are confirmed in views they had perhaps tentatively formed before they left home; they, like the first, have seen one nation, not two.

This difficulty of communication is not peculiar to Rhodesia. It exists in England even today between classes; it must have been stronger a hundred years ago. Dickens never quite bridged it; everyone knows that he could not draw a gentleman. Disraeli wrote from the other side of the barrier; the brilliance of the opening chapter of *Sybil*—the talk in the club on the eve of the Derby —was quite beyond Dickens. But though the young Disraeli had tried to look across the barrier, though he wrote with sympathy and understanding of the other nation, though he achieved, perhaps from his Jewish ancestry and his own sense of separation, a certain detachment, his working men are no more convincing than Dickens' gentlemen. Yet both Dickens and Disraeli were men of far more imagination and sympathy than most; for most the barrier was as absolute as in Miss Austen's novels.

The analogy between Rhodesia in the twentieth century and England in the nineteenth could obviously be carried too far; so indeed can every historical analogy. Here what is different is perhaps as important as what is like. Yet no one who studies the two sets of circumstances can fail to be impressed by the similarity of the responses which are often made by the privileged as well as by the people. In Chapter II of this book there is an example. The farmers in England in 1838 said to a Commission just what the farmers in Rhodesia said in 1925: 'You must not give the labourer land of his own or he will not work for us.' The sentiment, almost the words, are identical; that one set of labourers was black and

the other white makes no difference. And the more one reads of
the two periods the more one is struck by the patience with which the
poor in both sets of circumstances endured their hardships and
the moderation with which—to begin with—they stated their
claims. And in both cases kindly and humane people among the
privileged were able to shut their eyes and ears to what was going
on around them and to persuade themselves—if they thought
about the matter at all—that the poor were beings of quite a
different order whose needs were quite different from their own.
In both cases there is tragedy; claims for redress were put moder-
ately and ignored, and from time to time patience gave way to
moments of impassioned bitterness. Richard Gray in this book
quotes a description of what happened in Bulawayo in 1948 which
needs only a few words of alteration to be applicable to the rising
of the southern farm labourers in Hampshire, Wiltshire, and
Dorset in 1830.[1]

Though the analogy must not be pressed too far, the re-
semblances are enough to make it worth considering for a moment
the solution—a partial solution, no doubt—which the English
found to the problem of containing two nations within one. It
was partial; the difficulty is still with us. Yet we can claim some
success; profound changes in the structure of English life have
taken place without Englishmen killing each other very often.
What happened is spoken of as due to Whig policy, a Whig revolution. But not the least interesting fact about it is the part
played by those who were by no means predisposed to the philosophy behind it. It was Disraeli who saw and expressed the
dilemma more clearly than anyone else on his side of the barrier;
he came to a solution not by way of theory but by the logic of
facts. He was not a man who supposed that democracy was in itself a good or bad thing; he would probably have said that on the
whole government should be for the people rather than by the
people. But he understood as well perhaps as any man in England
the meaning of politics and the compulsion of fact. It was in
criticism of Sir Robert Peel that he uttered one of his most famous
phrases, but he must have used it with a touch of admiration even

[1] J. L. & B. Hammond, *The Village Labourer* (Longmans, Green & Co., 1911).

at the time, and twenty years later he did just the same thing him-self. When he introduced the Reform Bill of 1867, he caught the Whigs bathing and walked away with their clothes more truly than Sir Robert had ever done. Nor was it an accident that he put into the mouth of a character in one of his novels a definition of a sound Conservative Government as 'Tory men and Whig measures'. He took over from the Whigs the policy of gradually extending the franchise from the few to the many; realist that he was, Disraeli saw that it was the only alternative to repression and made it his own. It was thanks to him that the policy of the first Reform Bill was not exclusively a party policy but became an English policy, in which both parties strove to outdo the other. It would indeed be possible to argue that, at least on this question of the extension of the franchise, there was really only one party in England.[2] There were those who accepted the policy as a matter of principle and those who saw that as a matter of common sense it had to be done. This was the distinction, and it is also to be seen among voters in Rhodesia.

For the Tories, the Reform Bill of 1867 was a leap in the dark. It meant sharing power and a gamble on the chance that the new electorate would prove a solid element in the body politic. It seemed a dangerous, almost a revolutionary step. But the logic of facts forced it on those who liked it least; it was bound to happen, so they decided to do it themselves and take the credit; a few make a similar calculation in Rhodesia. One may guess that Disraeli would have looked with a certain admiration at Lord Malvern. Here, too, was a man not in love with theory, no fanatical believer in democracy, one who felt his way as he went and who under-stood the realities of politics, who shaped his course according to the way votes might go but also moulded the thoughts of his con-stituents so that the votes would go as he thought they should. In both there is a dislike of priggishness, a genial refusal to be gentle with current insincerities; though Malvern's wit has a very differ-ent flavour from Disraeli's, both have the knack of expressing a situation in a terse phrase. And both, surely, found a certain impish

[2] It has recently been argued by Colin Leys that there has always been one political party in Rhodesia. I suspect that it has not felt so to those taking part and that they would find the judgement irritating; so no doubt would Victorian statesmen this of mine.

pleasure in using an adversary's own weapons to achieve his over-throw.

How far has the policy which the Whigs began and Disraeli stole succeeded? It is still true, as A. J. P. Taylor has lately pointed out, that in England you can as a rule tell in a few minutes by his accent, the turn of his phrase, the way he smokes a cigarette or eats a roll of bread, whether a man comes from either extreme of the two nations of which Disraeli wrote. Marriage between the extremes seldom occurs and still raises all kinds of difficulties. But between the extremes there is a world of shades and distinctions; what would become of the English novel without them? And to-day it is possible up to a point to move from one class to another, even within one generation; above all there is an overlying sense of unity which transcends differences of class. This over-riding unity was of course there before the Whig revolution began; without it neither Trafalgar nor Blenheim would have been won. It is possible to argue that that sense of unity between the two nations does not exist in Rhodesia and that without it a Whig solution by gradual sharing of power is unthinkable.

No one can honestly deny that the fusing of two nations in Rhodesia is far more difficult than it was in England. And yet something not dissimilar seems to have happened in some of the Caribbean islands and territories, where, although racial differences are often regarded as symbols of class difference, they are not in themselves a barrier to an individual's progress, either social or economic. In parts of Brazil, ' to be a white' means to have reached a certain level, and from hearing a man described as white one can infer with safety as much about his bank balance as about his pigmentation. It is not true then that racial difference in itself rules out a Whig or Disraelian solution. But it does add difficulties, which become even more formidable when they are combined with differences of language as they are in Central Africa. At least as great an obstacle to a Whig solution as pigmentation is social myth; two nations enclosed in the boundaries of one territory will remain obstinately two if they are locked up in separate worlds with no communications and with rigid pictures of each other which do not correspond to reality.

What is the alternative to a Whig policy? Rigid alternatives are usually to be regarded with suspicion; to the argument that one must choose between two courses it is usually a true answer that there is a third and better. But in the broadest sense it is true that Europeans in Central Africa, as in South, must either hold on to the power they have or give it away. If it is decided to hold, it must be done ruthlessly, though even here there is a choice between provocative brutality and tactful restraint. If on the other hand it is decided to give, there is an almost infinite number of gradations in the pace and manner of the giving. To give grudgingly is in the circumstances of Central Africa perhaps more dangerous than not to give at all. To give gracefully recognizes what is inevitable and makes the best of it; to give generously involves a recognition of where justice lies and sometimes an acknowledgement that it is overdue. It is between these three that Central African policy at present wavers.

Richard Gray's book is divided into two parts, the first dealing with the period during which separate development was deliberately adopted as a policy in Southern Rhodesia, when eyes were averted from the other nation and its very existence seemed sometimes to be denied. Part II deals with a growing awareness of the dilemma, a consciousness on either side that the other nation is there and a new recognition on the European side that the awakening African constitutes a challenge. This is the broad outline; first, averted eyes and separate development, then a first tentative movement towards something which might be called partnership. Within these strong tidal streams are various cross-currents and eddies. There is the paradox for the European that just when his economy is booming, when he sees Salisbury transformed from a collection of frontier shacks to a modern town with sky-scrapers and a parking problem, at the very moment when he begins to feel that his country is growing up and entitled to enjoy the sweets of adult life—at that very moment the rule of Europeans throughout Africa is beginning to disappear, the prestige of white civilization to decline, and every assumption of his society to be threatened. His personal problem in Central Africa has suddenly to be seen against a world pattern in which the Afro-Asian conference at Bandung is one important symbol and others are the reactions of Iran to the Anglo-Iranian Oil Company and of Egypt to the Suez Canal Company.

The background is the world-wide revolt of the have-nots against rule by the haves, the revolt against any suggestion of inferiority in the badge of colour; in the foreground is suspicion, the tragedy, for example, of African discontent even with a measure good in itself but carried through without the understanding of the people. Over all is the tragic fact that readiness to meet the African intellectual developed on the European side perhaps ten or fifteen years too late, when he was already beginning to move into a mood of bitterness and rejection.

But the reader will want to turn to the book itself and he is owed some explanation of how it came to be written. The Rockefeller Foundation accepted the suggestion, made by what came later to be the Institute of Race Relations, that a dispassionate examination of the development of race relations in Rhodesia and Nyasaland would be valuable. Richard Gray was chosen to help me and we agreed on a first division of spheres of interest, I taking the period up to 1918 and he that from 1918 to 1953. It must be rare for two people to collaborate in a book without one taking a far larger part than the other; it soon became clear that the results were likely to be much better if each of us wrote his own book, though with constant discussion between us. My book, *The Birth of a Dilemma*, appeared in 1958; Richard Gray's longer and more difficult book has taken longer to write.

The two books were bound to be very different. The periods do not lend themselves to the same kind of treatment, but apart from that there were differences between the two writers in age, temperament, and experience. Of the two streams of visitors already referred to in this Foreword, I belonged on the whole to the complacent, and Richard Gray to the suspicious; each of us had something to learn from the other.

It was, however, agreed that I should write two chapters in Richard Gray's book. One was to have been on the development of land policy and one on native administration. The first of these is included in the first part of this book as Chapter II. It needs only one explanation: although I fully agree with the division of the book into two periods, it did not seem to me that the development of land policy could be cut in half. The later part could only be understood in the light of the earlier, and to have separated the chapter into two halves in the two parts of the book would have been confusing. This chapter, therefore, attempts to cover the whole period of the book, from 1918 to 1953, and in this respect differs from the other chapters in Part I.

The chapter on native administration has never been written. The subject is one on which Lord Hailey and Dr. Lucy Mair have written with an authority that no wise man would wish to impugn or even to qualify. All that might have been possible would have been to supplement their account by something from quite another angle, on the day's work of the Native Commissioner and the District Commissioner, an attempt—necessarily imperfect—to visualize what the impact would be on, say, a Master Farmer or a Sub-Chief. This would have meant lengthy stays with officials in the three territories for which time was never available. In the winter of 1957–8, when this was to have been done, I became a member of a commission to inquire into the affairs of minorities in Nigeria and the visit to Rhodesia had to be postponed. It seemed better to omit the chapter altogether than to attempt something which could hardly have added much to what is known already. This leaves a notable gap in the book, for which I can only apologize, but since there seems no prospect of being able to complete that part of it, it is better to let the book go forward without it.

There remains a third book to be written which will deal with the first years of the Federation. Part of this is ready and I hope that it will be possible to publish it before the Constitutional Review in 1960.

Our thanks are due, above all to the Rockefeller Foundation, but also to all those who generously helped us with information, advice and hospitality; in particular to Dr. Lucy Mair for comments and suggestions, to the staff of the Central African Archives, and to Margaret Usborne and the staff of the Institute of Race Relations for preparing the manuscript for publication.

B

Part One
Averted Eyes : 1918–1939

I. SEGREGATION AND TRUSTEESHIP

I. RIVAL PHILOSOPHIES

The upheaval of the First World War was followed in Britain by a decade of intense examination of her imperial role in Africa and especially in the mixed communities of East and Central Africa. 'Trusteeship' and 'the paramountcy of native interests' inspired the pronouncements, and to a lesser extent the practice, of the Colonial Office. These ideas, going back through Johnston and Livingstone to the Abolitionists and Burke, now provided the nearest approach to a coherent theory of British imperialism. This theory of trusteeship encountered, however, another and yet older colonial theme. In the twenties it was still possible, and indeed common, to regard the highlands of Eastern Africa, extending in an unbroken belt hundreds of miles broad from Kenya to South Africa, as the last great area in the world ready and waiting for European settlement. For the first time, following the fall of German rule in East Africa, the map was virtually coloured red from Cairo to Cape Town; and, deep in the centre, copper promised to rival the revolutions brought about previously by gold and diamonds. There was little to show that the great impulse of European migration, which so recently and spectacularly had transformed the Transvaal, would slacken and fall away. Yet these high hopes of settlement were accompanied by uneasiness and fears which brought with them the practice, and, to a lesser extent, the theory of 'segregation'—the idea that European and African were best left each to develop on his own lines.

The clash and mingling of these two philosophies distinguishes the inter-war years. Though drawn from such opposite sources, the concepts of 'trusteeship' and 'segregation' shared two basic assumptions which marked them out from the previous and the following periods. The introspective questioning of Western civilization, induced by the catastrophe of the war, made men more ready to appreciate the new values and worlds which social anthropologists were beginning to reveal in African cultures. The period of the 'manifest' superiority of the European's way of life contrasted with the 'primitive savagery' of the African was passing. The doubts and questionings, and the new awareness of African potentialities, were reflected not only in the readiness of colonial administrators to delegate power to Native Authorities, but also in the positive, protectionist element in the thought of some advocates of segregation. It was partly this that led many men, including Smuts and Lord Lugard, to support elements of both theories simultaneously. Both theories also shared a confident expectation of long life. Their exponents were concerned with a very gradual development of relatively intact societies, with the progress and status of peoples rather than the aspirations and achievements of individuals and an emergent class. They envisaged decades of undisputed European control. They thought in terms of centuries rather than five-year plans.

Both philosophies also assumed an unavoidable, and at times an almost complete, clash of interests between 'settlers' and 'natives'. The harmonious and increasingly integrated development hoped for by Livingstone was on the whole replaced by the suspicious, somewhat negative, watchfulness traditionally represented by the Aborigines Protection Society. The exponents of Colonial Office 'trusteeship' felt that the essential role of the Imperial Government should be to preserve a balance of interests by acting as an 'impartial arbiter'. And although the advocates of European settlement maintained that their leadership was the only sure means of bringing lasting benefits—and thus an element of trusteeship—to all the inhabitants of Africa, it is evident that the concept of segregation presupposed at least a temporary, and generally a permanent, incompatibility between the races.

Neither of these two approaches was defined or developed primarily for the territories of Central Africa. The practice of British colonial administrators of delegating power to Native Authorities—or 'indirect rule'—based partly on Lugard's experience in Nyasaland, Uganda, and Nigeria, was developed by Sir Donald Cameron in Tanganyika and was only later introduced in Northern Rhodesia and Nyasaland. The definitions of trusteeship were also occasioned by events elsewhere. The League of Nations' Mandate for Tanganyika, by accepting a 'sacred trust' for 'peoples not yet able to stand by themselves under the strenuous conditions of the modern world', was soon held to have prominently reaffirmed an 'axiom of British policy'.[1] Lugard's looser use of the term 'mandate' gave it a wider circulation. For him the Mandate—dual in its obligation to foster the welfare of the colonial inhabitants and to develop for the world the potentialities of a dependency—was universal in application and economic in emphasis; and in the British conception of it as a slow continuous process there was little emphasis on the advance to self-government already implied in the phrase 'not yet able to stand . . .'

The policy of trusteeship was brought into focus by the situation in Kenya. Here the small group of European settlers, with their numbers augmented by a settlement scheme for ex-soldiers, claimed an increasing share in the government of the Colony. Indian immigrants, however, originally encouraged with a disregard for political complications, now heavily outnumbered the Europeans and it was realized in Whitehall that any attempt to discriminate against them might have serious repercussions in India. The declaration of 1923 issued by the Secretary of State, the Duke of Devonshire, sought to counter these claims by the assertion of imperial responsibility.

Primarily Kenya is an African territory, and His Majesty's Government think it necessary definitely to record their considered opinion that the interests of the African natives must be paramount, and that if, and when, those interests and the interests of the immigrant races should conflict, the former should prevail. Obviously, the interests of the other communities, European, Indian or Arab, must severally be safeguarded. . . . But in the administration of Kenya His Majesty's Government regard themselves as exercising a trust on behalf of the African population, and they are unable to delegate or share this trust,

[1] *Memorandum on Native Policy in East Africa* (Cmd. 3573, 1930).

the object of which may be defined as the protection and advancement of the native races.[2]

Partly as a result of this declaration, the Kenya settlers concentrated their hopes on achieving power through a closer union of the East and Central African territories, and in response to their agitation a Commission was appointed in 1927 to examine the problem. Under the chairmanship of Sir Edward Hilton Young, its members included Sir George Schuster and Mr. J. H. Oldham, secretary of the International Missionary Council. The report was of major importance not only for its recommendations on the subject of closer union, but also for its comprehensive and authoritative discussion of the implications of trusteeship. It provided also a striking example of the difference in viewpoint between Parliament and the man on the spot. Immigrant communities, with their initiative, knowledge, and material resources, were regarded by the Commission as 'necessary instruments' in the fulfilment of the dual mandate; their importance was rigorously confined to this function. Economically their main contribution would be the stimulus they could give 'to the vast potentialities of native production';[3] politically the leadership claimed by the European community would 'never be secure until it rests on consent and not on privilege'.[4] The argument that strong white settlement was essential to ensure the permanence of 'white civilization in Eastern Africa' was repudiated. The strongest foundation of Western civilization and British rule was seen to lie not 'in the size of the white community, which must always remain a relatively small island in the midst of a greatly preponderant black population, but in the establishment of a rule of justice which will enlist the loyalty of the native people, and strengthen their confidence in British rule'.[5]

With the Imperial Government alone capable of creating this atmosphere of 'disinterested justice', a parallel form of political development was envisaged. Both immigrants and natives would be encouraged to develop local self-governing institutions in their

---

[2] *Indians in Kenya* (Cmd. 1922, 1923), p. 10.
[3] *Report of the Hilton Young Commission* (Cmd. 3234, 1929), p. 18.
[4] Ibid., p. 208. [5] Ibid., p. 39.

own areas, while power at the centre would be retained by the representative of the Secretary of State. The native areas were seen as 'a first charge on the territory', where Africans would be able to 'develop on their own lines in a process of continuous evolution'.[6] If this Dual Policy was followed honestly, it was felt that it was 'only a question of time before the natives will have to be admitted to a share in the whole government which fairly balances that accorded to the immigrant communities', and the Commission 'would not close the door' to the ideal ('though many would consider it visionary') that 'if white and black can some day meet on equal terms, intellectually, socially and economically, the racial and economic antagonisms may be merged in a community of interests which will admit of some form of free representative government'.[7] Since, however, there might remain even in that far-distant future 'fundamental differences of outlook', and since the dangers of a premature or wrongly directed advance for Africans were manifest, the whole emphasis of the Report was on parallel development of the different communities within their own areas under the control of the 'impartial arbiter'. The benefits of closer union, it was suggested, could be better obtained by the institution of a central authority in East Africa to provide for a more effective exercise of the Imperial Government's powers, than by delegating these powers to a settler-dominated Assembly. The immediate practical implications of this policy of parallel political development would be similar in some respects to those of segregation as conceived south of the Zambezi, but the assumptions and ultimate objectives of trusteeship were vastly different.

Segregation, as slogan and theory, had become widely accepted by 1918 and not only in Africa. Across the Atlantic, in the Southern States, the compromise of 1877, by which Southerners regained control of their affairs after the brief upheaval of Reconstruction and the reign of the Carpet-baggers, was followed by a period in which Southern Conservatives and their opponents, the Populists, alike advocated programmes which were by no means

---

[6] *Report of the Hilton Young Commission*, p. 46.
[7] Ibid., pp. 78, 84.

Negrophobe. Paternal Conservatives, to whom class distinctions
were sometimes more important than those of race, defended the
Negro franchise and wooed the Negro voter. Radical Populists
strove to establish an alliance based on an 'egalitarianism of want
and poverty'. By the end of the century, however, both these
alternatives were rejected: Northern liberalism, already on the
retreat and keen to seek reconciliation with the South, fell back
before the doctrines of Anglo-Saxon superiority which were used
to justify imperialism in Cuba, Hawaii and the Philippines; in the
South the economic discontent caused by agrarian depression
vented itself in hostility to the Negroes and white supremacy became a rallying cry. Virtual disfranchisement of the Negro was
accompanied by segregation in public institutions and employment, in residential areas, in parks and trams. By 1907 segregation was regarded as the immutable foundation of the 'folkways'
of the South, a way of life manifestly appropriate to a white man's
country. During the First World War a visitor from South Africa
to the United States found that 'the separation of the races in all
social matters is as distinct in South Africa as in the Southern
States' and saw separation as the solution of the common problems
of both countries. After the First World War racial violence intensified and racial hostility began to spread throughout the
United States. Labour in the North resented Negro competition,
and Negroes were excluded from unions; the Ku Klux Klan,
which reached its peak of activity in the mid-twenties, had a
larger following outside the South than within. In the North
there was uncertainty, guilt, and anxiety; segregation could never
be accepted whole-heartedly because the contrast with egalitarian,
democratic, and Christian ideals was too sharp. But it seemed probable that a hesitant enforcement of segregation would continue
to be the American response to the problems of race relations.[8]

In South Africa, segregation had a longer and more complex
history. In the early nineteenth century missionaries had supported measures of segregation to protect the Hottentots. In
Natal, Sir Theophilus Shepstone, recognizing the need for a
special treatment inconsistent with full citizenship, attempted to

---

[8] C. Vann Woodward, *The Strange Career of Jim Crow* (New York, 1955).

carry out a protective policy towards the Zulu, and Cape Colony policy in the Transkei was based on the same principle. Ultimate objectives were not fully stated, but segregation was regarded as a temporary measure designed to aid an inevitable and beneficial transition. In the twentieth century the will to protect persisted among some officials and missionaries, but doubts about the beneficence of the transition became common. Segregation came to be thought of as a necessary, permanent institution, even among those South Africans who were primarily concerned to protect the Bantu. The first descriptions of tribal life by anthropologists, continental theories of 'primitive mentality' and the 'group mind', as much as ideas embodied in Lugard's concept of indirect rule— initially designed for territories where there were virtually no immigrant European communities—all seemed to suggest the permanent necessity of different institutions for the Bantu; the destructive effects of contact with Western materialism were only too evident, and Western institutions themselves were under criticism. Segregation came to be thought of as a permanent protection, a means of preserving cultural roots, a provision for a full and free existence, and a panacea against racial tension. In this form it would involve, it was realized, sacrifices by all communities. And it was still not clear to many in the twenties that these sacrifices were impossible or unacceptable.

Others were concerned to protect white rather than black. In the Orange Free State and Transvaal segregation came to be regarded as something designed to defend the Voortrekker principle of not 'creating equality' in Church and State: the sources of power were to be closely guarded. It became linked with the growth and survival of an Afrikaans nation. This defensive aspect was powerfully reinforced by the demands of European labour, led by trade unionists on the Rand, that the inflated wage structure of 'civilized labour' should be protected by a colour bar. The intercolonial commission of 1903–5 recommended segregation in the franchise and in land-ownership. The Native Land Act of 1913 prohibited the African from purchasing land in European areas, and postulated somewhat vaguely that other areas would be provided in return. The Mines and Works Act of 1911 consolidated the colour bar. The defences were going up, and now they seemed to be protecting privilege alone.[9]

Besides segregation and trusteeship a third theme, at first faint but of increasing importance, was beginning to influence Central Africa. The ideas of popular sovereignty, propagated with increasing success in Europe in the nineteenth century—and particularly among the English with their memories of Byron and their support of Garibaldi—won their greatest recognition in the Allies' settlement of the Balkans after the First World War. The twenties witnessed an extension of these ideas to the peoples of Asia and also to those of African descent. In India the Congress under the leadership of Mahatma Gandhi developed into a mass movement, and in America Negro and African race-consciousness emerged. This took two widely differing forms, but both rejected the pre-war spirit of co-operative acquiescence in the programme of discrimination and the meek acceptance of an inferior status. The fierce, flamboyant, yet defensive pride in 'a pure black race' proclaimed by a Jamaican Negro, Marcus Garvey, with slogans such as 'Africa for the Africans at home and abroad' and 'Wake up, Ethiopia! Wake up, Africa!', was enthusiastically received. Garvey's pre-eminence in the States was brief and his 'Back to Africa' movement foundered ignominiously; but his conventions, his church, his newspaper, his bombastic self-confidence, and his delegations to the League of Nations produced a revolutionary stirring of the imagination, a vision of a future power which eclipsed past and present degradation. The philosophy and approach of Dr. Du Bois and the National Association for the Advancement of Coloured People (N.A.A.C.P.) were entirely different. A university professor, Du Bois attacked the racial ideologies of Gobineau and based his case on a thorough application of American democratic ideals. As chief publicist for the N.A.A.C.P., Du Bois deeply influenced thought and action in the United States, and his Pan-African Congress movements, started in the twenties, were a training-ground for West African nationalists.[10]

[9] W. K. Hancock, *British Commonwealth Affairs* (1942), Vol. II, Pt. II.
[10] G. Padmore, *Pan-Africanism or Communism* (1956).

Signs of this stirring were present in South Africa. The Native Land Act 1913 led to the formation of the African National Congress, then composed principally of intelligentsia with a moderate outlook. But a few years later the Industrial and Commercial Workers' Union was founded and it proved to be the first forward-looking movement to appeal to the masses. Founded in 1919 by Clements Kadalie, a missionary-educated Tonga from Nyasaland, it gathered in the twenties a membership of a quarter of a million. Combining political agitation with industrial activities, it paralleled the rapid impact of Garvey's movement, until it too declined at the end of the decade, weakened by internal dissensions. There remained, however, the vision, hopes, and ideas that it had produced and these reappeared elsewhere.[11]

2. SETTLERS AND SEGREGATION

Although outside observers were becoming increasingly conscious of this debate on ultimate aims and objectives, Central Africa was still surprisingly isolated from it in space, thought, and development. Europeans there were on the whole still unaware that their basic assumptions could be seriously questioned, and in 1923 the Europeans in Southern Rhodesia moved into a position where—it must have seemed to them—they could with a relatively free hand fashion their own future. Their struggle to free themselves politically from the rule of the Chartered Company ended successfully in a referendum on 27 October 1922, when by 8,774 to 5,989 votes they chose Responsible Government rather than admission to the Union of South Africa. As a result the country was formally annexed to the Crown on 12 September 1923, and was granted self-government in domestic matters, subject to certain limitations relating to native affairs.[12]

[11] E. Roux, *Time Longer Than Rope* (1948), pp. 161–205.
[12] 'This was provided in the Letters Patent in the following ways, viz.:
(a) Section 28 provides that 'any law, save in respect of the supply of arms, ammunition or liquor to natives, whereby natives may be subjected or made liable to any conditions, disabilities or restrictions to which persons of European descent are not also subjected or made liable', must be reserved for the signification of the pleasure of the Crown, unless the Governor, prior to its passing, shall have obtained instructions upon such proposed

Southern Rhodesia's choice of independence was influenced by fears of being completely absorbed by her powerful neighbour and of being involved in the bitter controversies of Boer versus Briton. There was also a feeling that in Rhodesia 'the native problem' was less acute and that there was more time and more land with which to achieve a solution. Despite its brief history and its close links with the South, the Colony had evolved a way of life which was already termed 'intolerably Rhodesian' by many in the Union. It was proudly conscious of its new, independent existence, of its peculiar experiences, and of its affection for British middle-class values—albeit of a past decade.[13] The country had become settled and sedate. Coats and starched collars, card cases and 'vanity bags' had become the rule in the towns. The family man was now typical. A second generation was coming of age: the 1921 Census showed that 8,308 out of the 33,620 Europeans had been born in the country. Motoring, telephones, and wireless were rapidly changing the pace and possibilities of life in the rural areas; people were now arriving not with hopes of a brief and profitable speculation but with the desire to retire and settle.[14]

Mining had become a more settled occupation. The itinerant prospector for gold had been to a great extent replaced by the small worker who either owned his plot or worked it on tribute to a larger company, in that case often owning land or a small farmstead nearby. Base metals, like chrome and asbestos, with a larger, more settled labour force, increased in importance. Above all, the Rhodesian had become 'eminently and typically a landowner'. Twenty-three per cent. of the Europeans gainfully

---

legislation through the Secretary of State, or unless it contains a clause suspending its operation until such pleasure has been signified.

(*b*) Section 40 provides that no such discriminative conditions shall be imposed, without the previous consent of the Secretary of State, by any proclamation, regulation or other instrument issued under the provisions of any law, unless they have been explicitly prescribed, defined and limited in such law.

(*c*) Certain supervisory and other powers in regard to native administration were vested in the High Commissioner for South Africa. . . . One important provision in the Letters Patent vested the Native Reserves in him.' *Bledisloe Report* (Cmd. 5949, 1939).

[13] E. Tawse-Jollie, *The Real Rhodesia* (1926), p. 7.

[14] *Southern Rhodesia and its Living Conditions* (Salisbury, 1932).

occupied were agriculturalists, and even the civil servant, business or professional man, miner or railway employee looked forward to retiring to a plot of land. In 1924 a third of the Members of the Legislative Assembly were farmers, while several others had a direct interest in the farming industry.[15]

This increased commitment to the country, together with their newly gained responsibility, produced in Europeans in Southern Rhodesia a desire to regulate and to establish on a firm basis their present and future relationships with the Africans in the territory. It was natural that this problem was seen primarily in terms of land-ownership; the African, too, was first and foremost a person who lived off the land. Out of an estimated total of 862,000 men, women, and children, some 47,000 were employed on the mines, in towns, or on European farms,[16] but much of this labour was annual or seasonal and, in this strange world which had so suddenly developed, the African's principal heritage was still the land. The 1920 Order in Council, which defined and allocated with finality the Native Reserves, in no way affected the right of individual Africans to 'acquire, hold, encumber, and dispose of land on the same conditions as a person who is not a Native', which had been established by the 1898 Order in Council. It was therefore still possible in theory for Africans to acquire land indiscriminately outside the Reserves, and in 1920 the Chief Native Commissioner in his annual report drew attention to the 'inevitable friction' this would cause. The delegation which went to London the following year to discuss the grant of Responsible Government suggested that specific areas should be set aside in which Africans alone could acquire land, with the clearly implied corollary that Africans would be prevented from acquiring land elsewhere. Mr. Winston Churchill, as Secretary of State for the Colonies, was unwilling to alter 'a long-accepted principle' but conceded that 'if full and impartial inquiry should show, after Responsible Government has come into force, that some amendment of the law is necessary, His Majesty's Government would be prepared to consider an amendment'. As a result a Commission

---

[15] *The Times*, 6 June 1924; Tawse-Jollie, op. cit., pp. 29–31.
[16] 1921 Southern Rhodesia Census.

under Sir Morris Carter was appointed in January 1925 to 'inquire into and report upon the expediency and practicability of setting apart defined areas outside the boundaries of the Native Reserves, (*a*) within which Natives only shall be permitted to acquire ownership of or interest in land, and (*b*) within which only Europeans shall be permitted to acquire ownership of or interest in land.'[17] The evidence submitted to the Commission by 233 influential Europeans and 1,753 Africans provides, at a highly formative moment, a broad panorama of opinion on a subject then central to race relations.

A small group of Europeans were surprised and appalled to discover that the African had an equal legal right with themselves to purchase land. For them Africans were uniformly 'idle and degenerate and lacking in all ideas of agriculture'. 'Natives', they said, 'never stay long in one spot and leave a desert behind them.' With their scrub cattle and scanty crops, they and their children were often half starved.[18] All available land should be reserved for European settlement; Africans should be 'deprived without any compensation' of the right to purchase land;[19] the Reserves were too large already. 'If they are crowded out so much the better, for then they will come out and work and so they will be able to get a fair wage and good food.'[20] 'Natives will only work when they find the Reserves are too small for them,' declared the manager of a large mining and land-owning company,[21] and a Roman Catholic missionary warned the Commission that there was 'a large body of representative men' who regarded the native 'as a mere asset of the labour market' and wanted 'a thriftless, homeless, and unattached class with one single tie, the interest of their master'.[22] Again, men like this could not envisage the need for the provision of married quarters for Africans in urban areas. 'As far as I have seen of the native women in this country,' said a Bulawayo merchant and farmer who had been in Rhodesia since 1892, 'they are nearly all prostitutes. You will never make them anything else.'[23] Another Bulawayan felt that since Europeans

---

[17] *Report of the Land Commission, 1925* (Salisbury, C.S.R. 3–1926).
[18] Central African Archives, ZAH 1/1/4, pp. 1364–5.   [19] Ibid., p. 888.
[20] Ibid., p. 1158.   [21] Ibid., p. 889.   [22] Ibid., pp. 225–6.   [23] Ibid., p. 712.

had lived in the pioneering days without their womenfolk, 'we might reasonably expect them to do the same.'[24]

Nearly all the men who took this line had arrived in the country in the nineties, and some of them quoted previous experiences in South Africa. Their attitude was formed in an earlier age. Engrossed in their own concerns, they had remained blind to African potentialities. For them there was no question of providing a sphere for African development, nor was there even a realization of the necessity to create a definite limit to African advancement. By right of conquest and by inherited and immutable inability, the African, they thought, was condemned to remain for ever the servant of the white man. To these men the problem of landownership simply did not exist, but most Europeans who gave evidence to the Commission realized that they were faced with a far more complex situation.

An overwhelming majority of Europeans supported segregation for many diverse reasons. There were the practical difficulties which arose when African holdings were scattered among European farms. Stray cattle trampled crops, interbred, and carried disease; fires were started and crops were pilfered; beer was brewed and the labour on European farms became unruly.[25] Some farmers, both European and African, declared that they had experienced no difficulties of this kind, but many cases of friction were reported and some Africans felt that in such cases they were 'sure to go under'.[26] From the Europeans' point of view there was always the danger that land would lose value if a farm near by was sold to an African. There were an increasing number of 'progressive natives' desirous of purchasing land and there had been cases where Europeans had been willing to sell, and had actually sold, their land to Africans 'very much against the opinion and sentiment of their neighbours'. That, the Assistant Chief Native Commissioner felt, was 'a power which the individual white man should not have'.[27]

---

[24] Central African Archives, ZAH 1/1/4, pp. 552–5.
[25] A Zulu who owned part of a farm seven miles out of Salisbury admitted that the fourteen families in his private location brewed beer and were a nuisance to neighbours; ibid., p. 440.
[26] Ibid., p. 447.   [27] Ibid., pp. 73–4.

C

The operative factor was, however, not so much irritation over present discontents as concern for the future. Several witnesses referred to the trend in world opinion by which segregation of land-holding was 'regarded more and more as the only practicable solution at the present time of the problem of the inter-relations of black and white'.[28] The Chief Agriculturist based his views on the position in America, where he thought 'the educated Negro was a most undesirable neighbour' and the educated, rather than the raw, native 'very often becomes a nuisance to his European neighbours'.[29] An American missionary recorded the belief that there was a tendency towards segregation between the races in every community, and a settler with experience of India felt that segregation alone could prevent Rhodesia from becoming a native country with all Europeans ousted within thirty years.[30] Many people also had been influenced by their experiences in South Africa and by the trend of policy there.

The Europeans who advocated segregation were divided into three main groups. Two of these groups considered that segregation should be a partial and perhaps a temporary measure; and the division between these two was mainly one of emphasis. Fears of African rivalry led the larger group to think of segregation primarily as a means of defence, whereas the smaller group thought of segregation as a temporary expedient and emphasized the possibilities of racial co-operation. Neither of these groups envisaged a total division of black and white into separate areas, and most members of both groups were content to leave the ultimate objectives undefined; but the first group we will deal with did believe that complete segregation would provide the only permanent solution to the dilemma of the white man in Rhodesia.

This first group included men who had thought deeply about the problem of race relations and had become convinced that the segregation of land-holding should be merely the prelude and basis for a thorough separation of all political, economic, and social interests. The most eloquent exponent of this view was

[28] *Report of the Land Commission, 1925* (C.S.R. 3–1926).
[29] Central African Archives, ZAH 1/1/3, p. 144.
[30] Ibid., p. 1448 and para. 5895.

N. H. Wilson, who, as an official in the Native Affairs Department, had launched *Nada*, a journal to stimulate discussion on
native affairs. In its pages, and in a long memorandum submitted
to the Commission, he developed his thesis. The position of
Europeans in Rhodesia was based, he thought, mainly upon the
assumption that their sole role was to supervise native labour.
Intelligence tests applied to the American Expeditionary Force
seemed to show, however, that not more than thirty-five per
cent. of any European race was qualified for supervising. The remaining sixty-five per cent. were capable of being trained to
skilled or semi-skilled artisanship, but so apparently were Africans
whose 'smaller spending power' gave them an overwhelming advantage. The history of South Africa and the United States
showed that Europeans would fall to the bottom of the ladder to
become 'poor whites'. 'To allow this to come to pass would be a
calamity to the state, a cruel injustice to our own race and children,
and a gross betrayal to the civilisation in which we may be supposed
to believe.'

Wilson thought that it was still possible in Southern Rhodesia
to forestall this development by joining the Native Reserves into
two or three large Native Areas where all facilities for 'native
development' would be provided. The native would be gradually
eliminated from the economic life of the rest of the country 'except as a hewer of wood and drawer of water'. Native Councils
within the Native Areas would 'furnish an outlet for the political
instinct that is bound to arrive', but elsewhere the natives should
have no franchise. 'We are in the country because we represent a
higher civilisation, because we are better men. It is our only excuse for having taken the land. For us to turn round now and ask
the natives to help us in directing the Government of ourselves is
ridiculous.' [31] Several other thoughtful officials, including Charles
Bullock, Peter Nielsen, H. S. Keigwin, and E. G. Howman—men
who had a keen interest in their work and a deep paternalistic
sympathy for Africans—supported the demand for as thorough a
separation as possible. [32]

[31] Central African Archives, ZAH 1/1/3, pp. 1625–8.
[32] Ibid., pp. 1408, 1444, 1694, and H. S. Keigwin in *Nada*, 1924.

In the Legislative Assembly, H. H. Davies, leader of the Labour Party, and Max Danziger, a Gwelo attorney, vehemently argued the case for one large Native Area, possibly adjoining Bechuanaland, which would provide temporary migrant labourers until European immigration made them unnecessary, and which would make possible a permanent separation. The position of the European artisans was uppermost in the mind of Davies, and Danziger was a man who demanded an honest appraisal of the dilemma confronting Europeans in Rhodesia. But the long-term attractions of a total separation were offset by a host of practical difficulties. Other Members pointed out the impossibility of the wholesale transference of tribal groups; small, separate units scattered throughout the country were more likely to meet the immediate and increasing demand for labour; and the Prime Minister roundly declared that complete territorial segregation was impossible. The sacrifices which the theory demanded were unacceptable.[33]

The opinions of the two other groups of European witnesses who supported partial segregation had not crystallized into theories. Like most people, they did not write lengthy memoranda, and many other aspects of life in a new country claimed their attention. The Mayor of Gatooma, for example, a merchant and farmer who had been nearly thirty years in the country, on being asked to express his views on the subject of the inquiry replied: 'I have no views whatever. I have not given the matter any thought or consideration at all. I did read over the Government Gazette containing the Terms of Reference of your Commission, but that is all.'[34] Their opinions were confused, their attitudes were often ambivalent, their approach was pragmatic, but their assumptions and votes largely determined policy. They shared a determination to protect and develop a white man's country: a country in which they and their descendants would enjoy the benefits of European civilization and a standard of living which on the whole was higher than in Europe. They were aware, un-

[33] Southern Rhodesia Legislative Assembly Debates, 14 May 1929, cols. 1113, 1171, 1218, and 25 May 1929, col. 1206.
[34] Central African Archives, ZAH 1/1/3, para. 6126.

like perhaps some of the small repressive group,[35] that the African had a share in the country, that he could not be merely exterminated or virtually enslaved. They were agreed that some form of segregation in land-holding would probably provide the surest means of averting the threat of competition and discontent. Unlike Danziger and Wilson they saw no necessity for seeking a permanent solution to all aspects of the 'native problem'; they preferred to ignore those aspects of life which challenged their assumptions.

Within this broad section which supported partial segregation there was a most significant division into two groups: on the one hand there were those whose attitude seems to have sprung principally from fear of the African as a danger and a rival; on the other hand those who, while regarding the African as a completely separate and, on the whole, inferior being, were prepared actively to foster his development and to view his prosperity and welfare as part of the country's well-being as a whole. Fears and hopes alternated, the emphasis varied with events, but the existence of this division was a fact of great importance. It preserved a measure of flexibility, of discussion as to appropriate means, and even permitted a certain amount of doubt as to the ultimate objective. It provided an atmosphere in which the old tradition of Cape liberalism could continue to make its voice heard.

For the majority of Europeans who supported segregation, fear was the most widespread and compelling factor, and its influence was predominant in the larger of these two groups who advocated a partial measure of segregation. It was not simply the threat of economic competition, or even of political infiltration; it was a combination of these factors together with the shadow of miscegenation and the presence of a vast mass of people across a cultural gulf which seemed unbridgeable. An abhorrence of miscegenation was general, it clinched the argument, and perhaps sometimes it was even a substitute for thought.

Darwinism coloured many of the pronouncements on this subject. We have already quoted a reference to 'political instinct' as

[35] See above, p. 14.

applied to a race,[36] and Charles Bullock,[37] later to be Chief Native Commissioner, favoured a land segregation policy to prevent 'the evils consequent on a fusion of black and white races'. 'Hybridization,' he said, 'however gradual, cannot be contemplated with equanimity. Apart from that danger, it is best and right that each race should develop (and, if possible, be given full opportunities of developing) according to the potentialities that lie within its biological inheritance.'[38] A farmer near Bulawayo complained that in his district a lot of white farmers were living with native women. It was, he thought, a serious menace that 'the several coloured children running about there' could inherit the land.[39] A Member speaking in support of Danziger in the Legislative Assembly surmised that 'if we do not face the position today, then I can see that in the future we shall have not a white race and not a black race but something undesirable to the Maker of humanity'. A back-bencher surgeon, Dr. Godfrey Huggins, summed up his feeling more temperately: 'Whatever the future may hold forth for the two races in the way of complete segregation or working side by side for an equal wage as they do in the Southern States of America, and where we are going nobody can tell, but we do know, whichever way we go, that social segregation will exist there all the time.'[40]

Apart from the biological hazards of miscegenation—whatever they might be—it was almost impossible to envisage a close political, economic, or cultural union. The phenomenon of the 'progressive native' was known to exist, but, apart from a few missionaries, practically no European had met one as an individual, and his existence was still for most people completely obscured by rigid conceptions generalized from the accounts of other settlers or from exasperating experiences with house-boys and unskilled

---

[36] Central African Archives, ZAH 1/1/3, pp. 1625–1628. See above, p. 17.

[37] After retirement Charles Bullock wrote a novel, *Rina*, with a romantic plot about early adventures in Central Africa, rather like *King Solomon's Mines*. The hero is saved by a beautiful white maiden with whom he falls in love. He arranges to rescue her from the tribe among whom she is living but discovers that she has African blood; his love disappears immediately but he feels he is committed to getting her away and says he will find her a post as a nursemaid in South Africa.

[38] Central African Archives, ZAH 1/1/3, p. 1408.

[39] Ibid., p. 493.   [40] S.R. Debates, 27 May 1929, col. 1167.

labour. Most Europeans had a fixed mental picture of what 'the native' was like, and to this conglomeration of characteristics, often contradictory, every African was expected to conform.

A farmer with experience of 'handling up to 150 natives on a big Rhodesian farm' maintained that

the Rhodesian native is not yet equipped, mentally or morally, for the franchise or political authority according to our standards. Whether he ever will be is a very moot question; the essential qualities of honesty, truthfulness, industry and sobriety are absent from his character, and, what is probably the greatest obstacle of all, the Bantu tongues hold no word for gratitude. That is what you are up against . . . the gigantic task of completely altering their nature, and that is not the work of one generation but of many, with very doubtful prospects of success.[41]

Or again, when there was the question of encouraging Africans to grow cotton, farmers maintained that 'natives only wish to cultivate what they can eat, and natives do not grow their crops for markets . . . perhaps in the next fourth or fifth generation he might do so'.[42] A Salisbury medical practitioner, who had been in the country fifteen years and had been 'able to form some idea as to the capabilities and the mental development of the natives', felt sure that they could not 'possibly reach the stage of the white man's development before at least another 150 years' and that it would be 100 years before native lawyers, doctors, or tradesmen would desire a house in the suburbs.[43]

A European's opinion on any aspect of the 'native problem' was therefore generally governed by his idea of 'the native's character'. He was unwilling and unprepared to distinguish between Africans on a basis of individual merit. The African was inherently different from a European, and, in the last resort, he remained merely a member of an undifferentiated, primitive people. The African school-teacher, the clerk who gave years of honest service, and the painstaking carpenter or artisan's assistant should be treated legislatively in the same way as the unlettered youth who had left his tribal kraal for the first time in his life.

[41] *Manchester Guardian*, 17 May 1928, letter of F. L. Barratt to the Editor.
[42] Central African Archives, ZAH 1/1/4, pp. 667–8, 941.
[43] Ibid., paras. 7936, 7962.

Most Europeans were, consequently, unable to adapt their response to a situation that was changing rapidly, and, by a process
which was perhaps all the more dangerous in that it may well
have been partly unconscious, they generally selected and carried
with them a mental picture of the African which conveniently
buttressed their vested interests. Europeans possessed very little
accurate information about Africans, and they were regarded as a
disturbing, separate form of existence, partly because their motives
seemed mysterious and their actions unpredictable. 'Their habits',
one witness said, 'are very different to those of Europeans.'[44]
These views were perhaps reinforced by the desire to make the
African seem different. Witchcraft cases received wide publicity
and although 'black peril' (attempted rape) cases were less frequent than before the First World War, the horror and dread inspired by them remained. Two witnesses at Gwelo thought that
a location for married natives might 'possibly lessen the cases of
"black peril"',[45] but other Europeans thought that 'as the native
becomes more sophisticated the danger increases'.[46]

These fears of miscegenation or contact with any member of
this race, so near yet so remote, united Europeans with a solid
sentiment which could be appealed to whenever it seemed that
the political or economic foundations of white supremacy were
threatened. The habit of regarding Africans as a uniform mass
fostered a sense of European solidarity which overcame the pull
of differing interests within the ruling class. As a result European
opinions were often illogical: 'I think', said one farmer, 'that it is
dreadful that in Gwelo, or any other town, a native can purchase
a stand cheek by jowl with white people, but on the other hand I
do not want to do away with the private locations on farms as it
will interfere with our labour supply.'[47] And these opinions
tended to make repressive action inevitable when a clash of interests occurred between the races.

Moved by these conscious and hidden fears, the members of
this group, which comprised the largest number of Europeans to

[44] Central African Archives, ZAH 1/1/4, p. 811.   [45] Ibid., pp. 825, 830.
[46] Tawse-Jollie, op. cit., p. 276.
[47] Central African Archives, ZAH 1/1/3, p. 815.

give evidence before the Commission and to which a majority of the Members of the Legislative Assembly seem to have belonged, thought of segregation primarily as a protection for the whites. 'A curb should be put on the activities of the native,' said Dr. Godfrey Huggins, and he should have the same right of progress as a European, but only 'as long as it is harmless'.[48] The General Manager of the British South Africa Company thought that the European settler was 'entitled to some measure of protection', and a farmer from Insiza bluntly declared: 'We must keep the upper hand.'[49] Their approach was far more tentative than that of those who advocated a complete permanent separation. With the Prime Minister they recognized the immense difficulties of an 'apartheid' solution, and they dismissed it as impracticable. Although concern to protect Europeans was generally uppermost in their minds it was combined, at least in public debates likely to be overheard at Westminster, with a desire to deal 'honestly and justly' with the 'native problem'. And in fact, if circumstances enabled them to take a comprehensive view of the problems of the country as a whole, their approach approximated to that of the other group who thought in terms of racial co-operation rather than competition: Huggins' approach was rapidly modified by the responsibilities of office.

There was no rigid line separating these two groups who advocated partial segregation; it was a difference of mood and emphasis rather than of fundamental doctrine. But it was a difference of immense importance. One approach fearlessly opened the way to friendship and a united country: the other, hampered by a host of fears and preoccupied with immediate self-interest, kept the country divided and estranged. Unable to construct a separate channel for the tide of African advance, the members of this group were also unwilling to launch their fragile shell of inherited tradition, skill and privilege on its rude waters. And perhaps the greatest danger of partial segregation was that it enabled so many Europeans to assume that it provided a satisfactory and 'fair' solution to the 'native problem'; awkward aspects of

[48] Central African Archives, ZAH 1/1/3, pp. 71–2.
[49] Ibid., para. 7706 and p. 1347.

economic inter-dependence could be ignored, especially if they
threatened the privileges of Europeans.

The group of those who thought in terms of hope rather than
fear, who emphasized the benefits of African development for the
country as a whole, was far smaller, but not without influence.
It included a few Members of the Legislative Assembly. There
was C. S. Jobling, a farmer from Bulawayo, and later a member
of Huggins' first administration, who ridiculed the conservative
mind—'a type of mind which is very common in Rhodesia today,
the man who says that the great thing to do today is to keep the
native in his place . . .' Whereas, in his own view, no form of
repression could be 'of any lasting value',[50] and he quoted Lord
Bryce's opinion that the American Negro had made progress in
the last two generations equal to that made by the Anglo-Saxon
race in 500 years. There was also R. D. Gilchrist, a rancher, who
declared: 'All over the world it is written in letters of blood that
you must either lift the barbarian up or he will drag you down.'[51]

The policy they advocated still implied that 'the native had a
place', but for the common good they were interested in his advance and welfare. They wanted a policy of controlled, but
actively encouraged, development. 'If one were asked to epitomise
what should be the native policy of this country,' said Gilchrist
on another occasion, 'the reply would be the establishment of an
intelligent native peasantry.'[52] People who thought on these lines
wanted Africans to be encouraged to grow cotton, for which
there was thought to be a great future,[53] and to improve and increase their holding of stock, perhaps in conjunction with the
newly formed Imperial Cold Storage Company. The President
of the Farmers' Association of Gatooma District felt: 'If we are
going to make a success of our export trade then we want every
beast that a native can produce.' He added that a government had
no right to prevent an African from growing cotton provided
that it was grown under proper supervision.[54] The Chief Agriculturist thought that Rhodesia would never be a large exporting

[50] S.R. Debates, 27 May 1929, cols. 1183–8.
[51] Ibid., col. 1201.   [52] Ibid., 4 May 1926, col. 329.
[53] Central African Archives, ZAH 1/1/3, para. 5508.   [54] Ibid., p. 966.

country unless the natives were encouraged 'to help us in that production', and other farmers urged that Government experts, at present 'more or less at the call of the white farming community . . . should be equally at the call of the natives'.[55] Successful farmers with adequate capital behind them were unperturbed at the thought of African competition, but farmers struggling without capital felt differently and the slump was to emphasize this aspect of affairs. Later a similar difference in outlook could be discerned between the professional and artisan Europeans, but in the last resort most white men had an over-riding interest in maintaining white prestige.

Advocacy of a progressive policy of development was not confined to those who wanted increased peasant development. Perceptive people realized that the shortage of labour would be solved not only by providing better working conditions but also by creating new wants, by integrating the African ever more closely in the economy of the country. Education would play its part in this: there was 'only one way in which to force him to play his part in the economic life of the country; that is by civilising him'.[56] Some people too were already stressing the benefits and efficiency which a settled, married labour force would bring to the towns and industrialists. They pointed out that the wealthiest people in Rhodesia were not the mining magnates nor the Cabinet Ministers but 'the Kaffir-truck people', that is, those engaged in trade with the African.[57] From here it was not such a very long step to a way of thought which regarded the State as an increasingly integrated unit.

I hold that our present policy of spending money on introducing white settlers and ignoring the native, who is and always must be the real base of the structure, is equivalent to standing the pyramid on its point, which will keep the white people busy running round to see that it does not fall over. It certainly will fall over unless we can make the native, who constitutes about nine-tenths of the population, into a good producing tax-paying citizen. How on earth can any sane man con-

[55] Central African Archives, ZAH 1/1/3, para. 5507 and p. 138.
[56] Tawse-Jollie, op. cit., p. 262. Cf. also Smuts, *Africa and Some World Problems*, pp. 44–53.
[57] Central African Archives, ZAH 1/1/3, pp. 743, 1635, 64–5, 96.

template a State with nine-tenths of its population mere unintelligent beasts of burden? [58]

People who shared these views supported the policy of segregation mainly on account of the practical difficulties which seemed to be a temporary phenomenon.   Just as much as those who were primarily concerned with protecting the European's position, they and their families had made the country their home, and they too were determined to stay permanently. They hoped, however, that in the long run their safety and prosperity could be guaranteed more securely by co-operation. Difficulties would gradually solve themselves. A company manager who had been in the country thirty-four years[59] thought:

The intelligence of the native will gradually increase as it has done within the last thirty-three years, and when the time arrives the people in the suburbs will have no hesitation in allowing a native doctor to live alongside them, the same as is actually happening in Cape Town today. Time alone can evolve that sort of thing.

Another European felt that as the country became bigger people would become more liberal.[60] The door should therefore be left open for a flexible evolving relationship. A district surgeon representing the Marandellas North Farmers' Association perhaps summed up the opinion of this group: 'We have the natives in the country; we cannot do without them, and we must live in the future in a sort of mutual partnership with them as part owners of the country.'[61]

So far this survey has included all those Europeans who actively supported a policy based to a greater or lesser extent on segregation. The purely repressive group, men who in the main had formed their opinion in the previous century, saw no reason or justification for the measure of protection which segregation bestowed on the tribal African. They could, however, be brought to recognize that some *quid pro quo* was necessary, if only to appease the qualms of the Secretary of State. The small group of men who advocated a total and permanent separation realized

---

[58] Central African Archives, ZAH 1/1/3, pp. 1683–4, a local journalist quoted by the Rev. A. S. Cripps.

[59] Ibid., pp. 537–8.   [60] R. A. Fletcher, ibid., p. 633.   [61] Ibid., p. 1152.

that every year that passed rendered such a solution ever more difficult, but hoped that the supporters of partial segregation could be converted to their standpoint. The majority of Europeans devoted little intensive thought to the problem of race relations; they felt that segregation in respect of land would be the fairest means of protecting themselves from too close a contact with the advancing mass. And a smaller group of men accepted segregation as a temporary expedient, but hoped for an increasing measure of co-operation between the races which would lead to the gradual disappearance of cultural differences. There remain those who accepted segregation with reluctance, and those who rejected it. The evidence places the majority of the Africans in these two groups.

A very few Africans gave an active welcome to the idea of separate areas. These were mainly 'colonial natives': Fingo, Xhosa, and Sotho from South Africa, who were afraid that Europeans were rapidly buying out all available land and who had already experienced difficulties with European neighbours.[62] James Situmbi, a Fingo, said:

In the Cape Colony, where I come from, the natives have farms there among Europeans, and there is no trouble at all, but in this country it is very different. . . . The white people in this country are not so kind to the native as the white people in the Cape Colony.[63]

A leading Wesleyan Mission preacher, Matthew Rusiki, conscious of the friction caused by proximity and the impossibility of having schools 'amongst the white people', was in favour of separate areas, but felt that Africans working in the towns should be able to buy small plots nearby on easy terms.[64]

Most of the tribal authorities questioned were primarily interested in increasing the size of the Reserves. Many of them thought that the Government should set aside further areas, but felt it unfair that they should be expected to purchase the land. 'I am only a dog of the Government, and I do not think it is right that I should have to buy land,' said Mkombo, a Ndebele chief,[65]

---

[62] Central African Archives, ZAH 1/1/3, pp. 447, 725, 617-8.
[63] Ibid., p. 398.   [64] Ibid., para. 6164.   [65] Ibid., p. 527

and other tribal Africans had a similarly passive and abject attitude.

When a man wants a wife he pays a dowry for her, and we, being the 'women' of the Government, where are we going to get the money from? . . . We consider that the Government should settle us on some land as living on the farms is rather troublesome. We are simply 'women' and 'women' must be looked after.[66]

In Lomagundi district farms were being purchased rapidly by Europeans, but Africans with wages at five shillings a month could see 'no prospect of improvement', and natives whose work was 'much harder than that of a white man' could not be expected to purchase land.[67] A headman of the Wabotcha near Umtali, after repeated questions about the Reserves, summed up his disgust: 'I have come here for nothing. I thought that there might be some land added to the Reserves where we are living, but I find that there is no such thing going to happen.'[68] Most tribal Africans did not as yet desire to purchase land and they accepted segregation as inevitable; of those who were adopting an individualistic approach to life, some accepted it as apparently necessary; apart from the few from the Union none were enthusiastic about it.

Some Africans were completely opposed to any measure of segregation. Teachers, chief messengers, and a tennis-court builder, earning about £3 a week and prepared to purchase about 2,000 acres of land, were unafraid of European competition on the open market.[69] They were afraid, however, that separate areas would leave them with inferior land remote from markets, 'dry, sandy, and sickly' like the Reserves.[70] They had experienced no difficulty with European neighbours; instead they thought that proximity was an important means of enlightenment: 'If I do not understand a thing I simply go to my white neighbour, and I ask him to explain something to me, and he does so.'[71] One of them, a Mosutho, carried the argument on to a higher plane:

---

[66] Central African Archives, ZAH 1/1/3, paras. 5835–6.
[67] Ibid., pp. 396–7, 1440.   [68] Ibid., para. 6369.   [69] Ibid., pp. 482, 622.
[70] Ibid., pp. 683–4, 472, 621.   [71] Ibid., pp. 687, 609, 621.

I do not see why the subjects of any one king should be separated. Seeing that all the natives are ruled by the British Government there should be no distinction in regard to their being able to purchase land. If a native is a neighbour to a white man, he should look to the white man as his guardian and adviser, and not as his enemy. The same thing should happen as regards the white man to the native. He should look to the native as his adopted child, and he should act as a true guardian.[72]

Missionary opinion was similarly divided. A few missionaries, like the American already quoted and those of the Dutch Reformed Church, thought that segregation was natural and in accordance with a world trend. The majority accepted it as offering the best practical chance in which a progressive policy of development could be attempted. They recognized, even though they also deplored, the existence of prejudice and practical difficulties; and some may have been influenced by a paternalistic and proprietary attitude towards their converts and the heathen. They realized, however, that a policy of separate development could only succeed if a generous amount of land was set aside for African use, and it was to this aspect that many directed their energies. Shearly Cripps, an Anglican priest who for over twenty years had lived in Franciscan—or African—poverty on his mission near Enkeldoorn, was, with the Methodist, John White, the most outspoken champion of African rights. He was representative in accepting segregation as a policy which, 'however defective in idealism, may obviously carry at least the Christian hall-marks of heroism and sacrifice'.[73] He urged that Africans should be allocated at least half the unalienated land, and pointed out that 'half a loaf is likely to be considered better than no bread by the hungry'.[74]

Some Anglican priests, however, opposed segregation on principle, and the most coherent criticism came from the Community of the Resurrection at Penhalonga. They held that total segregation and even a fair partition between Europeans and Africans was impossible. Any partition should not be based on purely racial grounds but should be a partition between two different systems

[72] Central African Archives, ZAH 1/1/3, pp. 683–4. [73] Ibid., p. 1694.
[74] *Manchester Guardian*, 3 July 1929, Cripps to the Editor.

of development, the communal life of the Reserves and an open individualistic freehold and tenancy system. A priest, who had witnessed the effects of the 1913 Natives Land Act in South Africa, urged the Commission to permit the ordered development of African tenancy on European farms. A carefully supervised system of share-cropping tenants could, he thought, avoid the evils of uncontrolled 'squatting'. Improved farming methods could be enforced, and wise regulations would permit long leases and 'permanent home-making in those parts of the country which were to be accounted as white areas'. The alternative of reducing the African outside the Reserves to the status of a mere wage-labourer would retard the country's agricultural progress, would create a host of social problems connected with vagrancy and an unsettled family life, and would destroy the African's confidence in the white man and the possibilities of a close paternal contact.

From what I have seen in the district within a radius of 30 miles around Umtali, I should judge that the natives here are superior as land cultivators to the Basuto, Zulu, or Cape natives, with whom I was familiar in the South. The well-kept gardens I have seen in the forest, and in the valleys and on the hills, suggest to me that they are now ready, at any rate, to *begin* to take advantage of a good system of leasehold or of land purchase, whereby the initiative and the diligence of the individual is stimulated. . . . What is wanted, I believe, is European farmers who will take the English Squire, at his best, as a model. Some of their ground they would lease or hire to natives on terms worked out by the Government. . . . They would form a healthy aristocracy which might exercise a potent, perhaps even a dominating influence on the development of the country for many generations.[75]

Three settlers held similar opinions. One, a general dealer at Chipinga, a predominantly Afrikaner neighbourhood, who had been in the country for sixteen years, thought that just as in India and Assam, where there were 'native tea farms sandwiched between European-owned estates' which seemed to work very well, so in Rhodesia Africans should be encouraged to imitate and emulate the white man. Successful African farmers were more

[75] Central African Archives, ZAH 1/1/3, pp. 1076–9. See also a letter from Father Cotton to the Editor, *Manchester Guardian*, 2 July 1929.

desirable, he thought, than 'poor white settlers'.[76] A farmer and surveyor who had been thirty years in the country thought that no African could be a worse neighbour than a limited liability company,[77] and another farmer who had been a Native Commissioner thought that it was 'wrong for a European to say that he would not have natives as his neighbours'. If Europeans were pinned down, he thought, they would give in or retract from this generalization. 'There are quite a number of natives in the Nyamandhlovu district whom I would not mind helping and teaching because, in my opinion, the more we produce, even if produced by natives, so much the better will it be for the country.'[78]

Most Europeans, however, would have dismissed such men as at the best impractical idealists, and summing up the results of this broad survey of opinion the Land Commission concluded that segregation of land-holding was expedient, practicable, and desired by 'an overwhelming majority of those who understand the question'.[79] Southern Rhodesia moved forward therefore into a determined attempt to prevent racial conflict and competition by a policy of separate development, of giving priority to the interests of each main racial group within their respective areas. Few Rhodesians, however, passionately believed, as did the Afrikaners in the Union, that segregation was the one hope for national survival. Most of them rejected the thorough-going doctrinaire approach; their whole attitude was far more pragmatic, even though its foundations may not have been a matter of conscious reasoning. The flexibility lessened, perhaps, but persisted, and when after the Second World War the difficulties and inadequacies of the policy were revealed, this flexibility became increasingly significant.

3. COLONIAL TRUSTEESHIP

South of the Zambezi, then, the principal object of policy was to protect and develop a white man's country; the Government was seen as the guardian or trustee of European civilization, and

---

[76] Central African Archives, ZAH 1/1/3, p. 1503.   [77] Ibid., para. 7668.
[78] Ibid., pp. 755–6.   [79] *Report of the Land Commission, 1925*, para. 49.
D

European settlers and capital provided the 'steel framework' of the superstructure.[80] North of the Zambezi the official aims of policy were in theory determined after 1924 by the Colonial Office; His Majesty's Government exercised a trust on behalf of the African population and was seen in theory as an impartial arbiter, controlling the development of the different racial communities. Political and economic facts, however, tested and challenged this claim.

Nyasaland, with no mineral wealth so far discovered, with its broken and uncompleted line of communications and its climate, which rendered the greater part of the territory unsuitable for white settlement, was far removed from the world of Southern Rhodesia. After the First World War there was a small influx of planters attracted by the high prices of tobacco and cotton, and the 1921 Census registered 1,486 Europeans. Of these 399 were planters, 229 were engaged in commerce and industry, 107 were missionaries, and 141 were Government officials.[81] In 1923 European planters produced approximately four-fifths of the exported tobacco, all the tea, and rather more than half the cotton, taking value as the basis.[82] Their position, however, was precarious; in 1924, for the first time for four years, the majority of them were only able 'to make both ends meet',[83] and the Ormsby-Gore Commission endorsed the Governor's opinion that

the prosperity of the Protectorate depends on the development of its tropical agricultural resources, partly by a limited number of European planters, but principally by the natives themselves with European instructors.[84]

Uganda, rather than Rhodesia or Kenya, was taken as an example. The future, so far as Europeans were concerned, lay with the companies and big estates which could afford the large capital outlay involved in tea-growing, or the supervisory, marketing, and processing functions undertaken by the British Cotton-Growing Association, the Native Tobacco Board, and

[80] Smuts, *Africa and Some World Problems*, pp. 49, 63.
[81] Results summarized in Nyasaland Census Report 1926.
[82] *Report of the East Africa Commission, 1925* (Cmd. 2387).
[83] Ibid., p. 103.   [84] Ibid., p. 109.

the Imperial Tobacco Company. With hardly an exception, Europeans did not come to settle permanently in the country, but to make money and retire elsewhere. By 1931 the number of planters had decreased by over a hundred,[85] and their place was taken by African peasants.[86]

Apart from the complicated question of tenants on European estates in the Southern Province,[87] the challenge to the doctrine of trusteeship came not from the presence and claims of European settlers, but from the extent to which the need for African economic and political development was met. Nyasaland Africans enjoyed a reputation for being 'naturally progressive' and 'second to none in Africa in their capacity for education and improvement',[88] and although this may well have been due to their early start in education and the absence of frustrating restrictions rather than to any 'natural' factors distinguishing them from other Africans, the reputation was well merited. Out of a male population estimated at 625,537 on 31 December 1929, some 32,000 were growing cotton, 48,419 were registered as tobacco-growers, and 10,655 were working as clerks, bricklayers, mechanics, and skilled labourers. Many engaged in trade on their own account: not less than 10,000 caught, dried, traded, and hawked fish from Lakes Shirwa and Nyasa all over the country; in the Blantyre district and the larger markets there were butchers, market gardeners, canteen owners, bicycle repairers, carpenters, cobblers, blacksmiths, all working on their own account, with average incomes of fifteen shillings to four pounds a month; several already owned motor-lorries, and in Blantyre an African-owned laundry 'well patronized by Europeans' employed fourteen labourers and had an income of about ninety pounds a year.[89] In much of the territory, however, and especially in the districts north of Kasungu, large numbers of Africans—in the twenties it was thought that they totalled not less than 30,000—left the country in search of work. It was gradually realized that the numbers involved

---

[85] 1931 Nyasaland Census; G. H. Wilson, 'The Labour Problem in Nyasaland', in *The East and the West*, Vol. XIX, 1921.
[86] See below, Chap. II, p. 83.   [87] See below, pp. 75–8.
[88] *Report of the East Africa Commission, 1925*, pp. 104–5.
[89] Nyasaland Census, pp. 27–8.

were much larger than this, that many became completely lost to the territory, 'that the waste of life, happiness, health and wealth was colossal', and that the state of affairs constituted a 'flagrant breach' of the ideal of trusteeship.[90]

The other serious trouble was political, or administrative. The 'awful upset' caused by the war had been but the latest of many factors breaking down the tribal system.[91] Many Africans had been recruited as carriers in the East African campaign, where conditions had been often unavoidably bad,[92] and at home there had been the ferment of John Chilembwe's rising. The old respect for chiefs and elders seemed to have disappeared and 'with it nearly all the old village discipline'; youths were 'bumptious and intractable', stealing and housebreaking were increasing 'beyond belief'. One missionary knew only two chiefs who had much power in their villages and both were 'notorious rogues and anti-European'.[93] Missionaries perhaps over-stated the case, but that the problem was real cannot be doubted. The Hilton Young Commission thought that the tribal organization was 'beyond re-call',[94] but eventually, in 1933, in a somewhat belated attempt to deal with the situation, powers were given to Native Authorities in Nyasaland to make rules for the 'peace, good order and welfare' of their areas, to administer Native Treasuries for specific local services, and to establish Native Courts with extensive powers of civil and criminal jurisdiction.

The increased prosperity of some African districts with their production of cotton and tobacco was reflected in a rapid increase in the number of Asian immigrants, who created and captured 'almost the whole of the retail trade' with Africans.[95] Their growth can be seen in the following census figures of Asians in Nyasaland:[96]

---

[90] *Report of the Committee to Enquire into Emigrant Labour, Nyasaland, 1935*. See below, Ch. III, pp. 120–4.

[91] G. H. Wilson, op. cit., p. 31.

[92] 'Even native fighting troops were quite frequently on half-rations and less.' Ibid., p. 30.

[93] Ibid., pp. 31–2.

[94] *Hilton Young Report*, p. 271.

[95] L. S. Norman, *Nyasaland without Prejudice* (1934), p. 140.

[96] Census reports, 1926 and 1931.

1911	.	.	.	481
1921	.	.	.	563
1926	.	.	.	850
1931	.	.	.	1591

In the twenties the number of Asian traders increased from 361 to 1,037 and in the same period one barrister and three medical practitioners entered the country.[97] Almost every European plantation had its Asian store, and numbers were dotted round isolated markets. As individuals and as a community the Asians fitted easily into the Protectorate's way of life. 'There has never been, as in Kenya, any "Indian" question. The traders stick to their own quarter in the townships, and do not, as in Natal or Kenya, attempt to invade the European residential areas.'[98] A few Asians purchased freehold farmland, but, like the Europeans, few of them at that time intended to make a permanent home in the country. There were only 149 adult females as against 1,257 adult Asian males;[99] the wealthier ones retired to India and they sent their children to be educated there.[100] Their interests did not clash with those of Europeans; it was recognized that they had an important role in the country's development, and they were content that Europeans should represent them in the Legislative Council. A few Goans were clerks in banks and stores and in 1931 more than eighty were working on the railway; but these were not sufficiently numerous to constitute a serious barrier to African advancement. Business experience, hard work, a desire for money as such, a capacity to live thriftily, a readiness to reinvest profits, the facility with which they could obtain credit from each other, and the fact that they escaped the extensive demands from kinsmen which were the downfall of many African storekeepers, helped them to run their stores more efficiently than did most Africans. These advantages do not then seem to have aroused jealousy among Africans, and among the villagers, peasants, and plantation-workers the Indian's store became a meeting-place for news and gossip comparable to the village inn in England.[101]

[97] Census reports, 1926 and 1931.   [98] Norman, p. 144.
[99] 1931 Nyasaland Census.   [100] Norman, p. 144.   [101] Ibid., pp. 140–1.

The relationships between Africans and Europeans were also on the whole easy-going. Africans were passing through revolutionary changes, but their response was becoming increasingly positive and forward-looking. The yearning for a return to the past, the rejection of European values, and the desire to escape from the restraints, frustrations, and insecurity that they involved, had erupted explosively but ineffectively in 1915. The future now seemed to lie with a new leadership, with the clerks, teachers, ministers, and small entrepreneurs who were beginning to form associations throughout the country and were taking a lead in demands for increased educational facilities—the door into the white man's world. They did not challenge European leadership, but they criticized, in a respectful manner, certain of its policies.[102]

On their side, many Europeans seem to have viewed African advancement with benevolent approval. Africans were thought of as 'a cheerful and jolly lot', their potentialities were evident, and there was a somewhat *laissez-faire* attitude towards their progress.[103] There was, however, a mysterious side to their nature: an ability to keep a secret, while Europeans remained in ignorance (as had happened in Chilembwe's rising), and a manner of forming their ideas which seemed 'entirely different from that usual to white men'.[104] The gulf was there, but it was not yet significantly exacerbated by political or economic barriers; the small planters were not sufficiently numerous to protest successfully against African competition in cotton and tobacco-growing, they turned to other crops, and in any case few of them had become rooted in the country. Although the Shire Highlands were climatically quite suited to Europeans, the atmosphere could never be described as that of a white man's country. 'It is probable', thought a writer who knew the country well,

that what residents in Nyasaland, or any similar territory, really need is an occasional change, perhaps more for mental reasons than any other. The constant presence of the African seems to bring to some Europeans a kind of mental exhaustion, or inanition.[105]

---

[102] See below, Chap. V, pp. 172–3.   [103] Norman, p. 116.
[104] Ibid., p. 115.   [105] Ibid., p. 105.

And this exhaustion is often felt in different contexts by those who stand in a paternal relationship with other people—by schoolmasters, priests and even parents.

One other problem, which was to develop into the most crucial test for trusteeship in Nyasaland, was beginning to appear. The Kenya settlers' demand for a closer union of the East African territories was sympathetically received at the Colonial Office, where the administrative and economic advantages of larger units were already obvious. As has been seen,[106] the Hilton Young Commission rejected the settlers' demands for political reasons, but it was realized that Nyasaland and Northern Rhodesia were in a position different in some respects from that of the three territories later regarded as East African. In Nyasaland the Commission found European opinion 'divided and uncertain'. The Merchants' Association at Blantyre and the Chamber of Agriculture and Commerce, representing the trading interests and the large agricultural companies, favoured an eventual federation with East Africa; they apprehended 'that the interest of the natives would suffer if Nyasaland were drawn into the orbit of Southern Rhodesia', where it was thought a 'colour bar' would develop. The smaller farmers and planters, however, were opposed to any union with East Africa on account of the 'pro-native' policy of Tanganyika and Uganda; they did not advocate an early change in status, but thought that the first step should be union with Northern Rhodesia, 'leaving the question of federation with Southern Rhodesia for future consideration'.[107]

The Commission itself was divided on the future alignment. The Chairman recommended that the Governor of Southern Rhodesia should be appointed High Commissioner for Nyasaland and Northern Rhodesia, and conferences should be held at Salisbury between representatives of the legislatures to settle differences on important matters of policy. He envisaged the development of two administrative unions: the eastern area of North-Eastern Rhodesia would be joined to Nyasaland, and the rest of Northern Rhodesia, with the exception of Barotseland, which would retain a Protectorate status similar to Bechuanaland, would

[106] See above, pp. 6–7. [107] *Report of the Hilton Young Commission*, p. 279.

be joined to Southern Rhodesia.[108] The majority of the Commission, however, feeling that there were 'so many reasons for eventually linking Nyasaland and a part at least of Northern Rhodesia with the Northern territories', could not recommend 'the forging of any fetters which might bind them permanently to the South'. Instead they recommended the maintenance of the *status quo*.[109]

The problems facing the greater part of North-Eastern Rhodesia were similar to those of Nyasaland. There were two small groups of European settlers at Abercorn and Fort Jameson. Both were virtually separated from the rest of the European community; those of Abercorn exported their produce through Tanganyika, those at Fort Jameson through Nyasaland, and since there was no road joining Fort Jameson with the rest of Northern Rhodesia, the quickest means of transport to Livingstone—the capital—was by rail via Beira and Bulawayo. The Africans of the area, unable to produce cash crops and with practically no means of earning enough locally to pay their tax, were forced to migrate in search of work. Family and tribal life was disrupted, and the area became more impoverished. The Ormsby-Gore Commission concluded that the only solution for both Europeans and Africans was the construction of a railway from the north of Lake Nyasa to some point on the Central Railway of Tanganyika, but finance was not forthcoming.[110]

These problems seemed, however, almost insignificant compared with the dramatic clash which developed in the rich Central and Western Provinces between the ambitions of the European community and the doctrine of trusteeship. At the end of the First World War the mineral wealth of Northern Rhodesia was still largely an unknown quantity. Lead-mining at Broken Hill was increasing in importance, and by 30 September 1923 lead to the total value of £2,259,198 had been produced.[111] Ancient copper-workings at Kansanshi and Bwana Mkubwa were being worked on a small scale, but this was overshadowed by the rapid

---

[108] *Report of the Hilton Young Commission*, p. 261.   [109] Ibid., p. 284.
[110] *Report of the East Africa Commission, 1925*, p. 11.
[111] *Report of the Pim Commission*, p. 18.

development of the rich oxidized ores over the Congo frontier in the Katanga. The railway, however, had been extended by the British South Africa Company to link up with the Belgian system, and in 1923 the Company granted exclusive prospecting rights over large areas to substantial companies. The largest prospecting operation yet attempted, including an aerial survey and trained geologists with modern equipment, was immediately undertaken and in 1925 sulphide ores containing 3 to 5 per cent. of copper were found at a depth of 100 feet.[112]

This discovery ended the period of speculation. By 1929 the *Economist* concluded that Northern Rhodesia would be one of the principal suppliers of copper to the world market and the Copperbelt was entering its first boom.[113] The 1931 Census enumerated 13,846 Europeans, of whom 1,291 had been born in Northern Rhodesia, 4,225 in Great Britain, and 6,824 in the Union of South Africa and other British African territories. About sixty per cent. of those born outside the territory had entered it within the past two years, and eighty-four per cent. within the past ten years.[114] This influx and this boom awoke among Europeans throughout Southern Africa hopes of 'another Transvaal on a smaller scale' which 'may give an opening for strengthening our civilization and reclaiming Africa from barbarism such as has never been dreamt of before'.[115] For the first time in the history of Northern Rhodesia there was a strong economic basis for the settler's hopes. The tenuous railway link with the white man's world of Southern Africa had suddenly become enormously strengthened.

The transition from Chartered Company to Colonial Office rule in 1924 made little immediate difference to the hopes of the European community. The Advisory Council established by the Company in 1919 became a Legislative Council, with nine Official and five Unofficial Members elected on a franchise restricted to British Subjects who fulfilled certain requirements of residence, financial standing, and literacy; and as Africans had the status of British Protected Persons, the electorate was composed of

[112] L. H. Gann, 'The Northern Rhodesian Copper Industry and the World of Copper: 1932–1952', *Rhodes–Livingstone Journal*, No. 18, pp. 4–5.
[113] Ibid.   [114] 1931 Northern Rhodesian Census Report.
[115] Smuts, op. cit., p. 43.

Europeans and a few Indians.[116] These Unofficial Members felt
confident that they were moving along the same path as Southern
Rhodesia towards responsible self-government. 'We are to all in-
tents and purposes a Parliament and likely to become a Parliament,' declared Leopold Moore, their most influential representative.[117] And to these Unofficials it seemed almost self-evident that
democracy would be restricted to Europeans.

It seems to me to be a well established fact that Europeans are the only
people in the world who are capable of exercising the right of election.
The electoral system is generally successful when applied by people of
British origin or descent and in almost every other case, with the
possible exception of Japan, it has been found a failure. Non-European
peoples can only be represented satisfactorily by some method of
nominating Europeans to do so.[118]

The policy of territorial segregation, commenced under the
Chartered Company, was further implemented in 1928 by the
Crown Lands and Native Reserves Order in Council, and alienated
Crown Lands were regarded by the settlers as exclusively European.[119] The threat of economic and political competition leading
to a class of poor whites was, as in Southern Rhodesia, mingled
with fears of miscegenation, and with the supposition that African
primitiveness was ineradicable. Settlers felt that they dwelt among
'masses of uncivilized and ignorant natives',[120] and that 'there is
not one intelligent native in the country'.[121] Their fear was put
succinctly by a Mr. Norris:

The white man simply cannot contemplate the possibility of the black
man being allowed to buy a stand beside him in his township, or elsewhere, to build thereon a house and to rear therein a family. The origin
of this aversion may be said to be race prejudice. It may be. The outcome is nevertheless a fact. An abattoir is not a pleasant place, but steak
and chops are justifiable facts. . . . However, is it not rather a profound

[116] J. W. Davidson, *The Northern Rhodesian Legislative Council* (1948), p. 24.
[117] Quoted by Davidson, op. cit., p. 34. A Londoner who had settled in Livingstone as a
chemist in 1904, Moore was the founder of the *Livingstone Mail*.
[118] Northern Rhodesian Debates, 20 May 1925, col. 106.
[119] See Debate, 18 November 1930, speech by Mr. Norris.
[120] N.R. Debates, 20 May 1925, col. 106.
[121] Moore, quoted by Davidson, op. cit., p. 68.

biological truth? Are not biology, history, anthropology all leading us to an appreciation of the supreme importance of heredity, the supreme value to civilization of superior racial stocks? . . . Both socially and economically we are conscious of the danger of unregulated mingling, of unregulated competition between the races. . . . It is not the fear of competing on even terms. It is the desire, the determination to maintain his standard of living, health and cleanliness, to preserve his racial heritage, and hand it on unimpaired to his children. Unless the white erects and maintains some artificial barriers, with the free intermingling of the races there would creep in the spectre of miscegenation, leading inevitably to the complete absorption of the higher by the lower.[122]

Upon this community, confident and determined to follow the policy of Southern Rhodesia, there broke Lord Passfield's 'Memorandum on Native Policy in East Africa', published in June 1930. Not that there was anything new in the doctrines that were expressed. The Labour Secretary of State in essence did no more than reaffirm the doctrine of trusteeship and the paramountcy of native interests as it had been developed in the twenties by previous administrations and commissions. What was new was the fact that these principles were now to be applied to Northern Rhodesia and that 'immediate steps to ensure strict conformity' were to be taken. On the issues of land, labour, and development the Memorandum was uncompromising. There was to be equality of opportunity in the disposal of Crown lands 'irrespective of race, colour, and religion', and 'effective opportunity' was to be given to Africans to take up plots on lease or by purchase on easy instalments. Great importance was attached to the principle that the African should be 'effectively and economically free to work, in accordance with his own wish, either in production in the Reserves or as an individual producer upon his own plot of land, or in employment for wages'. Taxation was to be limited by capacity to pay 'without hardship, and without upsetting his customary method of life'. African development was to be considered as a 'first charge' on the territory.[123]

The Memorandum shocked European leaders in Northern

---

[122] N.R. Debates, 18 November 1930, col. 40.
[123] *Memorandum on Native Policy in East Africa* (Cmd. 3573, 1930).

Rhodesia, and produced a hardening in their racial attitudes. It was pointed out by Lord Winterton, a large land-owner in Northern Rhodesia and a former Parliamentary Under-Secretary of State for India, that it was calculated to cause alarm 'especially to men and women from Southern Rhodesia and the Union',[124] and it evoked an explosion of indignation from the Unofficial Members of the Legislative Council. A cable expressing dissent and demanding an immediate conference in London was dispatched to the Secretary of State.[125] The Members held that:

The British Empire is primarily concerned with the furtherance of the interests of British subjects of British race and only thereafter with other British subjects, protected races, and the nationals of other countries, in that order. . . . To subordinate the interests of civilized Britons to the development of alien races, whose capability of substantial further advancement has not been demonstrated, appears to be contrary to natural law. . . . The policy is doomed to failure, except on one hypothesis, viz. that the white races are first expelled and the British Government provides the requisite financial resources.

They uttered the warning that:

faced with the declared determination of the Imperial Government to prefer the interests of barbarous races to those of their own, they may seek and find sympathy and aid (interested though it be) from neighbouring colonies enjoying freer institutions and more equitable opportunities.

The Unofficials' request for a conference was rejected, since the views expressed were 'wholly irreconcilable with the considered policy of His Majesty's Government'.[126] Thus rebuffed, they embarked in the following December on a campaign for amalgamation with Southern Rhodesia, and against this background of conflict over basic aims and objectives Northern Rhodesia entered upon its industrial revolution.

[124] *Empire Review*, December 1930.   [125] Cmd. 3731, 1930.   [126] Ibid.

II. LAND POLICY by Philip Mason

I. IN SOUTHERN RHODESIA

(i) *The Land Apportionment Act*

By 1925 almost everyone in Rhodesia who gave the matter any thought at all was agreed that something ought to be done about the land. But there were very varied opinions as to what. The outline of the problem can be stated simply. The land of Southern Rhodesia, in round figures, was ninety-six million acres. Thirty-one million were already in the hands of Europeans, twenty-one and a half reserved for Africans. Forty-three and a half million acres remained undistributed. Africans were entitled by law to buy land outside the Reserves, but in practice they found it almost impossible. The law as it stood was felt as a danger by Europeans, while to Africans it gave encouragement to hopes that in practice could hardly ever be realized. Such a situation must lead to vague apprehensions on one side, sooner or later to active discontent on the other; it could hardly be allowed to go on indefinitely. Should not provision be made for Africans to buy land and own it in the same way as Europeans? And if so, should it not be in a special area and should it not be settled—in their own interests as much as in the Europeans'—how much they might have? If it came to a scramble, long purses would tell and the Europeans would buy up all that was worth having. And if Africans were to be protected, should not Europeans too? Ought not more land to be reserved for Africans and the rest be kept exclusively for Europeans?

These were the arguments commonly used, and on 8 January 1925, the Land Commission was appointed.[1] The Commission was instructed 'to inquire into . . . the expedience and practicability of setting apart defined areas outside the boundaries of the

[1] Southern Rhodesia: *Report of the Land Commission 1925*. Presented to the Legislative Assembly 1926 (C.S.R. 3–1926).

Native Reserves (*a*) within which Natives only shall be permitted to acquire ownership of or interest in land and (*b*) within which only Europeans shall be permitted to acquire such ownership or interest'.

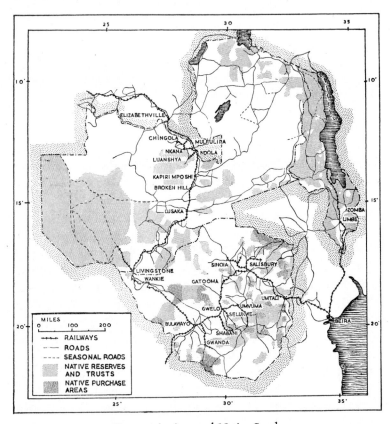

Communications and Native Lands.

In principle, this question could be answered quickly. The Commission found that

the overwhelming majority of those who understand the question are in favour of the existing law being amended and of the establishment of separate areas in which each of the two races, black and white respectively, should be permitted to acquire interest in land. Missionaries, farmers and town-dwellers, the officials of the Native Department, the

Natives in the out-districts and Reserves, so far as they can grasp the subject, and the more advanced Natives are, generally speaking, all of one mind on this subject.

Farmers—that is, Europeans—the report continues, fear disease among their cattle and damage arising from the natives' careless methods; they dislike their neighbourhood for social reasons; they fear their own property will lose value. On the other hand, the natives themselves prefer to be among their own people and dread the worry and trouble that would arise if their herds and flocks strayed on to European farms.

The Commission had heard a great deal of evidence, representing many shades of opinion. It was their duty, not to analyse every element in this composite whole, but to reach conclusions, which of course involve some simplification, but which as conclusions can hardly be impugned. Having concluded that segregation was the wish of the majority, they go on to a discussion of the general principle of segregation which is enlightened and humane. They recognize the growing dependence of the races on each other and the constriction of the world by modern means of travel; they perceive that relations between races will become of increasing and vital importance. Closer association is inevitable, yet in the intermediate stage it is essential to remove as far as possible all causes of friction; some measure of segregation is therefore desirable—though it will not be permanent. They quote with approval Basil Mathews, Lord Lugard, J. H. Oldham, Edgar Brookes, in support of this thesis.[2]

Some segregation, then, is necessary. And alike from two points of view—one bearing on the production of food and the other on the progress and education of the natives—it seemed right that there should be an opportunity for 'the more advanced native' to buy land where he could hold it in his own individual right and improve it. In the Reserves land was still held in common and (said the Commission) vested in the Chief; there were as yet few who wanted a change. But communal tenure prevented all progress, and it was wrong that the few who were ready to learn, who were anxious to improve their stock and their methods, should be held back.

[2] Land Commission, 1925, paras. 51–60.

The principle, then, was settled. There should be separate Native Purchase Areas in which Africans could hold land in individual right; part of the unalienated land should be set aside for this purpose; the rest should be kept for Europeans exclusively. But it was not so easy to decide how much should be set aside for each race. At present both Europeans and Africans had a legal right to buy alienated land; in practice a European could buy anywhere and an African could not. Africans would be required to give up a theoretical right over the whole area in return for an actual right in a specified part; what value should be assigned to what they surrendered? And though Europeans might regard the loss of some part of the area as a fair exchange for exclusive rights in the rest, they would look with jealousy at what they lost. The Commission were clear that the allocation must be carried out 'with a firm determination to do justice'; they were also aware that its terms depended on the decision of white voters, who were one party to the suit, and 'it will only be natural that a fair and equitable apportionment of land in the Colony will seem to many Europeans a generous and perhaps over-generous provision for the Native. . . .'[3]

It was not easy—with the best will in the world—to see where justice lay and on what basis assessment should proceed. What is justice as between a conquered people and their conquerors? Opinion varied widely and proceeded from varied sets of assumptions. One African said in evidence that 'the loaf should be cut in half',[4] a proposition that appeared to embody a simple rough justice and was endorsed by most of his people and by most missionaries[5]—though its exact meaning might have caused controversy if it had been put into force. Lionel Cripps, Speaker in the Legislative Assembly, who for thirty-four years had farmed near Umtali, went further.

I suppose, [he said] if you were to act fairly you would have to give them more than you would give to the white people really . . . it is very hard indeed for them because after all, it amounts to this, that we

---

[3] Land Commission, 1925, para. 77.
[4] Central African Archives, ZAH 1/1/4, p. 1559.
[5] Ibid., pp. 1518, 1597, 1609, and Land Commission, paras. 80–100.

took the country from them by force, and when they endeavoured to regain it, we said that they were rebels.[6]

In these opinions the criterion was justice as between two bodies of people, irrespective of their needs or numbers. Other witnesses reached a less generous conclusion, without specifying very clearly the basis of computation. The most common opinion was that less than a quarter would be enough, while the General Manager of the British South Africa Company thought that 10 per cent. would meet African requirements 'for many years to come'.[7] The Executive Council of the Rhodesia Agricultural Union looked at the matter differently. They thought that to provide 'adequate areas' for the natives would mean there would be no labour on the farms; they thought that not more than one million acres should be set aside.[8]

Here it is worth noting the opinion of the Poor Law Commission in England in 1834: 'We can do little or nothing to prevent pauperism; the farmers will have it: they prefer that the labourers should be slaves; they object to their having gardens saying: "the more they work for themselves the less they work for us".'[9]

The Commission were not impressed by the farmers' arguments; they thought in the first place that those who would buy farms in the Native Purchase Areas would not otherwise have worked as daily labourers, while their younger sons would do so and would provide labourers much more skilled and responsible than those now available. They thought that an adequate provision would not reduce the flow of labour and that in any case it was right in itself. They abandoned the illusory and unreal idea of fairness as between races and decided that they would endeavour to provide, in areas that seemed suitable, holdings of reasonable size for the numbers they thought likely to be ready for individual tenure. On this criterion, they recommended that just over 16 per cent. of the unalienated land, or about seven million acres, should be set aside as Native Purchase Areas; here individual Africans should be permitted to acquire farms of up to 1,000 acres freehold. There

[6] Central African Archives, ZAH 1/1/4, p. 1103.
[7] Central African Archives, ZAH 1/1/4, p. 1250.   [8] Land Commission, paras. 92–7.
[9] J. L. and B. Hammond, *The Village Labourer* (1911), p. 160.

E

would also be allotted for European purchase 17,400,000 acres, and about 19 million acres would remain unassigned; most of the unassigned area was dry, remote, fly-infested Low Veld.[10]

There might—the Commission considered—be two kinds of holdings for Africans, differing mainly in respect of size, though there would be slight variations in the kind of tenure, that for the larger holding resembling freehold and that for the smaller resembling copyhold. Neither could be mortgaged; the Commission refer to the example of the Punjab, where freehold rights were created wholesale after the Sikh Wars and a whole peasantry became enslaved to money-lenders. Neither kind of holding should be sub-let, and in both cases (though with some differences) title would be made dependent on development. But the larger holding might be bought outright and might be sold or disposed of by testament, subject to the approval of the Land Board; this approval would be required in order to prevent sub-division. The allotment, however, would be subject to an annual quit-rent and would pass by intestate succession to one heir; it might be resumed if not beneficially used, but could not be sold.

In considering size, the Land Commission took it as a rough standard that a beast required fifteen acres of rough grazing. This figure would in fact be optimistic in much of Matabeleland, in parts of which twenty-five or even fifty acres are reckoned to a beast; it would be conservative in eastern Mashonaland, and in much of Mashonaland ten would be nearer the usual figure. Another rough standard, applied later, was based on the dung needed to keep arable land in good heart; one beast to an acre of arable was found in practice to be usually enough. By this standard, if in a particular district it is believed that ten acres of rough grazing will support a beast, then there should be one beast and ten acres of grazing for every acre of arable.

The Commission were careful not to recommend a fixed size

[10] The exact figures of the Commission's unanimous recommendations were:

Native Area:	6,851,000
European Area:	17,423,000
Unassigned:	17,793,000

Two of the three members wished to add 117,000 acres to the Native Area and to create a neutral area of 1,099,000 acres.

either for the larger or for the smaller holdings, because the nature of the country varied. They did, however, record the opinion 'that only in exceptional cases should a Native be permitted to hold more than 1,000 acres in freehold, and that if, for the accommodation of his stock, he requires a larger holding, the additional land required should be upon leasehold'. They go on to mention that some Chiefs have as many as 3,000 cattle, and they speak of the danger of the land of the whole country falling into the hands of a few families; it is clear that the intention of the limitation was a laudable concern at the dangers of social inequality, against which Africans required protection. Europeans of course were in need of no such care, partly because they were better able to look after themselves and partly because there was more land allotted to them; a ranch of 20,000 acres in European hands did not constitute a social danger. An African farm of a thousand acres might, according to its district, provide up to 100 acres of arable and grazing for eighty to 100 beasts, a herd that might be increased as the pasture was improved by the use of fencing and controlled grazing. The allotment or smaller holding was more carefully defined; it was to provide grazing for six beasts and arable of 'about ten acres at one time'; the Commission supposed that the arable would be moved from time to time. There was as yet no developed doctrine as to the proper management of an African holding.

Most of the witnesses had thought that the land now to be divided—the unalienated land—should be divided between the two races as though each race was a unit: half to one and half to the other, or three-quarters to one and a quarter to the other. Looked at this way, the recommendation was that the Europeans should have 72 per cent. and the Africans 28 per cent.—rather more than a quarter—of what was now divided. Or the sum could be set out a little more favourably as follows:

European:	Acres in thousands African:
31,033 already alienated	21,594 Reserves
17,423 now allotted	6,851 Native Purchase Areas now allotted
149 urban	406 Missions
	224 Matopo National Park
48,605	29,075

Forty-eight to twenty-nine is 62 per cent. to 37 per cent., not a harsh division as between conqueror and conquered, and there were still 17 million acres unallotted of which use might some day still be made.

But the recommendation had not been reached by so arbitrary a calculation as this implies; it was based on what were believed to be individual needs. It had been estimated that some 50,000 persons now cultivating land in the Reserves would sooner or later move into the new Native Purchase Areas, and that some 200,000 were at present living either on land owned by Europeans already or on the unalienated land which was now to be reserved for Europeans. All these would eventually have to move; that was part of the concept of separate areas. The new Native Purchase Areas should therefore provide for some 250,000 persons, which, reckoning about 100 acres to a family of three and a half persons, meant about seven million acres. There is of course an important assumption behind this bare statement; it was felt just and proper to allot what he needed to the native; all that remained was to be kept for European development, because the land would thus be put to the best use and goods produced for export.

The Report was debated in the Southern Rhodesian Parliament and in general terms accepted; a Bill was drafted, discussed, and passed, but for a technical legal reason had to be re-submitted and passed again. It thus happened that Members, as one of them observed plaintively, had to make three second-reading speeches on the same measure. In all this discussion there was unanimity as to the importance of the subject—'perhaps the greatest of all problems for this young colony', said the Premier[11] (Mr. H. U. Moffat), moving the second reading, and on this at least the Opposition were wholly at one with him. There were some who argued that, because it was so important, the debate and the Bill should be delayed to give a fuller opportunity for discussion—but as to that, the Premier's answer was surely conclusive; the Commission sat in 1925 and the Bill was introduced in 1929. And a number of Members insisted that—in marked contrast with the Union—Rhodesia was in the fortunate position of being able to

[11] Southern Rhodesian Debates, 25 April 1929, col. 71 et seq.

divide the land while there was still plenty of land to divide—an argument, and a strong one, for acting at once; on this the majority were agreed.

There was really only one consistent argument put forward in opposition to the measure. Mr. Danziger,[12] in a speech that as an analysis was thoughtful and far-sighted, contended that it was a mistake to suppose that 'the native' would always be interested solely in pastoral and agricultural occupations; he was quite capable of skilled industrial work, and the 'solution does not lie in keeping him always a hewer of wood. We could not do this if we tried.' Competition with the white artisan was inevitable and as 'the native' became more organized, each reserve would be 'an island of unrest'. 'Once we sell land in any quantities' to the native, 'we can say that in fifty to 100 years Rhodesia will no longer be a white man's country'. 'The native' was intelligent and he was a million strong to 50,000 whites. The only solution—and here Mr. Danziger abandoned analysis—was complete political separation; all African Reserves should be added together to make a solid African State, which would lie to the west of Bulawayo and to which one day a benevolent British Government would add Bechuanaland.

To this the Premier and others replied that the present Reserves were vested in their African inhabitants for ever and guaranteed by the British Government; even if it were legally possible to expropriate their inhabitants—as it was not—it would mean bloodshed to move them, because 'the native' was devoted to his home and the bit of land where he was born. Total segregation might sound attractive, but it was not common sense; the Bill provided a practical, sensible compromise.

This was the view of most of the Members. Almost all spoke, and much in the debate is worth quoting. 'We are the guardians of the natives,' said Mr. Eickhoff,[13] who opposed total segregation on the grounds that it was a breach of trust. 'We govern them; we have assumed responsibility for their upbringing; and when they are grown up that responsibility will be shifted to their shoulders.'

[12] S.R. Debates, 14 May 1929.
[13] S.R. Debates, 23 May 1929, col. 1112 et seq.

'We could not', he went on, quoting J. H. Hofmeyr, 'uphold a European civilization on a basis involving a solemn,[14] discontented and hostile native population.' Mr. Mitchell added a more mercenary consideration; it would be difficult, he said, to maintain the revenues of the State without the large amount paid by the natives in indirect taxation. He was not alone in this view. 'Take away the native,' said Mr. Thomson, 'and the whole structure collapses.'[15] Mr. Gilchrist told the same story; the natives were already a more important element than the Europeans in the revenues of the State, consuming, he argued, nearly twice the value of imports; 'the elimination of the native would be stark ruin'.[16] And he went on: 'All over the world it is written in letters of blood that you must either lift the barbarian up or he will drag you down . . . there is only one hope of salvation, to take the native with you.' If the present Bill were rejected, the alternatives, alike unpleasing, were extermination and miscegenation.

There were other arguments against Mr. Danziger's solution; strategically it would be madness to concentrate the natives all in one area, and besides, the native had a right to stay where he was born; both these points were made more than once. Perhaps the most far-sighted speech was that of Mr. Jobling,[17] who began—as almost everyone did—by emphasizing the importance of the question. How, he went on, can the two races inhabit the same territory with the minimum of friction and the maximum of goodwill? The eventual solution 'must come by slow evolution . . .' and 'we here today may not like it'. The native was progressing very rapidly and there were no limits to his possible development. Repression had never worked and never would; competition was inevitable. Complete segregation was out of the question; for one thing, the Reserves were guaranteed in perpetuity by the British Government. It was no use hoping to get rid of the native; all that could be done was to go step by step, not trying to legislate too rigidly for posterity and 'erring if at all on the side of generosity'.

All were agreed that there must for the present be 'two streams'.

---

[14] Possibly misreported for 'sullen'?   [15] S.R. Debates, 1929, col. 1178.
[16] Ibid., col. 1195 et seq.   [17] Ibid., col. 1182 et seq.

But while the supporters of the Bill thought that one step at a time was all they could take, or—if they looked further—believed that the two streams would gradually come closer together, their opponents felt that the right answer was complete segregation. In this Mr. Davies of the Labour Party was at one with Mr. Danziger. His views were developed more fully in 1930, when the Bill was returned by Parliament in the United Kingdom and Members in Rhodesia had their chance of a third second-reading speech. 'The force of race consciousness and nationalism', said Mr. Davies, 'could not be denied; it could not be repressed.' Competition was inevitable, and must mean the 'disappearance from this country of the white working class'. Segregation—as complete as possible —was therefore the only solution; he thought that the Union, South-West Africa, and Southern Rhodesia should become one country and that representatives of this area should meet to discuss their future and should

set aside a part of Africa capable of being developed to the fullest extent for the free use of the native, with all the culture we can give him and all the experience we have at our disposal, helping him to become a race with a race consciousness and with no fear in his mind that he shall always be regarded as a hewer of wood and drawer of water.

Here is a classical statement of the case for complete territorial 'apartheid', urged as necessary to protect the 'white working people' from 'disappearing' or becoming 'poor whites'; some twenty years later the South African Bureau of Racial Affairs at Stellenbosch were preaching the same doctrine, with the difference that disappearance was ruled out because the Afrikaner 'had no-where else to go'.

What stands out from the debate as a whole is the anxious concern with which all Members looked at the problem and their expressed desire to be fair—whatever that might mean. It is true, of course, that in a debate in Parliament everyone puts the best face he can on his motives; it is equally true that in unbuttoned speech, or even in considered speech privately expressed, the same speaker may expose distinguishable motives. That is not to say that he is deliberately insincere; there are few people in the modern world

who do not do business in more than one currency, in the sense of
a set of basic assumptions. A man who is trying to persuade someone else will suit his argument to his audience, and part of the
interest of this debate lies in the evidence it provides of what was
thought likely to appeal to the audience. And the audience was
primarily the newspapers and voters of Rhodesia; Westminster
for most of the speakers and for most of the time was probably
secondary.[18]

There are various lines of division between the speakers. Some
argue with more and some with less imaginative vision of the
future; some are more conscious of immediate fears than of any
ultimate goal. One division of considerable importance lies between those who think in terms of mixed class and race and those
who think in terms of pure race. The supporters of the Bill, who
had their farms, their businesses, their professional practice, were
employers as much as Europeans; to them the natives were not as
yet personal rivals so much as a working class distinguishable by
skin colour. But to Mr. Davies on the Labour front they were
rivals already, and Mr. Danziger and those who thought like him
regarded a threat to the 'white working people' as a threat to the
whole conception of Rhodesia as a white man's country.

In spite of criticisms, the Act was passed. It embodied an idea of
segregation distinguishably different from apartheid; it was not
based on a difference absolute, ordained by God and eternal. It was
a temporary arrangement, convenient for the moment; those who
had thought about it most deeply believed it would not last. The Act
embodied the recommendation of the Morris Carter Land Commission with a few slight simplifications; the total allotted to the
Native Purchase Areas was 7,444,000 acres, while the Commission
had unanimously recommended the grant of 6,851,000. The Act,
then, was not unfair in its interpretation of the Commission's
views. And there can be little doubt that those who took part in
the debates were persuaded that the Act was fair, or, if anything,
that it 'erred on the side of generosity'.

---

[18] Not everyone will agree with this. Some will suggest that speeches on the Government side were all made with the effect on Westminster in mind throughout. I find this
hard to believe.

But it is difficult to see what exactly 'fairness' can mean in this context, particularly if one is judge in one's own cause. There is a scene in *Sense and Sensibility* in which Mr. John Dashwood discusses with his wife the provision he shall make for his step-mother and his three half-sisters. They are to set up house on their own; they have a small independent income, but he has promised his father on his death-bed that he will do something more for them. He is minded to be generous; he decides to give them a thousand pounds apiece. But his wife points out to him how little four women living alone will need. 'They will live so cheap! Their house-keeping will be nothing at all. They will have no carriage, no horses, and hardly any servants . . . no expenses of any kind.' He halves his first thought; they shall have five hundred. On further consideration he allows himself to be persuaded that what his father had really meant was that he should send them 'presents of fish and game and so forth, whenever they are in season'.

The voters of Southern Rhodesia were very much more generous than Mr. Dashwood; they had none the less been judges in their own cause. The division on which they decided was certainly more favourable to the African than that which had taken place in the Union; there the land available for each African was 5·8 acres, while in Southern Rhodesia it was thirty-five. And the Union had allowed the natives $8\frac{1}{2}$ per cent. of the total land as against 27 per cent. of that so far divided in Southern Rhodesia. Put in this way, the comparison is not altogether fair to the Union; fertility and rainfall ought to be taken into account, and in South Africa the European area included both desert and mountain. The fact remained that Southern Rhodesia had dealt with the problem while there was still land to divide and had been able to provide more than the Union. But the comparison is not very valuable. The Commission had in fact abandoned the idea of 'fairness' and had substituted that of 'sufficiency'; they had reached their total on the basis of providing a reasonable holding for 200,000 Africans who would have to be moved from the European area and for 50,000 eager individualists from the Reserves. But neither of these figures had much reality. The latter was admittedly a guess and the 200,000 did not in fact move—not at any rate until these estimates of what was needed had become irrelevant.

The Land Apportionment Act became law on 1 April 1931, and those paying rent on European land then had six years' notice to quit. But whereas there were 185,000 natives on private European land in 1930, there were 197,000 in 1939, and the increase was probably more than the figures would indicate, because in 1936 there was a change in the method of making estimates which reduced all the figures. In 1930 there had been thought to be 146,000 on Crown land, wherever it might be; this was sub-divided in 1933, when there were thought to be 48,000 on Crown land in the Native Area and 132,000 on Crown land in the European area. By 1939 the 48,000 had grown to 67,000 and the 132,000 to 141,000.[19] Until the outbreak of war, then, in spite of the Land Apportionment Act, the number of Africans in the

[19] The figures are in each case arrived at by a calculation from the number of tax-payers and the method of calculation was changed in 1936; in that year it looks as though there had been a reduction, but in fact there is no reason to suppose there was any drop in total numbers, and the redistribution between different areas must therefore be assumed to be slightly misleading. The figures are given in thousands. No figures are given for the unassigned area until 1944 and it is not clear whether this 60,000 was previously left out of account or included under another head.

African Population: In thousands:

	In the Reserves	On unalienated land i.e. Crown land		On land alienated to Europeans	
		Crown land, Native Area	Crown land, European Area		
1930	621	146		185	
1931	641	154		179	
1932	656	161		182	
1933	675	48	132	185	
1934	688	30	163	192	
1935	732	35	154	178	
		Native Purchase Area			
1936	719	54	136	169	
1937	755	59	136	184	
1938	781	65	132	194	
1939	793	67	141	197	
1940	819	69	not available	not available	
					Unassigned Area
1944	932	113	74	159	60

European area had increased, while in the Native Purchase Area it was already 67,000, against the 50,000 for which provision had been made. But few of them were on their own land. When the Act had been in force for four years it was said that 'rather remarkable progress had been made' and that 250 grants to natives had been made.[20] By the end of September 1944 the number of farms surveyed was 2,024, of which 316 had been sold and paid for and 1,352 were held on leases or agreements of purchase.[21]

The assumptions on which the Land Commission had based their recommendations regarding the amount of land needed thus proved to be mistaken. The question of what land was available for Africans and how many it would really hold was discussed in 1935 in an article in the *Journal of the Royal Africa Society* by A. C. Jennings, Assistant Director of Native Lands in Southern Rhodesia. He pointed out that overall figures were misleading, because holdings of the same size would carry much more in the east than in the west; in the east a holding of 100 acres might support as many as ten beasts and ten people, but in the west five or six hundred acres would be needed to feed as many men and cattle. Having allowed for this, he thought the seven million acres of the Native Purchase Areas must be supplemented by twelve million acres of the seventeen million unallotted; this would have to be cleared of tse-tse—a gigantic task—and when that was done there would be the possibility of 50,000 holdings of an average size of about 400 acres, supporting half a million people. The old Reserves, of about the same size, that is about twenty-one and a half million acres, would hold more—say, one person to twelve acres and ten persons to a holding of 120 acres, or a total of one and three-quarter million people. Add, say, half a million employed by Europeans, and you reached a total of two and three-quarter million Africans as the maximum the country would hold. The estimated native population in 1936 was one and a quarter million; it was supposed that this figure would double itself in thirty-five years. Mr. Jennings' article proceeded on the assumption, already challenged, that 'the native' would always be either a peasant or

[20] A. C. Jennings, *Journal of Royal Africa Society*, 1935.
[21] *Report of Native Production and Trade Commission, 1944* (C.S.R. 2–1945).

an employee of Europeans; the moral of his calculations—though, being an official, he left it unsaid—was that Southern Rhodesia had about thirty-five years in which to reclaim twelve million acres from tse-tse and completely reform the use of land in the Reserves.

Mr. Jennings also gave, almost without comment, some facts about European ownership of land. About thirty-two million acres were then in European hands, carrying an agricultural population of about 11,000—a density of one person to 1,800 acres. He added that a good deal of this land was quite unsuitable for small holdings; the best economic use in these areas was extensive, in huge ranches. In the Midlands of Rhodesia, European farms should be between one and two thousand acres, and some twelve million acres there should make 10,000 holdings and carry 40,000 people—one person to 300 acres. About two-thirds of the European area was 'actively and beneficially occupied'.

In the course of his article, Mr. Jennings discussed the vital question of cattle in the Reserves. When he wrote, the twenty-one and a half million acres of the Reserves carried an estimated total of 676,000 persons and 1,085,000 cattle; this was thirty-two acres to a man and nineteen to a beast. If the land was properly used, he thought the human population might increase until there were twelve acres to a person and the cattle until there were fifteen acres to a beast. There was thus clearly very little room for an increase in the number of cattle, up to one and a half million at the most. But in fact cattle were increasing very much more quickly than human beings; estimates put the cattle in native hands at 33,000 in 1911 and 1,555,000 in 1938[22]—already over Mr. Jennings' maximum, and the excess was worse in some Reserves than in others. Too many cattle lead to erosion of the top soil; they strip the land of its protective covering of herbage so that the rain tears off the stored humus; they walk to their watering-places and dipping-tanks on paths which storm-water carves into deep gullies. The Commission of 1939 estimated that by 1937 16 per cent. of the total arable land in the Reserves had been destroyed by erosion.

Mr. Jennings ended his consideration of the Land Apportionment Act by the remark that the problem was really becoming one

[22] *Report of the Commission on the Natural Resources o ¹the Colony.*

of marketing. If natives became exporters on a large scale of agricultural produce there would be a rise in everyone's standard of living; it was a mistake to suppose that if there was more for the native there would be less for the immigrant. This was true; he might have added that there was also a basic problem of the proper use of land which the Land Apportionment Act was bound to bring quickly to a head. It was usually for lack of capital that the European had not developed all his land; it was through ignorance that the African, on the other hand, was seldom making the best of his holding. The Africans in the Reserves in the main still continued their old system of joint ownership and communal grazing, which had worked very well when they could roam at will over many thousands of acres that were now European farms, but which quickly became inefficient when they were restricted to a fixed area. Neither Africans nor Europeans were making full use of the areas allotted to them, yet in some Reserves the land was over-stocked and its fertility was being destroyed; a process had begun which must lead steadily towards the ruin of the soil.

The ingredients in this approaching disaster were not merely bad husbandry and an obsolete system of land tenure; they were psychological and social. Africans still thought that it was the duty of a chief—or in this case of the Government—to supply every one of his subjects with enough land to feed him and his wives and children; they still thought of the land as something to be used and left to rest for long periods; they would hardly—until they owned it—work to preserve its fertility. Europeans on the whole still thought of all Africans as immutable in their habits. Few on either side perceived that while the land could produce far more if farming became more specialized, the revolution in land tenure and farming methods which this would involve would mean the growth of a new class of urban and industrial African divorced from the land. To the eventual numbers of this kind of African there need be no economic reason to set the kind of limit Mr. Jennings envisaged. Both an agricultural and an industrial revolution were needed, and they must go hand in hand. The revolution in agriculture might have been postponed if it had not been for the Act; but the Act limited the land available for

Africans, and thus made increased production an immediate necessity. By the time Mr. Jennings wrote, both revolutions had made an unobtrusive start.

(ii) *The Revolution in African Farming*

The Land Apportionment Act made inevitable that revolution in land tenure which had to take place before there could be a real improvement in agricultural methods. In England, too, the medieval system of village strip cultivation and common grazing was an obstacle to improved methods and had to go; in England, too, its going meant an improvement in the total wealth of the country, but immediate loss to many poor commoners. And it meant also a loss to the commoners in independence and happiness that could not be measured in terms of money, nor very sensibly weighed against the gains in wealth and leisure of their grand-children.

The African of Rhodesia could hardly go through a similar period of change without losses which might be even heavier; he might, however, avoid some of the dangers if those who guided him had their eyes open to what was happening.

The Native Purchase Areas recognized the existence of 'the progressive native', and the scheme for African ownership avoided the worst mistakes of the Glen Grey Act in the Union; Edgar Brookes, from the standpoint of South African liberalism, wrote in 1933 that on the whole Southern Rhodesia's policy regarding the division of land was 'good, informed with a spirit of equity, a real wish to be fair'. It was 'a sober agrarian policy capable of defence in certain circumstances or at certain stages of development'.[23] Segregation in its Rhodesian form was sometimes called possessory segregation, because it meant that the races were segregated in the matter of possessing land, but not divided into separate states; it was also called evolutionary segregation, because it was not meant to last for ever.

But, as we have seen, the distribution of farms in the Native Purchase Area went slowly; those Africans who had the money to buy and stock such farms seldom had the experience of modern

[23] E. H. Brookes, *The Colour Problems of South Africa.*

farming they needed and there was no machinery for providing them with advice. It was to the Reserves that the State directed such effort as it made to produce the needed revolution. It was a need that had been seen for some time by a few, but it was not easy to turn that realization into action.

As far back as 1913, the Chief Native Commissioner had written in his annual report: 'The conversion of native land tenure from the communal to the individual system is the true basis on which the progress of the natives is to be evolved. . . .'[24] And he reverts to the point again several times, recommending in 1920 that areas near existing Reserves should be set aside for individual purchase and commenting on the dawn of the idea that crops could be improved by better methods of agriculture.[25] It was in this year that a beginning was made by the appointment of a Director of Native Development and the setting up of the first industrial school at Domboshawa. Here at first the emphasis was on building and carpentry; agriculture was a poor third.

At some of the mission schools, however, agriculture was being taught, notably at Mount Silinda, where the American Board of Missions employed an agricultural missionary, Mr. E. D. Alvord, who by 1921 had already established a five-year course in agriculture and a four-year rotation of crops on a school demonstration plot of six acres. His ideas were of great influence in the subsequent development of Domboshawa and the other industrial schools which followed it; it was he who developed a system of agriculture which was suited to African methods and to small plots, a system which could be easily taught. This last aspect was very important; critics of the Southern Rhodesian system forget it, but the point was brought home to Alvord at a very early stage in his career as an instructor, when he was still a missionary.

He had an excellent crop of maize in the school demonstration plot; he arranged a meeting of Africans from all over the neighbourhood. They had never seen such maize before; they were filled with admiration. He explained how it had been done. His methods

---

[24] *Report of the Chief Native Commissioner for 1913* (A8–1914).
[25] *Report of the Chief Native Commissioner for 1920* (A10–1921).

were simple: the secret was simply thorough cultivation and plenty of dung. The audience shook their heads and laughed; they knew that the real reason was magical. He told the pupils who had dug the fields and worked the manure into the soil to describe the processes they had carried out, but they too asserted that it was all due to magic; they were sure, they said, that Alvord had crept out in the night to sprinkle medicine on the fields. He was in despair; he felt he could never teach them. And then there occurred to him a simple thought, which to anyone not accustomed to Rhodesia in the twenties would seem obvious, but which in the time and place was revolutionary. So long as a white man tried to teach the peasants, they would not believe that they could do what he did. It must be an African who taught them. He must be a trained professional demonstrator.

The Mission Council at Silinda agreed to the plan; the man was found and trained; he in his turn found six others, each of whom he persuaded to manage a plot of one acre on the lines laid down for him. The six did as they were told; what they were told amounted simply to thorough cultivation with plenty of well-rotted cattle manure from old kraals; the results were startling, in spite of drought which did much damage to surrounding crops, being in light land with little humus and little power to retain moisture. Others came and begged to be shown how to do the same; ten more plot-holders were chosen, and the original six moved on to the second year of a four-course rotation.

Alvord entered the service of the Southern Rhodesian Government as Agriculturist for Instruction of Natives; he was at first a member of the Department of Agriculture, which had so far been conceived as solely for the benefit of Europeans, and he found it hard to make much progress until he was transferred to the Native Affairs Department. This was in 1927. Here he developed and taught more widely the simple system of agriculture of which he had already proved the success.

The system is based on the kind of country usually found in the Reserves. It is mostly the light, sandy soil originally preferred by the Mashona; there is usually a good deal of rocky and broken ground not suitable for arable. The arable is a fraction of the total land available in the Reserve, varying according to the climate and geographical position, usually from about one-tenth to about one-twentieth. The arable plot will usually be from about five to ten acres, and for every acre the farmer should keep one beast. The cattle are to be penned at night; during the day they graze over the uncultivated land, except after the harvest, when they are turned on to the arable. The dung from the pen is composted with what vegetation is available and once every four years a quarter of the arable is heavily manured. Maize is grown on that quarter after manuring and maize again the next year, preferably with a fertilizer; next year comes a leguminous crop such as ground-nuts to fix the nitrogen in the soil, and finally a millet, which, according to Alvord, 'smothered the weeds and filled the soil with a dense growth of fibrous roots', and, when eventually ploughed in, had an effect similar to a grass ley.

The system is open to theoretical criticism on the ground that it progressively robs the grazing for the arable; further, one might expect the yields from the arable to get steadily less. On stiffer soil with more rainfall there can be little doubt that better results would be obtained by alternate leys. But it is claimed that on the sandveld which constitutes most of the Mashonaland Reserves a grass ley does not in fact improve land once treated in this way, while there are plots which have been under this course for twenty-five years and show no sign of falling off. The best of them give thirty bags of grain to the acre, while by the old method the average obtained from the Reserves is less than two bags to the acre. There are two determining points in favour of this system: it is easy to teach and it is suited to the terrain. In some of the Reserves it would be difficult to find sites for an alternate ley.

The progress made by persuasion was in one sense considerable. It was the task of the demonstrator to establish 'plot-holders', peasants whose work on their own holdings he would supervise closely; there was an outer circle of 'co-operators', who followed the general lines of the teaching without such close supervision; the best plot-holders were awarded the title of Master Farmer and given a badge. In 1927 there were two demonstration centres and eleven plot-holders; in 1946 there were 103 demonstration centres

F

and 5,393 plot-holders. The average return from an approved plot over twenty years was nine bags of grain to the acre, while the average for land farmed by the old methods was estimated at between one and two bags.[26]

This represented an immense amount of hard work, but in a sense—looked at from the point of view of the colony as a whole —it was depressing. The acres under cultivation in the Reserves fluctuated slightly, but broadly speaking had increased from about one and a quarter million acres in 1927 to about one and a half million in 1939; it could not be said, however, that there had been a corresponding increase in the total produce. In 1932 it was estimated that the Reserves produced 3,298,000 bags of grain; that total had not been beaten by 1939. The greatly improved results on the approved plots had been on too small a scale to affect the total.

At the same time, two parallel developments had been taking place. They concerned the consolidating of holdings, or centralization, and the conservation of the soil. The first was an essential part of the reform of land tenure which had so long ago been recognized as necessary. The land 'belonged' to the tribe; the individual—with the permission of the tribe, expressed as a rule by the Chief—had the use of certain plots, often scattered widely and in small fragments. Not only was much time wasted in going from one to another, but if the cattle were not to damage crops on these scattered plots they must be kept till after the harvest in an area often very confined, which they would over-graze, while in other areas, between the crops, the grass lost its protein content and was wasted.

Alvord has described[27] how in 1928 he persuaded a sub-chief of the Selukwe Reserve, Mhlolo, of the advantages of consolidating into single holdings the scattered plots of each individual and at the same time bringing together into one block all the holdings of arable which came under one headman. While the grass was growing and at its best, the cattle could graze everywhere except in the arable block; they could be turned on to that after the

[26] *Report of the Chief Native Commissioner for 1946* (C.S.R. 48–1947).
[27] In an unpublished paper in the possession of the Institute of Race Relations.

harvest. 'Mhlolo deserves a monument erected to his memory,' wrote Alvord, 'for ... he stood up against the antagonism of Paramount Chief Nema, his Witchdoctors and all his followers, and stated that he and the thirteen Headmen under him had decided to centralize.' Nema had already opposed the presence of a demonstrator and the practice of new methods of agriculture, on the ground that, if the land proved to be good, the Government would take it away and give it to white men; he was described by Alvord as 'an old conservative reprobate, steeped in superstition, witchcraft and taboos'. In 1930, only a year after his opposition to Mhlolo, Nema and all his forty-four Headmen demanded that their land too should be centralized; they had seen the effect on Mhlolo's cattle and the prices he was getting for them. By the end of 1943 the total area 'centralized' was 7,386,250 acres, representing 34·9 per cent. of the total area of the Reserves;[28] having at first been carried out by persuasion and later been eagerly sought, this was a remarkable achievement.

The second development concerned the conservation of soil, and that in its turn fell into two clearly defined parts, positive and negative. The positive aspects consisted mainly of ridging the land along the contours and ploughing parallel with the ridges, thus forming embryonic terraces to hold the maximum of water, providing at the same time storm-drains to carry away sudden excess without damage. With this went a careful siting of the dipping-points for cattle and the provision of new drinking-places, so that cattle could use a wide area of grazing and avoid making paths which would turn into torrents. But this could be of no avail unless the numbers of cattle were limited, and so a great part of the energies of the Native Affairs Department was turned into the thankless task of persuading the people of the Reserves to keep down the numbers of their cattle.

The figures are revealing. At first the cattle increased much faster than the people in the Reserves: in 1911 it was estimated that the cattle in the Reserves were over 330,000; by 1926 they had become 1,197,000. The increase continued steadily until 1932, when the estimate was 1,755,000: next year, for the first time,

[28] *Report of the Native Production and Trade Commission, 1944.*

there was a slight drop, and from that date onwards there was a
very slight annual decrease to 1,555,000 in 1938, followed by a
rise to 1,824,000 in 1943. The decrease was at first the result of
natural causes; foot-and-mouth disease was bad in 1931 and 1932,
while 1933 was a dry year, and for 1934 the Chief Native Commissioner reported that the main reason for the smaller number of
cattle was deaths from poverty. But for years the Chief Native
Commissioners had reported that many Reserves were over-
stocked and it became an object of policy to de-stock 'by administrative persuasion'. Briefly referred to in the Report for 1938, by
1946 de-stocking had become an important section of the Report;
under the Natural Resources Act it was no longer a matter of
'administrative persuasion' but a statutory power. The 'excess' of
native cattle at the beginning of this year was 341,000, which had
been reduced to 267,000 by the end, a net reduction of 70,000
after accounting for a natural increase of probably 120,000.[29]

The social importance of this agricultural policy is considerable.
'Cattle are and always have been a symbol of wealth and position
among the Matabele and in a lesser degree among the Mashona,'
wrote the Commission on Native Production of 1944. They were
intimately connected with marriage by the custom of *lobola*; in
some sections the cattle of the *lobola* were divided among the
senior relatives of the woman's family and were due to be
returned to the man's if the marriage failed; what complications
might ensue if a Government official considered that one uncle's
beast ought to be sold and not another's! And again, cattle were
often dedicated to an ancestor, and something worse than disrespect might be involved in sending to the butcher an animal that
had already been given to a grandfather.[30] But these were not the
only considerations. By the fifties much of Alvord's teaching on
agriculture had soaked through; it was no longer difficult—most
Native Commissioners would agree—to persuade a Chief that
his land ought not to carry more than so many beasts. It was not so
easy to answer him convincingly when he went on to assert that

[29] *Report of the Commission on the Natural Resources of the Colony* (C.S.R. 40–1939),
Report of the Native Production and Trade Commission, 1944, Reports of Chief Native
Commissioners, 1913 to 1946.
[30] Gelfand, *Medicine and Magic of the Mashona.*

the remedy was not fewer cattle but more land and to point down the valley to land still undeveloped in the European area. Here, in something very near to his heart, was a cause for the rural African to feel resentment.

Next to cattle came the marketing of maize. This was controlled by a series of Acts of great complexity, the details of which may be disregarded, but of which the broad effect was that though the African grower might part with his maize to a neighbour who wanted to consume it himself, if he sold it as a cash crop it must go to the Maize Marketing Board, either direct or through certain licensed traders or 'trader-producers'. The Board paid an estimated price, a conservative price which would leave a safe margin for the cost of acquiring the maize and would make it possible to build up reserves. This was reasonable enough if it operated, or appeared to operate, impartially, but there were several ways in which it did not.

In the first place, most Africans in the Reserves sold their grain to trader-producers, who 'almost invariably pay for it as grade D',[31] the lowest of six grades. The assumption that native-grown maize would always be dirty and of poor quality had once been justifiable, but by 1944 it was out of date. A second practice, defensible in the office, was difficult to explain in the kraal; the European grower usually delivered in bulk at railhead, while maize from the native was bought in small quantities near the field where it was grown; a lower price was paid for grain collected at a distance from a railway station or siding. This produced an apparent discrepancy which a peasant in any country in the world might find hard to understand. A third genuine ground for discontent may have often escaped notice; the prices were fixed for the bag of 200 lb., but sales in the Reserves were usually measured by the capacity of four-gallon petrol tins, reckoned as six to the bag; these tins were sometimes hammered all over to stretch the metal and increase the capacity; a trader using a tin like this with the grain well shaken down might get 228 lb. to the bag and pay for only 200 lb.[32]

But beyond all this lay a differentiation which arose from the

[31] *Report on Native Production* (C.S.R. 2–1945).   [32] Ibid.

distribution of the Board's grain between export and local consumption. The price realized for grain sold within the country
was often much higher than the world price, but no record
was kept of which producer's maize went overseas and which
producer's actually brought in the high local price. The total
result was shared; but it was assumed that the native share of
the higher prices—or 'quota allocation'—was considerably less
than the European. The provisions of the Acts were extremely
complicated and disguised the result; shorn of complications, this
was stated by the Native Production and Trade Commission as
follows:

> From the Native point of view there can be no valid objection to the
> control of the marketing of maize. But his confidence has unquestion-
> ably been very seriously shaken by the differentiation in price, grade
> for grade, which, when export is necessary, arises from the lower quota
> allocation.[33]

The Commission go on to list 'the reasons given to justify the
differentiation', of which the two most startling were that 'it
being essential to restore the fertility of European maize farms,
European maize-growers necessarily require a higher price than
the Natives' and that the standards of living were different. Both
these reasons were of course unhesitatingly condemned by the
Commission.

If, with that detachment which distance in time and space can
confer, one considers the Land Apportionment Act of 1931 and
its results, it becomes apparent that a measure that was designed to
achieve segregation in fact brought integration closer. The Act
aimed at the restriction of Africans to their own area; this was only
justifiable if there was enough land in their own area to support
them, but it now became apparent that in some parts they were
overcrowded, and thus it became essential to increase African production. Since the amount of land for Africans was limited, this
made a revolution in African farming and land tenure inevitable.
Such a revolution in its turn was bound to produce a class of professional farmers and leave no place for those who alternated

[33] *Report on Native Production* (C.S.R. 2–1945).

uneasily between a badly managed fragment of land and a half-hearted job in a town. A new class, the permanently urbanized African, was the logical consequence of the Land Apportionment Act—and the urban African hardly fitted into a scheme of segregation.

The agricultural and agrarian revolutions grew in momentum during the thirties and forties. At first, such progress as was made was due to the efforts of a small band of enthusiasts led by Alvord; their altruism met with much opposition from those European farmers who took the short-term view that the more grain the native grew, the poorer would be their own sales. There were conservative elements in the Native Affairs Department who shared this outlook, but there was always enough support at the top to overcome difficulties and to continue with a progress that might be small in relation to the whole territory but which provided a growing body of experience, and which made possible the Native Land Husbandry Act of 1951. There was no such body of experience in the Colonial Office territories; Nyasaland in the fifties was still making experiments in centralization on the scale of Alvord's first effort in the twenties; in East Africa it was revolutionary that the Royal Commission of 1956 should put individual tenure of land in the forefront of their proposals. But by 1951 Southern Rhodesia could speak with authority of what was possible and how it could be done.

The Native Land Husbandry Act of that year summed up the teaching of thirty years and made it possible to enforce what so far had been mainly a matter of persuasion. The Act would come into operation in stages; in a typical area a survey would first collect information—the number of residents, the number of families entitled to cultivate, the amount of land available, and how much was fit for cultivation. This would make possible decisions as to the size of an arable holding and the number of cattle that might go with each holding. There would be a great deal of practical work to be done: demarcating holdings, contouring and terracing, providing boreholes and dipping-tanks; eventually, the crucial stage would be reached when cultivation was prohibited throughout the area except by the registered holders of farming rights in specified plots. These rights are transferable and heritable, but the holder may be forced to sell if he has three times been convicted for failure to protect his land or to use it properly.

It remains to be said that seven years after the passing of the Act there were reasonable grounds for believing that it would be in operation everywhere in another three years. In a justification of the Act published in 1955 it was calculated that some 200,000 male African workers retained an interest in the Reserves and worked for about eight months of the year in a town. This figure, it was believed, would be reduced to about 75,000 in the eighth year from the Act's full implementation; presumably it would continue to get less. Thus the growth of a permanent urban class was clearly envisaged. The Act provided for villages, towns, and business centres in the Reserves in which Africans would be able to buy land outright, but by 1953 no steps had yet been taken to make it possible for an African to live near the great industrial centres in a house which he could regard as his own.

The Native Land Husbandry Act was perhaps bound to be unpopular with urban or half-urban Africans, just as the enclosure of the commons in England would perhaps have been impossible in a true democracy; the policy embodied in the Act seems to have been carried out with a good deal more concern for justice than the enclosures were in England. But for the rural African the good of the agrarian revolution was often obscured, partly by the fact that it was imposed from above and partly by the culling of cattle and the marketing of maize.

At about this time, the mid-fifties, India and Pakistan were proving that a revolution in agricultural methods which has made no progress when imposed from above can take place with dramatic swiftness if the psychological approach is changed. If a village community thinks that better seed is what the Government want them to sow, they will dislike it; once they think it is something they have found for themselves, they will compete for it eagerly. To this simple proposition and all that it implies, the authorities of Southern Rhodesia were still strangers.

As for the marketing of maize, here surely was a differentiation that grew solely from the concept of the two nations. To grading no one could reasonably object, but it was quite unfair to assume that of a given grade which had sold at two prices, more European grain sold at the higher price. It would have been easy to be fair about this. And the financing of the policy embodied in the Native Land Husbandry Acts reads strangely if the words 'European' and 'Native' are replaced by 'big farmers' and 'little farmers'. The scheme for improving little farms was recommended by the Minister as 'a carefully planned attack on the squandering of our most valuable asset'. 'Implementation of the Act means not only far better use of vast resources, it means also a greatly increased contribution to national welfare through the better employment of human resources.'[34] Such a scheme for small farmers in England today is being financed by loans on easy terms and some capital grants from national resources—national resources, not funds collected only from small farmers. The Southern Rhodesian scheme is financed differently because the small farmers are thought of as a different nation; the cost of speeding up the scheme was estimated in 1953 to be £6½ million, of which £3½ million was to be contributed from national income and the rest from the Native Development Fund, two-thirds by borrowing and one-third from current income. The income of the Native Development Fund is mainly derived from levies on native produce—that is to say, it comes from the pockets not of the nation as a whole, not of the farmers as a whole, but of the small farmers only.

It is an article of belief with almost every European in Southern Rhodesia that 'the native is not taxed'. It is equally an article of faith with every African that Africans are over-taxed. The truth is difficult to reach because in addition to direct taxes such as poll-tax and dog-tax, Africans pay a share of indirect taxation which can only be estimated. An estimate puts the taxes believed to be paid by Africans as a percentage of their income at about one per cent. less than the percentage of their income paid by Europeans—whose income is of course many times greater. The figures can be challenged and claim no accuracy, but they do invalidate the

[34] *What the Native Land Husbandry Act means to the Rural African* (Government, Salisbury, 1955).

belief common among Europeans. Looked at from a different point of view, in a homogeneous modern state it is taken for granted that the lowest income-group pays no taxes and receives many benefits from the national income.

2. IN NYASALAND

In Nyasaland the course of events was very different. The note had been struck long ago when Sir Harry Johnston distinguished between tropical dependencies, such as Nyasaland, Northern Rhodesia, and Uganda, and 'white man's country', such as Southern Rhodesia and South Africa. He was thinking mainly of climate, but quite apart from that there was another difference. Here in Nyasaland there had been no one paramount chief, no Lobengula or Lewanika, to cede rights over the whole country; here there had been no Company's rule. In Southern Rhodesia there was one claimant, the Company, which was for most purposes also the Government. But in Nyasaland, when the British Protectorate was proclaimed in 1891, there was already a confusion of European claims to have 'bought' land from various chiefs. They came from both companies and private persons.

These claims were investigated by Johnston, and with a certain austerity. He was the detached agent of an Imperial Government, acting as a trustee both for the Government and for the inhabitants. He represented neither shareholders nor settlers. 'There are claimants', he wrote to Lord Rosebery, 'whose demands it would be impossible for me to satisfy to the full unless I handed over to them thirty, forty, or fifty square miles of territory, with all the native inhabitants as serfs, with exclusive mining rights, road-making rights, and in some cases a right to exclude all other Europeans from the land.'[35] He visited the site of each claim and made sure that the chief had known what he was doing and that a fair price—which meant between 3*d*. and 1*d*. an acre—had been paid. If the land included African villages, he usually disallowed the claim, but found other land for a claimant who genuinely meant to develop it. When he was satisfied, he gave a 'certificate

[35] Quoted by Roland Oliver in *Sir Harry Johnston*.

of claim'; this always provided that African inhabitants already on the land must not be forced to pay rent or disturbed.

Even when Johnston had whittled down these claims so far as he could, the area alienated came to fifteen per cent. of the Protectorate. Thereafter it was Johnston's policy to relinquish as little land as possible in freehold; he believed its value would rapidly increase and that the profit should accrue to the State, not to speculators. But for all his care there were already grounds for African suspicion which events in Rhodesia did nothing to dispel. 'They are going to take away our land and give it to Europeans'— that was the fear that was to haunt African minds in Nyasaland for the next sixty years.

In Rhodesia, one of the first acts of the self-governing colony had been to inquire into the setting apart of African and European land; in Nyasaland, too, the question had to be considered, and a Commission was set up in 1920 to report on land policy in general and in particular on whether it was desirable that special areas should be set aside for 'non-natives', and whether Reserves should be created and natives settled on them. The Chairman was a judge; the Commission included officials, a missionary, European residents; they were all people who had lived and worked in Nyasaland, with no direct importations from Britain. But they were unanimous and emphatic in rejecting the idea of Reserves. They would be 'an unwarrantable interference with the free occupation by the people of their native land'. They would be 'totally unsuited to their way of life', of which they would involve 'a complete disruption'.[36]

Emphatic though this was, the Africans of Nyasaland would not have been altogether reassured if they had read the report. There had been an increase in European settlement since the war; the land held under lease, almost all by Europeans, had been 13,757 acres in March 1919, and in March 1921 had risen to 118,506 acres. The Commission assumed that this was beneficial; it was European settlement that stimulated all development and progress; it also provided a market for African labour close at hand. There was a total surplus of cultivable land in the Protectorate and in many

[36] Zomba 10582, Report dated 21 October 1921.

districts there was more—it was believed—than Africans could reasonably need in the next thirty years; in these districts the land suitable for Europeans should be surveyed in blocks of about 1,000 acres each and marked off. This would give the Africans security of tenure in what remained and allay anxiety. It was calculated that there was still a total of about two and a half million acres of surplus land in the Protectorate.

These were the arguments the Commission used. They were based on a calculation that African needs were normally limited to eight acres a hut; this included a system of alternate leys and provision for increase of population.[37] The figures are, incidentally, hardly comparable with those for Southern Rhodesia because most of the population of Nyasaland live in districts where there are no cattle, while rainfall and fertility are higher. This rate of eight acres was for tribal holdings. It was accepted that some Africans would one day want individual tenure—indeed, a few wanted it already—and the recommendations included the provision of small holdings of ten acres each and small farms of 100 acres. But these were exceptions to the general rule, which was 1,000 acres for a European and eight for a native.

The recommendations would be known and would hardly allay African suspicion. It is true that the Commission did not think many Europeans would come and that they emphasized Sir Harry Johnston's old point that Nyasaland was not 'white man's country'. 'The nature of European settlement is not permanent,' they wrote, arguing for leases rather than freehold, and they made it clear that a settler would have many difficulties to face and that only 'the right kind' of settler was wanted. The recent influx of Europeans had produced a disturbance of conditions and it would be wise to reorganize labour, improve communications, and let recent immigrants find their feet before encouraging more to come. There is no hint of racial rivalry, no suggestion of the need for reinforcements; the Commission's object in demarcating blocks of 1,000 acres at once was to give Africans confidence that the rest of their land would not be taken. But such confidence

[37] Two acres per hut in cultivation at one time; two acres fallow; four acres for the future.

would only arise if Africans believed the assurance that this was positively the last time and that what remained to them would be respected for ever. And events elsewhere surely gave them little ground for supposing that such finality was likely; surely in fact the demarcation of farms for Europeans would be far more likely to increase than reduce suspicion.

The possibility of an influx of Europeans was the main reason for the Commission's appointment, and that in itself, whatever their recommendations, was disturbing to Africans. And their suspicion was continually kept alight by the grievances of the natives who lived on private estates. Johnston had tried, as far as possible, to confine the estates to areas where few natives lived, but since this could not always be ensured he had given certificates of claim on the condition that residents were not to be disturbed. But a variety of causes soon combined to confuse this simple arrangement.

In the first place, shifting cultivation was still the rule, so that after even twenty years it was not easy to identify either the residents or the land they had occupied when the certificate of claim was granted. Secondly, most of the tribes involved were matrilineal and matrilocal; it was not the bride who came to her husband, but the man who came from outside to join his wife's group—and was he then 'resident' in the terms of the certificate or was he not? Next, it was a widespread custom in Southern Africa for a European landowner to permit 'squatters' to live on his land, each being allowed to cultivate enough to feed his family, perhaps graze a few animals, and work so many days a year in return. The 'residents' could not, under the certificate, be forced to work in this way—and so others were brought on to the estate for that purpose. And the distinction between these two classes was quickly blurred. To complete the confusion, throughout the first half of the century there was a steady influx of Africans from Portuguese East Africa—and many of them drifted on to private estates.

Such a situation was bound sooner or later to produce irritation and a sense of injustice. To the estate-owner, or more often his manager, this was private property, which had been bought from the Government and in which money was being invested— usually the money of shareholders or trustees. He considered that anyone who came on to the estate to live there—as opposed to full-time hired labour and domestic servants on contract—should pay rent in cash or kind or labour and should be subject to eviction at will. There was usually a good deal of truth in his contention that, apart from the destruction of timber, African occupation destroyed the fertility of the soil. By the twenties he could hardly ever distinguish the original residents, or say who were their successors in interest, even if he wanted to; if, as various Commissions suggested, he had made the distinction, it would surely have been difficult to explain its justice to people who had moved on to the estate soon after the certificate of claim, when there was little if anything to show that it was an estate. In practice it usually happened that no distinction was made, that everyone on the estate was required to work or pay rent, in cash or kind—and to the African mind the injustice was not that there was no distinction between newcomers and the original occupants, but that there *was* a distinction between those who lived on the estate and those who did not. A mile away, outside the estate, on Crown lands, no rent was charged, while the unfortunate resident on the estate paid his taxes just as much as the man on Crown land. There were of course subsidiary grievances, but that was the main point.

None of this would have mattered so much if there had still been plenty of land. But the population increased steadily, both by natural means and by incursions from Portuguese territory, all through the first half of the century and by the census of 1945 there was serious overcrowding in the Southern Province, where most of the estates lay. In Cholo District, of which two-thirds was included in private estates, the density of population was 191 to the square mile, contrasting with eighty-nine for the whole Southern Province, twenty-seven for the Northern Province of Nyasaland, and thirteen for the adjoining Eastern Province of Northern Rhodesia. Cholo is an agricultural district and there was thus in 1945 roughly one person to three acres, reckoning the whole district as land, although of course not all of it is cultivable and much of it is in large estates.

The history of this sore spot was bedevilled by the concern of the administrative authorities and of successive Commissions with the legal and administrative untidiness which had arisen because the original residents had been confused with later comers. Various Commissions were doubtful whether the exaction of rent was always legal; from 'residents' it was clearly not legal, but it was generally agreed that it would be extremely difficult to decide who were the original residents or their successors. It was not till Sir Sidney Abrahams was appointed Commissioner in 1946 that it was recognized that the problem was not really legal at all; 'the true difficulty', he wrote, 'has not been to effect a reconciliation between the legal rights of the landlord and tenant respectively but to appreciate that there is here a conflict of ideas which cannot be adjusted by statutory means.' He found that there was now a very widespread tendency to question the validity of any private rights on the side of the estate-owners. 'Who sold this land? What right had he to sell? Was he a Chief? Did he consult his people? And what did he get for it?' were the kind of questions asked, just as Johnston had asked them fifty years before—but these questioners would have been even more difficult to satisfy and were far from thinking it just that a man whose grandfather had paid a penny an acre should have the right to keep thousands of acres to himself for ever.

To return to 1920, the Jackson Commission[38] did not find a solution to this problem. They saw the dangers of the situation and proposed that it should be made law that only a limited proportion of the tenants on an estate could be evicted at one time; an endeavour should be made to give the tenant a fixed contract with security for a given period. There was much discussion; the East African Commission of 1925[39] recorded their doubts about the legality of much that was happening on these estates, and made the more radical recommendation that enough land to accommodate the resident natives should be re-acquired, the measure being financed by a more sharply graduated land tax. In fact, however, an agreement was reached between the estate-owners and the Government, who were taken to represent the African; this was

[38] Zomba 10582.   [39] *Report of the Ormsby-Gore Commission* (Cmd. 2387).

embodied in an Ordinance of 1928,[40] which obliterated—if it did not wholly extinguish—the distinction between those with a right to residence and those without, but limited and defined the estate-owners' rights to exact rent or service and to evict. No one was particularly pleased; some of the estate-owners soon raised objections and the main African grievance was untouched. Let us for the moment leave unsolved this serious contribution to African suspicion and dissatisfaction.

The Jackson Report had been clear against Reserves for natives but did contemplate the demarcation of areas for European settlement; the Commission thought that about two and a half million acres might be available. The Ormsby-Gore Commission of 1925, which of course dealt not only with Nyasaland but also Northern Rhodesia, Tanganyika, Kenya, and Southern Rhodesia, took a more positive line. Throughout the territories with which the Commissioners were concerned they found the 'trend of local European opinion wholly against industrial segregation or the colour bar'. The great distinction between these territories and those south of the Zambezi was the presence in the latter of Europeans of the wage-earning class. 'In South Africa', they wrote, 'one never sees a native engine-driver or skilled mechanic', while in 'East Africa' (in which term they included Northern Rhodesia and Nyasaland) an increasing number of engine-drivers, skilled mechanics, and chauffeurs were Africans. But throughout 'East Africa' there was an over-riding necessity for clear definition of rights in respect of land; in Kenya in particular great anxiety had been caused by a judgement of the High Court in 1921 that 'all native rights in reserved land had disappeared' and that natives in occupation of lands reserved for the use of a native tribe 'had become tenants at will of the Crown'.

Though less acute elsewhere than in Kenya, a feeling of insecurity was general. In Nyasaland five-sixths of the Protectorate was Crown land, over which the Crown had assumed rights 'in most cases without any cession of ownership of land by treaty'. The Crown had acted as guardian of the natives and there was 'no reason to suppose that native interests had suffered'. But there was

[40] The Natives on Private Estates Ordinance, 1928.

general uneasiness and insecurity. And, believing that the territory must look principally to the natives themselves for the development of its tropical agriculture, the Commission recommended that, with a few exceptions, all Crown lands not yet leased should be vested in a Trust Board. This recommendation was given effect in the Nyasaland Protectorate (Native Trust Land) Order in Council of 1936 which stated that, with certain exceptions, the whole of the lands of the Protectorate should be 'native trust land', and that all such land should be vested in the Secretary of State, 'to be administered and controlled for the use of common benefit, direct or indirect, of the natives of the Protectorate'.

Meanwhile, another affair had at last come to a head, and was finally settled in 1937. Among the lands covered by Johnston's certificates of claim were over three million acres in the North Nyasa District which had been granted to the British South Africa Company. A special Commission was appointed to deal with this question in 1929.[41] There were a number of Africans living on this land, and the question was really whether it was best to excise the land in their actual occupation, leaving the Company free to let the rest to Europeans, or whether some more radical step was needed. In evidence, the District Commissioner thought that the right policy was to encourage the small-holder rather than the large farmer employing labour; he thought there was little land available for alienation and was supported in his opinion by missionaries. Evidence was given that Africans were making rapid progress in new methods of agriculture, in the possession of ploughs, and in growing wheat, rice, and vegetables as well as traditional crops; one was planting gum trees, one chief employed about 100 people growing cotton; there was a future for native cattle. With one exception, the European planters who were called took the same general view: 'any economic development in the district must be by the natives themselves encouraged by the Government';[42] though some added that a few blocks of 200 to 300 acres each here and there in European hands would help to bring new methods into the district.

[41] *Nyasaland Protectorate Native Reserves Commission on North Nyasa District* (roneoed).
[42] Ibid.

G

The African witnesses understood and approved of such a point of view as this, but they were bitterly opposed to the claims of the Company. One chief did not object to Europeans coming but wanted to know what kind of Europeans they would be. 'Will they be Europeans of Nyasaland or of British South Africa?' he asked—a distinction that was often to be made in Nyasaland thirty years later. This chief questioned the Company's claim in principle. He understood (he said in a letter to the Commission) that 'North Nyasa was sold to the British South Africa Company between 1890 and 1893 and that North Nyasa was proclaimed British territory in 1895. How could Queen Victoria sell it before it became hers?' And, in the same spirit, he asked how Mr. Rhodes came to sell 100 square miles of territory to Dr. Laws of the Livingstonia Mission.

The accuracy of these dates and assumptions is less important than the radical and inquiring turn of mind they display. Another chief, who also questioned the Company's claims in principle, thought that Europeans should be permitted to come and settle, but on African terms. They should be given leases and then 'the chiefs would report to the Government who would cancel the lease if the European was not a good one'.

The settlers have left their own country and are now our people and should conform with our customs. For instance, if a European wants an African woman he should marry her publicly. There are many half-caste children here of African mothers. The European who comes here should become an African and not stand aloof and treat the African like a dog.

The result of this Commission was that the British South Africa Company renounced its freehold claims in this land in return for confirmation of its possession of the mineral rights. This decision of a long-standing question was embodied in a second Order in Council of 1936 and the land then became Native Trust Land. Other renunciations and reductions reduced the area of land held in freehold, until by 1946 the total, instead of 15 per cent., was 1,207,000 acres, only slightly more than 5 per cent. of the whole of the Protectorate, while more than 87 per cent. was Native Trust

Land. But there were still over 200,000 Africans, or 10 per cent. of the population, resident on private estates, and this was in the most crowded part of the Protectorate. Objection to these estates was more and more often raised as a matter of principle, while evictions, or the threat of them, had caused serious incidents near Blantyre in 1943 and at Cholo in 1945. Why should we pay rent as well as tax when on Native Trust Land only tax is paid? Who sold this land? Had he a right to sell? What is the justice of maintaining for ever the sale fifty years ago for a few rolls of calico of vast areas now worth many thousands of pounds? Why should those who came to teach Christianity have been given thousands of acres at our expense? It was questions of this kind that were asked.

Sir Sidney Abrahams was appointed Commissioner in 1946 to report on the need of the inhabitants with regard to land, but with special reference to those resident on private estates. He thought, very wisely, that there was little point in entering into historical controversy about how the estates had been acquired. Nor did he consider that the landlords in general evaded the law or enforced it severely. But he had no doubt that there was a real sense of injustice and insecurity, and indeed many said they regarded life on a private estate as 'little more than slavery'. As already explained, he was the first to recognize that this was not a legal question so much as a conflict of basic assumptions about justice, 'which cannot be adjusted by statutory means'. A radical operation was therefore needed; the clear-cut solution was to 'emancipate' the 'resident native' and bring to an end the whole class and a legal status which by now was virtually a fiction. Where possible, land in the occupation of resident natives should be acquired from the estate and become Native Trust Land; where this was not possible, the resident native must be given the choice of staying on as a tenant under contract or moving to Native Trust Land which the Government would provide. This would sometimes be land which had not been developed by the estate owner and which also would be re-acquired for this purpose.

These recommendations were not immediately put into effect in their entirety. Indeed, in 1952, Ordinance No. 8[43] carried the

[43] Ordinance No. 8 (Africans on Private Estates) of 1952.

principle of 1928 somewhat further, finally extinguishing the right
to free residence by descent and defining and regulating more
closely the exaction of rent or service and providing that eviction
could take place only by order of a Board of Arbitration, of which
there were to be African members. But—to carry the story slightly
beyond the scope of this volume—in 1954 the principles of Sir
Sidney Abrahams' recommendations were embodied in a declaration that the *tangata* system, of rent paid by labour, was to be
extinguished, and a considerable beginning was made in the resettlement of the tenants or residents on Crown land. But so long
as any 'residents' remained under the system, there existed a
source of bitterness and the possibility of trouble.

It was this system which had been an important factor in John
Chilembwe's rising of 1915; it was this system, as much as any
other single cause, which had led to the riots at Cholo in 1953. It
contributed to that suspicion in respect of their land that influenced
the Nyasalanders so markedly in their attitude to the Federation.
It might be the official doctrine that, as Johnston had said, this was
a tropical dependency and not white man's country. But many
Nyasalanders went every year to Southern Rhodesia, which was
'white man's country' and where they saw—as they would have
put it—that the land had been taken by white men. Throughout
the Union and widely in Southern Rhodesia farms and estates
had been granted on which there had been 'resident natives',
who had woken up one morning to find themselves trespassers,
or at best tenants, where they had thought themselves at home.
They had been forced to accept the inevitable. It was hard to
persuade the Nyasalanders that this could not happen in their own
country.

All the same, they had already done much to show that in the
agricultural future of the country the peasant had a big part to play.
In 1923 Europeans produced four-fifths of the exported tobacco,
all the tea, and more than half the cotton. By 1937 these three
crops still made up 98 per cent. of the value of Nyasaland's exports,
but cotton and tobacco had become mainly African crops. In 1936
there were only 2,000 acres still under cotton owned by Europeans,
while there were 90,000 acres of African cotton. In 1923 the

figures had been 20,900 and 9,400 respectively. Tobacco in 1923 had shown 17,300 acres European and African 2,970. By 1936 the corresponding figures were 7,350 to 32,900. From six to one in favour of the European the acreage had become four to one in favour of the African.

In the case of cotton the startling change was due to the fact that this crop does best in a rotation with other crops, which can easily be arranged when it is a subsidiary cash crop grown in conjunction with subsistence farming on a small holding. This is not so easy in a big plantation. In the case of tobacco, the Europeans had tried to grow the bright tobacco, which must be flue-cured and is largely used for cigarettes; the land and climate were in most areas more suited to the dark tobacco, fire-cured, which is used for pipe tobacco. Tea, on the other hand, is usually a plantation crop; a bush gives no return until its fourth year and does not reach maturity till later, while the leaves are dried on the estate by expensive machinery. In Nyasaland it has always been a European crop and as yet has made no headway as a peasant's crop, though there is really no reason why a co-operative society with some capital should not operate a tea estate—and in Kenya a beginning is being made with this today. Tea has steadily increased in importance, the value of exports rising from £57,000 to £326,000 between 1924 and 1937. These tendencies continued until the eve of federation, when tea was still a European crop and cotton African, while tobacco was mainly African, only the bright tobacco being still grown and cured on estates.

On the eve of federation, then, it was possible to say that Nyasaland had on the whole retained the character of a tropical dependency; in 1952 88 per cent. of the acreage was Native Trust Land; while the 12 per cent. that remained included reserved forests and towns and only 3·8 per cent. was for private estates. While the development of peasant crops had not gone so far as in Uganda, Ghana, or Western Nigeria, substantial progress had been made. But there had been dangers, from the African point of view; wide claims to land had been made and there had been talk of European settlement which had aroused African suspicion; the question of 'resident natives on private estates' had been a continual sore point.

And Nyasalanders, who had developed a rare sense of unity as a people, a unity over-riding tribal differences, showed a robust possessiveness in regard to the land of the Protectorate and a sense of their special status as protected persons. They were jealous that theirs should not become a 'white man's country'; their relationship with the officials, planters, and missionaries was different on both sides from what was usual farther south. The European was hardly ever a resident who meant to live in the country and he was more conscious of his trusteeship; he was the guardian rather than the rival or the master; there were hardly any European artisans and the African therefore became bricklayer and printer in Nyasaland, while he was prevented in Southern Rhodesia. He felt that the way was open for his development, that the country was his own and had a future, that time was on his side. But he must—he thought—be continually on the alert that the land was not sold over his head, as it had been in the south.

3. IN NORTHERN RHODESIA

Of the three territories, Northern Rhodesia is probably the one in which the allocation of land has had the least influence on the development of race relations. The territory as a whole is thinly populated and most of the soil very poor, but the areas are vast and there have been only a few districts in which overcrowding has been serious. The question of whether land had been fairly allocated was a matter of vital importance mainly in the Angoni country and near the railway line.

The British South Africa Company held Northern Rhodesia by virtue of its charter, which permitted the Company to exercise any rights conceded by Chiefs. Lewanika, King of the Barotse, had long wished to be given the protection of Queen Victoria; he was much less sure that he wanted the protection of the Company, but he did at last doubtfully accept the assurances he was given that the two were much the same. In 1900 he signed a treaty with the Company by which Barotseland was accorded a special status but rights were also assumed over a wide area in much of which the Barotse had occasionally raided and over which both parties

asserted that Lewanika had sovereign rights.[44] The rest of the
territory the Company held either by virtue of a series of agreements with Chiefs—whose interpretations of what they had
agreed to must have varied widely—or, in one case, that of the
Angoni, by conquest.

Outside Barotseland the Company was free to make grants of
lands to purchasers and it was a definite policy to 'open up' the
country by such grants. It was a condition of the Orders in
Council of 1899 and 1900 that proper provision should be made
for the needs of the natives of the territory, but the point really
arose only where settlers were expected in large numbers. In 1923,
when Company rule came to an end, there were three groups of
Reserves established for Africans: the first along the line of the
railway, the second in the Angoni area—that is to say the Fort
Jameson and Petauke Districts—and the third in the extreme north-
east in what was then the Tanganyika District. The rest of the
country, apart from Barotseland, whose special status was reserved
by treaty, was Crown land. The Reserves were extended from
time to time, and areas were demarcated as Forests or Game
Reserves.

In 1936 the position, in the broadest terms, was that the land of
Northern Rhodesia might be thought of under the three heads—
African, European, and Crown. The African land consisted of
seventy-one million acres, including Barotseland, thought to be
about thirty-seven million acres, and the Reserves, thirty-four
million; the European land was nearly nine million acres, of which
five and a half million was held by two companies, and rather
more than three million in farms; the Crown land consisted of
over eleven million acres of forests and game reserves and ninety-
four million unallotted. The Pim Commission recommended that
with some slight exceptions the Crown land should all be made
Native Trust Land, as in Nyasaland, and the substance of these
recommendations became law some ten years later.[45]

The usual method of cultivation, known as *chitemene*, consists
of felling or lopping trees, piling and burning the timber and

---

[44] This agreement is printed in full in L. H. Gann, *The Birth of a Plural Society*.
[45] The Northern Rhodesia Native Trust Land Order in Council of 14 October 1947.

brushwood, and throwing seeds in the ashes; this of course involves long periods of fallow in which the timber can grow again, but so poor is the soil that some such methods seem inevitable until cheap fertilizers are available and animal husbandry is well organized with good paddocks. An attempt was made by the Company in 1907 to change the system, and lopping was prohibited; the immediate consequence was a famine. An estimate made by the agricultural department for the Abercorn district is quoted in the Pim Commission's Report of 1938[46] and is probably of wider application than to one district; it is that when the population exceeds 6·4 to the square mile the soil is likely to be robbed and erosion to occur. In the 1946 Census it was only in one Province of six, the Eastern Province, that this figure was exceeded for a whole Province, and, if the mining districts and the central Barotse plain are excluded, it was only in the Eastern Province and the Mazabuka district, on the line of rail, that this figure was seriously exceeded throughout a whole district. In the Eastern Province, Fort Jameson district had an average density of 25·1 persons to the square mile and some areas of the district were seriously overcrowded.

It is thus in the Eastern Province that land problems have been most acute. Here an area of over 10,000 square miles was conceded by Mpeseni, Paramount Chief of the Angoni, to what eventually became the North Charterland Exploration Company. The consideration was £200 a year, which works out at a penny for 130 acres. Since it was the intention of the Company to make grants of land to farmers, it was clear that something must be done for the African population, and from 1903 onwards Reserves were established, only to be successively proved inadequate. By 1936 the total areas included in these Reserves came to some 3,500 square miles, but a quarter of this was uninhabitable because there was no water, while a third was infested with tse-tse. The calculations on which these reservations had been based allowed only one and a quarter acres per person and eight acres per beast, which was clearly insufficient in an area where fifteen to twenty years was needed for regeneration of the bush after burning; it gave, in theory, a density of forty persons to the square mile. The land

[46] Colonial No. 145.

reserved was thus certainly not enough, particularly for cattle-owning people, but the result in practice was even worse than it appears at first because of the waterless and fly-infested areas; in quite large tracts the Pim Commission found concentrations of 120 or even 150 persons to the square mile, while other parts were uninhabited because intended for Europeans who had never come. Eventually, in 1941, the Government re-acquired all the land in the Company's possession except that actually alienated; this is only about 624 square miles out of a total for the Eastern Province of 22,770 square miles. Some of those who had crowded into the Reserves could now move back.

In the old Tanganyika District a somewhat similar problem never became acute. Here the British South Africa Company had 4,310 square miles; there was a valid certificate of claim and at first the Company was successful in persuading settlers to take up land. Reserves were therefore established into which Africans were moved; some were overcrowded and deteriorated. But various enterprises having failed, the settlers became fewer; by 1938 only 500 acres were actually under European cultivation; the Company gave some of the land as a gift and some was bought by the Government; after the Pim Commission of 1938 and the Land Commission of 1946 and the various measures which followed, only 145 square miles remained as alienated, 546 reserved as Crown land and 3,467 as Native Trust or Reserves.

The remaining group of Reserves lay near the railway line, where again a much greater influx of settlers was expected than in fact appeared. Sixteen Reserves were established with over 38,000 square miles for a population of 268,000, giving over ninety acres per head or 6·89 persons per square mile; this in general terms should have been enough, but again there was in practice too great a concentration in certain areas.

In all three groups of Reserves the recommendations for their demarcation had included conditions. It had usually been said that the land would be sufficient if certain things were done; the provision of bore-holes and wells was almost everywhere recommended, sometimes anti-tse-tse measures were needed; in Tanganyika Province it had been suggested that when Reserves were allocated and Africans moved into them, village industries, and in particular the smelting of iron, should be encouraged. But in all three areas the Pim Commission found that these supplementary suggestions had been neglected. The position, they said, was nowhere satisfactory; some Reserves were definitely inadequate. There was damage by too much ploughing and by too much felling and lopping; large areas were uninhabitable for lack of water or because of tse-tse; there were large areas from which people had been compulsorily moved and which were now quite uninhabited. Comprehensive plans for rehabilitation and the supply of water were widely needed.

This was the situation in 1938. By 1950 the re-classification of Crown land as Native Trust had improved the position and the economy of the territory had been transformed by the prosperity of the copper industry. But so far only a very small beginning had been made in the comprehensive schemes which were so clearly needed. And the unadorned recital of the historical facts presents a picture of natives being constantly moved about, shepherded from an area that was meant for settlers to a Reserve where the bore-holes had been forgotten, moved back again when a commission had reported that they were crowded and ruining the land. But land was not the sore point here that it was to become in the other territories. Northern Rhodesia was too big and the population too scattered for the people to have acquired the sense of unity of the Nyasalanders. They were less articulate and their grievances were less clearly expressed, if indeed they were consciously formulated. If they had been expressed, they would probably have been directed less to the land policy of the Government than to lack of education and to the Government's attitude to the urban African.

III. LABOUR

1. THE DEPENDENCE ON AFRICAN LABOUR

In the twenties it was thought that land policy would broadly determine the differing destinies of the racial groups throughout Central Africa. In Southern Rhodesia the policy of segregation was conceived primarily in terms of land-ownership, and in Northern Rhodesia, despite doubts inspired by Colonial Office pronouncements, most European settlers hoped to follow a similar policy. Ownership of a farm or small-holding had become the hall-mark of a typical Rhodesian, and it was presumed that all African needs would be supplied by the Native areas. In Nyasaland the success of the peasant producer and the limited role of the immigrant planter seemed to imply a future far removed from that of the Rhodesias.

Yet although the Land Apportionment Act was the corner-stone of segregation in Southern Rhodesia, it had been adopted in response to a wide variety of hopes and fears. Relatively few of these were directly concerned with the problem of land-owner-ship; many were of a much more general nature. There was the paternalism of some missionaries and officials in the Native Affairs Department, who hoped that the Reserves would protect their charges from complete contamination by the baser aspects of an alien culture. Among other Europeans there were the fears of social contact, of miscegenation, of increasing economic and political competition from a race which was already showing an astonishing power of adaptation to the modern world. The Land Apportionment Act was to be the defensive *laager* separating the races in the twentieth century. For most Europeans in Rhodesia it provided the only sane 'solution' to the 'native problem'. It was hoped that all other aspects of racial contact could be made to conform to this basic pattern. Difficult, awkward facts were often

minimized or overlooked; in some respects there almost seems to
have been a conspiracy of blindness. The eye, if not closed, was at
least averted. In theory territorial, possessory segregation seemed
to offer a complete solution; the problems caused by racial interdependence could be ignored.

The dependence on African labour was the aspect of life which
most profoundly challenged the theory of segregation. The daily
contact on farms, mines, and in the towns was already the crucial
encounter between the races, and in these inter-war years industrial activity was beginning to shape the pattern of the future.
This activity, though deeply influenced by the concept of segregation, was based on the practice of private enterprise and the
dictates of economic individualism. In Southern Rhodesia African
wage labour was already creating problems to which the theory of
segregation could provide no final answer, and north of the
Zambezi it was disclosing the weakness and inadequacy of a policy
of remote trusteeship. On the Copperbelt, Government intervention was conspicuously absent, and many rural areas of both
Northern Rhodesia and Nyasaland, deprived of their able-bodied
male population, declined miserably. The money economy was
beginning to demand a new synthesis among the peoples of
Central Africa.

Throughout the inter-war period the economy of Southern
Rhodesia remained dependent on mining and agriculture. In 1926
the country's total exports amounted to about £5·4 million, of
which £4 million were minerals and £1·3 million agricultural
produce grown on European farms. Of the 17,000 Europeans
gainfully occupied, 23 per cent. were engaged in agriculture and
12 per cent. in mining. The depression, with its sharp fall in world
prices of primary products, seriously affected the country's export
of base minerals—asbestos, coal, and chrome—and agricultural
products; but with the increased value of gold the economy
recovered relatively quickly. In 1935 gold production was a record
for the third year in succession and as late as 1943 it was estimated
that 50 per cent. of the national income was derived directly and
indirectly from gold. In 1936, as in 1926, two-thirds of the African
labour force was employed in mining and agriculture. The contri-

bution of the 7,000 Europeans and the 160,000 Africans who worked in the mines and on the farms was crucial: they supported practically the whole of the remaining employment, and without the cheap labour of the Africans much of the gold mining would have been impossible. In 1943 a former Minister told a Commission of Inquiry that if there was no African labour, and if consequently wages were similar to those in Australia, 'something like 80 per cent.' of the gold mines in Southern Rhodesia would go out of production.[1]

Before the First World War labour was a problem in Southern Rhodesia mainly on account of its scarcity. The immediate postwar influx of immigrants prolonged this aspect, but by 1924 the Ormsby-Gore Commission to East Africa reported that there were 'now no serious labour difficulties' in Southern Rhodesia and that they had been overcome principally 'by education and habit'. The recovery after the slump was accompanied by an increased dependence on large supplies of cheap, unskilled labour. The figures of Africans in employment at each census year [3] show that Africans from within the territory were gradually providing a greater proportion of the labour force. 'Education and habit', in the shape of new needs and fresh interests, may well have contributed to this process. But it seems possible that taxation and the pressure on the resources of the Reserves were equally effective, and in some areas 'a hint from the Native Commissioner to some of the headmen' was needed to 'bring out the desired number of young ones' to meet the seasonal demands of the maize-growers, 'always the loudest complainants of the shortage of the eternal and necessary Kafir'.[4] Despite this increased use of local labour, farms and mines remained dependent on the labour of Africans from out-

[1] R. D. Gilchrist in evidence to the Howman Committee, p. 24; see also C. H. Thompson and H. W. Woodruff, *Economic Development in Rhodesia and Nyasaland* (1954), pp. 11–17.
[2] Op. cit., p. 45.
[3]

	S. Rhodesian	Alien
1921	47,374	92,302
1926	78,233	93,737
1931	76,184	102,908
1936	107,581	144,901
1941	131,404	168,106

[4] Tawse-Jollie, op. cit., p. 148.

side the territory. In 1937 the mining industry employed an average
of 30,777 Nyasaland Africans, and it was estimated that 25,000 men
from Nyasaland were working in agriculture. Twenty thousand
Africans from Nyasaland were also in the towns, providing at
least half the African population of Salisbury.[5] In the same year it
was estimated that 45,000 Africans from Northern Rhodesia were
working in Southern Rhodesia.[6]

The transformation taking place in Northern Rhodesia also
involved a dependence on African labour. By 1930 the Copperbelt was in the midst of a construction boom. The mines at
Bwana Mkubwa, at the Roan Antelope, at Nkana, Mufulira,
Nchanga, Chambishi, and Kansanshi were all on the point of production or were being developed, and in September over 29,000
Africans were employed by the copper mines, mainly on construction work.[7] The collapse in the price of copper from over £70
to under £30 per ton, which accompanied the slump of 1930,
suddenly arrested this activity. By the end of 1931 work was proceeding only at the Roan and Nkana mines, and in July 1932 the
African labour force had shrunk to a little less than 7,000.[8] The
shock produced momentary despair and, as will be seen, it profoundly influenced the strategy of future development. But
recovery was swift. By 1937 the future was considered bright:
the average price of standard copper on the London market had
risen to over £50 a ton, and the prospective earnings for the
ordinary shares of the Rhokana Corporation were in the neighbourhood of 80 per cent. with expectations of 115 per cent. in the
immediate future.[9] In the same year Northern Rhodesia rose to
fourth place among the world producers of copper.[10]

This recovery was aided by imperial preference on a favourable

---

[5] G. N. Burden: *Nyasaland Native Labour in Southern Rhodesia* (Zomba 1938).
[6] *Pim Report*, p. 36.
[7] J. Merle Davis, *Modern Industry and the African* (1933), pp. 143, 151.
[8] Ibid., pp. 144, 151.   [9] *Financial News*, 11 June 1937.
[10] L. H. Gann, 'The Northern Rhodesian Copper Industry and the World of Copper:
1932–52', *Rhodes–Livingstone Journal*, No. 18, gives the following figures for production:

	1928–9	1937
United States	855,000	750,000
Northern Rhodesia . . .	5,000	210,000
World	1,810,000	2,240,000

British market, but it was based on the fact that Northern Rhodesia was one of the lowest-cost copper-producing areas in the world. Production costs at Nkana and the Roan Antelope were about £20 per long ton at Beira, and it was expected that this could be reduced when the mines were working at full capacity. Chile produced more copper and at a price less than £20 per ton, but the average operating cost for all American mines, including those in the United States, Mexico, South America and Canada, was over £40 a ton.[11] This low cost in Northern Rhodesia was partly due to the vast quantities of unusually rich ores containing nearly 4 per cent. of copper compared to those of the United States which contained approximately 1·4 per cent. In addition these ores were at no great depth, were easy to mine, and could be crushed, concentrated, and smelted by simpler methods than those used with oxidized ores of other areas. But above all the low cost was due to the availability of 'cheap and increasingly efficient labour'.[12] By 1937, 14,000 Africans were again employed on the Copperbelt, and it was thought that 20,000 would be needed to sustain full production.[13]

Difficulties had been experienced at first in persuading Africans to work underground. Desertions were numerous; food supplies were scarce, living conditions for Africans and Europeans were difficult, and 'the atmosphere of construction was one of hard men living hard'.[14] The vast majority of workers were completely untrained, but the employment of Nyasalanders from the mines of Southern Rhodesia set 'a high standard of efficiency', and by 1932 mine officials with Rand experience considered that the Northern Rhodesian African was already 'almost, if not wholly, equal' in efficiency to the average worker in the Rand.[15] 'Native labour', concluded Sir Alan Pim after a thorough official survey of the economy of Northern Rhodesia, 'is the foundation of the whole great industry.'[16]

---

[11] Merle Davis, op. cit., pp. 145–6; *Financial News*, 11 June 1937; *Pim Report*, p. 20.
[12] Merle Davis, op. cit., p. 145.
[13] *Pim Report*, p. 20; Merle Davis, p. 153.   [14] Merle Davis, p. 172.
[15] Ibid., p. 172; F. Spearpoint, 'The African Native and the Rhodesian Copper Mines', *Journal of the Royal African Society*, Vol. XXXVI (1937), p. 9.
[16] *Pim Report*, p. 118.

Demand for labour from Central Africa came not only from Rhodesian mines and farms but also from the Union of South Africa. As early as 1903 the Witwatersrand Gold Mines entered into an agreement for the recruitment of Nyasaland Africans, and in the next ten years a total of about 9,000 workers were recruited, while considerable numbers of Africans travelled under great difficulties to seek independent employment. The Immigrants Act of 1913, however, refused Africans from territories north of latitude 22° South admission into the Union, and the migration stopped for the duration of the First World War. After the war it commenced clandestinely. The resumed and increased activities of mining and agriculture and the new secondary industries caused an ever-increasing demand for African labour, and the magnet of higher wages attracted men from as far as the north of Nyasaland. They evaded measures taken to prevent them from entering the Union and by 1928 it was thought that there were 11,000 Nyasa-landers in the Union. Official policy was modified in the thirties. Complaints from Farmers' Associations of the high wages which they were not always able or inclined to pay, and the extent to which the supplies of African labour within the Union were already drawn upon, made it clear to the authorities that the labour needed to develop large new gold mines could only be found from the north. In 1934 limited recruiting started in Bechuanaland and Southern Rhodesia, and in 1936 the Witwatersrand Native Labour Association extended its operations into Nyasaland and Northern Rhodesia. By 1939 it was estimated that 12,000 Africans from Nyasaland and 3,000 from Northern Rhodesia were working on the Rand and that in the Union as a whole there were between 29,000 and 33,000 Africans from Nyasaland.[17]

From Karonga to Cape Town Europeans and Africans were becoming increasingly interdependent. European industries were expanding so rapidly that their demands for labour continually threatened to exceed the supplies available from an African population small in relation to the vast area concerned.[18] The whole structure of government, European settlement, and, at least to

[17] G. N. Burden: *Nyasaland Natives in the Union of South Africa* (Zomba, 1940).
[18] *Pim Report*, p. 34.

some extent, African advancement depended on this economic interdependence. It is time to consider more closely the strains which the theory and assumptions of segregation imposed on this process, the points at which rivalry and a clash of interests occurred, and the policies, private and official, which sought to foster, control, and use the African in industry.

2. THE COLOUR BAR

In 1930 the Government of Southern Rhodesia invited a distinguished economist, Professor Henry Clay, then of Manchester University, to visit and advise them on industrial relations. His report lucidly exposed the basic economic facts which confronted the European population. Government, the professions, and all the appurtenances of European civilization were maintained by four fundamental branches of economic activity. Inside the country there was, first, the trade with the indigenous population, which offered a growing field not only for European traders but also for local manufacturers. Second was the mining industry; third, agricultural production for export, and lastly the transport supplied by the railways for Northern Rhodesia and the Katanga. These four industries set the limit of economic activity; all else was derived from them, and in every case, except that of African trade, their expansion was limited by costs. This was most clearly the case with gold mining, where any increase in costs reduced the amount of ore it would pay to mine. More than a quarter of the agricultural produce of the country was exported, but on a harshly competitive world market expansion was again curtailed by the costs of production. Rhodesia Railways had the advantage of a virtual monopoly of the carrying trade of the Copperbelt and the Congo, and roughly half the traffic on the railways consisted of consignments to and from these territories; but with the construction of the Benguela railway this monopoly would be curtailed, and in any case an increase in the volume of traffic largely depended on a reduction of costs.

The country was 'in the position of a firm with heavy overhead expenses and an inadequate turn-over'. Living costs could be kept

H

low only by those who, like 'the natives and some Dutch farmers', contrived 'to live as Africans—mainly on the produce of African soil'; for the rest of the European population a large part of the food, drink, and manufactures had to be imported. The high wages earned by European artisans kept up the prices of secondary industries: newspapers had a ready sale at threepence, and even artisans paid £100 and upwards a year in rent; and these high prices in their turn kept up wages. The country had to maintain all the services of a civilized community without being able to utilize them enough to make them cheap. Railways, commerce, and banks could all have handled a much greater volume of trade, and administration would have cost little more for a much larger population. 'The only ultimate remedy is to increase turn-over, which in this case means secure an increase in population.'

Immigration and settlement were, however, a 'necessarily gradual process'. Rhodesia, with its small European population, could not rapidly absorb a large number of immigrants; in proportion to its population it was already absorbing them at a high rate. The average immigration for the previous five years was 3,350, or 8·2 per cent. of the 1926 European population. There were few countries, if any, in which the population was increasing at a greater rate. Yet this rate of expansion did not solve the difficulty of overheads, and with the slump the numbers of immigrants declined, while there was a large number of emigrants too. There remained only an expansion of trade with the African section of the population, and this depended on increasing the productivity and economic capacity of the African population. As the African's skill and pay increased he would become ever more closely integrated into the economy of the country, and increasingly able to support and enjoy European civilization.

If the natives all lived on a European standard the population of the country would no longer be 45,000 Europeans and 850,000 natives, with an aggregate spending power equivalent to that of perhaps 80,000 Europeans, but 900,000 persons with a combined spending power perhaps ten times that of the present population. That state of things may never arrive, and at best must take generations; but every increase in the native's economic capacity, every extension of his economic range, by increasing his output, increases in the same degree his power to purchase. If the Europeanisation of the native population must be slow, so far as it goes, it is equivalent economically to the immigration of more Europeans, and has the same effect of spreading the burden of the necessary costs of government, trade and transport.[19]

The economist of 1930 might well have been surprised could he have foreseen the development of world markets, the demand for primary products, and the consequent prosperity and rapid expansion which two decades were to bring to the Rhodesias. But even the realization that he was standing at the brink of an industrial revolution would merely have reinforced his plea for a rational use of the total population of the country. It was already beginning to be obvious that a dependence on large supplies of unskilled labour caused a dangerous lack of balance in the country's economy, that labour's cheapness, although encouraging rapid development in certain directions, was ultimately an illusion and a grave disability, and that a resolute effort should be made to take every opportunity to improve African skill as the only means of permanently securing a high standard of living for the community as a whole. As will be seen, this argument was given added urgency, and perhaps compelling force, by the conditions to which the system of labour migration and temporary urbanization gave rise. But besides the inherent difficulties of imparting industrial skills to a largely illiterate, rural, and primitive population, a rational use of African labour challenged the assumptions of both segregation and indirect rule, cherished by the official and upper classes, and it also seemed to threaten the vested interests of European workers.

Though small in numbers, European artisan wage-earners held a strong position in Southern Rhodesia. They earned high wages: in the neighbourhood of £32 to £40 a month for skilled work and £25 for semi-skilled. These money wage-rates were more than double those of London; real wages were slightly higher than in Johannesburg and correspondingly higher than in London.[20]

[19] H. Clay, *Report on Industrial Relations in Southern Rhodesia* (Salisbury, 1930).
[20] Clay, pp. 32–4. In 1925 the relative level of real wages was 141 in Johannesburg to 100 in London.

Artisans' wages were high also when compared with agricultural incomes: a farm manager, for instance, generally received only £15 a month, free quarters, and a 'problematical share in the profits', this additional remuneration usually being very small at that date. The average European farmer could expect to make about £300 in a good year, and since several made much more than this average, many must have made considerably less.[21] The high wages of the artisan could partly be explained and justified by claiming that they showed more enterprise and ability than those who stayed at home. Many white wage-earners had to supervise large numbers of unskilled workers and consequently carried a greater degree of responsibility than they would have done in similar work in Europe. It was also partly true that, in common with other Europeans, they were using African labour as a source of wealth, one of the 'natural and indigenous resources' of the country.[22]

But more important than these considerations was the fact that European wage-earners were organized. The high level of wages was originally established by the necessity of attracting skilled workers to a new country and of providing them with a standard of living consistent with white health and prestige: servants, imported food, drink, clothing, and, later, a car. Just as in the nineteenth century the Rand had to pay high wages to attract workers from Kimberley and overseas, so did Rhodesia in the twentieth. Trade union organizations maintained and increased this advantage. The Rhodesia Railway Workers' Union, with Mr. J. W. L. Keller as its organizing secretary from 1920 to 1945, was the most powerful European union. It dominated the early growth of the Rhodesia Labour Party, providing ten out of the party's fifteen candidates for the 1924 election,[23] although it was 1928 before Keller became one of the party's first representatives in the Assembly.

Keller's thought and background were strongly anti-capitalist. Born in 1885, he worked on the London and North Western

[21] Clay, op. cit.
[22] Professor Clay seems to have underestimated the part played by this factor; op. cit., p. 37.
[23] *The Times*, 6 June 1924.

Railway as a youth for eight years and in 1912 he emigrated to start work on the Rhodesian Railways at Umtali. Almost immediately he began to demand better conditions of service and, according to one account, he was as a result 'continually transferred, temporarily or otherwise'. During the First World War he was given overseas war leave, was wounded, and taken prisoner. In September 1919 he returned to Bulawayo, and the following February he organized a remarkably successful strike which won for the European workers 25 per cent. on substantive pay, increased overtime pay, a shorter working day, a cost-of-living allowance, better leave, and other concessions. After this success separate agreements were entered into with the postal workers, the miners' union, and the police, and in 1939 it could still be claimed that 'every trade has built upon the foundation of the benefits gained in this great strike'.[24] Thus before the publication of Clay's report and the crisis of the 1931 depression white wage-earners had established their claim to a 'civilized' standard of living; already they were the first line of a defence in which all Europeans were to some extent involved, for white solidarity minimized the importance of European class differences.[25]

After this victory in 1920, therefore, European artisans became less interested in direct warfare with capital and management. Instead they became more concerned with preventing the infiltration of lower-paid Africans into skilled or semi-skilled work. A scarcity of skilled workers explained the origin of the European's high wages; an artificial or controlled scarcity prolonged them. The building workers were well organized, shared in the advantages which such workers enjoyed in South Africa, and assiduously defended them against any encroachment. In 1928, for instance, the Salisbury Municipality was persuaded by the Rhodesia Labour Party not to entertain any tender for new cottages in the native location which included the use of 'Coloured or native labour employed on bricklaying or plastering'.[26]

The issue was even clearer in the case of the railways. When

---

[24] *Rhodesian Railways Review*, Christmas 1939.
[25] Cf. Huggins' speech in 1938, below, Chap. V, pp. 151–2.
[26] *Manchester Guardian*, 9 May 1928, letter of J. Harris to Editor.

Keller made his first complaints in Umtali, the traffic manager, in refusing to consider the men's demands, is reputed to have curtly informed the deputation that 'he could obtain "niggers" to do the same work they were doing at a much cheaper rate, and just as efficiently'.[27] The same point was made, though with much more tact, in a report submitted to the Legislative Assembly in 1926 by Brigadier-General F. D. Hammond, an experienced railway administrator. Hammond had been asked to state whether a reduction of working expenses could be made without loss of efficiency, and he reported that in one particular direction they could be reduced, namely by an increased employment of the African. 'There is', he wrote, 'a very large class of so-called skilled work, which . . . can be performed by natives under periodical supervision after a short period of instruction . . . the work of firing a locomotive is easily within the scope of the native, and he is probably better suited physically for this work than the men of English descent.'

Hammond estimated that in two or three years the European wages bill of the Engineering and Locomotive Departments, which totalled £450,000 per annum, could be almost halved, and that if Africans were trained and employed as fully-skilled tradesmen still larger economies could be made. The effect of this on railway rates, and hence on the economy of a land-locked country, was obvious, but he realized that a such a course would involve 'a complete reversal of present policy; the Railways alone could not embark on it; the change would have to be supported by the people of the country and the Government'.[28] Clearly if the change had been carried through in 'two or three years' it would have involved a considerable amount of hardship and unemployment, and European railwaymen must have felt that only their united organized strength could avert this threat.

It was therefore extraordinarily difficult for white wage-earners to grasp the logic of an academic economist's argument which maintained that it was in their ultimate interest, as well as that of

[27] *Rhodesian Railways Review*, Christmas 1939.
[28] Report of Brigadier-General F. D. Hammond on the Railway System of Southern Rhodesia (Salisbury, 1926), p. 38.

the rest of the European community, to encourage the development and use of African potentialities. They saw themselves placed between the capitalist's desire to decrease labour costs and the willingness of the African to accept wages below the minimum needed to support the accustomed European standard of living. Their natural reaction was a firm determination to defend with closed ranks their precarious privileges. It was also particularly unfortunate that Clay's report was followed by the slump of 1930–1, which caused a certain amount of European unemployment. In these circumstances it was even harder to appreciate the fact that in an expanding economy, which was the country's normal condition, there was no rigid limit to the amount of work awaiting additional resources of labour and capital. It was by no means clear to the European worker that wider and more rational use of African labour would increase the openings for supervisory and skilled workers in a broadening economy; the possibility of displacement and the difficulties of readjustment were far more obvious.

The artisans' reaction to the phenomenon and possibilities of African advance was moreover not merely a matter of defending a sectional vested interest. At that time their attitude appears to have been questioned by few responsible Europeans; the diverse interests of settler and native were taken for granted. The emergence of a 'poor-white' class caused by African competition was feared not only by the man with little technical ability or qualifications, but also by every white man who saw it as a direct threat to white prestige, a prestige basic to his whole position and way of life. White solidarity drew its strength not merely from sentiment but also from a rational awareness that in many situations colour alone was a man's greatest asset. Any damage to this prestige could not be restricted to the individual alone. 'I do not think that anybody loves the farmer because he is a farmer, or a "brickie" because he is a "brickie". In these capacities they have not much claim, but as white men they have a claim to fair treatment in this country.'[29] It seemed self-evident that the surest means of pre-

[29] A Member of the Legislative Assembly in the debate on the Industrial Conciliation Bill, *Southern Rhodesian Debates*, 10 April 1934.

venting such a development was to protect the European wage-earner from infiltration: to rely on restrictive practices rather than on greater opportunities.

This negative, easier course was chosen not only to protect the European, but also because the idea of vigorously aiding African advancement was alien to most Europeans. The pretensions and even the existence of 'educated natives' aroused considerable hostility,[30] and it needed little imagination to recognize that white supremacy could be maintained in its entirety only by retaining full control of strategic occupations and industries. Segregation was conceived primarily in terms of land policy, but it soon also afforded a theory of industrial defence. Economic facts were disregarded; uncomfortable realities were banished from the realm of consciousness.

After a strike of European employees in the building industry the Government passed the Industrial Conciliation Act in 1934. In introducing this measure the Minister of Justice said it was 'an effort to do three things: to maintain harmony in industry, to provide for apprenticeship, and to help to maintain a white standard of living in this country'.[31] The Act provided for the creation by trade unions and employers' associations of National and Local Industrial Councils, somewhat on the lines of the Whitley Councils in the United Kingdom. It explicitly excluded the African from its definition of employee.[32] Its effect therefore was to introduce a modern and progressive method of industrial conciliation for European wage-earners and employees while leaving the mass of the labour force under the Masters and Servants Act, which resembled the legislation of Elizabethan England.

The 1934 Act did not directly institute a colour bar. Instead it provided, indirectly, a two-fold protection against African competition. Wage-rates and conditions of employment negotiated by the Industrial Councils could be made applicable to Africans if it seemed likely that African infiltration into skilled or semi-skilled work would threaten European wages. And since no European

---

[30] See below, Chap. IV.   [31] Southern Rhodesian Debates, 10 April 1934.
[32] For the purposes of the Act an 'employee' was defined as 'any person engaged by an employer to perform . . . work . . ., but shall not include a native'. *Statute Law of S. Rhodesia*, 1934, p. 43.

employer would employ an African if, for the same wage, he could obtain a European, the Act made it possible for European artisans to erect an effective colour bar. To some extent African interests were, at first, protected by the fact that the Minister had to be satisfied that the wage-rates fixed by an Industrial Council were not 'so high as likely to deprive natives of such reasonable prospects of employment . . . as would have been open to them'. In 1937, however, an amendment abolished this proviso and enabled an Industrial Council to petition the Governor to enforce an agreement in any municipality where European wage-rates, fixed by an Industrial Council, were threatened.[33] In addition to fixing wage-rates at a level which would support a European standard of living, and thereby make the employment of Africans extremely unlikely, the 1934 Act gave the Industrial Councils the power to regulate the conditions of apprenticeship. 'With the view to absorbing to the fullest the youth of this country' and in order to train 'youths to become efficient craftsmen and operatives for the future requirements of industry', the following industries were officially urged to set up Industrial Councils: bookmaking, building, clothing, carriage building, electrical and mechanical engineering, food manufacture, leather-working, motor car, printing, mining, and commercial distributive.[34] And since the African was excluded from the Act it was tacitly understood that the youths in question were white.

As a result of this Southern Rhodesian policy 'operating in the main centres of European occupation and exemplified in the Industrial Conciliation Act', an officer sent by the Nyasaland Government to act as Nyasaland Labour Officer in Salisbury reported in 1938 that 'there is little remunerative employment available for the skilled native artisan or the native with a sound clerical education. In fact the term "native clerk" is not used in business or in the Government service, being replaced by the designation of "messenger interpreter".'[35] In contrast to the countries north of the Zambezi, Africans in Southern Rhodesia

---

[33] Statute Law of Southern Rhodesia, 1934, 1937.
[34] *Handbook on the Industrial Conciliation Act, 1934,* Part II (Salisbury, 1934).
[35] G. N. Burden, *Nyasaland Native Labour in Southern Rhodesia* (Zomba, 1938), p. 7.

were as a rule not employed in any position, however humble, which carried any responsibility. There were no African foremen, telegraphists, postal sorters, salesmen, typists, printers, dispensers, 'or even trained mechanics employed either by Government or in industry'. Africans were employed to drive cars and lorries, but mechanics in the motor workshops were rare, 'the native usually being required only in order to fetch and carry for the European worker'. Outside the towns, however, and particularly in the small mining areas, the position was different. There African craftsmen and even clerks were accepted, and Nyasaland provided the majority of them.[36]

In Northern Rhodesia, except on the railways and in the mining industry, the problem of competition from African labour hardly existed. As in the rural areas of Southern Rhodesia, Africans were generally encouraged to work as carpenters and bricklayers, though European standards were seldom enforced, and in the Government service Africans were commonly employed as clerks and telegraphists. In motor transport the infiltration was gradual and aroused little comment. A European Member of the Legislative Council described the situation in his constituency in 1938: 'One of the Government lorries is driven by a native. The others are driven by Europeans. I think it is very largely a question of efficiency and economy. If it is found that the native can do the work satisfactorily he is given a chance of taking the post.'[37]

But on the Copperbelt Europeans were moving into defensive positions. As early as 1931 it was being said that the profits of the copper companies were dependent in a very large measure on the employment of Africans in semi-skilled jobs. Some unskilled and semi-skilled European labour was crowded out, and in these circumstances other European workers saw no security for themselves and still fewer openings for their sons. There was, therefore, 'a strong movement' in favour of trade unions to protect white tradesmen, and an Anglican priest spent his time on the mines 'trying to explain that Northern Rhodesia is not a suburb of

[36] G. N. Burden, *Nyasaland Native Labour in Southern Rhodesia* (Zomba, 1938), p. 7.
[37] Evidence to Bledisloe Commission, XCVI.

Johannesburg or a northern extension of the Rand'.[38] But there were still two courses of action open to the European workers. Theoretically it would have been possible for them to have accepted the inevitability of African advancement and to have attempted to bring skilled Africans into a common union organization; the alternative was to organize themselves in an exclusive defence.

These alternatives were reflected in the attitude of Europeans to a strike of African mine-workers in 1935 in which several Africans were killed. In the opinion of the District Commissioner, Ndola, 'a good many of the Europeans on the mines were probably in sympathy with the strike'. There had previously been 'a lot of foolish talk among the Europeans'; letters suggesting equality of pay between Europeans and Africans had appeared in the local papers, and another witness corroborated the fact that in public and in private conversation Europeans were 'most sympathetic towards the natives in their present circumstances'.[39] At Nkana, however, a section of the European population 'was inclined to talk about shooting the strikers',[40] and it was this mood which prevailed.

In 1936 Charlie Harris, the secretary of the South African Mine Workers' Union, visited the Copperbelt and established a branch of his union there. With the support of Rhodesian Railway workers he declared that he was determined that the Colonial Office 'should not have its way' in the matter of skilled trades. He said that he had come 'to help make Northern Rhodesia a white country. He was surprised to find that the Native had actually encroached upon not only unskilled labour, but skilled labour . . . and he asked what was going to happen to the white men if they were not organised.'[41] He also foretold that 'in the near future, union men only would be employed on the Copper Belt', but this device of enforcing a colour bar was only conceded by the

---

[38] W. F. Ellis, 'Missions and our European Population', *Proceedings of the Northern Rhodesia Missionary Conference 1931*.

[39] *Copperbelt Disturbances, 1935*: evidence, Vol. I, pp. 160, 224.

[40] Ibid., evidence of A. T. Williams.

[41] Press reports quoted in J. Lewin, *The Colour Bar in the Copper Belt* (South African Institute of Race Relations, 1941), p. 5.

Companies during the Second World War.[42] In the meantime the South African Mine Workers' Union discovered that it was precluded by its constitution from operating outside South Africa, so its mission was handed over to the Northern Rhodesian Mine Workers' Union, which was founded in 1936 and recognized by the four leading copper mines the following year.[43] In July 1938 its president claimed a fluctuating membership of about 1,000 men, or approximately 50 per cent. of the daily paid Europeans, and it had concluded 'a gentleman's agreement' with the mine management that 'the relation between white and black will not be interfered with for a period of another two years'. Its spokesman maintained that the union was very contented with the management and that conditions were unequalled in any other part of the world.[44]

Thus in the vital spheres of economic activity—on the railways and the Copperbelt, and in the municipalities of Southern Rhodesia—European artisans were able in the thirties to entrench themselves in privileged positions with the support of the rest of the European population. This development, inspired by the protectionist feeling of the trade unions, and accentuated by the temporary effects of the slump, was accepted as an inevitable component of the racial situation in the Rhodesias. South of the Zambezi the Government actively fostered the process; on the Copperbelt the Colonial Office administration silently acquiesced.

3. THE URBAN ENVIRONMENT

While this issue of the colour bar and African advancement was still in its early stages, the movement of vast numbers of Africans on to the mines and farms and into the towns was beginning to raise a host of problems both in the towns and in the remote rural districts from which the workers came. The problems would have been grave in any case, for the increasing use of African labour involved a revolution even more profound than that which had

---

[42] See below, Part II, Chap. II, pp. 241–2.
[43] *Financial News*, 22 November 1937.
[44] Evidence to Bledisloe Commission, CXV, 20 July 1938.

occurred in Europe; but they were made even harder to solve by
the fact that the whole system of migrant labour was widely regarded as an inevitable and permanent institution in Central
Africa. At the turn of the century the African was still wholly a
tribesman. Only with considerable difficulty could he be persuaded to venture forth for a brief spell of work on the farm or in
the mine. Originally it was he who was anxious to return quickly
to his tribal life. As we have seen, however, labour gradually
became more plentiful and many Africans soon became accustomed to this new environment. After the First World War
some Africans were already seeking to make permanent homes for
themselves and for their families in the towns.[45] Here, however,
they encountered an insuperable obstacle. Migrant labour, which
at first had been accepted, albeit reluctantly, by the European
employer as a simple matter of fact, was now thought by the
Europeans to have positive and vital advantages, and the idea of a
permanent African urban population was often abhorrent and
alien to official and unofficial Europeans in both the Rhodesias.

In Southern Rhodesia the system of migrant labour was an
essential part of the scheme for segregation. The 1930 Land
Apportionment Act deprived Africans of the chance of obtaining
permanent rights in the European areas, and thereafter it was taken
as axiomatic that the towns should be regarded as white areas. 'I
think', said Mr. Robert Tredgold, then a young and newly-
elected Member of the Legislative Assembly, 'almost every Hon.
Member in this House would be prepared to accept that as a
premise.'[46] The African was therefore permitted to visit the towns
only under stringent control and his temporary residence was
made conditional on his being in full-time employment. As has
been seen, opinions differed as to whether he should be enabled to
bring his wife with him on these periodic visits.[47] The larger
municipalities made a very limited provision for married quarters,
and other amenities were severely restricted, for, as the Mayor of
Umtali pointed out, the Councils did not wish to lose money on

[45] See above, Chap. I, p. 27.
[46] Debate on the Natives Registration Bill, S.R. Debates, 2 April 1936.
[47] See above, Chap. I, p. 14 et seq.

the location, 'as it would not be fair to the white population'.[48]
The towns belonged to the Europeans, and as late as 1930 educated
Christian Africans were asking missionaries to persuade the
Government to rescind the notice of 1906 which made it an offence
for an African to use any sidewalk or pavement within a municipality.[49] Even in 1935, when plans were prepared in Bulawayo for
expanding local industry and the first sites were sold, the problem
of native housing was barely considered.[50] The whole weight of
European thought was against recognizing the social and human
needs of African labour. The African, it was thought, had his
home elsewhere.

Working and living conditions varied considerably. Domestic
servants, although they were expected to work long hours, were
comparatively fortunate. They earned from one to three pounds
a month, and usually received good food and accommodation.
Government departments, such as the Post Office, Roads, and
Native Departments, and the larger firms also had a good reputation. For the most part, however, the average wage for unskilled
adults was fifteen shillings a month with food and shelter, or
thirty shillings a month without.

And when it is realized that the rent of the meanest room is ten
shillings a month, that firewood and mealie meal alone for two persons
cost ten shillings a month, it will be understood that hardship verging
on semi-starvation often occurs amongst this class of urbanized native,
particularly if they happen to have wives and children.[51]

Housing was already the biggest problem. In Salisbury government and municipal housing provided accommodation in 1938
for about 5,400 Africans. But there remained at least 6,000 men,
exclusive of domestic servants, living in the back of premises of
shops, factories, and warehouses in the business quarter of the
city, in 'private locations' consisting of huts erected on farms outside the southern and eastern boundaries of the commonage, and

[48] Central African Archives, ZAH 1/1/3, p. 1493.
[49] *Proceedings of the S. Rhodesian Missionary Conference*, June 1930. In 1934 a conviction
under this notice was set aside 'on the grounds that as an African was entitled to enter a
European shop it was unreasonable to request him to keep off the sidewalks'—B. W.
Gussman, *African Life in an Urban Area* (typescript, Bulawayo, 1952), p. 3.
[50] Gussman, op. cit., p. 5.   [51] Burden, op. cit. (1938), p. 9.

in the 'crowded and filthy hovels surrounding the brickfields . . . an area which constitutes a menace to the well-being of the city'.[52]

Outside the towns conditions were equally varied. Some of the biggest mines, such as the Wankie collieries, the Shabani asbestos mines, and some of the larger gold mines, compared 'very favourably' with the Rand; wives and children were welcomed, and facilities for sport and education were provided. At Wankie during the economic depression the management adopted the policy of rationalizing the labour force and making greater use of machinery, with the result that rates of pay compared favourably with the Rand and the Copperbelt; some 40 per cent. of the labour force were accompanied by their wives, and long periods of employment were encouraged.[53] On other large gold mines, however, where economy was the ruling factor, the welfare of African workers was not considered. The housing, latrine, and washing accommodation was less than the minimum required by Government regulations; 'men with wives and others with temporary female associates' were herded together in one quarter along with single Africans. The granting of unlimited credit by store-keepers was encouraged by some employers so that the employee was kept in a position of bondage and was unable to save either to support his family or to return home.[54]

For the most part, however, labour relations were still dependent on the immediate, personal relationship of employer and employee. Much of the gold mining was undertaken by small workers rather than large companies, and on the smaller mines, as on the farms, there were many employers who, treating their employees fairly, had no difficulty in finding and retaining their labour. In these cases the personality of the individual European was 'a most important factor'. The Labour Officer of the Nyasaland Government reported in Salisbury that:

Natives will often work contentedly for low wages with unvaried food and dilapidated quarters if the employer or shift boss is a man who

---

[52] Burden, op. cit. (1938), pp. 5, 10.

[53] J. C. Abrahams, *Report on Nyasaland Natives in the Union of South Africa and in Southern Rhodesia* (Zomba, 1937).

[54] Burden, op. cit., p. 16.

does not harry them or lose his temper easily. Many of the smaller mine compounds resemble typical native villages surrounded by gardens of maize, pumpkins and sweet potatoes. The mine continues to function after a fashion even in the absence of the owner who is often the sole European on the property and the employees appear to consider that their own interests are bound up with those of their employer.[55]

This was a paternal relationship in which both parties found a certain satisfaction and happiness. But it was already far from universal. In the towns and the compounds of the railways and larger mines there were 'thousands of children growing up without ever experiencing village and tribal life'.[56] There were many workers with their families who never visited their tribal homes. They were ignored by Government and employers alike. According to the theory of segregation they were not there. Government responsibility towards urban children was thought to end with attempts at 'exportation' to the Reserves. No location or compound in Southern Rhodesia had any provision for a children's amusement park.[57] The African, upon whom so much depended, was an alien. Migrant labour alone made segregation, in the sense of parallel development in separate areas, seem even remotely plausible. But although the assumptions encouraging the use of migrant labour were the most vital part of the theory of segregation, they were also the most vulnerable. As this type of labour became increasingly uneconomic and impracticable, as workers became more permanently urbanized, and as the African rural areas turned towards a more permanent system of peasant agriculture, it became more and more difficult to persist in the belief that segregation was working. Either the eye had to be closed to many unwelcome facts, or the theory of segregation had to be thought out afresh. But this was a process which was only begun several years later, when the problems had become far more acute.[58]

In Northern Rhodesia Europeans were equally unwilling to recognize the necessity for, and the needs of, a permanent African urban population. In the period before the Second World War

[55] Burden, op. cit., p. 19.   [56] Ibid.
[57] B. Grimston, *Survey of Native Educational Development* (duplicated, Salisbury, 1937), para. 50.
[58] See below, Part II, Chap. IV.

this reluctance does not seem to have arisen directly from either the theories of segregation or the defence of the position of European artisans. It is true that in town-planning Northern Rhodesia broadly followed the example of her southern neighbours, but the reluctance to recognize the strength of the flow to the towns or the emergence of the urban African was here primarily a result of the attitude of the administration.

The development of the Copperbelt coincided with the attempt to revitalize and govern through the bonds of tribal control, and these bonds could be maintained only if the adult male Africans returned regularly to their tribal homes. Respect for traditional customs and morality, obedience to the older generation, and the natural good manners of African rural life which appealed so strongly to many European officials, rapidly—and it seemed inevitably—disappeared when the African found himself an uprooted individual in a heterogeneous collection of employees. Officials tended to rationalize in language at once more altruistic and more sophisticated than that of farmers and industrialists.

Unless we are very careful [said the District Officer at Mufulira] we are going to get an industrial community consisting mostly of Wemba boys who will in course of time lose contact with their own people, but will still remain very aggressively Wemba, and who will be a strange people in a strange land. A wholly industrialised Wemba is, I should think, a very unpleasant person indeed, and it will come when this generation grows up here. He will require very strong discipline, he will lose the very powerful discipline of the White Fathers' Mission in the Wemba country, and he will find himself down here an individual instead of as in his own country a section of his family group. I think he will be a very difficult man indeed to manage, and his son will be worse.[59]

The solution which officials put forward was to encourage workers to leave their wives and children behind them and to introduce a system of deferred pay, with the worker returning home after a year's work.[60]

[59] *Copperbelt Disturbances, 1935*: evidence, Vol. 1, p. 281, J. S. Moffat—now Sir John Moffat.
[60] Ibid.

I

Urbanization therefore ran counter to the whole trend of official thought, and in addition to this there was a strong current of *laissez-faire*. As the Chief Secretary put it: 'None of us wish to see interferences with our employees by public authority. It has been the custom in Africa for servants of the white man to be more or less entirely under the control of their master.'[61] This might well have been a satisfactory policy in calmer days, but it was, surely, completely inadequate for a country immersed in an industrial revolution. The administration, trying to make both ends meet with very scanty resources of finance and personnel, suddenly found itself confronted with a scale of employment which, as the Chief Secretary himself admitted, went beyond 'anything in any Crown Colony in Africa'.[62] The administration's share in the newly-discovered wealth only accrued slowly, and with a serious shortage of staff contact was lost with the African workers. This was clearly revealed by the strike and riot of 1935, which were touched off by an admirable, but inadequately explained, decision to increase the tax in the urban areas while lowering it in the country. The whole group of problems connected with labour was largely 'ignored, or treated only in conjunction with other matters', the mine management was compelled 'to undertake duties and responsibilities which should scarcely come within its sphere', and, as a result, by 1938 there was 'a certain lack of mutual comprehension in the relations between the industry and the administration . . . a perceptible air of suspicion in the transaction of business'.[63] The firm initiative and control of Government were non-existent; an unfortunate precedent had been created.

The basic strategic direction of the industry and its labour force remained therefore in the hands of the Companies. Their policy was influenced by their early experiences. Both Government and outside observers were deeply impressed by the slump. As we have seen, it caused a dramatic fall in employment on the Copperbelt, but its impact on Africans had been greatly lessened by the ease

---

[61] *Copperbelt Disturbances, 1935*: evidence.
[62] Ibid.
[63] G. St. J. Orde Browne, *Labour Conditions in Northern Rhodesia* (Col. No. 150, 1938), pp. 4, 5.

with which they had been able to return to a life of subsistence agriculture. This was the obvious and only means of social security then available, and it would have been extremely dangerous to have broken the unity between town and country suddenly and

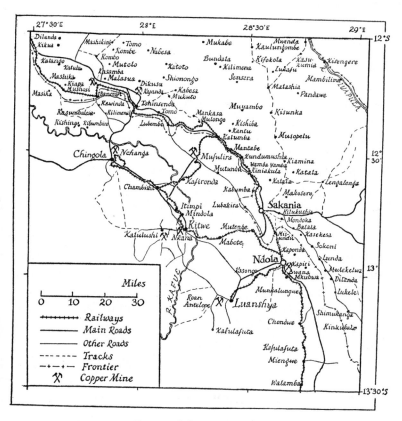

Towns of the Copperbelt.

completely.[64] Giving up the Reserves would have meant providing social insurance, and even in England the Welfare State was not yet accepted. But it was perhaps even more dangerous in Central Africa to make no provision for the future.

The policy of the Companies varied. All provided good and

[64] E.g. Merle Davis, op. cit., p. 177.

varied food, excellent medical arrangements, recreational facilities, and good working conditions. A high proportion of men were accompanied by their wives, in contrast with the custom on the Rand, but whereas at Luanshya and Mufulira employees were encouraged to go in for gardening and to settle for longer periods, at Nkana it was preferred that men should return to their villages after two years. Free rations were provided for families. Housing was varied; most workers lived in single-roomed huts, unsuitable for bringing up families, although, as one observer cryptically remarked, 'native custom is necessarily modified under urban conditions'.[65] At a time when it was difficult to estimate future labour requirements it was in the Companies' immediate interests to preserve an elasticity in the supply of labour: they wished to retain freedom to increase or decrease the force as rapidly as possible.[66] They aimed at a flexible, contented, and increasingly healthy and efficient labour force. Provision was therefore made for women, and, if necessary, younger children, to live with the men, but their living quarters were essentially conceived as labour camps.

For women—and by 1938 there were 10,000 of them—life on the mines was demoralizing. Many of them contracted temporary unions, and few were able to undertake new constructive interests and occupations. In education a great opportunity was being missed. In 1935 there was one school in the mine compound at Nkana, but the D.C. admitted that it did not meet 'the educational needs of the people to any extent'; at Mufulira the Compound Manager expressed himself as 'definitely against all education', and at Luanshya there was a school in the town location but no direct provision for education on the mine.[67] In 1937 the United Missions collaborated with the Government in starting 'a certain number' of schools, but Sir Alan Pim reported that they would only provide for 'a small proportion' of the 8,430 children on the Copperbelt, of whom some 3,000 were of school-going age.[68] Both the Government and the Companies appeared to be reluctant to encourage and guide the emergence of a permanent African com-

---

[65] *Pim Report*, p. 41.   [66] Orde Browne, op. cit., p. 30.
[67] *Copperbelt Disturbances, 1935*: evidence Vol. I, p. 161.   [68] *Pim Report*, p. 47.

munity whose interests and institutions would be attuned to their new environment.

This was in sharp contrast with the policy pursued by the Belgians in the Katanga just north of the Copperbelt. As early as 1922–3 concern was being felt there over the wastage caused by a high labour turnover and the need of industry for more and more skilled workers. At the same time, from a thorough investigation of the rural areas from which the migrant workers were drawn, the conclusion was reached that not more than 5 per cent. of the adult male population could be removed from their villages without gravely disturbing the economic and social balance of the community. In the light of these clear economic conclusions, the Government, the missions and the Union Minière du Haut Katanga were able to make a planned, united attack on the problem. This was the more effective in view of the close control exercised from Brussels. A policy of both rural and urban stabilization was adopted and was put into force by the Union Minière in 1927. Social services were carefully planned: maternity wards, infant-welfare clinics, refectories with two meals a day for children, and compulsory primary education for all children between the ages of five and twelve. From the age of fourteen, boys started on light employment and were gradually trained for more skilled work. Until 1932 the proportion of Europeans to African employees was between one to seven and one to nine, but by 1938 a proportion of one to twelve, compared with one to eight or ten on the Copperbelt, was considered normal. Besides these measures taken by the Union Minière, the Government established a 'centre extra-coutumier' at Elisabethville which facilitated the growth of a permanent urban community.[69] There was no sudden or complete break with the rural areas, contracts were renewable after three years, but in the Katanga the foundations for the future were being carefully and consistently provided.

Yet, although it was not recognized or encouraged, a haphazard urbanization was taking place on the Copperbelt. Even in 1935

[69] F. Grévisse, *Le Centre Extra-Coutumier d'Elisabethville* (Bruxelles, 1951), pp. 1–18. *Pim Report*, pp. 42–3.

the evidence was incontestable. A Bemba chief carefully explained to the Commission which inquired into the riot of 1935 that, although the people were pleased about the tax reduction in the rural areas, they were annoyed at the increase on the mines, because 'most of these people working on the mines have no desire to return home'. On being asked if the tax had been reduced recently in Nyasaland, a Musisya from Chinteche angrily replied: 'I have been here over twenty years, and how can I know the things that are going on in Nyasaland? I regard this as my home now.'[70] On the mines new links were formed, new interests were arising. These sprang up and were developed most clearly among the clerks and *capitaos*, many of whom came from Nyasaland. But the influence of these men percolated down and determined the outlook which, most observers felt, was in the background of the disturbances. Men who had left their tribal homes and had come to live in the towns were bound to feel frustrated and resentful in a society which did not recognize their existence. Signs of 'unrest', 'defiance', and 'definite increased disrespect for Europeans' were reported, a larger number of complaints were made by European women of 'the insolence of native servants', and the officer in charge of the police at Mufulira noticed 'a growing class-consciousness amongst the educated and progressive natives during the last year. It is merely something one observes and cannot explain. It is an atmosphere. There are certain classes of natives who are proud of being Africans.'[71]

This new sense of a common racial solidarity doubtless had several sources, but its economic source, in the contrast between European and African wages, was already apparent. The common attitude of Europeans towards African wages was expressed by the Provincial Commissioner:

Their pocket is a different one from ours, and the money they put into it still remains for almost the whole population of this territory an unnecessary luxury, that is as far as living is concerned. They can live comfortably without any money at all—not at Nkana for instance, but when they return to their homes—apart from their payment of revenue.

[70] *Copperbelt Disturbances, 1935*, evidence.
[71] Ibid., evidence of J. C. Maxwell and A. H. S. Goslett.

If I am deprived of my salary I starve, but the native in similar circumstances can go home and live as happily as ever.[72]

At Nkana, however, and on the other mines and in the towns, any mode of living above a purely animal existence demanded considerable sums of money. By 1940 a married man on the Copperbelt earning the minimum of 12s. 6d. a month was actually on the subsistence level, spending his whole wages to supplement his rations. And even the single man found his wages insignificant when confronted with the whole host of new needs. Raincoats, shoes, pullovers, and handkerchiefs were beginning to be essential articles of clothing for people expected to be out in all weather and to take part in an urban life. Enamel and ironware inevitably took the place of pottery and gourds: pots, basins, dishes and knives were all necessities.[73] These needs were felt most compellingly by the educated cadre, especially those who were attempting to bring up families remote from any rural 'subsidies'. More sophisticated forms of recreation soon became popular, the new urban forms of prestige demanded extravagant clothing and lavish hospitality, while among all Africans there were many 'very fond of beer', because beer was their 'only food', a social as well as a nutritional 'necessity', and the cups in the 'Government' beer-hall were 'very small for 6d. or 1s.'[74]

Men with these varied needs, said a clerk from Nyasaland,

have seen that they started to work at the same time as the European and the European at once is able to buy a motor car and he gets a lot of food at the hotel. The natives complain about this. They compare the wages of the Europeans with the wages of the natives.[75] They do the same kind of work, for instance the natives working underground are supervised by a European who only points out to them the places where they should drill holes. After doing this the European sits down and the natives drill the holes. The natives know where the holes should be

[72] *Copperbelt Disturbances, 1935,* evidence.

[73] R. J. B. Moore, 'Native Wages and Standard of Living in Northern Rhodesia', *African Studies,* Vol. I, 1942.

[74] *Copperbelt Disturbances, 1935*: evidence, p. 757.

[75] In 1937 the average pay at Nkana for European workers was £506 p.a.; the average pay for all mines to Africans was £10 16s. p.a. for surface labour, and £18 18s. for underground labour. *Pim Report,* pp. 51–4.

drilled, they have been doing that work for some time and they know and understand the work.[76]

Only a few Africans as yet made such comparisons and voiced similar complaints, but their number steadily increased.

Away from the mines, life in the towns was even more strange and difficult for the African worker. The rhythm of the mine and the rule of the compound manager supplied a discipline which to some extent replaced that of tribal life, and the worker's immediate physical needs were well looked after. In the towns, however, there was little discipline and often the living conditions were appalling. In 1938 Livingstone was surrounded by a variety of compounds, some of which were 'a permanent threat to the health of the town'. In one of the buildings, 'long rows of cells about $7\frac{1}{2}$ ft. square ... built with a soft mortar ... a refuge for ticks, bugs, and all sorts of pests' formed 'a squalid courtyard' which had been taken over by the Municipality at a total valuation of £1. In the other municipal compound the tenants paid a shilling a month and built their own houses: the result was 'an extraordinary collection of huts of every size, shape, and condition, connected by a labyrinth of paths' with obviously inadequate bucket latrines on the outer edges. The compounds belonging to the railway and the Zambezi Saw Mills were deemed 'satisfactory', though badly sited. At Lusaka, the newly-built capital, conditions were better, but the huts were small, with communal kitchens and there was a 'lack of suitable sites, permanently allotted; indecision as to appropriate type of hut; variations in sanitary instalments, and a tendency to experiment with quite unsuitable types; inadequate or unwholesome water supply; and unduly high rentals'. Municipal and administrative officers were alive to these shortcomings but funds were restricted and there had 'apparently never been any definition of responsibility for doubtful cases; administration, municipality, and private employers all endeavour(ed) to avoid expense for which they (were) not certainly liable.'[77]

All these conditions were part of a situation in which low wages were paid to inefficient labour. On farms and towns, desertions

[76] *Copperbelt Disturbances, 1935*, evidence Vol. II, p. 825.
[77] Orde Browne, op. cit., pp. 63–5.

were a common occurrence, for although they involved penal
sanctions they were punishable only by action in the Courts. This
procedure caused the employer considerable trouble and merely
ended in the deserter spending a short spell in jail, which carried
no sort of social stigma. In fact most employers found such action
so profitless that resort to the courts was rare. 'In most cases the
delinquent is simply written off, and the employer pockets the
loss; the whole standard of performance deteriorates and the
labour market is flooded by men who leave work immediately
the task becomes irksome.' On small farms it was not unusual to
find an average working week of thirty hours or even less, and
this 'cheap' labour used unproductively was in fact going far to
cripple certain industries.[78] In Southern Rhodesia most deserters
were apprehended by the police, and often employers paid the fine,
deducting it from the employee's pay.[79]

Thus in these two inter-war decades the fears of the European
artisans, and the determination of the Europeans in general to
avoid any development which might threaten white supremacy,
led to the colour bar. A desire to keep the towns white, the policy
of strengthening tribal authorities, sympathy for rural simplicity,
fears of a slump and a reluctance to face the immediate difficulties
and expenses involved in providing education and social security
—all these resulted in a refusal to accept a permanent African
urbanization. But the ever-increasing interdependence of Europeans and Africans in industry was beginning to produce a situation which challenged the system of segregation root and branch.
The urban African was a fact, as were on the other hand the
vicious circle of African poverty and inefficiency and the whole
complex problem of a new generation emerging chaotically in an
urban environment where they found themselves denied access to
its essential techniques. The implications and urgency of these problems were as yet by no means universally apparent and were
virtually ignored. With an averted eye responsibilities were
evaded.

But already another whole aspect of migrant labour was causing
acute alarm. Far away from the towns and mines, a slow paralysis

[78] Orde Browne, op. cit., p. 22.   [79] Burden, op. cit., p. 14.

was creeping into thousands of remote African villages denuded of their young men: a paralysis which challenged the doctrine of paramountcy and trusteeship.

4. THE RURAL PARALYSIS

In his 'Memorandum on Native Policy' Lord Passfield, it will be remembered,[80] had attached great importance to the principle that the African should be free to work on his own land and that taxation should not oblige him 'to labour for wages as the only practicable means of obtaining the money wherewith to pay his tax'. African development was to be a 'first charge' on any territory and the provision of access to markets 'a primary consideration'. In 1930, when these principles were enunciated, the extent to which they were being disregarded was unknown. Missionaries, however, were drawing attention to the plight of the rural areas. For example, as early as 1924 the Bishop of Northern Rhodesia was demanding a radical reassessment of taxation,[81] and in 1935 the Nyasaland Government appointed a Committee to Enquire into Emigrant Labour. The members of this Committee—local officials, settlers, and a missionary—confessed that on their appointment 'there was not one of us who realized the seriousness of the situation: as our investigations proceeded we became more and more aware that this uncontrolled and growing emigration brought misery and poverty to hundreds and thousands of families and that the waste of life, happiness, health and wealth was colossal . . . a state of affairs which, viewed from any standpoint, constitutes a flagrant breach of that ideal of trusteeship of native races "not yet able to stand by themselves under the strenuous conditions of the modern world".'[82]

In the 1931 Census it was estimated that not less than 30,000 adult male Africans were temporarily working outside the Protectorate; in 1935 the Committee, with no exact evidence before it, had 'no hesitation' in stating that the number abroad was in the

---

[80] See above, Chap. I, pp. 41–2.
[81] *Proceedings of the Northern Rhodesia Missionary Conference.*
[82] *Report of the Committee to Enquire into Emigrant Labour, 1935* (Zomba, 1936), p. 7.

neighbourhood of 120,000. It was a 'spectacular jump',[83] and a second inquiry was made in 1937, which revealed a total of 90,000.[84] This latter figure, which was officially accepted, was based on an 'occupation census' carried out in each district of Nyasaland, and the following table gives its results as compared to the Committee's estimates:

	1935 Estimate	1937 'Census'
Southern Rhodesia . . .	75,000	64,078
Northern Rhodesia . . .	2,000	4,108
South Africa . . .	20,000	13,938
Tanganyika	17–20,000	5,792
Belgian Congo . . .	unknown	599
Other countries . . .	2–3,000	1,582
	120,000	90,097

The findings of the Committee were to some extent discredited by this later census; yet if one compares the estimates with those compiled by officials of the Nyasaland Government in Southern Rhodesia and South Africa, the Committee is found to err if anything on the conservative side,[85] and it seems probable that the 'census' figures may well have been too low. Yet even the 1937 figures showed that 18·3 per cent. of the adult male population were employed abroad, and the incidence of this migration fell far more heavily on some districts than others. Of the nine districts in the Southern Province, only four had a percentage in double figures, rising to 27·1 per cent. in South Nyasa, but all the districts in the Northern Province were in double figures and the districts of the 'dead north' were as follows:

Mzimba	45·4 per cent.
West Nyasa . . .	60·9 per cent.
Kota-Kota . . .	43·1 per cent.
Kasungu	43·8 per cent.

These were a serious contrast to the figure of 5 per cent. which the Belgian authorities considered, at least in theory, to be the permissible maximum.

[83] Sir John Harris, *The Times*, 12 August 1936.
[84] *Bell Report*, p. 96.
[85] Cf. above pp. 91–4.
[86] *Bell Report*, Appendix A.

The effects were felt by all sections of the communities involved. For the labourer himself there was a long, tiring, and often dangerous journey. In self-protection the emigrants generally went in small bands of five or more. Until the twenties these bands were frequently attacked, robbed, and murdered as they passed through Portuguese East Africa. This became a serious menace to the labour supply of Southern Rhodesia, so that in 1923 the Southern Rhodesian Government appointed a 'supervisor of facilities for the passage of Northern Natives'. This officer was able to establish ferries over the Zambezi, put down the robbers, and open a medical post at Fort Darwin. There were no suitable rest camps, however; the migrants slept in the bush, and if a man fell ill his life depended on his companions' efforts. In the thirties, lorry transport was beginning to be used, but passengers were apt to find themselves 'dumped' at isolated spots unless additional fares were forthcoming.

Even with these difficulties, however, the journey was by 1935 perhaps the easiest part of the labourers' adventure. On the frontier they were approached by recruiters' messengers and touts who wore uniforms bearing 'a marked resemblance' to those worn by the African police and messengers in Nyasaland. The unwary or unsophisticated were thus carried away for 'cibalo'[87] to work for employers whose behaviour was such that they could not obtain voluntary labour. The majority evaded the clutches of the recruiters, registered, and obtained a pass to seek work. Employment was not always easy to find, however, and, unless a friend or 'brother' helped the immigrants, they had to beg, borrow, or steal. Many of them worked for other Africans in return for food and shelter; 'not a few Europeans' took advantage of a labour glut and employed them at rates far below the average and, in some cases, for food only. Until they found regular employment they had to re-apply fortnightly for renewed permits to seek work; if they neglected to do this they were imprisoned, and they could not stay in any township for more than a fortnight unless they obtained work. Other Africans, especially those in subordinate

[87] 'a term of opprobrium originally denoting "forced labour" and now indiscriminately applied to all recruited or attested labour', Burden, op. cit., p. 2.

positions of authority, often treated them unjustly because they were foreigners. They did not always receive compensation for injuries received at work, and on the mines in Southern Rhodesia the death rate among Nyasaland Africans was double that of the indigenous.[88]

For many Africans from Nyasaland life in Southern Rhodesia was therefore a strange and sometimes vicious form of existence; one might find riches and excitement, but seldom a home and security. Life in a 'white-man's country' was in harsh contrast with that in the lakeside Protectorate. The exiles met and mingled, their tribal differences were lessened and, as on the Copperbelt, a new sense of unity emerged. There was also a personal grievance against the Governments of the Union and Southern Rhodesia. When in 1935 Nyasaland Africans were declared prohibited immigrants into the Union, men who had been there for many years and who looked on it as their home were suddenly uprooted. They came back to Nyasaland 'with a strong feeling of grievance against all European Government'. Those who returned through Southern Rhodesia often had to pay Southern Rhodesia taxes for the years they spent in the Union unless they could prove that a pass to visit the Union had been obtained, a proceeding which, reported the Nyasaland Labour Officer, accounted for 'a spreading distrust of the Southern Rhodesian Government amongst Nyasaland native migrants'.[89]

Deep as were the effects on the man who emigrated, more damage was caused to his family and tribe. The Committee estimated that 25–30 per cent. of the men who left Nyasaland lost their connexions with the country and did not return. This figure was confirmed by the 1937 'census', when it was found that a quarter of the emigrants had not been heard of since 1930.[90] Some of these 'machona' or 'lost ones' married local women in the countries to which they went, settled, and, in Southern Rhodesia, even obtained a local inhabitant's pass. Many others entered into temporary unions, which brought them into debt and prevented them from saving money to return home, where a man who

[88] *Report of Labour Committee, 1935*, p. 28. [89] Burden, **South Africa**, pp. 8, 19.
[90] Committee's report, p. 29; *Bell Report*, p. 96.

returned penniless found himself in disgrace with his family. After two or three years of absence the migrant discovered that he was free from all communal responsibilities and all too often he was loath to return to them. Whatever the causes, the migrants' absence enfeebled their tribe and brought misery to their families. Huts, grain-stores, and fences fell into disrepair; gardens and farms were not properly cultivated; attempts to affect improvements in the villages were stopped by lack of manpower. The whole balance of obligations was disrupted. Elderly parents and relatives were left to fend for themselves, in patrilineal tribes children found themselves forsaken and grew up without discipline or respect, and never having experienced the traditional way of life they remained ignorant of its positive values.

Above all, 'the most pathetic effect of emigration', the Committee felt, was its responsibility for 'the tragic lot of thousands of women'. For them the highest fulfilment of life was motherhood. Yet for many women motherhood was now impossible save through illicit connexions. As a result divorce was becoming the 'commonest of occurrences in some districts'. Utterly unable to do all the work of house and garden, many women could sustain themselves only by brewing beer or by prostitution. One woman whose husband had been away for seven years exclaimed: 'Money is nothing. I want my husband to give me children.' This was 'endorsed emphatically' by other women and several expressed indignation at the injustice of their position. The Committee summed up in sombre words the probable evils which would occur if emigration continued unchecked and uncontrolled:

In the northern half of the Protectorate the moral, social and physical life of our Native population will be so affected that any attempts by Missions, Government or other agencies to maintain, let alone improve upon, the present low standard of health and happiness, will be abortive.

Home life will cease to exist; all belief in the sanctity of marriage will disappear. Immorality will be the rule. In consequence, venereal disease will affect one hundred per cent. of our Native population. The birth rate will fall.

Large tracts of land will be rendered unfit for habitation and in consequence the economic life of the whole country will suffer seriously.

As the Native population will be dwindling, the country may be able to sustain, along the Lake Shore and river banks, the remaining inhabitants.

And, resident chiefly in other lands, the Nyasaland-born Natives will have acquired a complete mistrust in and loathing for administration by white people which has made a wilderness and called it peace.[91]

What, then, were the causes of this emigration and what steps could the Government take to remedy the evils? Taxation, the factor for which the Government was most directly responsible, was still in 1935 an important cause in certain areas. The Committee thought that 'from the point of view of immediate necessity' taxation was still a prime cause: the five most northerly districts of the Northern Province obtained only £14,000 in wages and from sale of produce, and yet they paid £18,379 in hut and poll tax, the balance being supplied by remittances from abroad. In the Kota-Kota district tax collection was a 'most depressing experience' for the Native Authorities, since the only result that they could see was 'a continual stream of their able-bodied population emigrating', and among the Chewa at Kasungu taxation was 'probably the paramount cause for emigration'.

But in other districts other economic influences were even more important. Among the Tonga, the Tumbuka, and the Ngoni, communal obligations and the necessity to earn '*lobola*' were the prime incentives: with the Tonga, emigration had become a part of 'the natural order of things' and half the emigrants were prospective bridegrooms. As communal ties weakened, other incentives took their place: bicycles and sewing-machines were becoming necessities and could be obtained only by wage-earning abroad. Finally, in the Southern Province the large influx of Alomwe from Portuguese East Africa to work on European estates had prevented wages from rising, and the native Nyanja preferred, in consequence, to seek higher wages abroad.[92] In the Northern Province of Northern Rhodesia taxation was thought to be the main cause of emigration, and among the Fort Jameson Ngoni it was considered to be 'still very important' but outweighed by other economic incentives.[93] The economic background to emigration was therefore harshly obvious; and to these hard facts some observers added

[91] Committee's report, pp. 30–8. [92] Ibid., pp. 18–23. [93] *Pim Report*, p. 39.

other less tangible influences: a love of travel and a desire for adventure. But, as the Committee pointed out, most men who undertook the 'grand tour' of the white man's world would return and settle down were it not that economic realities pushed them forth again.

Faced with this situation, the Committee recommended action at two levels: emigration should be regulated and the workers cared for and kept in touch with their rural homes, and at the same time fresh resources should be directed towards the development of the rural areas. In order to prevent the numbers of 'machona' from increasing, an inter-territorial agreement with Southern Rhodesia, and if possible with the Union, should provide for compulsory deferred pay, family remittances, and repatriation. Recruiting under licences, which provided for medical attention and transport facilities, should be permitted. At home every effort should be made to open up the Northern Province, and taxation should be readjusted. Most constructive of all was the suggestion that the tax payable by migrant workers should be considerably increased and that recruiters should pay a capitation fee of £1 in respect of each labourer recruited, both sums to be paid into a Native Trust Fund.[94]

The report, with its outspoken indictment of the situation, aroused considerable interest in the United Kingdom,[95] particularly as it coincided with Sir Alan Pim's report of a very similar situation in the High Commission Territories and with Miss Monica Hunter's work in Pondoland, all of which underlined the difficulties of a system of segregation dependent on migrant labour. In August 1936 an inter-territorial agreement was signed in Salisbury between the Governments of the Rhodesias and Nyasaland, which went some way towards rectifying the worst abuses. Southern Rhodesia agreed to admit only those Africans who were provided with identity certificates and recognized the desirability of repatriation after two years, with exceptions in particular cases. Rest camps and rapid, cheap transport were to be provided. In its

---

[94] Committee's report, pp. 48–51.
[95] E.g., *The Times*, 6 May 1936, 12 August 1936, *Manchester Guardian*, 22 July 1936, *International Labour Review*, July 1936.

financial provisions, however, the agreement did not come up to the Committee's recommendations: only a voluntary system of remittances was instituted and the Government could merely recover tax at the basic rate payable in the worker's own territory.[96] In September 1936 agreements were entered into with the Transvaal Chamber of Mines, as a result of which the Witwatersrand Native Labour Association was permitted to recruit 10,000 workers from Barotseland and 2,000 from Nyasaland. In 1938 the Barotseland figure was reduced to 1,500 and that of Nyasaland was increased to 8,500. The W.N.L.A. paid the whole cost of transport and a pass fee of 6d. a month per labourer, and arranged for compulsory deferred pay.[97] In Nyasaland itself there was a full inquiry on taxation, but no immediate action was taken.[98] For the rest the Secretary of State drew attention to the fact that £4,200,000 had been spent, mainly with the aid of grants from the United Kingdom, on development of roads and railways in Nyasaland since 1930,[99] and the problem of the 'dead north' remained.

In this chapter attention has been concentrated on the problems which industrialization was beginning to bring to Central Africa. Yet it also brought the possibility of revolutionary improvements in the lives of the people of this territory. A new era could be contemplated in the age-long battle against pest, disease, and environment. It was possible to envisage a rapid closing of the gap which distinguished European from African standards of living. The problems were to increase in urgency, but so also were the material resources available for their solution. It was not yet certain whether the evil effects would outweigh the good, but the dangers of beginning a rapid industrialization when men lacked the desire to create a united nation were, surely, apparent.

[96] The text of the agreement is reprinted in Appendix IV of the *Pim Report*.
[97] *Bledisloe Report*, pp. 186–7.
[98] *A Report on the Direct Taxation of Natives in the Nyasaland Protectorate* by E. Smith (London 1937). Smith criticized the 1935 Committee's emphasis on taxation, but it is difficult to see what evidence Sir Robert Bell had for concluding that taxation was nowhere 'an appreciable factor in emigration': *Bell Report*, p. 97.
[99] *The Times*, 16 October 1936.

K

IV. AFRICAN EDUCATION

I. THEORY AND ATTITUDE

In this inter-war period European rule was firmly established; the initiative belonged to the Europeans, and in land policy and labour relations it was being used in such a way as to transform the lives of Africans throughout Central Africa. It was a time of European dominance and African malleability: a fleeting moment, though most contemporaries assumed it to be permanent. In the realm of African education, the Europeans had in these years a unique opportunity to influence profoundly the future thought and outlook of Central Africa. For about so long as it takes a man to grow from infancy to maturity African minds were open to receive with gratitude the teaching of the West. The most spectacular of the early African reactions to the arrival of European settlers and domination—the rebellions of 1896 in Southern Rhodesia and 1915 in Nyasaland—had turned towards the past. The passionate and violent rejection of the new order had failed; a fresh response was forming, a response moulded by men looking towards the future. Africans were gradually realizing that a different set of tools was needed and a new horizon of thought had to be mastered before they could begin to take an effective share in determining their way of life.

In the twenties African apathy and suspicion of schools and missionaries were changing over wide areas into interest and enthusiasm. In 1927 a speaker in the Legislative Assembly of Southern Rhodesia pointed out that whereas twelve years previously missionaries had to seek for students, they now had to refuse them by the score.[1] 'Wherever you go', it was said on another occasion, 'you will find the keenest interest on the part of the native in the question of education.'[2] Even the traditionally-

---

[1] Southern Rhodesian Debates, 5 May 1927, col. 86.   [2] Ibid., 4 May 1926, col. 331.

minded Matabele realized that the basis of their former ascendancy had disappeared. They discovered that they were 'lagging behind, while others are forging ahead', and they demanded schools so that they could 'thrive like other tribes'. As one of them put it: 'My fathers came here and put their earmark on local Natives. We want Government to put its earmark on us.'[3] Previously the only girls who were brought under mission influence were those boarders who had, for various reasons, run away from home, but in most areas by 1925 the strong initial prejudice against education for girls was weakening.[4] Whereas in 1905 there was in Southern Rhodesia 'a mere handful' of vernacular village schools, by 1925 there were over 1,000. The stirring was general, and an observer compared it to the situation in England in 1816, when a 'Select Committee on the Education of the Lower Orders' found 'the most unquestionable evidence that the anxiety of the poor for education continues not only unabated, but daily increasing'.[6]

It is one of the sober paradoxes of Central African history that just at the moment when Africans were thus beginning to demand better education and more opportunities of sharing in the white man's world, Europeans were becoming less and less ready to give active and confident help in this transition. The task of fostering a new understanding between the races seemed immense and formidable; some Europeans even felt that it would prove impossible. Segregation and indirect rule sought therefore to preserve the African's traditional way of life, or at least to mitigate the abruptness of the transition. This emphasis was strikingly reflected in the accepted educational theory of the period, which, as will be seen, was primarily connected with the tribal, village, peasant community. Yet the pace of development was set not by administrators, teachers, or political theorists, but by the economic system which drew Africans and Europeans together. To bolster up tribal ways, to try to maintain the past, to oppose the growth of a class of skilled, urban Africans, to neglect the needs of the emergent individual was to resist the march of events instead of guiding it.

[3] *Report of Commission on Native Education, 1925* (Salisbury).   [4] Ibid.
[5] Ibid.   [6] Quoted in A. V. Murray, *The School in the Bush* (1928), p. 82.

Before the First World War African education was regarded as almost exclusively the concern of the missions. In Nyasaland no official was responsible for education; the Government paid a grant of £1,000 in 1907, rising to £3,000 in 1924, but this was a minute part of the total sum, one of the missions alone spending well over £21,000 per annum.[7] In Southern Rhodesia the 1899 Education Ordinance provided for small grants to mission schools: by 1909 eighty vernacular schools were earning grants totalling £1,744. The 1910–11 Native Affairs Committee recommended that the Government should establish a teacher-training institute and should foster agricultural instruction in the Reserves, but no steps were taken to implement these recommendations.

After the war, however, there was in Europe and America a growing wave of interest in African education. It was felt that education was a challenge that involved the basis of trusteeship, and this feeling was matched by a realization that the resources of tropical Africa could be developed fully only if a measure of Western knowledge percolated through to the mass of the population. Although the United States received no mandated territory from the League of Nations, she played a leading part in establishing the new idealism, and in view of their own experience in Negro education, many Americans felt that their country could contribute uniquely to the solution of Africa's problems. The trustees of the Phelps-Stokes Fund, an American charitable foundation which in 1917 had prepared a two-volume report on Negro Education in the United States, decided in 1919 to appoint a Commission to survey education in Africa. Under the leadership of Thomas Jesse Jones, an authority on Negro education who had directed the research department of Hampton Institute, the Commission included British and American missionaries and an African member, Dr. Aggrey of the Gold Coast. Concentrating on West and South Africa, the Commission's report awakened both missions and governments to a new and broader conception of the role that education could play in Africa. The literary and narrowly evangelistic education previously provided was shown to be 'inadequate and to a considerable extent unreal so far as the

[7] T. J. Jones, *Education in East Africa* (New York, 1922), p. 199.

vital needs of Africa' were concerned. Education, the report emphasized, should be related to the environment of the masses; soil and sanitation should be emphasized as much as the three Rs. 'If the world is to be Christian, then Christianity must broaden its conception of mission possibilities.' The missions had a chance to take a central part in the shaping of a new Africa; they must seek to convert not only individuals but also the community. Since the overwhelming majority of Africans lived on and by the soil, agricultural training should be regarded as fundamental; the Commission also recognized the special needs of urban communities and the vital importance of a far greater provision for secondary education, but in Central Africa these aspects of the report were subsequently overlooked. Above all, the report urged the missions to eliminate the inefficiency due to denominational rivalry, and advised the Governments to bring their resources into action and co-ordinate policy.[8]

The report of the Commission was well received in both official and missionary circles. At the Colonial Office in 1923 Mr. Ormsby-Gore, the Parliamentary Under-Secretary of State, appointed a permanent Advisory Committee on Native Education in Tropical Africa to consider policy in conjunction with leading missionary representatives, educationists, and colonial experts. Another Phelps-Stokes Commission visited East, Central, and South Africa in 1924, and this, together with the Ormsby-Gore Commission of the same year, laid a new emphasis on a policy of active educational, economic, and technical development. At a conference at Le Zoute in 1926 representatives of every Protestant mission working in Africa approved the policy of adopting professional standards in education and of partnership with the Colonial Governments. The following year the Congregation of Propaganda Fide established a 'Conférence des missions catholiques d'Afrique'; Mgr. Hinsley was appointed Visitor Apostolic to the Roman Catholic Missions in the British Colonies in Africa, and vigorously set in train an active co-operation with the new policy.[9]

---

[8] T. J. Jones, op. cit., pp. 10–46.
[9] R. Oliver, *The Missionary Factor in East Africa* (1952), pp. 263–76.

But the new approach needed money to give it effect, and in Central Africa this was found grudgingly and sparingly. In Nyasaland an Education Department was formed in 1926 with the modest staff of a Director and an African clerk. In the following year an Education Ordinance provided that the payment of grants should be based on the number of qualified teachers and instructors and the number of students in training. The funds available were, however, quite insufficient throughout the inter-war period to meet the full grants earned by the missions.[10] In Northern Rhodesia a sub-department of Native Education under the Department of Native Affairs was established in 1925. In 1930 native education became the responsibility of a separate department and approval was given to a five-year scheme. This was to have entailed an expenditure of £32,179 in 1931–2, rising in the fifth year to £71,346, nearly half of which was to be spent in grants-in-aid, but the inauguration of this scheme was immediately postponed as a result of the slump.[11]

In Southern Rhodesia, too, there was an interest in African education in the post-war years that was certainly greater than it had been before. Here the initial impulse came not only from Europe or America but also from the officials of the Native Affairs Department. In 1919 H. S. Keigwin, a Native Commissioner, put forward a scheme for the development of native rural industries, and the following year he was appointed Director of Native Development. Under his guidance two Government centres were established, at Domboshawa and Tjolotjo, to train agricultural and industrial teachers and demonstrators. The Government, however, still took no direct part in the main field of native education: mission schools were given increasing grants, but they received relatively little attention from officials in the Education Department, who were primarily concerned with the work of European and Coloured schools. In 1925, soon after the end of Chartered Company rule, a Commission on Native Education was appointed, and as a result of its report a Department of Native Education was formed, grants-in-aid were made more dependent on scholastic efficiency, and grants for super-

---

[10] *Bell Report*, p. 16.   [11] *Pim Report*, p. 278.

visors and capital equipment were started. But the total financial contribution remained relatively small throughout the inter-war period.[12]

TABLE 1
Government Expenditure on Education

Financial Year	Southern Rhodesia		Northern Rhodesia		Nyasaland	
	Non-Native	Native	Non-Native	Native	Non-Native	Native
1923	£207,029	£27,176	£7,835	Nil	Nil	£2,137
1938	£360,825	£89,539	£55,594	£44,223	£1,946	£19,270
Per head of population in 1938	£6	1s. 5d.	£5	8d.	11s.	3d.

Source: *Bledisloe Report*, p. 83.

Thus the Governments still played a very minor role in African education; the missions remained by far the most important educational agent in Central Africa. Their financial contribution was still considerably greater than that of the Governments. In Nyasaland it was estimated that the cost of the schools in 1936 was met to the extent of five to ten per cent. by fees, thirty per cent. by Government grants, and for the rest by the missions from their home resources.[13] In Southern Rhodesia missions were often represented by hostile critics as financing their church work largely by appropriating educational grants; the reverse was in fact the case. In 1936 nine of the largest missions received £44,000 in Government grants and £12,000 from native members; but they themselves contributed £40,000 from home funds and, even more important, 400 full-time workers.[14] On the other hand, the growth of church membership was intimately linked with the missions' educational work: schools were their best evangelistic agents, and it was thought in Southern Rhodesia that probably 90 per cent. of the Christians came into the Church by way of the school.[15]

The schools themselves were originally designed to teach Africans to read the Bible, and at a higher level to train evangelists.

---

[12] *Report of Native Education Commission 1925.*
[13] *Bell Report*, p. 17.   [14] Grimston, op. cit., Chap. 2, p. 43.
[15] E.W. Smith, *The Way of the White Fields in Rhodesia* (1928), p. 153.

At the same time the missions, with their increasing need for school-buildings, mission houses, and churches, provided a certain amount of incidental industrial training. In the inter-war period the desirability of such training as a part of education was increasingly recognized. Largely as a result of the reports of the Phelps-Stokes Commission, the declared aim of the period was to raise whole communities 'by placing emphasis on the "essentials of education", namely the improvement of health, family life, use of the environment both human and material, recreation and religion'.[16] Interest was therefore focused—in theory at least—on the village rather than the individual, on the tribe rather than the town, on the small school rather than the large. It must have seemed most convenient that educational theory harmonized so smoothly with the official policies of indirect rule and segregation. While officials sought to revitalize tribal authority and to restrict the ambitions of the emergent few, black and white teachers were encouraged to regard African children as members of a traditional, rural society, which slowly and cautiously would adopt the modern blessings of hygiene, morals, and manure.

The Jeanes-trained teacher was the chosen tool for this policy of community education. In the Southern States of the U.S.A. the Jeanes Fund, a charity founded by Miss Anna T. Jeanes, a wealthy Philadelphian Quaker, especially trained Negro 'demonstrators' to visit and assist other teachers in the work of community development. Following the Phelps-Stokes reports, the Jeanes Fund and the Carnegie Corporation extended this work to East and Central Africa. With their aid Jeanes Training Schools were established in Kenya, Northern Rhodesia, and Nyasaland, while in Southern Rhodesia the Government school at Domboshawa became a centre for this training, and Hope Fountain Mission near Bulawayo provided a similar course for women teachers.

This concern with the wider responsibilities of education was undoubtedly an improvement on the former limited aims of the missions; but the emphasis on the rural village community diverted attention from far more urgent realities. The competitive

---

[16] *Village Education in Africa*, a report of the inter-territorial 'Jeanes' conference (Lovedale Press, 1935), p. 13.

demands of the twentieth century, the routine of European farms, mines, and slums, and the frustration of playing so restricted a role in the modern world were on the whole overlooked. The European awakening to the strength and possibilities of tribal life came a generation too late. The task of preserving traditional values was of immense importance; but the African's cultural inheritance would survive as a living force only if it took part in a genuine, equal synthesis with the twentieth century. The immediate problem was to help Africans in the transition to a modern way of life and to an active share in the life of the European minority. It was this help that Africans demanded from education, and which economic developments made it imperative for them to obtain. Instead, in Nyasaland, the Jeanes training scheme retarded the development of secondary education,[17] and in the Rhodesias the problem of urban education was largely neglected.

The broad educational aims of the various missions were also profoundly affected by differences in their political and cultural philosophies. In all three territories the approach of the Dutch Reformed Church missions was deeply influenced by their South African background. Of all the Protestant missions, they were making the largest contribution: in Southern Rhodesia they had fifty-four European and 539 African workers with 324 schools, compared to the Anglican mission—the next largest—which had forty-seven European and 261 Africans workers with 277 schools. In Northern Rhodesia the Dutch Reformed Mission had forty-one European workers and 509 schools; in Nyasaland 713 schools with 38,000 enrolled pupils, compared to the 401 schools and 20,000 pupils of the United Free Church of Scotland, the next largest Protestant mission in that territory.[18] In Dutch Reformed opinion, African education was 'a matter to be proceeded with cautiously'; the school was the handmaid of religion. But in two important respects the schools of the Dutch Reformed Church were unequalled. Some of the missionaries had been farmers in South Africa and most had grown up on farms, and as a result they

[17] *Bell Report*, p. 273.
[18] Smith, op. cit., Appendix iii; Jones, op. cit., p. 200. The figures refer to the period 1923–5.

brought with them an appreciation of the importance of agriculture and simple village industries.[19] One of their missionaries expressed their aims in the following words:

Our Church is composed of farmers, the Boers. We grew up with the Natives, and had an idea that the Native was the servant of the white man; that was wrong. We believe they have souls to be saved. Other people say to the Native, 'Oh! my brother!' We say that we must preach the Gospel and educate him too. He is not equal to us and we cannot make him so. We must turn the flood of the Natives' desire to learn to good purpose. Education is to improve the Native; to improve his body and soul; I want to make him pure, I want to make him intelligent so that his fears of spirits will have no hold upon him. I want to make him ambitious to lift up his people.[20]

In their industrial training the missions of the Dutch Reformed Church did not aim at turning out skilled artisans. 'We would far rather see', wrote their Superintendent in Nyasaland, 'one of our boys setting up for himself as carpenter in his own village . . . than have him enter the employment of a European, and ultimately compete with the European.'[21] And it was not only the Afrikaner who was influenced by South African experience. The Seventh-Day Adventist minister at Solusi in Southern Rhodesia, a Britisher from Natal, said that he did not think 'that we should teach or allow a Native to think that he is as good as a white man. You would be spoiling him if you did that. He should be brought up in the proper way. If this were done I consider that it would be the means of eliminating a large number of the so-called "black peril" cases.'[22]

At the other end of the scale there were those missions who believed that education should prepare the African for integration with the Europeans. Often this belief was combined with a feeling that it was impossible to apply Christianity to the traditional system, the best and the worst customs being inextricably interwoven. Man would be made new not only by the Gospel but also by literary and industrial training, which would completely

[19] Jones, op. cit., p. 212.
[20] *Report of Commission on Native Education, Southern Rhodesia, 1925.*
[21] Ibid.   [22] Central African Archives ZAH/1, p. 809.

change his whole outlook and ultimately enable him to take his place in the body politic. A prominent member of an American mission operating in Eastern Mashonaland thought that

a large part of educational work is to train and educate Natives to take the proper place they must take in the political body . . . to fit them to get the franchise and to take part in the administration of the country. . . . We teach them civics and methods of self-government, and have always done so.[23]

These differences in approach and ultimate objectives were partly discounted by the varying conditions under which the missions worked, so that while the contrast between missions remained significant, that between territories was even more important. The greatest contrast was in the spheres of employment open to educated Africans. In Nyasaland the Church of Scotland Mission at Blantyre arranged an apprenticeship course of four years which included printing, book-keeping, and clerical work. From this course Africans passed out to become overseers, engineers, builders, carpenters, drivers, interpreters, and clerks. Strong in the belief that Nyasaland was 'not a white man's country', the mission could pursue a policy of training 'the native both educationally and industrially to meet the coming influx of civilisation and take his share in it for the development of his country's resources'.[24]

European planters employed men educated at Blantyre Mission and elsewhere as *capitaos* or overseers, and a leading planter expressed his satisfaction with their work: 'They were honest and more intelligent than the average uneducated native.' As a result this planter was anxious to open schools on his estate and to help them financially, adding that his offer was not purely philanthropic, as he realized that only by using better agricultural methods could the country compete with other East African territories.[25]

[23] *Report of Commission on Native Education, Southern Rhodesia, 1925.*
[24] Letter from Dr. Alexander Hetherwick, *Report of Commission on Native Education, Southern Rhodesia, 1925.*
[25] *Report of Native Education Conference, Zomba, May 1927,* Captain Humphrey in discussion on agriculture.

In Southern Rhodesia, however, the advance of educated Africans into skilled work was vigorously obstructed during this period,[26] and as a result there was a persistent doubt in the minds of both missions and the Native Education Department of the advisability of specialist industrial training.[27] The determination to prevent Africans from infiltrating into European jobs was accompanied by a fairly general prejudice against the 'educated African'. The 1925 Commission on Native Education in Southern Rhodesia reported that

a clear majority of Rhodesian women, a large number of whom are fair and indulgent mistresses, have the opinion that mission-trained Natives are self-assertive and impudent. It is also said that mission Natives are not as honest as 'raw' Natives.

Many employers would not wittingly employ a mission boy, and one 'kindly and just employer of over two thousand Natives' told the Commission: 'If you want to spoil a good nigger send him to a mission. He is casual and approaches you as an equal.'[28] The 1,000 odd boss boys on the farms in Southern Rhodesia at the best were merely semi-literate and in 1937 were paid about £1 a month, and, although a few farmers were beginning to ask the missions to supply them with a better type of boss boy, the general opinion was summed up by the president of the Matabeleland Farmers' Union, who remarked that up to about the beginning of the First World War there were 'natives in this country whom it was a pleasure to have work for one, but the better educated the native became the lazier he seemed to get'.[29] As late as 1937 it was reported that

if the average European wants to engage, say, a messenger he will turn down the capable applicant as 'sure to be a rogue' and engage the cringing illiterate one with the remark, 'useless, but you can't expect more of a native'.[30]

This prejudice against education took various forms. Among Europeans in Southern Rhodesia there was, and indeed in some

---

[26] See above, Chap. III, pp. 100–4.   [27] Grimston, op. cit., Chap. 2, p. 79.
[28] Report of Commission.   [29] J. Bazeley's evidence to the Bledisloe Commission.
[30] Grimston, op. cit., Chap. 5, p. 53.

quarters there still is, a flat refusal, or at the best a great reluctance, to speak to an African in English. Even someone like Mrs. Tawse-Jollie, who was a strong advocate of the policy of paternal development and official aid to and control of African education, confessed to 'a strong prejudice against speaking English to a native'.[31] In Nyasaland, by contrast, missionaries like Laws supported a policy of spreading the use of English as a *lingua franca*, rejecting alike the Swahili of East Africa and the Kitchen Kaffir of the South. Africans themselves were most anxious to learn English, and at Blantyre it was thought that 'in two or at the most in three generations nothing but English would be used'.[32] Thus in Southern Rhodesia the young semi-educated African often found himself in a society whose rulers despised the gifts and qualifications which he had, laboriously if imperfectly, acquired; whereas in Nyasaland and to a lesser extent in Northern Rhodesia there was a far greater readiness to appreciate his value.

2. RESULTS

Despite the varied opinions on the aims and usefulness of African education, the mission schools continued to extend the bounds of literacy and rudimentary knowledge. The Jeanes teachers encountered many difficulties: Government officials were apt in Southern Rhodesia to suspect them of usurping authority; denominational rivalries interfered with their work; envy, misunderstanding, superstition, and suspicion often hindered them in their relations with the village communities, village women in particular being tenaciously conservative.[33] In Nyasaland the Jeanes centre at Domasi introduced courses for chiefs in an attempt to enlist their active co-operation, and as a result a leading Dutch Reformed Church missionary thought that by 1935 headway was being made in linking up school and community, but the centre's sphere of influence was restricted.[34]

Gradually the Jeanes teacher became accepted as a trained

[31] Tawse-Jollie, op. cit., p. 265.
[32] R. Laws, 'Native Education in Nyasaland', *Journal of the Royal African Society*, July 1929.
[33] *Village Education in Africa*, pp. 60–74, 211.   [34] Ibid., pp. 74, 158–76.

deputy-superintendent of 'untold value to the cause of Native education',[35] but the philosophy on which his training rested was increasingly challenged, especially by Africans who became impatient with what seemed to them an attempt to consign them perpetually to an inferior status. Grimston records how even one of the most promising Jeanes teachers in the country eventually asked him:

> Why do you teach our children only to use the Native axe and knife, and prevent us from using saws and hammers? Why do you tell us to make wooden spoons? Do you not want us to climb the ladder of civilisation? We buy metal spoons from the store. Is it wrong for our children to want to have chairs and beds and be like the European? Are there many natives in England who do all the work for you white people? It is not easy for us to tell our children, 'No, you must want to be natives; no, you must make spoons because it is hand and eye training; no, the Pass Laws are not all bad because they are made to protect you.'[36]

But the specialized Jeanes training reached only a minute proportion of the teachers, and the small remote bush schools continued their important yet haphazard work. A typical school, four hours away from Livingstonia at the north end of Lake Nyasa, consisted of a mud building, 30 feet by 16, with three square holes in the walls for windows, and earth floor and platform with a table for the teacher, and a blackboard hanging on the wall. On the seats, which were branches of trees stuck in the floor, there were young men and maidens, old men and children, 'as eager for the new learning as the Florentines of the age of the Medici'.[37] As a result of the work of these schools, Nyasaland had a higher percentage of literacy in the vernacular than most other parts of Africa. The 1937 Commission on Higher Education in East Africa estimated that sixty per cent. of the population in Nyasaland could read and write. This was almost certainly an over-estimate: in 1938 a survey of twenty-nine villages in a progressive area gave 37 per cent. literacy, yet even this figure was high by African standards.

[35] Grimston, op. cit., Chap. 3, p. 105.
[36] Ibid., Chap. 4, p. 6.   [37] Murray, op. cit., p. 79.

But with the scanty supply of vernacular literature, literacy by itself was no great gain. Apart from a very few magazines produced by the missions there was little to satisfy the interest and curiosity of the newly-literate. Much of the valuable, spontaneous enthusiasm in the schools was wasted. Very few of the schools earned any assistance from the Government, and supervision was scanty: one mission with over 700 schools had a single European engaged full-time on educational work.[38] The schools varied enormously in quality. Overcrowding, mixed age groups, irregular attendance, and the lack of trained teachers ensured that few children reached the higher standards of even elementary education, and there was no provision for those who could have progressed farther.

In Southern Rhodesia there was a greater degree of control. There were no 'bush' schools properly so called: all the village schools, with the exception of a mere handful, were aided, and the Government steadily opposed the missions' agitation for the right to establish uncontrolled, unaided 'schools of religion'. Even here, however, there was a great variety in the quality of the schools. Some of them were said in 1925 to be 'really excellent'. 'The pupils are taken far beyond the Native section of the code. Some of the teachers have made a useful start in agricultural and industrial work. Simple lessons on hygiene are given, habits of discipline and cleanliness are enjoined, conversational and book English are taught, even recreations are not forgotten.'[39] Other schools, however, consisted of 'a number of children, dirty and undisciplined' crowded into a hut 'with neither charts, books, nor slates, under a teacher possessing little more learning than the scholars themselves and almost as untidy'.[40] With the creation of the Native Education Department in 1927 a determined, and to some extent successful, effort was made to improve the standard of teachers: in 1928 seventy-six per cent. of the teachers had an academic attainment lower than Standard IV—the fourth year's work at an elementary school—but by 1934 this had been reduced

[38] Murray, op. cit., p. 80.
[39] *Report of Commission on Native Education, Southern Rhodesia, 1925.*
[40] Ibid.

to thirty per cent.[41] There remained, however, an enormous wastage in educational effort: in 1937 about sixty per cent. of the children who enrolled in village schools left before they passed Sub-Standard A, a further twenty per cent. left before they reached Sub-Standard B. Those who did pass Sub-Standard B took about five years to do so, and only then were they in a position to start a full elementary education. The school was generally staffed by a single teacher, probably not fully trained, and expected to take four classes. This deadening stagnation could be overcome, it was thought, only by setting up central village or intermediate schools that would bridge the gap between kraal school and the principal school at the mission station.[42]

Time had brought a new interest and understanding to African education. No longer was it thought of solely as a mission responsibility, and the missions themselves were gaining a wider view of their educational opportunities. It was seen that the school must be intimately linked with the life of the community, and even though the community was often envisaged in unreal and static terms, this was a considerable advance on the previous limited aims. Much effort, however, continued to be wasted, and only a very few pupils gained more than the haziest impression of the new world they were entering. In 1939 there was still no secondary education for Africans anywhere in Central Africa. In the Colonial Office territories a six-year course of secondary education was planned but not in being; in Southern Rhodesia the absence of secondary education was a direct result of the Government's policy of segregation.[43] Not only was this seriously hindering administration and development, through the lack of well-educated clerks, accountants, and assistants in the scientific and medical departments,[44] but it also deeply affected the relationship between Africans and Europeans. Apart from a very few Africans who were able to obtain further education in South Africa, there were few who could easily and confidently enter the intellectual heritage of even the average European. The sights

[41] J. Lewis, *A Short History of the Development of Native Education in Southern Rhodesia* (cyclostyled, F.A.W.S. Bulawayo).

[42] Grimston, op. cit., Chap. 3, p. 28.

[43] See for example *Bledisloe Report*, p. 88.

[44] See *Bell Report*, p .270.

were still set very low. Education was doing very little to bridge the cultural gulf which separated the races and which was becoming more and more dangerous in the face of their growing economic interdependence. Few Europeans as yet appreciated the urgency of the situation, and in all three territories funds for education were very short. This was partly due to the slump, which in Northern Rhodesia led to the abandonment of the ambitious plans of 1930.[45] It was only in the 1940's that Northern Rhodesian expenditure on African education equalled that spent on the far smaller number of European children, and African education occupied a low place in financial priorities throughout Central Africa.

In Southern Rhodesia between 1930 and 1936 the number of African schools decreased by 133, and although revenue collected directly from Africans increased by £60,000 between 1932 and 1937, the grants to missions only increased by £3,000. The ability of African families to pay the school fees largely determined which pupils should proceed beyond the village school.[46] In the Legislative Assembly there was in the thirties a great reluctance to devote funds to African education. Jack Keller, the Labour Member, pointed a warning finger at Northern Rhodesia, where there were 'not only native Civil Servants, and telegraphists, but even surveyors', and the extremist viewpoint was put by Sir Hugh Williams, Member for Gwanda:

Who wants the native to buy a pair of black trousers to cover his black legs? His black legs are infinitely preferable as a worker and as an individual. The native will continue to be honest if you leave him with his beads and blankets. . . . It is we who are battling out on the veld. . . . If we could clear out every mission station in this country, and stop all this fostering of higher native education and development, we would much sooner become an asset to the Empire. . . . We are simply committing suicide.[47]

In one of his earlier budget speeches as Prime Minister, Huggins expressed his reluctance to aid African development as long as it

[45] See above pp. 131–2.
[46] Evidence of the Rev. H. Carter to the Bledisloe Commission.
[47] Southern Rhodesian Debates, 30 April 1935, cols. 1446, 1448.

L

remained possible for the Imperial Government to interfere with legislation affecting Africans:

> If I am allowed to protect my own race and find a niche in this country for every grade of white civilisation, then I will dip into the pockets of the hon. Minister of Finance and see that the native gets more money; but until I know that I am not moving. That is why you find a standstill in the Native Development Vote. . . . I cannot stand the dead weight of wondering if someone is going to censure what I do. . . . We claim the right to run our own domestic affairs for which we pay.[48]

Yet while doubt and hostility lingered in some European circles, among Africans enthusiasm for education increased. Disregarding the denominational and other differences of opinion among Europeans, Africans were gradually supplying the impetus and assuming the initiative. Education often involved both teachers and pupils in hard work and sacrifices. There were, for example, the several hundred road workers in the north of Nyasaland who built successive school-houses for their own use, several miles apart, as the road progressed.[49] In all territories there were many cases of African village communities going to great trouble to secure and maintain a school, and of African families educating their children at very considerable expense. In the towns of Southern Rhodesia there were night schools where waiters, houseboys, and manual workers paid 1s. to 2s. a month in an attempt to satisfy their desire for education, and though the educational attainments of these schools were often limited, they did at least provide 'a compensatory feature of sojourn' in the towns.[50] At Maronda Mashanu Mission, where the Rev. Shearly Cripps preferred independence to a Government grant, kraal schoolteachers worked without pay, and at other missions there were examples of similar sacrifices.[51]

Educational and Church work gave Africans their fullest opportunity of bearing responsibility and achieving a new sense of self-respect. In both spheres there were remarkably few Europeans in

[48] Southern Rhodesian Debates, 24 April 1934, col. 531.
[49] Laws, op. cit., p. 365.
[50] *Report of Commission on Native Education, Southern Rhodesia, 1925.*   [51] Ibid.

relation to the amount of work undertaken, and inevitably Africans were often encouraged to hold responsible posts. In Nyasaland, for example, the Anglican Church had in 1938 twenty-one African priests and deacons, four of whom were in sole charge of large districts.[52] In Southern Rhodesia the biennial missionary conference, which was a valuable means of consolidating missionary effort and presenting missionary opinion to the Government, also ran a similar conference for African pastors and priests where the leaders of African opinion in the thirties met together and discussed political and social, as well as religious, issues. In Nyasaland an African, Mr. Levi Mumba, was on the Government's permanent Advisory Committee on Education. Yet even north of the Zambezi this devolution and sharing of responsibility had not gone very far, and in Southern Rhodesia it was thought that 'there are not many Native leaders who have complete confidence in the good intentions of their European masters'.[53]

The challenge to the Europeans' paternal control over the Africans' education and adaptation to the modern world was vividly illustrated by the continuous growth of separatist and independent religious movements. As in the Union of South Africa these sects could be divided into two main groups: the Ethiopian and the Zionist.[54] The Ethiopian sects, generally led by educated men, sought to maintain the doctrine, and the pattern of church organization, received from the missionaries; but, confronted with the many denominational differences of European Christians, they contended that Africans also had a right to organize independent Churches ruled by Africans for the mass of Africans. Their inspiration seems to have been racial rather than theological; not so much a repudiation of Christian teaching as a reaction against European leadership and the total situation in which they found themselves. To the insults and the pin-pricks of the colour bar were added frustrated personal ambitions. There were also opportunities for serious misunderstandings with the missionaries over finance. The married missionary's standard of living—his housing,

---

[52] Memorandum submitted to Bledisloe Commission.
[53] Grimston, op. cit., Chap. 4, p. 5.
[54] Cf. B. Sundkler, *Bantu Prophets in South Africa* (1948).

food, clothing, and transport—was on a far higher scale than that
to which most Africans could aspire. It was not easy, therefore,
for the African to realize that mission funds were limited. The
marked decrease in subscriptions from Europe and America
which followed the slump imposed a great financial strain on the
Christian African, and he found that 'he was continually being
badgered by the "rich" who pose as his benefactors for endless
subscriptions and fees'.[55]

One of the oldest and most typical of the Ethiopian sects was
the African Methodist Episcopal Church, founded at the beginning of the nineteenth century by Richard Allen, a Negro in the
Southern States of America. In 1894 an off-shoot was formed in
Johannesburg by the Rev. M. M. Mokone, who had seceded from
the Wesleyan Church, and during the inter-war period a branch
was formed in Nyasaland by Hancock Msokera Phiri. Born in
1897 at the village of Chief Mwase in Kasungu, Phiri was educated
at the local Presbyterian mission school and became a leading
member of the Church. In 1916, while still a youth, he left for
the Transvaal, working on a gold mine in Johannesburg, and
there attended the services of the African Methodist Episcopal
Church. Two years later he moved up into Southern Rhodesia.
He next taught for two years in a mission school at Livingstone,
and then traded fish, and subsequently worked as a bricklayer.
At the end of this brief, varied, yet typical career he entered the
African Methodist Episcopal Church as a full-time worker. In
December 1923 he was appointed a deacon in South Africa and
the following year he was made a pastor and instructed to return
and carry on work at his home village. Within five years he had
over 400 adherents with two schools which were progressing
'chiefly because English was taught'. By 1940 he directed fifteen
schools, one of which qualified for Government assistance, and no
schisms had appeared among his followers. The movement as a
whole was well ordered and law-abiding; Phiri worked in close
harmony with his influential Chief Mwase and a D.C. reported
that he was of 'great assistance in many ways'.[56] In all, he was a
striking example of the way in which a young, able, ambitious

[55] Grimston, pp. 35–7.   [56] Central African Archives, Zomba, Miss. 12/10.

African found in these Ethiopian sects an outlet for initiative and a basis for independence and self-respect.

The Zionist type of separatist sect often combined the racialist undertone of the Ethiopian sect with a rejection of at least some aspects of Christian doctrine. They sought to combine Christian ritual with traditional modes of thought and behaviour; faith healing, speaking with tongues, taboos, and purification rites were their distinguishing features.[57] A typical example of a Zionist sect was the 'Last Church of God and His Christ', which started operating in the Karonga District of Nyasaland about 1926. Its doctrine was founded on the parable of the ten virgins, which was interpreted as justifying polygamy. Some of its members were drawn from the Scottish missions, but most of them came from pagan communities. They were predominantly of the Nkonde group of tribes and, in the words of a D.C., chiefly consisted of 'uneducated and simple people having two or three wives and who like to attend a religious service where they are not condemned as adulterers'. By 1940 they claimed over 7,000 adherents.[58]

None of the independent sects scattered throughout Central Africa, of which the African Methodist Episcopal Church and the 'Last Church . . .' are merely two examples, caused much concern to the Governments. In this inter-war period it was the adherents of the Watch Tower doctrines who aroused more anxiety, with their emphasis on the imminence of the Second Coming of Christ and their repudiation of governments and churches as the organizations and emissaries of Satan. These doctrines were first introduced into Nyasaland in 1908 by Elliot Achirwa, who, on declaring that the end of taxation, the disappearance of British rule, and the formation of an African state would coincide with the final advent due in October 1914, was promptly deported to the Seychelles.[59] Similar teaching was introduced into Northern Rhodesia in 1918 by a group of Africans returning to the Northern Province from the mines south of the Zambezi. Their rejection of authority, with their refusal to pay tax, caused 'serious disorganization' in the districts of Fife and Abercorn,[60] and in 1919 ninety-

[57] Cf. Sundkler, op. cit.
[59] Ibid.
[58] Central African Archives, Zomba, Miss. 12/10.
[60] *The Times*, 9 July 1926.

nine Africans associated with Watch Tower were charged with sedition and assault at Kasama. In 1923, 1,000 Africans were involved in a disturbance at the Wankie colliery, believed to have been inspired by Watch Tower doctrines,[61] and in 1924 Watch Tower adherents held a mass meeting at Broken Hill where the leaders pressed round the local Magistrate 'shouting all at once, yelling defiance within inches of his face' and demanding a reduction of the tax.[62]

The European representatives of the Watch Tower Bible Society, or Jehovah's Witnesses, in South Africa disowned all responsibility for the actions of this 'so-called Watch Tower movement' and a European representative was sent to Northern Rhodesia to try 'to put the thing straight'. The Society, however, continued to flood the area with cheap, attractive literature, containing lurid pictures of white people being destroyed by an avenging Jehovah, and their doctrines were, perhaps, imperfectly understood by tribal Africans. In 1935 the D.C. at Ndola considered that 'nearly the whole country is affected now'. In his opinion the movement as it operated in Northern Rhodesia was 'only semi-religious . . . a sort of free masonry'. It had almost become 'part and parcel of native custom'; in the nearby Reserves whole villages were found calling themselves Watch Tower, permeated with 'a subtle influence that acts against authority'.[63] Most of the missionaries and officials who gave evidence to the Commission appointed after the Copperbelt disturbances of 1935,[64] considered that the Watch Tower movement had been an unsettling factor, at least partly responsible for determining the African's outlook towards authority, although there was no evidence that it was directly responsible for the strike. By 1940, in Nyasaland at least, the Jehovah's Witnesses under the leadership of a European representative were considered to be well behaved and gave no trouble,[65] but the movement continued to provide

[61] Central African Archives, Zomba, Miss. 12/10.

[62] F. Melland, 'Washing in Jordan', in the *African Observer*, September 1935.

[63] Evidence to Commission on Copperbelt Disturbances, 1935. Witnesses: J. L. Keith and Petrus Johannes de Jager.

[64] See above Chap. III, p. 112.

[65] Central African Archives, Zomba, Miss. 12/10.

for needs and emotions which found no satisfaction in the Christian Church as it was presented to large groups of Africans in Central Africa.

In the inter-war period, then, the independent religious sects and movements did not erupt in a rebellion like that of John Chilembwe and the Providence Industrial Mission in 1915. But they constituted a disturbing challenge to both missionaries and settlers. Their growth was a sign that the period of African malleability was drawing to a close, that European leadership would not be accepted unquestioningly forever. It was not yet clear how the African of the future would respond to the challenge of his rapidly changing environment nor what would be the motives and ideals that would inspire his leaders. But it should, surely, have been clear that if Africans were to move towards a unity of purpose with the Europeans in Central Africa, they would need assistance, encouragement, and opportunity on a quite revolutionary scale.

V. THE BLEDISLOE COMMISSION: SURVEY OF A DECADE

I. SOUTHERN RHODESIA

The concepts expressed in the two words 'segregation' and 'trusteeship', defined and crystallized as policies during the twenties, still divided Central Africa at the end of the inter-war period. It was realized that both policies were as yet incompletely implemented: in Southern Rhodesia a slow start was being made on the immense task of raising living conditions in the Native Reserves, but meanwhile Africans continued to flock into the European areas; while north of the Zambezi development plans were only just beginning to undertake some of the obligations implied in trusteeship. Both policies were also an inadequate answer to the new problems brought by industrial development. Increasing economic interdependence made racial segregation more and more difficult to achieve; the influx of European capital and workers made it steadily more impracticable for the Colonial Office either to persevere in a paternal policy of trusteeship or to enforce 'the paramountcy of Native interests'; the mass migration of workers destroyed inherited traditions, impoverished the rural areas, and posed the tremendous question of what the new kind of town should be like. All this demanded inter-territorial control and a thorough readjustment of policy. But incomplete and inadequate though these policies were, the difference between them still seemed acute to outside observers. A Royal Commission, under the chairmanship of Lord Bledisloe, was appointed in 1938 to report whether a closer co-operation or association between the Rhodesias and Nyasaland was 'desirable and feasible'; in the opinion of the Commission, these differences in racial policy were a formidable barrier to amalgamation. The divergence, which was one of aims even more than application, was seen to be of over-riding importance in determining the destiny of the three territories.

In Southern Rhodesia segregation was unhesitatingly accepted by all the European political parties. In 1933 the Reform Party, led by Dr. Godfrey Huggins, won the elections and ousted the Rhodesian Party, which under Sir Charles Coghlan and H. U. Moffat had governed the country since the grant of Responsible Government in 1923. Prime Minister at fifty years of age, Huggins had come to Southern Rhodesia in 1911 for reasons of health, leaving his post of Medical Superintendent at Great Ormond Street Hospital, London. After serving with the R.A.M.C. in Europe during the First World War, he continued his practice as a surgeon, and was elected to the Legislative Assembly in 1923. A vigorous back-bencher, he had in opposition criticized various administrative failings of the Government, but there was in fact little difference of opinion between the two parties on the fundamentals of policy. As if to demonstrate this, Huggins brought various members of the Rhodesia Party into his Government to form the United Party in 1934, a year after taking office. His own political and administrative ability was rapidly recognized; his personal ascendancy was quickly established. As early as 1937 an article in *The Times*, headed 'In Southern Rhodesia. The Huggins Era. Between Two Native Policies', described the 'quite unusual personal popularity' of the Prime Minister to which was added 'a faint disillusionment' with his Cabinet: a combination which persisted for the most of his twenty-three years in office.[1]

Huggins declared the 'native policy' of the United Party to be one of 'gradual, differential development',[2] and in a speech to missionaries and educated Africans in 1938 he expounded what was known as the Two Pyramid Policy. Fear of African competition and a pertinacious determination to preserve European supremacy were allied to a firm, paternalistic conviction that the presence of European settlers could provide the only structure for a permanent civilization in Africa. Huggins made it clear that segregation was conceived primarily in terms of defence for the

[1] *The Times*, 2 August 1937.   [2] *The Times*, 31 October 1934.

white electorate but, at least as he expounded it to this audience, it had also a positive, forward-looking aspect. It was designed to protect African institutions and enable them gradually to adapt themselves to 'civilization'.

The Europeans in this country can be likened to an island of white in a sea of black, with the artisan and the tradesman forming the shores and the professional classes the highlands in the centre. Is the native to be allowed to erode away the shores and gradually attack the highlands? To permit this would mean that the leaven of civilisation would be removed from the country, and the black man would inevitably revert to a barbarism worse than ever before. I say this because the ancient controls and inhibitions of tribal custom and superstition on which Bantu society rested are going, or have gone, never to return. But the white man's law, religion and example can take their place. Rightly or wrongly, the white man is in Africa, and now, if only for the sake of the black man, he must remain there. The higher standard of civilisation cannot be allowed to succumb.

Huggins went on characteristically to decry those 'earnest people who believe that the Shorter Catechism, the multiplication table and possibly a pair of braces are the only steps between barbarism and civilisation'. Policy, he said, should be continuously directed towards the construction of two separate social pyramids. In the African areas the African 'must be allowed to rise to any position to which he was capable of climbing'. The African might be his own lawyer, builder, journalist, or priest; he must be protected from white competition in his own area, and there 'every step of the industrial and social pyramid must be opened to him except only—and always—the very top. For what can be done we may point to Uganda, for what must be avoided we may look at Haiti and Liberia. The senior administrative officer must be white.' In the European areas the African should 'merely assist, and not compete with' the white man. 'If he wishes to stop in his own area, let him. The two races will develop side by side under white supervision, and help, not hinder, each other's progress. The interest of each race would be paramount in its own sphere.'[3]

---

[3] *Rhodesia Herald*, 31 March 1938. Parts of the speech are reprinted in the *Bledisloe Report*, p. 170.

The basis of this policy was the 1931 Land Apportionment Act,[4] but in 1933, when Huggins accepted office, few of its provisions were as yet being actively implemented and, partly as a result of the slump, little development was taking place in the native areas. Huggins himself was unwilling at first to provide funds for African welfare and development, until he could be confident that what he considered to be aspects of domestic policy would not be censured by Whitehall.[5] Hostility towards the tenuous control still nominally exercised by the Imperial Government over legislation affecting African interests had been aroused shortly after the grant of Responsible Government. Two Acts—the Native Juveniles' Employment Act, 1926, and the Native Affairs Act, 1927—had aroused criticism in the House of Commons, and although both Acts received the Royal Assent, there were demands in the Southern Rhodesian Legislative Assembly that these constitutional restrictions should be removed. Southern Rhodesians particularly disliked the opportunity for missionaries and others to 'go behind our backs to the Secretary of State'; they feared the possible effects of a Labour Government in the United Kingdom; and the most outspoken advocate of African rights in the Assembly said that the fear of being distorted by extremists 'restricted legitimate criticism at this end'.[6] In June 1934 on his first visit to London as Prime Minister Huggins discussed this question and by Letters Patent of the 25 March 1937 the supervisory powers of the High Commissioner were taken over by the Secretary of State. Huggins explained afterwards that he had become convinced that these powers did not matter and that with a single-chamber Government they had 'a very useful function'. 'They enable us', he said, 'to consult with somebody else not quite so close to the problem—though, of course, we are the only people who understand it.'[7] He was, it seems, beginning to realize the advantage of being the supreme mediator between London and Salisbury—one could be played off against the other.

Satisfied, then, that he would not be subjected to undue interference, Huggins was free to embark on an intensified effort to

[4] See above, Chaps. I and II. [5] See above Chap. IV, pp. 143–4.
[6] S.R. Debates, 4 July 1928, cols. 2035–9. [7] *East Africa and Rhodesia*, 10 June 1937.

enforce segregation in both its defensive and constructive aspects. The Natives Registration Act of 1936 was the piece of legislation which attracted most attention. Lord Hailey has remarked how in the Union the Pass Laws have served a wide range of purposes. Originally they were simply intended to assist the police in the task of identification; subsequently they were utilized to secure a supply of labour and to prevent desertion; and finally, with the Natives (Urban Areas) Act of 1923, they became part of the machinery of segregation seeking to prevent the influx into towns.[8] In Southern Rhodesia passes underwent a similar transformation. Before the First World War, apart from the function of identification, Europeans were principally concerned with the pass as an instrument for extracting better service from African labour. Every male African of fourteen and above was required to carry a registration certificate or *situpa* which also served as a tax receipt, and on which could be endorsed the contract of service.[9] The aim of the 1936 Act, however, was to protect more effectively the whiteness of the towns—to implement segregation. Henceforth in the principal towns every male African was compelled to have, in addition to his *situpa*, one of the following: a pass to seek work in the town; a certificate to show that he was employed within the town; a certificate signed by a Native Commissioner to the effect that he was earning a living in the town by lawful means; if employed outside the town, a written permit from his employer; a visiting pass. Wives and minors living with their families were not affected by these provisions, but in common with adult males they were constantly liable to be challenged by the police.[10] When introducing the Natives Registration Bill, Huggins gave an example of the type of change it would make. Africans, he said, would be able to bring their wares—'curios, baskets, and articles of that kind'—into the towns for sale, but the sale of chickens, eggs, butter, 'and things of that kind in the white towns' would be definitely discouraged.

I cannot visualize that this is the future of the native inhabitant of this Colony, because if it is, then I am afraid it will mean the gradual

---

[8] Lord Hailey, *An African Survey* (1938), pp. 664–7.
[9] Ibid., p. 669.   [10] *Bledisloe Report*, p. 173.

disappearance of the white race. . . . White people should be prepared to buy these things from other white people living on the white standard, and be prepared to pay for them on that standard.[11]

Huggins defended the Bill by saying that he believed that 'the administration of the law is far more important than any other part of it'.[12] But it was precisely its administration which aroused most criticism. Most responsible observers agreed that in a country 'where the great mass of the population is illiterate' and where most of the labour was temporary and migrant, some means of identification was desirable.[13] In Northern Rhodesia, too, along the line of rail, Africans were obliged to carry an identity certificate and if absent from their homes in the towns after 9 p.m. they were required to carry a pass. But the Southern Rhodesian system, with its multiplicity of documents, the constant liability to police interference, and the long delays experienced in obtaining the pass, was disliked as a symbol of indignity and servitude long before Africans objected to the ulterior purposes it served. 'It seems probable', reported the Bledisloe Commission, 'that if the number of passes could be reduced, and the procedure and formalities generally simplified, the unpopularity of the system would be considerably lessened.' As it was, it caused 'considerable discontent' which had, as will be seen, 'wide repercussions' north of the Zambezi.[14]

Other legislation passed during these years attracted less attention. The Sedition Act of 1936, by making it an offence 'to engender feelings of hostility between Europeans and others', placed a powerful, but seldom used, weapon in the hands of the Government. More constructively the Native Councils Act and the Native Law and Courts Act, both of 1937, enabled tribal chiefs and their counsellors to begin to exercise a carefully controlled judicial and administrative initiative in matters concerning the Reserves. For the more positive aspect of segregation, the active development of the Reserves as a sphere of African advance, Huggins relied principally on administrative action. Like his

[11] S.R. Debates, 2 April 1936.   [12] Ibid.
[13] *Bledisloe Report*, p. 175.   [14] Ibid., p. 176, and see below pp. 177, 191.

predecessors, he retained the portfolio of Native Affairs, and it was here that his influence was chiefly brought to bear.

In the Reserves the small beginnings of an agricultural revolution were tentatively supported,[15] and there was a spectacular and rapid increase in medical services for Africans. In 1936 there were only thirteen clinics in the Reserves which, as the Medical Director pointed out, constituted an 'infected reservoir' exposing the Europeans to constant re-infection: 'the native will not permit us either to ignore or forget him, unless under penalty of extreme peril to ourselves.' It was decided to train Africans as orderlies in charge of simple sub-clinics, and eighteen months later there were thirty-seven clinics treating more than double the 1936 number of patients, and the scheme was recommended as a pattern for the rest of Central Africa.[16] Rather larger sums were made available for African education, though secondary education was not as yet envisaged, in accordance with the policy of segregation.[17] Near Salisbury and Bulawayo the Government established the model Village Settlements of Highfield and Luveve, setting a relatively high standard of housing, sanitation, and amenities.[18] Aided by the growing prosperity of the country, these various improvements created a considerable impression on contemporaries. As careful and critical an observer as Lord Harlech agreed in 1939 that 'the native policy of Southern Rhodesia has been almost revolutionised by Mr. Huggins, and is among the most progressive and most enlightened in Africa'.[19]

These legislative provisions and administrative developments were, however, making relatively little impact on the basic problem of implementing segregation. Despite increasing attempts to move Africans into the Reserves, there were still in 1938 more than 300,000 Africans officially living on alienated or Crown land in the European area, while nearly 100,000 other Southern Rhodesian Africans were employed in mining and industry.[20] On

---

[15] See above, Chap. II.

[16] *Bledisloe Report*, p. 92. Even with this increase, however, rather less than a quarter of the African population still lived outside a radius of twenty-five miles from the nearest clinic.

[17] Cf. above, Chap. IV, p. 142.   [18] Ibid., p. 131.

[19] House of Lords Debates, 31 July 1939, col. 723.

[20] Annual Report of the Chief Native Commissioner for 1938.

the other hand, apart from a very few posts as teachers, orderlies, or demonstrators, there was still practically no opening for educated or progressive Africans in the Reserves. And by 1938 only 834 holdings had been taken in the Native Purchase Areas, which were still in a very primitive state of development.[21]

Despite these stubborn facts no alternative to segregation was placed before the European electorate. The Rhodesia Labour Party, the chief opposition to Huggins, was in the thirties almost completely preoccupied with the problem of defending the position of European artisans. In 1938 it criticized Huggins for accepting the restrictions in the Constitution which prevented, at least in theory, differential legislation; it promised to remove 'the menace to white labour', and it advocated a White Rhodesia.[22] The only dispute was whether the country was advancing at a sufficiently rapid pace towards the defensive objective of segregation. Europeans in fact had as yet little stimulus to re-examine the basic tenets of their policy. The 'two pyramids' theory comfortably protected them and provided an apparently fair solution to the 'native problem'; there even seemed to be no need for urgency in implementing it in all its ramifications. Unlike the Europeans in the Union, where during the thirties the issues were becoming more sharply defined, where the difficulties were far more pronounced and attitudes were becoming more intransigent, Rhodesians could still afford to remain relatively unconcerned with the strict logic of their policy. Insulated from harsh problems their approach still consisted of empiricism mixed with complacency. This was clearly reflected in their attitude to the franchise.

Southern Rhodesia had inherited from the Cape Colony a common roll and, despite attacks, the Company had preserved this inheritance, though the qualifications had been raised in 1912. There was a further move to raise them again in 1928, when the Cabinet proposed to increase the property qualification from £150 to £500. Their motives were stated 'very frankly' by W. M.

---

[21] *Bledisloe Report*, p. 36.
[22] E.g. J. T. Durward, 'Sidelights on Labour's Industrial Policy', a pamphlet dated 24 January 1938.

Leggate, the Colonial Secretary of Southern Rhodesia, who explained that with the provision of Native Purchase Areas considerable numbers of Africans might qualify at the lower figure.

> I am perfectly certain [he added] that neither the honourable members of this House nor the people of this country, nor indeed the Imperial Government, wish the natives to dominate the legislature of this country.[23]

There were difficulties, however, attached to this sudden increase to £500. The Leader of the Opposition maintained that 'on no account must we keep out a single white voter in this country'.[24] The oligarchy must be comprehensive or it would lose its main safeguard. White unity was essential. On second thoughts the Premier withdrew the Bill. There were, he agreed, merely sixty-two native voters against the 22,000 European voters. He thought therefore that:

> The way to deal with the question is when the time comes; that is, when it becomes necessary we should then definitely face it and decide whether the native is to be allowed to continue to have a vote on the same terms as the European, or whether the country will grasp the nettle, the difficult question, and decide upon some other form of franchise for the native.

He added that they would watch the South African method of dealing with the question, and the results obtained by it, and that would be 'a guide for future action in this Colony'.[25]

In South Africa at that date there were 15,000 African voters compared with 162,000 European in the Cape. Eight years later the Representation of Natives Act removed the Cape Native franchise. As a substitute a Natives' Representative Council was created, and in addition four European Senators were elected by Africans on an indirect communal vote to represent African interests in the Senate, with three European M.P.s in the House of Assembly elected by Africans in the Cape Province by direct individual vote. In Southern Rhodesia, however, the numbers of African voters actually declined—in 1938 there were only thirty-

---

[23] S.R. Debates, 15 May 1928, col. 34.
[24] Ibid., 26 June 1928, col. 1582.   [25] Ibid., 22 May 1928, cols. 222–4.

nine African voters out of a total electorate of 24,626[26]—so the institution of a common roll somewhat fortuitously survived. Land apportionment and an industrial colour bar preserved the economic bases of white supremacy, and it was thought that similar political machinery could, no doubt, be devised when necessary. So far as Europeans, busily intent on building up a new country, were concerned there was no cause for immediate anxiety.

Explicit African reactions to European policy in Southern Rhodesia were subdued, divided, ignored, and largely ineffective. The shattering events of the nineties, combined with the close and thorough enforcement of direct administration, had disastrously weakened the few significant tribal rallying-points. North of the Zambezi, tribal institutions still enabled many illiterate humble Africans to participate as active agents in local and even at times in national life. In Mashonaland, however, the small and broken tribes, scattered and restricted to their separate and distant Reserves, were prevented from developing any cohesion or a wider outlook, while in Matabeleland 'the only rallying point of national feeling'—the family of Lobengula—was becoming, in the words of an official, 'more a family and sentimental affair than a national aspiration'.[27] Chiefs felt themselves to be helpless, incapable of independent initiative, the 'dogs' or 'women' of the Government,[28] and the mass of the people had no means of formulating or expressing an opinion on questions of national policy. It is significant, for instance, that while the Bledisloe Commission interviewed numbers of chiefs and Native Authorities north of the Zambezi, not one was consulted in Southern Rhodesia.

Only in Bulawayo, with the 'Amandabele Patriotic Society', was there an attempt to organize a response to new problems along tribal lines. This was a group of educated Matabele who sought to influence tribal opinion on various issues. In 1915 for example they issued a proclamation in Sindebele blank verse:

[26] *Bledisloe Report*, p. 15.
[27] N. H. Wilson, 'Native Political Movements in Southern Rhodesia', *Nada*, 1923, pp. 17–18.
[28] See above, Chap. I, pp. 27–8.

M

Wake up, wake up, wake up, Mandebele!
Your people are in great danger of being wiped out . . .
Many of our old and young women are living on mines and Town
Locations as prostitutes. They are selling their bodies
To evil men for money, clothes and Utchwala (beer). They have
    brought
Disgrace to our nation. The white people are despising us . . .
Syphilis, the curse of prostitution, is showing itself in the children
That are born . . .
How are we to break down and kill this evil? The A.P. Society
Will lead you to break it down by the help of the Almighty God . . .

> (i) Tell the fathers or the guardian of the fallen women to report
> them to the Native Commissioner of Police.
> (ii) If you know any bad house point it out to the English detec-
> tives.[29]

Members of the Society also acted occasionally as spokesmen on
ceremonial occasions: on Kitchener's death they forwarded a
resolution mourning the passing of the 'warrior of warriors, the
fighter who made war with weapons . . . whose guidance of our
armies will ever be remembered by whites and blacks'.[30] Their
influence, however, was never very widespread, their activities
seem to have been complementary to the work of the Native
Affairs Department, and their more active members moved on
into the supra-tribal organizations which in the twenties were
gradually appearing.

At first the more articulate Africans were those who came up
from South Africa as interpreters or teachers. Some of these
formed themselves into the Union Bantu Vigilance Association
to guard the interests of Union natives in particular.[31] These, in
company with the secretary of the Amandebele Patriotic Society,
Thomas Mazinyane, and Africans from Salisbury and other parts
of the country, met together in Gwelo on 20 January 1923 to
found the Rhodesia Bantu Voters' Association, 'a constructive
and co-operative society, founded by persons desiring to work for

---

[29] Central African Archives, N.3/21/1–10. Proclamation dated 15 December 1915,
with translation attached.
    [30] Ibid., 10 June 1916.   [31] Wilson, op. cit.

the general uplift of the Bantus irrespective of tribe and status'. They resolved that a 'Native Women's League' be formed to co-operate 'with all individual societies directly or indirectly working for the native women's uplift morally, socially and educationally', and they forwarded resolutions to the Government asking for improved standards and aid for schools, modifications to the pass laws, and facilities to purchase land. They also complained that 'the qualifications for the franchise are almost beyond reach of many otherwise eligible natives'. Taken by themselves, these requests could hardly be described as extremist or revolutionary, but the movement as a whole seemed to strike at the very basis of European policy. For the first time Africans in Southern Rhodesia were asking for a greater share of the white man's world; their organization was founded on the political system of the Europeans, through which they sought to exercise their rights effectively; they were turning their backs on the shattered traditional basis of society and the life of the Reserves, and they faced the challenge of an 'open society'. In all this they were strengthened by a new spirit of racial solidarity, a consciousness of potential African unity spreading in from South Africa and indeed possibly even from the United States.[32]

The ultimate political objects underlying the movement [wrote the Chief Native Commissioner] are found in the expression 'Africa for the Africans', and these Associations are formed as a constitutional means of approaching that ideal by the operation of the Vote . . . the inevitable outcome of the movement will be to concentrate native opinion more and more upon the view that Africa should be mainly, if not exclusively, developed in the interests of its indigenous races.[33]

At about the same time the Rhodesian Native Association was founded, and was described in an official minute as 'a non-political body compared to the Union Vigilance Association consisting of the more advanced natives of purely Rhodesian origin . . . a reputable organization'.[34] Yet the same blend of ideas—a desire to

---

[32] Wilson, op. cit.
[33] Central African Archives, N.3/21/1-10, Memorandum by the Chief Native Commissioner.
[34] Ibid.

be recognized by the European's world, to escape from the
criterion of colour, and, at the same time, a racial reaction, a
dawning consciousness of African unity—can be seen in these remarks published by its President, J. S. Mokwile, in the journal of
the Native Affairs Department:

> 'Natives are all alike,' it is often said. This word 'native' is used
> without distinction. The man is black, and there's an end of it. High,
> low, rich, poor, Christian, non-Christian, uncivilised, educated and
> un-educated—they are all marked with one and the same brand: and
> justly so, we are just plain natives of Africa, sons of the soil. But we
> must not be too proud just because we own the title of being the sons
> of the soil.

And he tactfully added:

> Any opportunity for improvement alike of Indians or natives, we
> must thankfully admit is possible only by the presence of the white
> man in our country.[35]

In January 1922, when a delegation from Southern Rhodesia was
to be sent to South Africa to discuss the possibilities of fusion with
the Union, the Rhodesian Native Association respectfully requested the Administrator to select a delegate 'expressly charged
to safeguard the interests of the Natives', but in reply it was
pointed out that the Chief Native Commissioner would perform
that function.[36]

During the thirties these two Associations were superseded by
the Bantu Congress of Southern Rhodesia, which by May 1938
had 150 members, with branches in the chief towns and in some
of the Reserves. The president was Mr. Aaron Jacha, a farmer in a
Native Purchase Area who had been brought up and educated at
Waddilove Mission, and other leading members included educated Africans, ordained ministers, teachers, and clerks from
Matabeleland and Mashonaland. The Bantu Congress protested
against several laws which 'had been passed to the disadvantage
of the natives, in spite of the Imperial Government's veto'. The
Natives Registration Act, it said, 'irksomely restricted legitimate

[35] J. S. Mokwile, 'Native Ideals', *Nada*, 1924.
[36] Central African Archives, N.3/21/1–10.

freedom of movement', the Industrial Conciliation Act 'removed chances of employment from trained native builders even in the locations of the towns', and the Maize Control Act 'conferred no advantages upon the natives, who found difficulty in disposing of their crops at a remunerative price'. On the other hand, the Land Apportionment Act was 'perfectly satisfactory'. Congress members felt that the Africans were paying, in direct and indirect taxes, much more than was being spent on them, and 'hundreds and hundreds of native children got no education'. All this, they thought, happened because nobody directly represented Africans. They welcomed the establishment of Native Councils, but felt that 'the views of these councils should reach' the Legislative Assembly. They agreed that there were as yet no Africans qualified to act as M.P.s, but felt that there were 'some Europeans who have the interests of natives at heart, and if we had the right to elect them they could represent us'.[37]

Like their predecessors in the Associations, these men accepted as permanent the new outlook brought by the Europeans—including, in this case, segregation of land tenure—but they ardently wanted to play a recognized part within it. Like their colleagues on the Conference of Christian Natives,[38] they were concerned with the status of educated Africans: in 1934, for example, the Conference 'humbly requested the Postal, Native and other Government Departments to discard the use of the word "Native" in their communications with Africans, as its appearance on envelopes tends to offend'; with regard to the Pass Laws, they asked the Government to provide 'an Exemption Certificate of greater value by raising the qualification required, so that the holder be not required to carry any other passes, even in towns after 9 p.m.'; and they 'respectfully asked' the Government that when 'Royal or other highly placed Visitors came to this Colony, the Christian and enlightened Natives of the Colony should be given a full opportunity to meet them'.[39] The following year, on the occasion of the Inter-Territorial Jeanes Conference, a vote of thanks was

[37] *Rhodesia Herald*, 24, 25 May 1938. Evidence of Mr. Jacha and others to the Bledisloe Commission.
[38] See above, Chap. IV, p. 145.
[39] *Proceedings of the Southern Rhodesia Missionary Conference, 1934.*

passed to the Governor, Sir Herbert Stanley, 'who has been the first to invite us as honoured guests to Government House. He shook hands with us, and we felt that he was indeed God's representative and a Father of the Africans.'[40]

The extent to which the members of these organizations had accepted and were committed to the European system can be seen from the fact that the Congress and Conference delegations to the Bledisloe Commission preferred amalgamation with South Africa rather than with the Colonial Office territories to the north of the Zambezi: Africans in the Union 'were not so badly treated' and they were more advanced, whereas 'amalgamation with the north would mean a reversion to barbarism'. People in the north were 'primitive' and 'very backward indeed'; and their influx into Southern Rhodesia, which it was thought would greatly increase under amalgamation, lowered the local Africans' wage rates.[41]

All these African hopes of being recognized as advancing towards European civilization, of playing an active and integrated, if small and humble, role within the framework of the European state, ran counter to the theory of segregation. The Councils isolated in the Reserves were by nature concerned with particular, local affairs; in the towns there was no formal machinery for consulting African opinion, although many urban Africans held strong views on questions of vital importance,[42] and Africans had little hope of influencing decisions in the Legislative Assembly. The two-pyramid policy envisaged an attempt to direct the aspirations and energies of emergent Africans into the confines of the Reserves, where it was hoped that eventually small market towns might develop and absorb these awkward individuals. They were not yet seen as possible allies, the nucleus of an African middle class; instead, in the meanwhile, these moderate men emerged from schools and colleges into a world which ignored

[40] *Village Education in Africa*, p. 359.

[41] *Rhodesia Herald*, 24, 25 May and 9 June 1938. The fear was also expressed that 'the enlarged territory would get Dominion status and the power of the Imperial Government would disappear'.

[42] See for example the numerous recommendations on urban affairs forwarded by the Conference of Christian Natives.

their existence; they waited outside with patient, frustrated, and increasingly bitter resignation.

It is difficult to estimate the extent to which these Associations and the Bantu Congress were representative of African opinion in Southern Rhodesia, but it seems probable that relatively few Africans accepted so wholeheartedly the European state and system. The voice of the masses was seldom heard, their response had as yet little perceptible impact on the course of events, and the records available at present to a historian are scanty in the extreme. There was, however, one movement which, in its passionate, vague, ill-directed, and abortive protest, may have been an authentic register of the unformulated feelings of the mass of the people who, bewildered by the effects of conquest, were becoming painfully aware of the unrelenting discipline of wage labour and the new forms of insecurity and poverty.

In the early part of 1927 Robert Sambo and Mansell Mphamba, whose original homes were in the far north of Nyasaland, set out from Bulawayo to Johannesburg on a hurried, secret visit to their friend and fellow-countryman Clements Kadalie. At this time the influence and power of Kadalie's Industrial and Commercial Workers' Union[43] were at their height, and Kadalie himself was being given as much publicity in the South African Press as a Cabinet Minister.[44] Armed with advice and credentials from Kadalie, Sambo and Mphamba returned to Bulawayo and there established a branch of the Industrial and Commercial Workers' Union, known as the I.C.U. Their policy of appeal to the masses —large posters in the streets of Bulawayo announcing their existence, militant speeches to crowded public meetings—was an intoxicating innovation in Southern Rhodesia and they soon gathered a nucleus of indigenous leaders including Thomas Sikaleni, a clerk in the Native Affairs Department. Official reaction was swift: Sikaleni lost his job, at the end of 1927 Robert Sambo was deported to Nyasaland as an undesirable alien, and from henceforth the fortunes of the Industrial and Commercial Workers' Union in Southern Rhodesia were in the hands of local leaders.

[43] See above, Chap. I, p. 11.   [44] Roux, op. cit., p. 170.

One of the young men whose attention was caught by the posters was Charles Mzingeli. Born in 1905 at the Roman Catholic Mission in Plumtree district, he is said to have acquired from his father a general distrust of Europeans as unjust usurpers whom 'no sensible African could trust'. At the age of fourteen he ran away from home and worked for railwaymen in Bulawayo, Livingstone, and Broken Hill. Until he threw in his lot with the Industrial and Commercial Workers' Union he lived, as he himself put it, 'in a world of intellectual bewilderment'.[45] He was soon impressed by the official concern aroused by the activities of the Union, exemplified by the presence of a European detective taking notes at a meeting, and by the fact that, unlike other organizations, the Industrial and Commercial Workers' Union alone had a programme which apparently promised liberation to the African. In November 1929 Mzingeli was sent as full-time organizing secretary to the Salisbury branch, and it was a sign of the supra-tribal nature of the organization that he, a Matabele, was sent to Mashonaland, while in Matabeleland the organizing secretary was a Mashona. Within a year he had enrolled 200 members and the branch was holding meetings every week-end. In March 1932 the Union held its second conference in Salisbury. Its members complained of the very low level of wages, and asked the Government to appoint a Native Wage Board. As a result of 'the depression throughout the colony' they also requested a reduction in taxation. They complained of conditions in the Reserves and the Locations, and finally they asked the Government 'to consider the poor unemployed Natives who are discharged from their situations'.[46]

The Union also attempted to carry its activities into the Reserves and to organize resistance against unpopular measures such as destocking, but in 1935 the secretary of the Bulawayo branch was arrested in a Reserve and sentenced to one month's imprisonment, and after some encounters with officials Mzingeli

---

[45] Mzingeli, *Gandhi of the Africans*, an unpublished manuscript written in 1949 by Mr. Lawrence Vambe, Chief Editor of 'African Newspapers'. I have supplemented it by some facts given by Mr. Mzingeli to the *Sunday Mail*, 20 January 1952.

[46] Papers of the Anti-Slavery Society, at Rhodes House, Oxford. Letter from Nklova to Harris, 4 May 1932.

also abandoned the attempt to unite rural with urban discontent. The imprisonment brought the movement to an end in Bulawayo, and in Salisbury Mzingeli had to support his wife and himself by playing 'the violin, banjo, guitar, and piano with accompaniment' in a local African dance-band. These setbacks and official repression were the immediate causes of the movement's decline, but later, looking back on this early period, Mzingeli thought that incoherent policy was the basic reason for its ineffectiveness. None of the leaders had been trained in trade union practice, their ideas were vague, and they confined themselves

to making militant speeches merely calculated to have the effect of stirring up the feelings of the people against bad conditions. . . . Attacks were made on this or that Department for ill-treating the Africans. . . . Zealous but tactless, they seemed to think that what the working African wanted above everything else was better treatment by the police and the Native Department.[47]

Apart from this one brief, ineffective exception, the mass of the population in Southern Rhodesia were politically inert, passive, and virtually powerless. The sudden shock of conquest and the sustained, increasing alien regulations had disrupted their ancient way of life and intruded intimately into their beliefs and closest personal relationships. The negative, destructive aspects of this intrusion were growing; the Rev. A. S. Cripps thought that Africans preferred the days of Chartered Company rule to the situation in 1938, when there was 'such a lot of bureaucracy and such a terrific multiplication of laws'.[48] The ancient burdens of poverty, ignorance, and disease were still relatively unaffected by the narrow impact of modern science and industry, but the end of inter-tribal warfare and of widespread famines was perhaps reflected in the growing population. A few of the Africans, anxious to enter fully into the system brought by the Europeans, found themselves debarred, hindered, and frustrated, but the fierce challenge of an open society and the complex, dangerous transition it demanded had not yet convulsed the mass of the population. The rule of the white man was apparently accepted almost

[47] Vambe, op. cit.   [48] Evidence to Bledisloe Commission, LIII, 14 June 1938.

as inevitable, open resentment was rarely manifested; European privileges and prestige seemed inviolable, white supremacy appeared to be permanently established. South of the Zambezi the initiative remained wholly with the Europeans and they seemed certain of their white man's country and of its success.

2. NYASALAND

In Nyasaland Africans were already taking an active and increasingly influential part in determining their country's development. Strands of unity, new leadership, and independent self-confidence were beginning to be interwoven; the first tentative signs of a Nyasaland nationalism could be discerned. The new and spectacular importance of peasant rather than plantation production[49] provided a sturdy economic basis for the emerging sense of independence; the tenacious sense of land-ownership, confirmed and strengthened by Government policy, created an atmosphere of confidence and self-respect. The fact that much of the country had never been conquered, that it was a Protectorate, and that its traditional leaders had on the whole been confirmed in their positions and entrusted with further responsibilities, enhanced this spirit of independence. And the foundations of supra-tribal unity, which in the emerging African states was to become a rare phenomenon, were being laid by the experience of migrant labour.

As the thousands of workers streamed out of Nyasaland they encountered a world which made little or no provision for their particular tribal affiliations: to the Europeans on the Rand or in Southern Rhodesia they were simply Nyasa boys, to the Mashona or Matabele they were foreigners. Even the most humble migrant labourer, if only from the colour of his registration card, gained some impression, however hazy, of an entity, Nyasaland, to which at least in the eyes of others he belonged. Chinyanja quickly became a universal medium of communication among themselves, and such were their importance and influence that for twenty years it was accepted as the *lingua franca* of the Copperbelt.

[49] See above, Chap. II.

They gained a reputation for hard work and relative reliability, partly perhaps because they were separated from the immediate support and demands of their rural kinsfolk and because the tribal links continued or formed while at work were less distracting and exacting. It is interesting to notice that the Mashona and Matabele, who in Southern Rhodesia were often compared unfavourably with the worker from Nyasaland, shared in the Union the relatively high reputation of migrant labourers. Because of this reputation, and because of their greater degree of education and training, Nyasas often obtained the more responsible and better-paid jobs; in Southern Rhodesia and on the Copperbelt they supplied a very high percentage of clerks, teachers, trained artisans, and *capitaos*. They became accepted as the leaders of the new urban communities and they fashioned and assimilated new forms of social organization as traditional patterns became inadequate. They also carried with them into the white man's world the experience of a country where Africans felt securely that the future belonged to them. As prophets of so startling a hope they exercised a revolutionary influence.

Clements Kadalie, with his Industrial and Commercial Workers' Union, was by far the most prominent and influential of these migrants from Nyasaland. News of his activities filtered back home into the most remote villages and were animatedly discussed by even the humblest illiterate. A missionary, for example, recorded the following conversation in a remote village:

'We here have heard', said one of the local inhabitants, 'that black men are allowed to have a union so that they can speak to the whites as one clan speaks to another—through the leaders.' 'Yes,' broke in a small boy, of about 13 or 14, 'Kerementi, you know.' For a moment I was beaten. Who or what was Kerementi? Then it came to me; this insignificant goat-herd was referring to Clements Kadalie. . . . He did not even belong to the same tribe or territory as Kadalie, yet this boy knew about the labour leader who had gone out from Nyasaland.[50]

Kadalie's emissaries returned to Nyasaland, and although the Government attempted to restrict their activities, his impact

[50] T. Cullen Young, in *Africa*, Vol. XI, p. 68.

seems to have been widespread and enduring.[51] And he was but an outstanding example of the new leaders who emerged from among the migrant workers. Their influence was prevalent in Northern Rhodesia. It was evident on the Copperbelt before the disturbances of 1935,[52] and it was 'Nyasaland people' who drafted the Copperbelt clerks' and *capitaos'* memorandum to the Bledisloe Commission.[53] The African Civil Servants' Association, with headquarters at Lusaka and branches 'at nearly all the Bomas' in Northern Rhodesia, was led by two Nyasaland clerks educated at Livingstonia,[54] and even at Masama, in the centre of the powerful Bemba tribe, Nyasalanders were leading members of the Native Welfare Association.[55]

Yet the experience of migrant labour did not merely create a sense of a common homeland and foster the emergence of a new dynamic form of leadership: it also gave the migrants a deep affection for their own country. Wherever they went—on the Copperbelt, in Southern Rhodesia, or on the Rand—they found higher wages but also restrictive and discriminatory measures: pass laws, a sterner police force, stringent labour regulations, and 'colour-bar' practices which prevented some of the more proficient from rising as high as they could at home. Throughout Nyasaland, and Northern Rhodesia too,[56] Africans became keenly aware of the differences which separated them from, as it seemed to them, their conquered brethren south of the Zambezi. In Nyasaland they felt the Government 'made laws to suit the interests of the Africans, whereas in the Rhodesias, especially Southern Rhodesia, laws were made to suit the interests of the Europeans with very little consideration for the Africans'.[57] This contrast,

[51] Isa Lawrence, sentenced by the High Court to three years' intensive hard labour on 22 September 1926 for importing Industrial and Commercial Workers' Union literature, was in 1944 the first Treasurer General of the Nyasaland African Congress. Robert Sambo, deported from Southern Rhodesia for his Industrial and Commercial Workers' Union activities in 1927, was later a leader of the African National Church and a prominent farmer at Karonga. Central African Archives, Zomba, Miss. 12/10.

[52] See above, Chap. III, p. 112.

[53] Evidence to Bledisloe Commission, CXIX, 22 July 1938.

[54] Ibid., CXXIV, 25 July 1938.

[55] Ibid., CXXXV, 3 August 1938.   [56] See below, pp. 190–1.

[57] Evidence of Native Authorities and Native Associations of Northern Province to Bledisloe Commission, *Rhodesia Herald*, 5 July 1938.

more perhaps than any other factor, nourished and formed their national consciousness, and Nyasaland became loved not merely as a distant home but as a haven of security and a symbol of self-respect.

These strands of economic independence and self-confidence at home, and the new links and conceptions of unity brought by migrant labour, were gathered together and found expression in the various Native Associations which in the inter-war years spread through the country. As early as 1912 the North Nyasa Native Association was formed at Karonga with the encouragement of Robert Laws of the Livingstonia Mission, and it was followed in 1914 by the West Nyasa Native Association, which met in the mission-school house at Bandawe among the Atonga.[58] The war interrupted their activities, but in the immediate postwar years they flourished, and other Associations were formed at Mombera, Lilongwe, Zomba, Blantyre, Chiradzulu and Mlanje.

Like Kadalie and the other Nyasaland leaders of the migrant urban communities, the men who formed and led these new Associations at home were representatives of the new class of educated men who worked for the Government, the missions, or the planters. In June 1919 thirty-eight members of the North Nyasa Native Association gave an account of their war service: nearly all had served as interpreters or clerks.[59]

These men drew their prestige from the fact that they were successful pioneers in the new way of life, and as such they saw themselves as mediators:

Being Natives of the Country and acquainted with all the habits and customs of the people, (the Association) could adequately express their desires and needs to the Government; and being educated it could fully explain the mind of the Government to the people.[60]

[58] Central African Archives, Zomba, SI/1481/19, statement by A. S. Muhango encl. in Abraham to H.C.S., 24 March 1921 and SI/2065/19 Y. M. Bhango to H.C.S., 4 October 1935.

[59] Ibid., SI/1481/19, minutes of North Nyasa Native Association 17–20 June 1919. The constitution of the West Nyasa Native Association laid down that the members should be 'persons of good knowledge and character', and left it 'an open question for educated chiefs and Europeans either to attend or join it as full members'.

[60] Ibid., SI/2065/19, copy of constitution encl. in Brackenbury to H.C.S., 6 November 1919.

The potential value of this mediatory role was stressed by Robert Laws, who advised the Government to recognize their existence and to guide their development:

> No suppression can prevent the natives from discussing political and other subjects and the characters of individual Europeans in the country round their camp fires at night, and they do so often, with a shrewdness and accuracy which would be disconcerting were it known to the parties concerned. Very often however there is lacking in these discussions the guidance of a better educated person than his companions who could state the other side and a wider view of things. This counteractive the Associations can supply, as their discussions would be talked over throughout the district in small groups as above.[61]

Laws also envisaged that these Associations might 'be guided and led up to' a method of electing a European, and finally an African, to represent their interests in the Legislative Council.[62]

It is difficult to say to what extent the traditional tribal authorities welcomed the new men as mediators or despised them as upstart interlopers. On the whole their spheres of influence and activity seem to have been complementary rather than competitive. The Associations were generally concerned with supratribal affairs: they took a keen interest in educational questions, and when the hut tax was raised they urged the Government to increase the educational grant; they suggested that the wives of '*machona*' or lost migrant workers should be released from the hut tax, and that emigrant workers should pay their tax 'in the Foreign Country who would return it to the Nyasaland Government'; they requested the Government 'to lend a hand in giving loans of money, or find out where money could be borrowed' to assist the production of cotton, rice, and maize; they sent evidence to Government Commissions.

Like those of their counterparts in Southern Rhodesia, their methods were strictly constitutional: they 'regretted exceedingly the rising of John Chilembwe and others inasmuch as they knew that a High Court exists to which appeal could have been made'.

---

[61] Central African Archives, Zomba, SI/2065/19. Laws to acting C.S., 12 January 1920.
[62] Ibid.

But they aimed at changes that in the context of their day were radical, and, in contrast to Southern Rhodesian Africans, they were proudly self-confident. Their tone was by no means servile: Residents, they demanded, should be approachable by all 'without threats of *chikoli* [imprisonment] before the man states what he has come for'.[63]

In all this there would have been little ground for disagreement with the traditional authorities; in fact there is scattered evidence that on some issues, particularly those concerned with land-ownership, the chiefs were at one with the Associations,[64] while at Momberas in the twenties the chief and principal counsellors were all members of the Association. With the introduction of indirect rule it was decided by the Government that the resolutions of Native Associations would receive consideration only when supported by their respective District Councils,[65] and the importance of these local Associations seems to have declined. The one at Mombera became merged with the local authority. The West Nyasa Native Association, torn by personal rivalries, was reported to be 'nearly moribund', and others suffered from discontinuity of membership due to emigration and the transfer of clerks.[66]

But in Nyasaland the introduction of indirect rule did little to hinder the emerging sense of national unity. The ties of traditional loyalties were never so strong or so widely spread as among the Barotse or the Bemba in Northern Rhodesia. The traditional authorities were themselves influenced by the factors producing a

[63] Central African Archives, Zomba, SI/1481/19, Minutes of the North Nyasa Native Association, 20 June 1919.
[64] See for example an address by Principal Headman Mtenje to the Chiradzulu District Native Association, 23 May 1931: 'When I complain and ask for these burdens to be lightened on my people, they tell me I must go in Government land. As I look on the Crown land, I see no land remaining where so many of my people can go. I look in the air I see I cannot fly there, then I come to the point that I say what is the use of living. But I have come to put this matter before the Association, that they may put this matter before Government with a view that they pay whatever the amount of money may be necessary to pay the Company, and my people and I will pay the Government in instalments, so that we may not have to undergo these difficulties. I cannot help however to think that with the large sums of money and labour we have been paying the Company these many years we owe the Company nothing. . . .' ibid., SI/1598/29.
[65] Ibid., SI/1481/19 Chief Secretary to Provincial Commissioners, 31 January 1931.
[66] NAT 12/3 P. C. Lilongwe to H.C.S., 25 July 1935.

nascent nationalism. At times of crisis, when for example they submitted evidence to the Bledisloe Commission,[67] they acted in unison with the leaders of the Associations. And the declining status of the local Associations was more than offset by an institution at Zomba which began to centralize and give continuity to their activities.

Men from the Northern Province exercised an invigorating influence not only in the Union, in Southern Rhodesia, and on the Copperbelt, but also in the south of Nyasaland itself. In 1930 'a man from up-country' urged the Blantyre Native Association to remember that 'as natives of Nyasaland our wants are the same, because our mentality is the same',[68] and a few years previously Levi Z. Mumba had arrived in Zomba. This man, who was later to be president-general of the Nyasaland African Congress, had been secretary of the first Native Association, that of North Nyasa, in 1912. On his posting as a clerk to Zomba in 1924 he was instrumental in organizing the Zomba Native Association and other Associations in the Southern Province, and he was later a founder of the Native Civil Servants, Association. But his most important activity in these inter-war years was as president of the Representative Committee of Northern Province Native Associations. This Committee was authorized to act for the Associations 'in presenting the native point of view to Government or delegations from the United Kingdom'. Even after the introduction of Indirect Rule, the Government did not insist that the Committee's resolutions should be passed through the Native Authorities, but merely reserved the right 'to return for submission to the Native Authorities anything they considered proper for those channels'.[69]

The members of the Representative Committee echoed the Associations' interest in educational issues, and Mumba was the first African to be appointed to the Government's Advisory Committee on Education. They were also concerned with many other issues. In 1930, for example, they criticized the Governor's speech

[67] See below, p. 176.
[68] Central African Archives, Zomba, SI/3263/23, 18 January 1931.
[69] Ibid., NAT 12/3, Chief Sec. to Pres. R.C.N.P.N.A., 20 May 1935.

to the Legislative Council on the Passfield Memorandum on Native Policy,[70] and in the same year they initiated an agitation against Section 129 of the 1929 Code of Criminal Law. They pointed out that this Section

penalizes a 'white woman' who voluntarily permits a native to have unlawful carnal connexion with her while it leaves a 'white man' free to do with a native woman as he likes without being penalized. Similarly on the African side it seeks to punish a man while it says nothing about native women who so far have been the culprits.

The members of the Committee entirely agreed that 'any native who allows himself to be influenced by a "white woman" in this connexion should suffer the consequences', but added that 'since the law is just, it should also take into consideration the protection of the "native woman" from herself as well as from outside forces as it has done for the "white woman"'. They suggested therefore that the Section should be amended to extend the penalty of five years' imprisonment to native women and European and Indian men. This was an unqualified, outspoken demand for absolute racial equality in a matter which deeply affected their pride and self-respect. Their lead was quickly taken up by the other Associations, and although it was pointed out that the Code was made for East Africa as a whole, that no aspersion was cast on the morals of either Africans or Europeans in Nyasaland, and that native women were adequately protected by Section 113, which punished any one guilty of procuring, the 'stigma' continued to be the subject of resolutions for several years.[71]

It was, however, the Bledisloe Commission which called forth the clearest manifestation of national unity and revealed the significant role of the Associations and their fundamental harmony with the traditional authorities. Six months before the arrival of the Commission in Nyasaland, the Zomba Province Native

---

[70] 'They consider that such an important matter should have been conveyed to your African subjects at the same time as the other communities were being informed' and they trust that 'in spite of the threats and the animus shown by Europeans' H.M.G. will stand firm. Mumba to H.C.S., 28 October 1930, SI/1481/19.

[71] Central African Archives, Zomba, SI/1481/19, Jere to H.C.S. 29 November 1930, and D.C. Karonga to P.C. 27 January 1931, SI/3263/23 Blantyre Native Association, 11 May 1935, NAT 12/3, Mumba to H.C.S., 26 November 1933.

N

Association held a special meeting to consider the question of amalgamation. It was attended by five of the more important local chiefs and by fifty-three other members, including Charles Matinga, its secretary, and James Sangala, who were both in later years to be prominent members of the Congress. All the speeches opposed amalgamation. The chiefs expressed fears of further land alienation; some members thought amalgamation would increase labour migration, and all speakers warmly defended the policy of indirect rule. Amalgamation or some sort of federation, Matinga thought, 'might even remove the policy of Native Paramountcy now being enjoyed by our chiefs and also other privileges enjoyed by natives in Nyasaland such as Native Civil Service and absence of obnoxious pass laws'.[72]

At Blantyre in June 1938 the Bledisloe Commission took evidence from about 200 members of the Blantyre Native Association, who were unanimously opposed to amalgamation, and a few days later it

had its most spectacular sitting, when, in the little district court building at Lilongwe, it heard the evidence of the Native Authorities of the Northern Province of Nyasaland. Between thirty and forty Chiefs were assembled, most of them wearing their robes of office, particularly the official tarbush with its distinctive badge. There were grizzled veterans, slow of speech and movement, and there were younger men, keen and intent, who expressed themselves fluently and with a wealth of vivid gesture. . . . They answered the questions briefly and to the point, and altogether created an impression of general efficiency and pride in their work.[73]

They submitted a memorandum prepared by Levi Mumba and the Representative Committee for the Northern Province Native Associations, which expressed hostility to any form of closer union with Rhodesia, and their spokesman, Chief Gomani, expressed their desire that Nyasaland should continue to develop independently. Their opposition came not from any theoretical objections, but from the impression they had formed of the way

[72] Central African Archives, Zomba, NAT 12/33, Minutes of the Zomba Province Native Association, 29 January 1938.
[73] *Rhodesia Herald*, 5 July 1938.

Africans were treated south of the Zambezi, which was based on the experiences of migrant labour and was shared by the majority of their fellow countrymen. They were certain that Africans were badly treated in Southern Rhodesia.

This was evidenced by the pass laws and the congestion of Africans on infinitesimal land. . . . With all the wealth of the Rhodesian Government very little was being done for native education. In Rhodesia there was discrimination against the African regarding employment, and he had no trading rights.[74]

This fluent, consistent, vehement opposition, in common with that encountered in Northern Rhodesia, deeply influenced the members of the Bledisloe Commission. They reported their conclusions in words which might well have been remembered fifteen years later:

The average native is ill-equipped to form a proper appreciation of the effects of amalgamation, either on his own position or on the prospects of the Territories, and in his present stage of development even longer time for consideration would probably have made but little difference to his attitude. Nevertheless the striking unanimity, in the northern Territories, of the native opposition to amalgamation, based mainly on dislike of some features of the native policy of Southern Rhodesia, and the anxiety of the natives in Northern Rhodesia and Nyasaland lest there should be any change in the system under which they regard themselves as enjoying the direct protection of Your Majesty, are factors which cannot in our judgment be ignored.

If so large a proportion of the population of the combined Territory were brought unwillingly under a unified Government, it would prejudice the prospect of co-operation in ordered development under such a Government. We do not mean to suggest that amalgamation must necessarily be postponed until such time as a positive demand for it arises amongst the natives of all the Territories, but we are agreed in doubting the practical wisdom of such a step, until, through longer acquaintance with the issues involved, the fears and suspicions at present prevalent amongst the natives have been substantially removed, and they are themselves in a better position to form a considered judgment on those issues.[75]

[74] *Rhodesia Herald*, 5 July 1938; and Evidence to Bledisloe Commission, LXX and LXXVI.
[75] *Bledisloe Report*, p. 218.

Yet although the new and old African leaders, the Associations and Authorities, were thus already taking a decisive part in the development of Nyasaland, there was still no cry for freedom, no hint of active hostility to the colonial régime, no mobilization of the masses, no premonition of the hectic search for independence which was so soon to change the face of Africa. Their most extreme request was that 'a native should always be present at meetings at which Europeans discussed native affairs';[76] the possibility of supreme executive power being brought under their control was not as yet even remotely envisaged.

The political initiative and economic importance of Africans in Nyasaland were, in 1938, the most striking points of contrast between that country and Southern Rhodesia. But the whole tenor of European life and attitudes was also profoundly different in the two countries. In Southern Rhodesia policy was determined primarily by reference to the immediate, foreseeable needs of a sprinkling of European farmers reinforced by small rich pockets of mines, small towns, and a connecting railway. The 55,000 Europeans were defensively separated from African competition and the African was mainly thought of as a servant or labourer. Practically no consideration, outside missionary circles, was given to the part to be played by educated Africans in aiding the mass of the population to adapt itself to the inevitable transition to a new way of life; the only sphere for African initiative was the scattered, undeveloped, closely administered Reserves. The steady rhythm of everyday life and the many individual instances of virtue, courage, and contentment could blind neither black nor white to the realization that, reduced to the starkest terms, they constituted two rival groups with fixed membership and a rigid status.

In Nyasaland the 1,700 Europeans—officials, missionaries, company employees, and planters—had little group continuity or cohesion. They did not think of themselves as permanent settlers, and while they were in the country they could not ignore the mass of the population. Even the unofficial, non-ecclesiastical sections were far more concerned than were their Rhodesian

[76] Evidence to Bledisloe Commission, LXX.

counterparts with the need for African advancement into a new way of life; their prosperity was largely dependent on African potentialities and there was a much greater recognition of a community of interest. Thus, although the Convention of Associations, a European society 'formed of all the public bodies in Nyasaland', was fully conscious of the economic benefits which membership of a larger unit could bring to the country, it was very cautious in its approach to the problem of amalgamation. Its members recognized that 'any serious alteration or modification' of native policy 'might arouse grave concern in the minds of the natives' and lead to 'very serious trouble'. They thought that the Nyasaland native policy was 'enlightened and progressive . . . a real attempt to build up responsible native administration and native authorities capable of supporting responsibility'. And although they hoped that 'a time should come when the Imperial Government would find themselves able, with a clear conscience, to delegate their trusteeship of the native to the amalgamated Governments of the three territories', they suggested that for the time being closer co-operation might be effected by the appointment of a High Commissioner to deal with certain specific matters.[77]

Europeans in Nyasaland were willing to recognize and respond to manifestations of African adaptability, enterprise, and responsibility: the official recognition of Native Authorities, the freedom and even encouragement enjoyed by Native Associations, and the appointment of Mumba, and later Matinga, to the Education Advisory Board were paralleled on the unofficial side by the planter's relationship with his educated *capitao*, the traveller's reliance on an African engine-driver, the trader's interest in his peasant customer, and the tourist's appreciation of Blantyre Cathedral—built entirely by Africans. Instead of being an object of good-humoured contempt, the African was often seen as an interesting individual with a rich past and a hopeful future. The Europeans in Nyasaland were less inclined than those in the Rhodesias to allow their mental picture of the African to crystallize. There was a different

[77] Evidence to the Bledisloe Commission, LXXI, and memorandum submitted to the Commission.

climate of opinion, and this resulted in important differences of behaviour.

In Southern Rhodesia the fear of the 'black peril'—that is, of cases of attempted rape of white women—was one of the deeper motives supporting a policy of segregation.[78] Responsible citizens urged that, despite a possibly increased danger of miscegenation, African girls should replace men as domestic servants:

> It is surely an illogical mind which regards this imaginary danger (of miscegenation) as equal to the real evil which we term the Black Peril. Surely it should not be necessary to point out the difference between the terrible suffering involved when a white woman is assaulted by a male native, and the comparatively mild disapproval endured by a native girl who has had a liaison with a white man.[79]

The abhorrence of miscegenation and the fear of the black peril are amply documented in other replies to a questionnaire issued by the Women's Institutes. Mrs. Tawse-Jollie, for instance, gave as her principal reasons for opposing male domestic labour:

> 1. The Black Peril question. I do not think in recent years there has been a single Black Peril case which was not traced to a house-boy.
> 2. The incredible carelessness of new settlers in this matter, permitting these native men to enter their bedrooms and perform the most intimate duties. They are more prone to this than are colonial women because they do not understand native character and regard servants as automata. Quite recently I was talking to a patient in a maternity hostel, who sat up in bed in a flimsy nightgown, when a native of full age entered her room, without knocking, and proceeded to clean the floor etc. I consider the employment of such men in women's hospitals, girls' hostels etc. a positive scandal, and as long as women acquiesce in such things the Black Peril will grow. . . .
> The introduction of women servants would solve one of the greatest difficulties about life in this country. . . . No native would attempt to rape a white woman if a woman of his own race was anywhere near.[80]

In Nyasaland, however, there was no recorded case of this 'black peril' and Lord Bledisloe was assured that 'any white

---

[78] See above, Chap. I, p. 22.

[79] W. S. Bazeley in *Report of the Standing Committee of Domestic Service* (Federation of Women's Institutes of Southern Rhodesia July 1930).

[80] Ibid.

woman can go unaccompanied anywhere with perfect safety.'[81] There were doubtless many factors which contributed to this astonishing difference. There was, for instance, the fact that nearly all domestic servants in Nyasaland were accompanied by their wives. There were far fewer European women in the country, and those that were there were almost certainly accustomed to handling domestic servants and would possibly have exhibited a more maternal and commanding attitude than the wives and daughters of some Rhodesian settlers. But above all it would seem that the absence of the 'black peril' was a dramatic result of the different climate of opinion. In Southern Rhodesia the racial situation inevitably led to tension and conflict and a deep fear of what lay on the other side of the gulf—although of course in many individual instances these feelings were absent or at least submerged. In Nyasaland, despite some individual cases of friction, exploitation, and hostility, most Europeans thought of themselves as paternal trustees, and the general trend of relationships was towards co-operation. It was not a situation conducive to hysteria.

3. NORTHERN RHODESIA

Nyasaland and Southern Rhodesia were, therefore, following divergent policies; in each territory one policy was supreme and neither country felt sharply the challenge of the rival concept. In Northern Rhodesia, however, the two policies met and clashed. The Passfield Memorandum on Native Policy of June 1930, with its declared intention of taking the policy of trusteeship seriously, evoked a storm of protest from European settlers and their representatives in the Legislative Council.[82] But the intention was soon modified. In 1931 a Parliamentary Joint Select Committee reported that the 'paramountcy of native interests' meant 'no more than that the interests of the overwhelming majority of the indigenous population should not be subordinated to those of a minority belonging to another race, however important in it-

---

[81] Evidence to the Bledisloe Commission, CXIII. See also B. G. Hess, 'The Nyasaland Boy', *African Observer*, March 1936.
[82] See above, Chap. I, pp. 41–2.

self'; and in 1934 the Governor of Northern Rhodesia further reassured the settlers that the Select Committee's 'no more' also meant 'no less than that the interests of the non-native minority must not be subordinated to those of the native majority'.[83]

In practice the principles of the Passfield Memorandum were never applied wholeheartedly. Despite its statement that there was to be equality of opportunity in the disposal of Crown lands 'irrespective of race, colour, and religion' and that 'effective opportunity' should be given to Africans to purchase plots on easy instalments, settlers in Northern Rhodesia adamantly insisted that Crown lands should be sold exclusively to Europeans.[84] Most Africans still lived on unalienated Crown lands, but a small proportion had been compelled to move into Reserves which were seriously overcrowded and undeveloped.[85] Passfield attached great importance to the principle that the African should be 'effectively and economically free to work, in accordance with his own wish, either in production in the Reserves, or as an individual producer upon his own plot of land, or in employment for wages', and that taxation should be limited by his capacity to pay 'without hardship, and without upsetting his customary method of life'. Yet in Northern Rhodesia all able-bodied male Africans over the age of sixteen were compelled to pay a poll tax, and as the only extensive sources of employment were on the line of rail, the great majority of Africans had no alternative but to journey long distances to work in order to pay their tax.

Passfield had stipulated that African development should be considered as a 'first charge' on the territory. But in 1938 Sir Alan Pim reported that there was a 'very striking disparity' between the amount spent on development which would primarily benefit European enterprise and that spent on African development. From 1927 to 1936 the Government capital grant for development and public works was so allocated that £1,543,865 was spent in the small railway strip and Copperbelt, occupied primarily by Europeans, while only £421,762 was spent in the whole of the rest of the country and the greater part of that was used in road

[83] Davidson, op. cit., p. 72.   [84] See above, Chap. I, p. 40.
[85] See above, Chap. II.

construction which benefited Europeans and Africans alike. In the same period there was little difference between the revenue collected from native tax and that collected from European income tax, including the tax paid by all registered companies.[86] Maize marketing was instituted largely, as in Southern Rhodesia, to protect European farmers, agricultural research in African areas was practically non-existent, medical facilities made little impact on the vast problems of malnutrition and endemic diseases (at least fifty per cent. of the Africans presenting themselves for work at the mines were rejected for physical defects mainly due to malnutrition), for more than twenty years no organized campaign was undertaken to preserve the cattle wealth of the Barotse from the ravages of lung sickness,[87] and at Fort Jameson the European tobacco-planters exerted their influence lest the local Africans should be encouraged, as in Nyasaland, to plant tobacco themselves.[88]

In Northern Rhodesia no Industrial Conciliation Act was introduced, but the fact that Africans in Northern Rhodesia could be clerks, bricklayers, carpenters, telegraphists, post-masters, etc., was due less to Government protection than to the remote and undeveloped nature of the country, which had to compete with Southern Rhodesia and the Union for its supplies of white skilled labour. This was eventually realized even by Sir Leopold Moore, leader of the Unofficials, who admitted: 'We cannot develop this country with white Trade Union labour, nor can we afford to support a white army.'[89] The Government seldom intervened. When construction and development work started up again on the Copperbelt after the slump, the mining companies found it impossible to obtain white builders from the south, so they let the work out on contract. On the Roan a building programme of about £300,000 was done with 99 per cent. African labour, and the representatives of the Northern Rhodesian Mine Workers' Union admitted to the Bledisloe Commission that the building

---

[86] *Pim Report*, p. 95.   [87] Rita Hinden, *Plan for Africa* (1941), p. 80.
[88] Evidence to the Bledisloe Commission.
[89] Ibid., CVI. In 1910 Moore had declared:'We shall consistently oppose the employment of natives where they compete with or are substituted for white men.' P. Mason, *The Birth of a Dilemma* (1958), p. 253.

industry was 'absolutely lost to the white artisans'.[90] But on the crucial question of mining labour the Government were content to let the Union arrive at a 'gentleman's agreement with the mine management'.[91] This *laissez-faire* attitude was in striking contrast to the declaration of the Secretary of State in the House of Lords that: 'If there is one thing which trusteeship involves . . . it is the right of the African to have a free chance . . . to learn a skilled trade and to operate that skilled trade.'[92]

These discrepancies between professions and performance amply demonstrated the difficulty of implementing a policy of trusteeship in a country which was being so rapidly and unevenly developed by Europeans, and which, apart from minerals, was so deficient in natural resources. The 'paramountcy of Native interests' had conferred few immediate benefits upon the African population. Yet although the doctrine of trusteeship had little practical impact on the situation there was considerable discontent among Europeans with the colonial régime. In the Legislative Council Unofficials levelled charges of extravagance and inefficiency. The constant replacement of officials reduced their efficiency, their understanding of technical issues was often inadequate, and the need to refer 'many minor questions' to Whitehall shackled the administration.[93] £400,000 was spent on creating a 'luxury' capital at Lusaka, while essential services were disastrously curtailed through lack of funds. Settlers felt that law and order were insufficiently provided for; the 1935 riots on the Copperbelt took the Government by surprise and it had to depend on armed support from the South. Compared with Southern Rhodesia, the country, apart from the Copperbelt, was in a state of stagnation. The more liberal of the Unofficial Members deplored this lapse of trusteeship,[94] and the others seized upon these shortcomings in order to discredit rule from Whitehall. Having presented his re-

---

[90] Evidence to the Bledisloe Commission, CXV. They added: 'there were no men out of work over this transferring to natives, but we would not like to see it carried on ad infin.'

[91] Ibid., see above, Chap. III, p. 106.

[92] House of Lords Debates, 31 July 1939, col. 724.

[93] Ibid., Bledisloe, col. 710.

[94] E.g. Gore Browne quoted in Davidson, p. 73.

port, Lord Bledisloe delivered a weighty indictment in the House of Lords:

> Vitality and progress are to be seen throughout Southern Rhodesia and unfortunately stagnation in almost every direction throughout both the northern Territories but particularly Northern Rhodesia. . . . The trusteeship of the United Kingdom is ideal in theory and on paper, but the state of Northern Rhodesia and Nyasaland illustrates in somewhat glaring colours the extreme difficulty of exercising that trusteeship efficiently 'longa manu' at a distance of 6,000 miles.[95]

On the Copperbelt hostility to the Colonial Office régime was even stronger than in the Legislative Council and it found vehement public expression. Relationships between Europeans and Africans deteriorated after the 1935 disturbances. A mine-club manager thought that 'a considerable influx of the poor type of Afrikanders from the Union of South Africa' who had come up during the last few years might have been partly the cause, but most Europeans had no hesitation in ascribing the bad feeling to the insolent bearing of the Africans. The manager himself, who had worked 'with natives for forty years', said, 'I have never had trouble of any sort, but definitely on the Copperbelt I give it up. They are beyond all comprehension.' A metallurgical accountant described the 'dumb arrogance' among Africans: when told to do a job 'he simply stands and looks at the man who gives the orders. Or he says "pay me off" which is a very bad example to other boys.'[96] Since on the mines a European was legally liable to instant dismissal if he hit a native, the problem of keeping discipline in the face of this attitude was a constant strain, and Government policy, together with education, was blamed for this 'insolence and arrogance'. Europeans thought, for instance, that in the Courts of Justice there was a definite 'colour bar operating . . . against the white man'. The official attitude, they felt, was 'not to be suspicious of the native', who was given the benefit of the doubt to a greater extent than the white man, while the authorities were 'definitely disinclined to believe Europeans'.

[95] House of Lords Debates, 31 July 1939, Bledisloe, cols. 707, 711.
[96] Evidence to the Bledisloe Commission, CXIII.

We had a case in Mufulira only last week of a young girl of only five years being assaulted . . . by a native. The mother of the child, who we understand was a particularly careful mother, reported the matter to the Boma, who said it was nothing to do with them and she must go to the Police. She went to the Police and they arrested the native. They came back the next day and said that they regretted there was insufficient evidence and they were releasing the native. . . . A public meeting was called under the auspices of the Mine Workers' Union . . . where it was decided to submit the case to the Chief Secretary. In the afternoon prior to this meeting the pulse of public feeling had been high, and the Superintendent of Police came out and said that he would go ahead with the prosecution after the Police had already said there was not sufficient evidence. That case I believe was tried last Saturday, and the native was given twelve lashes and twelve months hard labour and five years banishment to his village. Yet if it had not been for that public meeting the native would have been allowed to go.[97]

The previous year the case of Douglas Bissett, a European youth of seventeen years sentenced to four strokes of the cane for assaulting an African and breaking his collar-bone, provoked mass meetings, a delegation to the Governor, a public disturbance, and an official inquiry. The report of the acting Attorney-General reviewed a series of cases in which complaints were made that action had not been taken against Africans, but on investigation it was found that the assaults had sometimes been committed first by the European or that the evidence was quite insufficient to lead to a conviction. The issue was summed up by a police inspector saying that the police frequently received notes to the effect that 'this boy has refused to wash the dishes, please give him a good hiding'.[98] Most of the Europeans on the Copperbelt came from the Union of South Africa and Southern Rhodesia and many of them may well have been accustomed to a more summary form of justice. Colonial Office practice was therefore all the more abhorrent and their antipathy to its servants was intense.

The tense, crude atmosphere of the Copperbelt was reflected in the fact that the alarm and apprehension aroused by the 'black

[97] Evidence to the Bledisloe Commission, CXIII.
[98] E. E. Jenkins, *Report of an Inquiry into the Causes of a Disturbance at Nkana on the 4th and 5th November 1937* (Lusaka 1937).

peril' were even more prevalent than in Southern Rhodesia. It was considered 'definitely foolish for a white woman to go walking unaccompanied on a quiet road or a bush path', and one witness said that there had been cases of attempted rape every year since he arrived in 1929. Later this was qualified by a spokesman for the barristers and solicitors of Ndola who said:

I do not think that the attitude of natives towards women which has been referred to was intended so much as to suggest rape, but undue familiarity and general misbehaviour such as coming up and handling them. I have known of few serious assaults on European women. . . . The main cases I have heard of were natives meeting them on the street, even in the streets between houses.[99]

Behind the criticisms of the Unofficials in the Legislative Council and the anger of Europeans on the Copperbelt there lay a basic lack of security and a fear of what might happen in the future. Although Colonial Office rule brought few immediate concrete benefits to the Africans, the very concept of trusteeship seemed to involve an eventual handing over of power when the ward could be deemed to be sufficiently advanced. On the political side the introduction of indirect rule could be seen as a gradual preparation for this transfer of power. The Governor sought to allay European fears by declaring himself 'rather a heretic on indirect rule, for it should be regarded more as a training for the natives to run their own affairs rather than an acceptance that they would eventually govern the country'.[100] But while Colonial Office rule lasted the Europeans could never be certain that the country would not follow a West African example rather than those to the south of the Zambezi. On the industrial side, the Northern Rhodesian Mine Workers' Union stated that they were 'nervous about the future, especially from our children's point of view'. With the 'famous white paper' and its reference to the paramountcy of native interests, there was, they feared,

nothing to stop the Colonial Secretary and Governor starting large industrial schools for natives, and to turn round to the Mining

[99] Evidence to the Bledisloe Commission, CXIII and CXIV.
[100] *The Times*, 19 February 1937.

Companies and say 'the interests of the whites and the natives are now clashing, you must employ a larger proportion of native artisans year by year', and gradually put us out of work.[101]

This fundamental sense of insecurity was, even more than the present discontents, the driving force in the Europeans' demand for amalgamation with Southern Rhodesia. In 1931 the Secretary of State informed the Unofficial Members in Northern Rhodesia and the Government of Southern Rhodesia that

a substantially greater advance should be made in the development of Northern Rhodesia before any final opinion can be formed as to its future. . . . At present the European population is small and scattered over a wide extent of territory, while the problems of native development are in a stage which makes it inevitable that His Majesty's Government should hesitate to let them pass even partially out of their responsibility.[102]

The demand, however, steadily increased, and in January 1936 a Conference was held at the Victoria Falls. It was attended by all the Unofficial Members of the Northern Rhodesian Legislative Council and by representatives of the three parties in the Southern Rhodesian Legislative Assembly. The Conference unanimously resolved in favour of 'the early amalgamation of Northern and Southern Rhodesia under a Constitution conferring the right of complete self-government'.[103] This demand for full autonomy, which also implied the removal of the Secretary of State's reserved powers in Southern Rhodesia, was supported, with only a few dissentients, in a subsequent debate in the Southern Rhodesian Legislative Assembly.

The Southern Rhodesians were doubtless partly influenced by economic considerations: the hope of sharing in the market and the riches of the Copperbelt, the desire to forestall Witwatersrand competition for Northern Rhodesian labour, and the advantages of being the senior partner in a larger unit. But their dominant motive was a sympathy for the aspirations of their fellow settlers and a fear that, as Mrs. Tawse-Jollie put it, 'the bogey of the

---

[101] Evidence to the Bledisloe Commission, CXV.
[102] *Bledisloe Report*, p. 111.   [103] Ibid., p. 113.

"Black North" would come south if there was no unity of government'.[104] Huggins felt that there was no time to be lost: 'If the territories are ever to be united, it will have to be in the very near future. Otherwise they will draw so far apart in different ways that it will become absolutely impossible.'[105] And the Bledisloe Commission was told that he argued at a meeting at the Colonial Office, 'giving rather confidential data', that unless closer union was embarked upon he might have to take into consideration the 'very strong feeling in Southern Rhodesia towards moving into the Union'.[106]

As a result of this pressure discussions were held in London in the summer of 1937 and the Royal Commission was appointed. Led by Lord Bledisloe, formerly Governor-General of New Zealand, the Commission consisted of Messrs. P. Ashley Cooper, a Governor of the Hudson's Bay Company, Ernest Evans, Liberal M.P. for the University of Wales, T. Fitzgerald, a former Colonial Civil Servant, W. H. Mainwaring, Labour M.P. for East Rhondda and Ian Orr-Ewing, Conservative M.P. for Weston-super-Mare. The Commission created a good impression in Southern Rhodesia:

When has the Colony known such a tonic since the visits of its Founder? In ten days they have given us a picture of the supple intelligence and moral integrity of England that has made one revise one's ideas both of the Mother Country and the Colony. They have reminded us that isolation and the environment of a million primitive natives will take mental and moral toll even of the picked European community of this Colony unless it continually faces the highest standards of life and thought. . . .[107]

It was, however, faced with an enormously difficult task. On the one side there were the impatience and fears of the Europeans in Northern Rhodesia, who, ably supported from the South, were determined to win recognition of their claim to establish a régime of prosperity and security for themselves and their children. To this was added the manifest shortcomings of trusteeship, partly due to the insecurity which hampered the investment of capital

[104] *Rhodesia Herald*, 7 July 1938.   [105] *East Africa and Rhodesia*, 3 June 1937.
[106] Evidence to Bledisloe Commission, CXLII.   [107] *Rhodesia Herald*, 27 May 1938.

in Northern Rhodesia, and partly to the economic plight of
Nyasaland, a small remote country, dependent on a few agricultural
products of no exceptional value and burdened with a very considerable public debt. The British tradition of granting self-government to settler communities[108] and the importance of creating
a united British 'block' in Central Africa strengthened the case
for amalgamation. On the other side there was the comparative
paucity and weakness of the Europeans, the long tradition and
ultimate implications of trusteeship, and the fears of the Africans.

As in Nyasaland, the Commission took evidence from Africans
in Northern Rhodesia representing a wide range of interests. At
every town or important centre they met members of the neighbouring Native Authorities, educated representatives from Native
Welfare Associations, clerks and tribal elders on the Copperbelt,
teachers and members of the African Civil Servants' Association.
Even in remote rural areas the issue had been discussed at meetings
between District Officers and Chiefs, and the Anglican Bishop of
Northern Rhodesia told the Commission how while he was on
trek he would hear, 'night after night', embittered discussions
based on the experiences of humble, unlettered Africans of life in
Southern Rhodesia.[109] Although in Northern Rhodesia there was
not as yet a sense of national unity such as was beginning to appear
in Nyasaland, there was already among Africans a deep and
articulate sense of human dignity and equality, a pride in their
status as unconquered, protected people, and a determination to
forge their own future under the guidance of the 'throne'. Not
one voice was raised in favour of amalgamation with Southern
Rhodesia. There were many wildly exaggerated rumours about
life in Southern Rhodesia; there was, naturally, much that was
narrow and parochial in their outlook; there were few who could
be expected to understand all the issues involved. But, as in Nyasaland, the Africans' opinions and objections were not the mere
egotistical whims of an unrepresentative minority, but the hard
fruits of an experience shared by the majority of their fellow

[108] Already in 1937 Northern Rhodesian Unofficials were members of the finance committee as in Kenya. Davidson, p. 51.
[109] Evidence to the Bledisloe Commission, CXXVII and CXVII.

Africans. Thousands of Northern Rhodesians had worked as labourers in Southern Rhodesia, several of those who gave evidence to the Commission spoke from first-hand experience, and there was a widespread interest in the trend of events south of the Zambezi. The *Bulawayo Chronicle* was 'read avidly', and an African said that his people preferred 'to read what the white man says about us in his own paper' rather than rely on *Mutende*, the newspaper aided by the Government.[110]

The Africans brought forward many aspects of life in Southern Rhodesia to explain their opposition to closer union: the 'very harsh' administration of the pass laws in contrast to East Africa and Nyasaland (though they complained also of the system of night passes in use in Northern Rhodesian urban areas),[111] the interferences and attitude of the police, the heavier taxation, the fact that native markets were discouraged in the urban areas of Southern Rhodesia while they were becoming a prominent and valued feature of life on the Copperbelt, and the lack of opportunity for exercising any skilled trade. For instance, an African sergeant-major from the Northern Rhodesian Regiment had been chosen to go to the Coronation, while there was 'nothing of the sort' in Southern Rhodesia.[112] 'We know that although they receive higher wages, they are suffering.'[113] There were the advances that were being made with the policy of indirect rule in Northern Rhodesia. Educated and uneducated Africans were 'very much satisfied with the power that has been given to our chiefs, because now we are being ruled by our chiefs'.[114] They were afraid, together with the chiefs, that this policy would be changed. All classes expressed fears for their land. Even when a group of chiefs were assured that their powers would be secure and that 'no obnoxious laws' would be introduced, they still obstinately would not agree to amalgamation because they wanted 'to live separately'.[115] All projected safeguards were regarded as inadequate, for they had proved ineffective in Southern Rhodesia and the Union.[116] And behind these specific fears and objections

---

[110] Evidence to the Bledisloe Commission, CXXVII.   [111] Ibid., CXXIV.
[112] Ibid., CXLVII.   [113] Ibid., CV.   [114] Ibid., CV.
[115] Ibid., CIX.   [116] Ibid., CXLVII and CXLVIII.

o

there was a factor, not apparent at a first glance, not evident from a comparative study of statistics and policies, and often unrealized, uncomprehended by most European settlers: a deep, intangible, powerful current of feeling.

This factor was early summed up for the Commission at Fort Jameson by Kawaza, Chief of the Chewa, who had himself worked in Southern Rhodesia: 'In Southern Rhodesia there is no respect like there is here in our country.'[117] Elsewhere in Northern Rhodesia this feeling found further clarification and expression. At Mongu, the capital of Barotseland, the Commission was told how in Southern Rhodesia 'they do not look upon the black man as a person, they just treat them as dogs. The only time they look after them, is when they want money from them. . . . I am a person, not a dog.'[118] Clerks and *capitaos* from Nkana and Mu-fulira said: 'We know Southern Rhodesia and it is not good. . . . They do not speak to you properly, just get hold of you and push you about, and it is not pleasant.'[119] At Mazabuka an Ila Chief thought that the reason was 'that the natives there had refused to make friendship with the white people and there was war, and they were overcome, and hard laws were made for them', and the African Civil Servants' Association added: 'Why we should run parallel with that conquered country we cannot under-stand.'[120] This passionate rejection of a servile status, the bitterness aroused by the absence of mutual respect and by the white man's denial of a basic equality, explained the Northern Rhodesian Africans' hostility to the Southern Rhodesian régime and also seemed to lie at the heart of the worsening situation on the Copper-belt. Miss Mabel Shaw, a pioneer of African girls' education who had spent twenty-three years at Mbereshi, said that she had not noticed any diminution in the feeling of respect shown by Africans to Europeans 'up country', but she had heard 'so much' about it in the industrial areas. She added:

There is something extraordinarily precious to the Bantu—he expresses it by the word 'buntu'. It is this deep respect for a common humanity which makes the chief greet the commoner with as great a

[117] Evidence to the Bledisloe Commission, LXXXVI.
[118] Ibid., CXXXI.   [119] Ibid., CXIX.   [120] Ibid., CIV, CXXIV.

respect as he would another chief. The Bantu in his tribal life is a self-respecting being, and if you kill that self-respect he loses his head entirely. That is what happens here—his self-respect is killed—and they are very bitter about it. Young men and older men come to me and beseech me to tell the white people when I go home on leave that they want their respect more than anything else.[121]

Faced with this direct clash between European demands and African fears, between segregation and trusteeship, two 'inherently different and divergent' policies (as Lord Bledisloe said in the House of Lords),[122] the Commission was unable to recommend any immediate decisive course of action. Their report expressed the belief that the three Territories

will become more and more closely interdependent in all their activities, and that identity of interests will lead them sooner or later to political unity. If this view should commend itself also to Your Majesty's Government in the United Kingdom, we recommend that it should take an early opportunity of stating its acceptance of the principle.[123]

In the House of Lords, Lord Bledisloe gave his opinion that this step was of 'immediate and outstanding importance' in order to dispel the prevalent feeling of insecurity in the Northern Territories, but, although the Report was signed unanimously, several of his colleagues had expressed their doubts. Neither Fitzgerald nor Orr-Ewing accepted amalgamation as the inevitable object of policy; Evans thought that amalgamation could only be effective 'if it be established on the basis of a practical recognition of the fact that settler and native are partners and the acceptance by both parties of the full implications of that fact'; in a long note appended to the body of the report Mainwaring asserted that the United Kingdom's responsibility for the welfare and development of the Protectorates could not be discharged by 'handing them over to the European settlers of Southern Rhodesia'.[124] The Report therefore merely recommended the immediate amalgamation of Nyasaland with Northern Rhodesia, with Europeans

[121] Evidence to the Bledisloe Commission, CXVII.
[122] House of Lords Debates, 31 July 1939.
[123] *Bledisloe Report*, p. 214.   [124] Ibid., pp. 248-60.

being more closely associated with the Government and representation of natives in the Legislature, and also suggested that an Inter-territorial Council should be established to co-ordinate Government services and to frame plans for future development.

The publication of the Report caused widespread disappointment among the whites in Rhodesia. Huggins came to London in July for further discussions. At a luncheon in his honour, the Secretary of State for the Dominions, Sir Thomas Inskip, mentioned the 'exploratory operation' which had been conducted by the Commission and added that he was 'undergoing a process of education by the kind and helpful Prime Minister of Southern Rhodesia which, he hoped, would lead his colleagues and himself to the right conclusion'. These remarks elicited a typical reply from Huggins:

The 'exploratory operation' as I see it is this: that certain people met and discussed the disease. They decided that a major operation was necessary, but owing to some of the consultants not being quite satisfied the whole lot lost their nerve, the operation was not performed, and the patient died.[125]

In Northern Rhodesia the Report was received with even greater anger. Sir Leopold Moore resigned in protest and was returned unopposed at the consequent by-election. In a subsequent debate in the Legislative Council several Unofficials dismissed African opinion as of no account and passed a motion deploring the indeterminate nature of the Commission's conclusions. The campaign for amalgamation spread outside the Council. On the Copperbelt public meetings were held and associations were formed.[126] But before the British Government could come to any further conclusion the Second World War had intervened.

[125] *The Times*, 26 July 1939.   [126] Davidson, op. cit., pp. 106–9.

Part Two
Awakenings : 1939–1953

I. THE CHANGING ARENA

As European rivalries developed into the Second World War only two states in Africa—Liberia and the Union of South Africa—were free to decide for themselves whether or not to take part in the conflict. European rule was the decisive, and virtually the undisputed, factor in the continent; Africa was still a pawn of the outside world. By 1953 the situation had radically altered. Europe, shorn of its Asian possessions, weakened by the devastation of war, and dwarfed by two rival giants both strongly critical of European 'colonialism', had lost its supremacy. In the Gold Coast, if not yet in the Congo, in the Sudan, if not yet in Mozambique, it was clear that Europe was no longer the unquestioned arbiter in the African continent. Africa had entered a period of political change, as rapid as that which, some six decades earlier, had divided her between the European powers.

This dramatic reduction in the status of Europe in Africa took place at a time when the importance of Africa to Britain and Western Europe had enormously increased. In 1938 Britain's colonies supplied only 5·8 per cent. of her total imports; she could still afford to treat the whole world as her market-place.[1] The war and the dollar crisis which followed reduced both her affluence and her area of choice. Together with the other countries of Western Europe, Britain was faced with overwhelming debts and trading deficits with the American continent, and at the same time there was a world-wide shortage of the raw materials produced by the colonies. Suddenly, for the first time since the eighteenth century, the colonies, and Africa in particular, were seen to be of supreme economic importance. Sir Stafford Cripps told a conference of Colonial Governors in November 1947: 'The whole future of the sterling group and its ability to survive

[1] Rita Hinden, *Common Sense and Colonial Development* (1949), p. 16.

depends in my view upon a quick and extensive development of our African resources.' The economies of Western Europe and Tropical Africa were interdependent. Africa possessed 'a great potential for new strength and vigour in the Western European economy' and the stronger that economy became 'the better of course Africa itself' would fare. The tempo of economic development in Africa should therefore be increased 'out of all recognition', and Cripps hoped for 'a really marked increase' within two to five years of all raw materials that could save or earn dollars.[2]

This demand by politicians faced with the metropolitan predicament was strengthened by other—and perhaps in the eyes of Africans more respectable—considerations. A few persistent prophets were already proclaiming that, in view of the world's food problem, Africa had an 'extraordinary part to play in the coming generation'.[3] It was estimated that in the second half of the twentieth century the world's population might increase by one thousand million. With little virgin soil to be used for food production and with soil erosion taking place all over the world, the problem could only be solved by an intensive, world-wide application of science and capital to agriculture. 'There is only a fifty-fifty chance of getting over this food problem,' said Sir John Boyd Orr when he retired from the Director-Generalship of the Food and Agriculture Organization (of the United Nations) in May 1948. 'Soil erosion is the big problem we are up against, but the Governments of the world are not interested. Their major problem is Communism versus private enterprise, and the next election.'[4]

But conditions in the colonies themselves were already beginning to change British colonial policy several years before the dollar shortage gave an unprecedented urgency to increased colonial production. The difficulties of under-developed areas precariously dependent on one cash crop were sharply revealed in the years of poverty which followed the depression of 1930-1. The Colonial Development and Welfare Act, passed in 1940, when Britain's fortunes were at their lowest ebb, made a decisive

[2] Hinden, op. cit., p. 9.   [3] Ibid., p. 5.   [4] Ibid., p. 5.

break in the long-established Treasury tradition that the colonies should meet their needs out of taxation or by loans raised by themselves. A sum of £5 million a year for ten years was to be provided as a direct grant for development plans in the colonies—for communications, housing, education, technical training, and social services. Shortages during the war prevented the full implementation of this scheme, but in 1945 a further Act made available a total of £12 million a year and plans were already being made for a balanced development. Africa was on the brink of an economic revolution.

In common with the rest of the continent, the Rhodesias and Nyasaland were affected by the greatly quickened tempo of political and economic change. In retrospect the inter-war period seemed to have been a time of unruffled, static calm. The principal exports of Central Africa—copper, tobacco, asbestos, chrome and gold—were valuable dollar-savers. During the Second World War they brought a greatly increased revenue which helped to stimulate a rapid development of secondary industries. Political developments in other African territories also altered the setting of race relations in the Rhodesias and Nyasaland. As the backdrop changed, its sharper contrasts exerted an increasing influence in the narrower arena of Central Africa. Events in the Gold Coast, with the report of the Coussey Commission in 1949 and the subsequent election of Dr. Nkrumah as Leader of Government Business in 1951, clearly foreshadowed the headlong rush towards political independence in West Africa. The discussions terminating in February 1953 in the Anglo–Egyptian agreement on a timetable for Sudanese independence marked the recession of British imperial power in the Nile Valley, and in Kenya Mau Mau underlined the precarious position of European settlers in East Africa. The Union of South Africa, on the other hand, elected in 1948 to follow Dr. Malan's programme of apartheid. This policy, and the reactions of its opponents, heightened racial consciousness throughout the continent. It turned widespread attention to the problems of race relations and the dilemma of peoples of European descent attempting to practise democracy in a world in which they were greatly outnumbered.

In the midst of these developments the creation of a British bloc in Central Africa seemed to be a matter of urgent importance. In Whitehall, Salisbury, and Lusaka it began to seem that a new state might form an island of stability and security at a point in the world where Western interests were by no means insignificant. It might foster an economic development which would substantially benefit its inhabitants and the sterling area in general. And it might provide the base for a policy of racial co-operation. Yet while Europeans were pondering over their response to the changed situation, the stirrings of a new continent were gradually reaching African ears. The isolation of Central Africa was rapidly diminishing.

On both sides of the Zambezi the declared objectives and the firm assumptions of the thirties were also being challenged by internal changes. The most striking difference from the previous inter-war period was the shift northwards of the economic centre of the Rhodesias. In the aftermath of the 1930–1 slump the future of European settlement in Northern Rhodesia seemed to be far from secure. The European population decreased from 13,841 in 1931 to an estimated 10,588 in 1936, and it was only slowly recovering at the outbreak of the Second World War.[5] Copper already formed over 80 per cent. of Northern Rhodesia's exports,[6] but in 1939 few people would have confidently echoed Smuts' hope, expressed a decade earlier, that copper might do for Northern Rhodesia what gold had done for the Transvaal. The Bledisloe Commission, for example, could only say that 'the industry appears now to have reached a more stable position'.[7] For most Europeans south of the Zambezi the Copperbelt was still a somewhat remote mining camp, a place where one could perhaps earn a rather higher wage than elsewhere, but an unproved, precarious base for a permanent European community.

With two million pounds of copper needed for a battleship and two miles of copper wire for a bomber, the Copperbelt was of vital importance to the British war effort. Production expanded, and between 1939 and 1944 the numbers of Europeans and Africans employed on the mines increased from two to three

---

[5] *Bledisloe Report*, pp. 3–4.   [6] Ibid., p. 57.   [7] Ibid., p. 56.

thousand and from twenty to thirty thousand respectively.[8] As the war came to a close the copper companies, faced with increased costs and fearing a sharp reduction in the world demand for copper, decided to cut down production. But the immense task of post-war reconstruction, followed by rearmament and the Korean war, pushed up the price of copper, and the Copperbelt was the only large source of supply within the sterling area. Mining expanded, milling capacity was increased, refineries for electrolytic copper—previously obtained by Britain from North America—were built at Nkana, cobalt production increased, and Northern Rhodesia entered one of the most spectacular booms in African history.

Europeans flocked into the country. In 1946 the European population was double that of ten years earlier, and by 1951 it had grown to 34,962, which was about the same total as in Southern Rhodesia when Responsible Government was obtained in 1923. More than 6,000 European immigrants were arriving each year. After the war the use of D.D.T. virtually eliminated any serious danger from malaria on the Copperbelt and a reasonably large permanent settlement was now a practical possibility. The increase

TABLE I

Exports from Central Africa (in £m.)

	1938	1946	1949	1952	1953
S. Rhodesia . . .	10·6	18·6	29·6	51·1	54·0
N. Rhodesia . . .	10·0	12·8	32·9	81·7	93·7
Nyasaland . . .	0·9	2·3	4·7	6·2	7·1

(Source: Thompson and Woodruff, op. cit., pp. 199–200; and *Central African Territories, Geographical, Historical and Economic Survey* (Cmd. 8234, 1951), p. 44.)

in European population was accompanied by an even more impressive increase in the country's wealth. By 1953 the value of Northern Rhodesian exports had become almost double that of Southern Rhodesia's[9]—a development which would have been almost unbelievable a decade earlier. With the Copperbelt as the

[8] L. H. Gann, 'The Northern Rhodesian Copper Industry and the World of Copper: 1923–52', *Rhodes–Livingstone Journal*, No. 18, 1955.
[9] See Table I.

economic centre of Central Africa, the idea of a union with
Northern Rhodesia became even more attractive to Southern
Rhodesia than it had been in the thirties, and it was increasingly
difficult for the Colonial Office to overrule the ambitions of
Europeans in Northern Rhodesia. A new formula had to be
found.

Despite the sudden turn in the fortunes of the Europeans on the
Copperbelt, Southern Rhodesia, with her larger, firmly settled
European population, remained the key to the European position
in Central Africa. In Northern Rhodesia it was obvious to anyone who gave the matter any thought that the future development
of by far the larger part of the country would depend primarily
on African initiative, and on the elimination of the tse-tse fly. But
in Southern Rhodesia the policy and attitudes of Europeans continued to be of supreme importance, and the immediate future
of race relations in Central Africa was largely dependent on their
response to the changing situation.

In the years following the outbreak of the Second World War
the Southern Rhodesian economy rapidly expanded in a quite
new sphere. Founded on the hope of inheriting the fabulous
golden wealth of the Monomotapa, by 1923 the colony had become a mixed mining and agricultural community with land
policy its principal concern. By 1938, after fifteen years of Responsible Government, the country still had a 'colonial' economy,
exporting primary products and importing nearly all its consumer
goods. It was hoped that it would prove possible one day to build
up a manufacturing industry and to process the raw materials
within the country itself, but at that time the 2,800 Europeans
working in 'industrial establishments' were employed, apart from
the large number in the Railway workshops at Bulawayo, in
small firms engaged in activities such as printing, milling, brewing, brickmaking, or engineering repairs.[10]

The shortage of consumer goods during the Second World
War stimulated the creation and expansion of secondary industries: metal manufacturing, food processing, and the manufacture of furniture, boots, shoes, and clothing were undertaken.

[10] Thompson and Woodruff, pp. 16, 162–3.

The Government also began to take an active part in encouraging industrial development. Plans were made for a State mill to spin locally-grown cotton and for a statutory commission to produce iron and steel from the large deposits of high-grade iron ore and limestone near Que Que. These two public enterprises, which started large-scale production in the post-war years, provided the materials for a series of other industries. A large Lancashire textile firm established a weaving factory at Hartley, the clothing industry expanded rapidly, and the iron and steel produced at Que Que went to factories producing wire, water-piping, agricultural machinery, constructional materials, and other commodities urgently needed in an expanding economy.[11]

After the war a pronounced increase in the value of Southern Rhodesian primary products assisted the continued development of secondary industries. Before the war Southern Rhodesia produced thirty million pounds weight of tobacco per annum; by 1950 production had increased to over one hundred million

TABLE II

Production in Southern Rhodesia

Year	Per cent. growth of European pop.	Index of volume of production		
		Agriculture	Mining	Mfg. industry
1938	100	100	100	100
1945	132	160	81	221
1949	187	209	89 *a*	330
1952	249	268	91 *a*	476 *b*

a Includes chrome ore stock piles in the years in which they were mined.
b Estimated.
(Source: *Survey of Rhodesian Industry*, published by the Federation of Rhodesian Industries (Salisbury 1955).)

pounds, worth approximately £20 million. Tobacco had become by far the most important export, a valuable dollar-saver for the sterling area and the prop for much of the rapid post-war development. By 1952 a total of 9,000 Africans and Europeans were employed in grading, packing, and selling tobacco, or in manufacturing cigarettes; the expansion of tobacco-growing was 'one

[11] *Southern Rhodesia's Economic Progress* (Public Relations Department, Salisbury, 1953).

of the primary causes of the high rate of immigration' and indirectly the wealth that it brought into the country helped to create an internal market for many secondary industries.[12]

The change in the economy of Southern Rhodesia is perhaps best illustrated in Table II, which shows the rapid growth of the manufacturing industries.[13] The extent to which European economic interests were broadening is shown also by an analysis of the 1951 Census. In that year the economically active European population of Southern Rhodesia consisted of—

7,582 employers, among whom over 4,000 were farmers, 1,000 traders, 700 engaged in building and other construction, and about 500 in manufacturing industries;

547 self-employed workers;

8,780 central Government employees;

43,858 other employees, among whom about 3,000 were on farms, 2,400 miners, about 9,000 in manufacturing industry, 5,700 in building and construction work, 10,000 in commerce, and 4,000 in transport.

The 'colonial' pattern of the economy had been decisively modified: the country was now producing a large proportion of consumer goods for itself and was building up a significant export of manufactured textiles to its neighbours.

This economic expansion resulted in a great increase in both the numbers and the wealth of the Europeans—between 1946 and 1951 their aggregate personal income increased from £20 million to £52½ million. In 1936 there were 55,408 Europeans in Southern Rhodesia, ten years later there were 82,386, and by 1951 the total had reached 135,596. Nearly a third of the Europeans living there in 1951 had been born in the country; but more than half of the remainder had been there less than five years. The United Kingdom and Ireland provided the larger part of this tremendous post-war influx, and the wave of immigrants fresh from the United Kingdom was perhaps one factor which facilitated a few tentative modifications of the policy of segregation.[14]

---

[12] Thompson and Woodruff, pp. 145–6, 169.   [13] Table II.
[14] See below, Part II, Chap. IV, p. 308.

The South African element in the country, however, remained strong. The total number born in the Union still exceeded those born in Britain, and many of the latter had lived in South Africa before crossing the Limpopo. At least one in every eight Europeans was a member of the Dutch Reformed Church, and hence presumably of Afrikaner origin.[15] In Northern Rhodesia the South African element was even stronger in proportion: in 1951, 16,167 of the Europeans there had been born in the Union compared with 9,238 born in the United Kingdom and Ireland, and the ratio of Dutch Reformed Church members was 1 : 4·6 (N.R. Census, 1951). But Malan's militant Afrikaner nationalism made the majority of the Europeans in the Rhodesias feel that the Limpopo was perhaps more of a dividing line than the Zambezi.

The change in the hopes and horizons of the Europeans was possibly even more important than the actual increases in immigration, industry, and wealth. They no longer felt that they were a handful of pioneer settlers in a vast and on the whole untamed country; they began to see themselves as the first citizens of a Dominion with a great and prosperous future. Under the chairmanship of Sir Miles Thomas a Development Co-ordinating Commission was appointed in 1946 to advise the Southern Rhodesian Government how 'to ensure the most rapid development of the Colony on sound lines', how to make the best use of the country's water, mineral, and agricultural resources, and how to effect 'a rapid increase in European population'. The Commission thought that the country, although 'no fantastic Eldorado', should be regarded as 'an extremely fertile field' which, properly husbanded, could repay 'a rich reward'. The vast coal resources were seen as the potential basis of an important chemical industry and as a source of motor spirit, fuel oil, and gas. Hydro-electricity would provide the cheap power essential for all branches of industry and would foster the production of nitrogenous fertilizers, ferrochrome, and other materials. The irrigation and mineral possibilities of the large Sabi River area were investigated as a long-term project, and the Commission pointed out that

[15] Southern Rhodesian Census, 1951.

smaller irrigation schemes could more immediately help the country to become self-supporting in food production. As evidence of the confidence felt in the economic future of the country the Commission instanced the fact that Government loans on the London market were rapidly over-subscribed, and in a speech in London in 1948 Sir Miles Thomas declared that Central Africa was 'simply asking to be turned into both treasury and armoury, a source of dollar reserve in peace, a steadfast fortress in war'.[16]

In this atmosphere of confident optimism the rigid concept of territorial segregation began to seem less relevant, and the problems of economic integration demanded increasing attention. The growth of secondary industries implied, as will be seen, the permanent urbanization of Africans. The focus of interest in race relations shifted from the land to the towns. Industrialists emphasized the value of the African as producer and consumer and so long as the Government was committed to a policy of rapid industrialization it was bound to give heed when possible to the views of industrialists. In contrast to the restricted opportunities of the years of the depression, an expanding economy could offer better prospects for all. But even industrialists had a limited conception of the possibilities of African advancement, and few Europeans envisaged any real devolution of power. The African, said Sir Miles Thomas, 'has the manipulative dexterity and mental agility to enable him to become a useful operator in the agricultural and engineering fields. In that way he will emerge as a wage-earning artisan who is a good customer for consumer goods.'[17] But would Africans remain content with such a partnership, or would there be time for the fact of economic co-operation to lead gradually to a more satisfying relationship?

Time was short, for the days of undisputed European initiative were drawing to a close. The final factor which sharply distinguished the post-1939 period in Central Africa from that which preceded it, was the development of a new response

---

[16] *Third Interim Report of the Development Co-ordinating Commission* (Salisbury, 1949), and Hinden, op. cit., p. 41.

[17] Quoted by Hinden, op. cit., p. 42.

among Africans. In part this was an inevitable result of the greatly increased opportunities for African education. In 1938 there were no secondary schools for Africans in Central Africa; by 1953 university education for a limited number of Africans was in sight. In 1938 the Governments of the three territories spent approximately £150,000 on African education; by 1953 they were spending more than ten times that sum. Elsewhere in Africa the advance was even more impressive, but here also education was opening up new possibilities. The whole emphasis had changed from the slow, steady uplift of the villages as envisaged by the Jeanes Teachers, to the rapid creation and training of an *élite*. The role of this *élite* was envisaged differently on either side of the Zambezi,[18] but on neither side of the river could the educators control the thoughts of the educated. African minds were opening to new, disturbing influences.

From the rest of the continent the wild wind of nationalism carried the intoxicating message of 'Africa for the Africans'. Some educated, 'detribalized' Africans were beginning to recover a pride in their ancestry and in the achievements of their distinctive culture. In remote, rural Nyasaland the idea of freedom slowly developed a new meaning and relevance for Africans until, under the stress of events, the whole basis of colonial rule began to be questioned. At the same time, in the Rhodesias, thousands of Africans were exposed to another formative, revolutionary experience. On the Copperbelt, in Lusaka, Livingstone, Salisbury, Bulawayo, and other urban areas of Southern Rhodesia, Africans, under a fresh leadership, were establishing types of mass organization, new to Central Africa, and were reaching out towards strange forms of power.

When it is realised that by virtue of numbers alone Salisbury and Bulawayo can each be assessed as Provinces, [wrote an official of the Native Affairs Department in April 1953] that the Salisbury aggregate is the equivalent of the combined adult male population of her seven neighbouring districts (Salisbury, Goromonzi, Marandellas, Hartley, Lomagundi, Mazoe and Mrewa), it becomes possible to appreciate

[18] *Report of the Native Education Inquiry Commission, 1951* (Salisbury, C.S.R. 6–1952), pp. 10–13.

P

what an enormous influence these (urban) centres are compared to the rural groupings.[19]

The future of Rhodesia was to be decided in the towns; industrial and urban life confronted both Europeans and Africans with their most critical challenge and an unprecedented opportunity. And during the Second World War the full nature of this challenge began to be apparent.

[19] R. Howman, *African Local Government in Urban Areas* (cyclostyled, Salisbury, 1953).

II. THE CHALLENGES OF INDUSTRIALIZATION

I. THE COST OF LIVING

Before 1940 the urban African's cost of living attracted relatively little attention from either Europeans or Africans. In the inter-war period European interests in Southern Rhodesia had been primarily agricultural, most African families were still peasant in outlook, and the policy of segregation was conceived principally in terms of land ownership. The challenges inherent in large-scale industrial enterprise were already apparent to a few who had eyes to see them,[1] but the problems were still relatively embryonic, and even on the Copperbelt, despite its rapid development, the African was still regarded as a basically rural being.[2] Few Europeans foresaw that within a decade the problems of the Copperbelt would be widely recognized as symbolic for Central Africa and crucial for the future of race relations, or that wages would suddenly become the dominant issue between black and white.

Then, suddenly, in 1940 there came an African strike on the Copperbelt. In its concerted demand for a dramatic increase in wages, the bitter comparison between the European and African standards of living, and the prominence given for the first time to the colour bar, this outburst was sharply distinguished from the disturbances of 1935.[3] And the change in Southern Rhodesia was even more startling. Previously African organizations had been mainly concerned with the problems and status of the educated *élite*, and even the Industrial and Commercial Workers' Union, with its brief, ineffective, yet authentic demonstration of mass aspirations, had been only partly concerned with 'wage rates and working conditions'.[4] But by 1943 widespread dissatisfaction

---

[1] See above, Part I, Chap. III.
[3] See below, pp. 224–5.
[2] See above, Part I, Chaps. I, III, V.
[4] See above, Part I, Chap. V, pp. 166–7.

among urban Africans of all classes was steadily accumulating. It erupted in the strikes of 1945 and 1948: two explosions which revealed to many Europeans the coming of the new era.

The old causes of racial tension continued: land policy, the fears of a privileged caste who had committed themselves to developing a new country, the resentment of a conquered people, the differences in cultural background, the badge of colour, the basic lack of mutual comprehension and respect. But this discontent over wages produced a new dimension in race relations. For both Europeans and Africans a window opened and the flat, monochrome landscape had changed for ever. Europeans began to realize that their actions and decisions were not the sole factors determining race relations. The cost of living was not merely an additional grievance; it initiated a revolution in African thought and reactions. Africans in Southern Rhodesia began to think of themselves and of their relationships with Europeans in a new way. Increasing numbers of Africans suddenly became aware that they were poor and the whites were rich, and this awareness bound them together. Gradually they began to realize that they had a common interest and a fresh purpose in the new urban, industrial world where their old broken loyalties were largely irrelevant.

In twentieth-century Rhodesia the initiative and power had hitherto lain wholly with the Europeans; the post-war strikes showed that this was no longer so. In Nyasaland Africans were beginning to become united and self-conscious under the influence of the ideas of self-rule and national independence; but in Southern Rhodesia Africans began to unite under the impetus of a colour-consciousness, all the more potent because colour seemed to constitute the one obstacle to an escape from poverty. And this new-found unity, based on a common economic interest, gathered to itself the other, older strands of racial pride and resentment. In Southern Rhodesia the frontier of the nascent African nation was not a territorial boundary, but a common level of poverty, demarcated by colour.

The extent of this poverty was first partially revealed in a survey carried out from August 1942 until June 1943 by the secretary of the Native Welfare Society, the Rev. Percy Ibbotson.

Questionnaires were submitted to a wide range of employers and house-to-house investigations were conducted which together gave particulars of 26,553 cases, a representative sample of the adult male Africans in the urban areas of Southern Rhodesia. It was found that 15·7 per cent. were receiving less than 20s. a month, and fifty-one per cent. less than 30s. a month. Most African employees who earned less than 60s. a month also received either rations or accommodation or both from their employers.[5] It was therefore often claimed that wages were mere pocket-money as the men were fed and housed, but the facts hardly confirmed this, even for those who were single. 'In very few cases' could the rations be considered satisfactory. Often employers appeared 'to regard 2 lb. of mealie meal per day and 2 lb. of meat per week as adequate', neglecting the necessity of a balanced diet; many Africans had therefore to spend a substantial portion of their wages on food and this gave 'an entirely false impression of the economic value of the wages paid'. At the same time war-time scarcities and rising prices made even the scantiest and most necessary clothing a hard-won 'luxury' for most Africans.

But it was married Africans with wives and families living with them in town—that class which represented the only hope of a successful adaptation to urban life—who suffered most acutely the degradation of real poverty. After a careful survey of prices and family budgets Ibbotson came to the conclusion that the average minimum wage required to maintain satisfactorily a married couple with two young children was £4. 15s., a total which, he pointed out, made no allowance for hut tax,[6] travelling, education, medicine, amusements, etc.

Fifty-seven per cent. of the married Africans earned cash wages alone; of these 50·7 per cent. received less than £3. Their condition must have been desperate. Only 8·8 per cent. received £4. 15s. or over. The 29 per cent. who were given rations seldom received any provision for their wives or families. The average

---

[5] Of the total survey covering all ranks of pay, 65·9 per cent. received wages, accommodation and food, but 21·7 per cent. received wages alone.

[6] One shilling and eightpence per month payable by all adult male Africans.

monthly wage in cash for married Africans varied from £3. 3s. 2d. in Bulawayo to £2. 3s. 9d. in Que Que, and several cases were encountered of tailors, store, and factory workers with their wives and anything from one to five children attempting to live on cash wages of 17s. 6d. to 27s. 6d. a month while paying 25 to 38 per cent. of this wage on rent.[7]

As Ibbotson's investigations were drawing to a close a member of the Southern Rhodesian Labour Party, Wing-Commander Eastwood, introduced a motion in the Legislative Assembly urging the Government to introduce a statutory minimum wage for adult Africans. As a result of this debate a Committee under a retired Provincial Native Commissioner, E. G. Howman, was appointed by the Government to report on the economic, social, and health conditions of Africans in urban areas. The Committee was provided with a great deal of evidence that many Africans were not earning enough to feed their families. The Junior Chamber of Commerce at Bulawayo told the Committee that 'the average wages paid to the majority of Africans' in that town were inadequate to supply the minimum needs of married Africans, and in Salisbury Major Tysoe, the Labour Officer of the Northern Rhodesian Government, stated that the economic position of the African was 'deteriorating rapidly'.[8] African wages were by no means keeping pace with the rising costs of living. In September 1941 the Government had instituted a cost of living allowance of 2s. 6d. per month to all their African employees not in receipt of rations. Some of the larger employers followed this example, but only about 5 per cent. of the total number of African employees received the allowance.[9] And 2s. 6d. was an inadequate amount. In the absence of satisfactory statistics it was impossible to estimate with accuracy the increase in the African's cost of living, but Tysoe suggested that it was at least 7s. 6d. per month. Essential clothing—a khaki shirt, shorts, blankets, and printed cotton cloth—had doubled or more than doubled in price since 1939, and food prices had increased considerably.[10]

[7] Percy Ibbotson, *Report on a Survey of Urban African conditions in Southern Rhodesia* (Bulawayo, 1943).
[8] Howman Committee evidence, pp. 306, 359.   [9] Ibbotson, op. cit., p. 8.
[10] Howman Committee evidence, p. 359.

There was no attempt, apart from Ibbotson's, to obtain a statistical survey of African wages. But from evidence submitted to the Howman Committee its members were able to form a fairly general picture. The Rhodesia Railways, the largest employers of labour in the country, employing from 2,000 to 3,000 Africans in Bulawayo alone, started their unskilled African labourers at 20s. per month, and their highest-paid grade of 'boss boys' rose to a maximum of 45s. per month. These workers were accommodated in compounds belonging to the Railways, and were given rations for themselves alone. Their conditions, hard as they were,[11] compared favourably with those in many smaller concerns. A building contractor in business since 1897, with ninety-eight labourers on his pay-roll, affirmed that he had paid 10s. a week as far back as he could remember, save that during the depression it had been reduced to 8s. Recently he had started to add 1s. per week cost of living allowance, but no labourers, however long they had been with him, were paid more than 15s., for otherwise he found that 'they reckon they own the firm'[12]—and no rations or accommodation were provided. The wages of tailors in a Salisbury clothing factory varied from 17s. 6d. to 25s. per month with rations of mealie meal and 6d. worth of meat per week, while the highest-paid tailor in one of the largest clothing factories received only 40s. per month after working there for fourteen years. Many Africans employed as tailors and store-boys at the Indian stores received even less than those employed in the factories.[13]

Ibbotson's survey was therefore supported by evidence from many sources, and the Howman Committee found that their main recommendations were identical with his. They agreed that the 15·7 per cent. who drew less than 20s. per month represented 'exploitation of labour by a certain class of employer, European, Asiatic and African'. They recommended therefore that a minimum wage of 20s. with specified rations and free accommodation should be statutory for all urban workers, men, women, and juveniles. This, it was felt, would 'give protection against the

[11] See below, Part II, Chap. III, p. 254.
[12] Howman Committee evidence, pp. 110, 299.   [13] Ibid., p. 359.

casual, inefficient rural visitor; lead to more efficient use of labour by certain employers; prevent exploitation; link up with a "compulsory education" recommendation by preventing the employment of juveniles'; and finally would 'provide a floor above which wages would be encouraged to rise' by various measures designed to increase efficiency. A Wage Board would determine the wages for individual industries and categories. The Committee agreed that the position of married men was 'very difficult, especially those earning less than £3 a month' who constituted over 50 per cent. They realized that 'if Mr. Ibbotson's calculation of £4. 15s. as the average minimum monthly requirements of a man and his wife and children was accepted then very large numbers of families must be perilously near starvation point'. They pointed out, however, that men who had wives to prepare their food were often less liable to deficiency diseases than bachelors, and they suggested that 'the inter-relationships between wages earned and standards of living maintained, between income and habits of spending, were much more complicated than sets of figures imply'.[14]

In so far, however, as figures could reveal the situation, Ibbotson's calculation was more than supported by the findings of a social survey of Salisbury carried out by Professor Edward Batson and a team of social scientists from the University of Cape Town in July to September 1944. Batson was primarily concerned to assess the 'poverty datum line' in Salisbury, that is, to arrive at 'an estimate of the income needed by any individual household if it is to attain a defined minimum level of health and decency'. He calculated the lowest retail cost of a budget of necessaries: sufficient food essential for health, the minimum of clothing necessary for protection of health and conformity with standards of decency, and the minimum requirements of fuel, lighting, and cleaning materials. This, as he pointed out, by no means provided a 'human' standard of living: it made no allowance for amusement, medicine, education, holidays, tobacco, gifts, newspapers, or comforts of any kind, nor did it make any provision for blankets, furniture, or crockery. It was merely 'the barest

[14] 'Report on Urban Conditions in Southern Rhodesia', *African Studies*, March 1945.

minimum upon which subsistence and health can theoretically be achieved'.

Batson came to the conclusion that an African household consisting of a married couple and two young children would need £7. 7s. 4d. per month, and an unmarried man would need £3. 2s. 5d. per month, if these basic minimum needs—leaving out of consideration housing and transport—were to be satisfied.[15] A year earlier, it will be remembered, Ibbotson had put a married couple's needs at £4. 15s. per month; he had also found that 50 per cent. of the married Africans earning only a cash wage received less than £3 per month, and that of the total labour force 51 per cent. earned less than £1. 10s. per month exclusive of accommodation and some sort of rations. Since African wages had remained virtually stationary, Batson's survey revealed an even more serious situation.

Along the line of rail in Northern Rhodesia poverty among urban Africans was similarly general, though some of its effects were slightly mitigated by certain factors. A survey of Africans in Broken Hill carried out in 1939–40 by Godfrey Wilson, the Director of the newly-founded Rhodes–Livingstone Institute, showed that nearly 10 per cent. of the labour force were juveniles earning less than 10s. per thirty working days and that 60 per cent. were adults earning less than 20s. Just over half the total male population were married and 40 per cent. had their wives living with them. Children in the compounds were 'a heavy economic burden on their parents', and a man with four or five children in Broken Hill was normally 'a very poor man indeed'. In contrast to Southern Rhodesia, however, the large employers—the mines, the Railways, the Government—provided half rations for wives. In Broken Hill some 7,000 Africans were able also to supplement their livelihood from the fruits of five-acre plots, and the provisions for marketing low-priced African produce in the towns were considerably better than in Southern Rhodesia.[16]

Until the strike of March 1940 the wages of African miners on

[15] E. Batson, *The Poverty Line in Salisbury* (Cape Town, 1945).
[16] G. Wilson, *An Essay on the Economics of Detribalization in Northern Rhodesia*, Parts I and II (Livingstone, 1941, 1942).

the Copperbelt remained at the level to which they had fallen
during the depression of 1931–2, 'even though the prosperity of
the mines during the years immediately before the strike showed
remarkable strides'.[17] After the strike the Companies raised
African wages in all grades, and considerably increased the increments to be earned by longer periods of service. As a result the
average wage at Mufulira in August 1942 was 35s. 6d. per thirty
working days for surface workers and 52s. 11d. for underground
workers, a considerable increase on the 22s. 6d. and 30s. which
were the average wages for surface and underground workers
before the strike.[18] In the same year a missionary estimated, after
a careful study of family budgets, that the minimum wage needed
by a married man on the Copperbelt was 35s. a month. This included 10s. to be spent on food with which to supplement the
rations for his wife and family. Thus by 1942 the average wage of
African miners on the Copperbelt covered the estimated basic
minimum needs; but of course many men earned considerably
less than the average. The starting rates for completely unskilled
surface workers had only increased from 12s. 6d. to 15s. and those
underground from 22s. 6d. to 25s.—and all those who earned less
than the average, if their families were with them, were living
below the estimated subsistence level.[19] In 1943 an official report
summarized the situation in the following words:

> The psychological effect of the gap between wages and minimum
> expenditure cannot be over-stressed. Africans working on the mines
> are becoming increasingly conscious of the great gap between the
> wages paid to Europeans and those which they themselves receive. I
> have been impressed by the bitterness with which Africans speak of
> their wages. They declare openly that although it is they who do the
> work, it is the Europeans who get the money.[20]

The average wage of miners compared favourably with most
of the other wages on the Copperbelt. Conditions outside the

[17] *Report of Commission on Copperbelt Disturbances*, July 1940, para. 120.
[18] A. Lynn Saffery, *A Report on Some Aspects of African Living Conditions on the Copper-belt of Northern Rhodesia* (Lusaka, 1943), p. 71.
[19] R. J. B. Moore, 'Native Wages and Standard of Living in Northern Rhodesia', *African Studies*, Vol. 1, 1942, pp. 146–7.
[20] Saffery, p. 154.

mines varied considerably. There were, it was thought, at least 1,200 independent workers on the Copperbelt—traders, shoe-makers, carpenters, market gardeners, and curio-makers. Most of these men were married and they earned an estimated average of 74s. per month, a rate equal to the wage of the majority of Government clerks, but out of this they had of course to provide food and accommodation for themselves and their families. In Ndola in 1942 wages in secondary industries started at 17s. 6d. per thirty working days, a rise of 2s. 6d. since 1939. 'Increments', it was reported, 'are haphazard and meagre and it is seldom that an employee attains the 25s. notch even after many years of service. Contractors pay notoriously low wages . . . picannins at 7s. 6d. per ticket and adults at 12s. 6d. . . . At Nchanga one contractor pays only 10s. and never gives increases.'[21] And the provision for food and shelter, especially for wives and children, was generally far below that of the mines.

Poverty and a harsh struggle to provide even the barest necessities of life were thus a constant feature in the experience of the average African urban worker. For many this struggle was made even harder by certain facets of their environment or way of life often overlooked by many Europeans. The distance from their rural homelands to the new urban centres forced many Africans either to spend relatively large sums on transport or to waste a great deal of time on long and exhausting journeys by foot. In 1939, for instance, transport from Kasama, the capital of the neighbouring Bemba country, to Broken Hill cost 35s., the equivalent of two months' wages, an expenditure which could be avoided only by a seven weeks' trudge.[22] In Southern Rhodesia, ULERE, the Government's Free Migrant Labour Transport Service established in accordance with the 1936 Inter-territorial agreement,[23] was beginning to lighten the burden; but many immigrant workers still had to face long journeys and many of the Native Reserves in Southern Rhodesia itself were several days' journey from the place of work. The cost of these journeys might properly have been a charge on the economy of the country as a

[21] Saffery, p. 93.   [22] Wilson, op. cit., Part I, p. 49.
[23] See above, Part I, Chap. III, p. 127.

whole, since it was the policy of segregation and the reluctance to accept permanent urbanization which made them necessary. The cost was in fact borne primarily and directly by the worker.

Contact with the rural areas, it was true, had provided a degree of social security and old age insurance which alone had rendered possible a system of low wages. But this security was steadily becoming less adequate, and even inoperative in some cases, while its maintenance laid upon most migrant workers the necessity of saving considerable sums for gifts before they could expect a welcome from their rural relatives. The urban worker was also beset by importunate demands when visited by his rural kinsmen.[24] The impression, sincerely held by many Europeans, of a care-free, thriftless 'boy' indulging himself amidst the gay city lights, free to return easily and at whim to the indolence of the kraal, was far from correct; in many cases his link with the rural areas was financially a mixed blessing.

Daily transport also presented a problem to Africans working within the towns. In Bulawayo the distance from the Location to the industrial sites was at least two or three miles, and it was 'no longer correct to assume that the African could walk this distance on his bare feet' twice a day and work efficiently. A generation was growing up accustomed to some form of footwear, a development warmly welcomed by health authorities, and the cost in shoe-leather of a daily five-mile walk was not inconsiderable. Others who lived beyond the Location, in compounds on farms or at the Government's Village Settlement at Luveve, were faced with a longer journey which almost invariably necessitated the ownership and maintenance of a bicycle or heavy expenditure on bus fares—1s. daily in the case of Luveve.[25] The segregation of Africans several miles away from their place of employment was undertaken almost solely for the convenience of Europeans, but here again it was the African who had to pay.

There was another major factor, also often unperceived by Europeans, which raised the African's cost of living. Through

---

[24] Wilson, Part II, p. 36, and B. W. Gussman, *African Life in an Urban Area* (Bulawayo, typescript, 1952, 1953), p. 98.
[25] Gussman, op. cit., Part I, p. 94.

lack of credit, capital, and space, Africans had to buy food in small quantities and, in the long run, the extra cost was considerable. Purchasing mealie meal in small packets, for example, he had to pay 2s. more per month than if he had been able to buy in 100 lb. sacks, the usual basis for computing his cost of living. He often had to buy something more expensive than he would have chosen. The cheaper cuts of meat were often in short supply, and even when available were of dubious quality: an investigation in 1951 showed that Africans were paying 1s. 3d. a pound for meat that was 83 per cent. bone.[26] Nearly all his purchases had, in addition, to carry very heavy overhead charges. These began at the frontier, where most imports for the African market carried a fairly high tariff. The profits of wholesalers and retailers were high: it was said that an analysis of income-tax returns showed that 'the biggest fortunes made in this country have been made by wholesaling native truck',[27] and, although in part this might have been due to the traders' enterprise, one industrialist described to the Howman Committee how by bulk purchases for his employees he had reduced the cost of certain commodities by 50 per cent.[28] Finally, African shop-holders in the Locations generally exploited the convenience of their situation by charging higher prices than those in the main towns.[29]

There was, moreover, one part of an African's food the price of which was enormously increased by legislative and administrative action. In both the Rhodesias it was illegal for Africans to brew their own beer in urban areas. The Municipalities established beer-halls in the Locations, but charged exorbitantly high prices. 'It is obvious', reported the Howman Committee, 'that a state of semi-prohibition is brought about when a man earning 6d. to 8d. a day is confronted with beer priced at 6d. a cup.' Beer which could be made for less than 7d. was sold for 2s. a gallon, and the profits, which by law had to be devoted to 'welfare' purposes, were so enormous that Councillors—perhaps satisfied that every welfare need was met—publicly admitted that they were an

---

[26] Gussman, op. cit., Part I, p. 98.
[27] Evidence to the Howman Committee, p. 24.
[28] Ibid., p. 127.   [29] Gussman, op. cit., Part I, p. 92.

220 Awakenings: 1939-1953

inconvenience. In seven years the Bulawayo Council took a gross sum of £161,845 from sales of beer, of which £112,796 was pure profit. 'Had the Africans been given value for their money,' the Committee commented, 'it is probable that malnutrition in the city would not have reached the extreme that it now has.'[30]

There were other reasons besides that of price which caused Africans to drink and brew beer illegally—the dislike of the beer-hall's rowdy atmosphere and its lack of privacy, the inconvenience of an often distantly situated hall, dissatisfaction with the quality or strength of municipal beer, and the relative ease with which African women could use their new-found urban leisure in brewing their traditional drink—but the Committee had little doubt that the financial factor was predominant. The high price of municipal beer and the prohibition of private brewing, led to the making of 'skokiaan' and other powerful alcoholic brews, which were seriously bad for health. Wilson reported that 'practically every African married couple in Broken Hill brews beer privately',[31] and in Bulawayo skokiaan parties of 1,000 strong were not uncommon, while 'the special police (liquor) detachment was reduced to travelling in an armoured vehicle and had on occasion to use tear gas to break up illicit gatherings'.[32] Thus, the institution of municipal beer-halls not only raised the cost of a traditional food, rich in vitamins, but was also a constant inter-racial irritant and a source of conflict with the authorities, affecting and alienating respectable married couples along with the masses of migrant workers. Constant police raids on African homes in an attempt to suppress illegal brewing aroused hatred among Africans. On the other hand, Europeans justified the institution of the beer-hall by the need for firm European supervision over a mild and limited supply, and there was perhaps a scarcely formulated impression that an ineffective law was better than none. The fear of an uninhibited, savage crowd breaking forth from its bounds lay deep in the European memory. But to Africans the beer-hall was a striking example of the way in

[30] *Howman Report*, paras. 58–63. [31] Wilson, op. cit., Part II, p. 31.
[32] Information taken from Dr. Hugh Ashton's notes on the compilation of population figures.

which segregation, or the belief that the towns were by right part of the European's preserve, resulted in a rigid refusal to recognize the needs of urban Africans, intruded into the intimacies of their lives, and destroyed their happiness.

In addition to these factors which increased African poverty there was the handicap—much more readily recognized by Europeans—of 'unintelligent' spending on the part of the Africans themselves. Gramophones, like television sets in England, were to be found in homes with very little 'essential furniture and few household utensils'; excessive amounts were often spent on seldom-used crockery; and a number of Africans entered into hire-purchase agreements which they could not possibly fulfil.[33] Gambling, although illegal for Africans, was becoming fairly prevalent and several professional gamblers were earning substantial incomes.[34] This expenditure on 'luxuries', involving a deprivation of 'essentials', was of course a phenomenon by no means restricted to Africans, but in the case of Africans it was aggravated by certain aspects of their situation. There was not only the thrill of ready cash in the hands of the freshly-arrived novice and the bewildering change from communal subsistence to a cash economy; there was also the deep yearning to live like Europeans. This ambition found few satisfactory openings. With the sparse and rudimentary education available, only a few individuals could grasp the intellectual substance of European civilization. Urban Africans were virtually precluded from making any substantial investments in the European's economy: they were not permitted to buy an urban home, commercial openings were limited, there was little incentive or opportunity to save. Only the trappings of European life remained. Clothes assumed an enormous significance and became the symbol of the search for dignity and respect. Wilson describes how in Broken Hill 'clothes are discussed unceasingly, in much the same way that I have heard primitive villagers discuss their cattle; they are tended lovingly and carefully housed in boxes at night'. Clothes were the chief presents given to country relatives, and thus incidentally were the principal mode of saving, and the search

---

[33] Ibbotson, op. cit.   [34] Gussman, op. cit., p. 238.

for a status comparable to that of Europeans reached its climax in the European evening dress worn at superior dance clubs.[35] Yet these extravagances should not obscure the realities of daily life for the urban African and, as Ibbotson pointed out, the fact that the majority of married Africans were in debt was due not so much to unwise spending as to the low wages received.[36]

By the end of 1943 there was, then, considerable evidence of widespread poverty among urban Africans. Married men and their families were particularly affected, but large numbers of men officially considered to be single were also receiving a totally inadequate wage. Many of them were in fact married and were expected to send money to their wives in the Reserves and to educate their children; those who were in fact unmarried were probably saving for 'lobola'. And whether married or not most 'single' men were living with a girl-friend in the town. The old assumptions on which the low wages had originally been justified were no longer valid. A whole range of new, and on the whole necessary, expenditure had developed, and the rising prices due to the war underlined the inadequacy of the old wages. In the face of this gap between wages and expenditure how in fact did the African manage to survive? It was a question which perplexed some Europeans. One industrialist, for instance, dismissed Ibbotson's estimate of the cost of living for a married man on the grounds that it could not be 'an actual fact', because, he said, 'our boys go on year after year, and there is always a gang waiting to come'.[37] To a large extent rural poverty explained the waiting, unemployed gang, drawn from the Reserves and all the neighbouring territories in Central Africa; but they survived in the towns only because of the various expedients they were driven to adopt.

Some wives took in European washing and others went out to work, leaving their children under the spasmodic care of a neighbour or an older child. Even more damaging to family life and parental discipline was the widespread device of augmenting

[35] Wilson, op. cit., Part II, p. 18.   [36] Ibbotson, op. cit.
[37] Evidence to Howman Committee, pp. 374–6.

the family income by juvenile employment.[38] Many men found odd jobs outside working hours such as haircutting, carpentry, teaching, photography, tailoring, porterage, and newspaper selling. A few men practised as witch doctors. Other households took in lodgers, and most unmarried girls and young women supported themselves by some form of concubinage. Liquor brewing was the commonest and most remunerative means of earning additional income, and although illegal it was by no means performed only by the more criminal or unstable members of the community. 'One highly respected woman resident of Luveve' admitted to one investigator that she could 'only keep her son at secondary school in the Union by brewing over week-ends'; and the African Welfare Society at Luveve, composed of moderate, middle-class leaders, petitioned the Government not to expel residents from their homes should they be found in possession of illegal liquor.[39] Petty thieving and pilfering, often from European employers, were widespread. In 1943 it was reported that petty theft on the Copperbelt had 'increased enormously during the last two years'.[40] Among the more respectable sections this expedient took the shape of requests for charity. 'A good, honest, and God-fearing man of high intelligence', with a wife and ten children to support, who 'if he were not so religious would probably be a successful criminal', was known by the Native Commissioner at Hartley to cover his monthly shortfall 'by debts at the local stores and polite begging'.[41] Above all, many Africans were forced to economize on essential foodstuffs. Shopkeepers reported a dramatic fall in the level of food consumption towards the end of the month,[42] and medical evidence given to the Howman Committee was 'almost unanimous in stating that malnutrition is seriously prevalent everywhere in the urban areas, particularly amongst the factory (labourer) class'. Domestic servants alone were well-fed, for the kitchen 'legitimately and illegitimately' provided a variety of foodstuffs. For the

[38] See below, Part II, Chap. III, pp. 264–5.
[39] Gussman, op. cit., pp. 101–4. [40] Saffery, p. 152.
[41] Evidence to the Howman Committee, memorandum submitted by the Native Commissioner, Hartley.
[42] Ibid., p. 348.

Q

rest low wages and inadequate rations meant hunger and in-efficiency.[43]

Engaged in this, at times, desperate attempt to meet the dis-crepancy between income and expenditure, Africans began to find in the question of wages a focus for their discontent. In March 1940, shortly after the European mine-workers had success-fully struck for a war bonus to meet the increased cost of living, African miners stopped working at Mufulira and Nkana. A state of confusion ensued during which the tribal elders recognized by the mine authorities were superseded at Nkana by a committee of seventeen 'ringleaders'. At a meeting with Government officials these men demanded a wage of 10s. a day. They alleged that African workers did all the work for which the Europeans were paid. They gave 'graphic descriptions' of the European ganger at work, of his alleged abuse of his natives and of his alleged laziness and inefficiency. They complained that no com-pensation was paid to relatives of men who died of sickness.[44]

Confusion and tension increased for several days and cul-minated in a riot on 3 April, when a crowd of about 3,000 Africans attacked the Nkana compound office. Twenty African policemen and soldiers were wounded by stones and clubs, seventeen African strikers were killed and sixty-five were wounded by rifle-fire. One missionary eye-witness of the riot described how 'a comparatively small minority of the Natives at Nkana had established an ascendancy over the minds of the majority of their fellows. . . . Any suggestion of reasonableness was howled down. One man who dared to suggest lowering the demand from 5s. to 3s. per day was roughly treated.' On Wednesday, 3 April, as the crowd moved up to the compound office, 'many of them were like schoolboys out for a rag,' but as the stone-throwing started they became 'a completely wild mob'. Tear-gas bombs had no effect. 'Smoke rose and passed away and the crowd came on. It was a glimpse of savagery we shall not forget. A few minutes later we heard firing. We were shocked and humiliated, but at the same time had to agree that at that particular moment the

[43] *Howman Report*, paras. 2, 34.
[44] *Report of Commission of Inquiry into Copperbelt Disturbances*, July 1940, para. 86.

officer in charge of the troops had no alternative but to give the
order. The room we were in was a mass of terrified Africans and
several Europeans, some of whom were in an abject state of
terror'. That night there was 'a reign of terror' in the Nkana and
Kitwe compounds. 'Compound clerks and police had to watch
their houses being looted and their belongings set on fire. . . .
Hundreds of frightened people ran away into the bush to spend
the night there. But this was the last of the trouble. . . . On
Friday 80 per cent. of the Nkana men were at work again (to
the amazement of us all) and on Monday 100 per cent. of the
employees were at work. . . . Our impression was of a real relief
being felt by the large majority who all along had been wanting
to resume work.' But the memories remained. 'We shall never
forget the absolute silence of Wednesday night', when dumb
sorrow 'seemed to hang like a pall' over the Africans at Mindolo,
a nearby compound. The missionaries felt keenly that 'confidence
had been lost and might be difficult to recover (perhaps it never
will be completely recovered) in relationships between white
and black'.[45]

In Southern Rhodesia African reactions to urban poverty were
at first less dramatic, and there was less criticism on a comparison
with the European's work and wage-packet. Here, it seems, the
white man's régime and standard of living were accepted as part
of the order of things with far less question than they ever were
on the Copperbelt.[46] Widespread discontent and resentment were,
however, unhesitatingly expressed by the Africans who gave
evidence to the Howman Committee. Aaron Koanza, chairman
of the African Welfare Association at Que Que, who had been
in the town for fifteen years said:

I want to talk about the living wage which is the trouble amongst the
African people. We don't just want to have high wages, we want
wages that will enable us to live. We don't only need mealie meal and
meat but other things too which are home and life necessities. . . .
There are many town people suffering in spirit and body owing to too

[45] A letter from the United Missions in the Copperbelt, 9 April 1940, to the International
Missionary Council, kept in their archives at Edinburgh House.
[46] Cf. above, Part I, Chap. V, pp. 190–2.

low wages. As a result of the low rates of pay we are forced to commit crimes such as stealing and gambling. There is a saying in English 'necessity knows no law' and that applies to the African. . . . We are forced to live in unhygienic ways which result in the death of young and old.

Proximity to Europeans was raising the Africans' needs and aspirations, education was passionately desired, but was a heavy financial burden, and prices, 'particularly in the Indian and Jewish stores dealing with Africans', were rocketing upwards.

'Our only purpose in coming to this meeting is that we want to speak about the money,' declared the Bulawayo representatives of the Native Welfare Society, the Matabele Home Society, Nyasa African Labour Council, Barotse Improvement, Railway Bantu Benefit Society, Manyika United Society, store-keepers, waiters, railwaymen, the *Bantu Mirror*, and the Ministers Fraternal. Their plight was common, their plaint was unanimous. 'The stomach is not like clothing . . . if we are stealing in the stores it is because we are starving.' Rations were inadequate and had in fact been reduced for eighteen months on the Railways owing to a shortage of mealie meal, yet 'the pay is not enough because it is said that rations are given'. Men found it difficult to return to their kraals because they had 'nothing to take back' and were therefore ashamed.

Many of these leaders had become permanent town-dwellers. Those with families found life particularly difficult: 'We are encouraged to send our children to school. We are encouraged to bring up our children in the right ways of cleanliness, but how can we do it?' Those who were growing old faced a desolate future: 'I have grown up under the white people. My wish is that the Committee should see to it that we get better treatment in the way of wages. Today I am getting older and I have done nothing. I have not saved anything. I might die and not know how my children are going to manage.' And a man who had worked as a tailor with the Bulawayo Clothing Factory for twenty-three years added: 'I have already been told I am getting an old man. What is going to be done?' There was bitterness also as they told how they had 'lost many people by the Limpopo River eaten by lions trying to get where there is money' (emigration to the Union was illegal), and later at Makabusi Police Camp as an African policeman told of a visit to a tobacco factory: 'I found little boys of about seven to eight years trying to work. They are trying to work because their fathers have no support for children. They live in dark and dirty places and most of them were coughing. They will not grow into good men. They will die before they come to be men.' Another policeman, who maintained that an urban African and his family could not possibly live under £5 a month, roundly declared that 'it would be better for us Africans to be unemployed than paid at £1 a month'.[47]

In nineteenth-century England, when country labourers found themselves immersed in urban poverty, there was bitterness against the employers. But even at Peterloo the magistrates and the mob had much in common—a long tradition of living together in the same land—and parentage did not inexorably divide individuals into two camps instantly recognizable at sight. In Rhodesia, with the rigid racial division, it seemed only too likely that the wave of African discontent would turn against the European community as a whole. White men would be blamed not only for their racial policies but also for the hardships for which the African's total unpreparedness for rapid industrialization was primarily responsible. It was nobody's fault that in Rhodesia employers were white and came from a far land; but the danger and the difficulties increased when black labourers were excluded from political power.

Most Europeans in Southern Rhodesia were either unconcerned or hostile to any idea of raising African wages. Eastwood's modest proposal for a minimum wage of 45s. where no housing or rations were provided was at first received with amusement in some quarters of the Legislative Assembly. This hostility was partly due to economic factors. Farming members maintained that they paid their natives 'remarkably well',[48] and the pervasive influence of the agricultural interest was further demonstrated in

[47] Evidence to the Howman Committee, pp. 238, 294–8, 336, 394.
[48] Southern Rhodesian Debates, 2 June 1943, col. 1364, and 9 June 1943, col. 1594.

evidence given to the Howman Committee. A senior official of the Native Affairs Department warned the Committee that if a minimum wage was introduced in the towns 'you are bound to have repercussions amongst the farming community and today the farming community rules this country so that flattens out the minimum wage straight away'. A divisional engineer described how the 'reactions of the public' influenced wage rates in the Department of Posts and Telegraphs, adding that the farmers particularly were 'inclined to be very critical' of any conditions more favourable than they were able to give, and a Bulawayo building contractor reported that builders in Salisbury said that 'they cannot increase their wages to a very high amount because of the farming industry'.[49]

In contrast to the farmers, the opinions of industrialists were somewhat ambivalent. Many recognized in general terms the advisability of increasing African spending-power and the desirability of a more stable and contented labour force. Some of them even admitted that industry could easily bear an increase in African wages, which were a small portion of the actual cost. Few, however, were prepared to give a lead or to advocate any real change which might affect the European's position. The manager of a large tobacco factory, for example, while declaring that he was 'willing to pay as well as anyone', for 'the more money a Native gets, the more money is put into circulation', insisted that the employment of picannins and juveniles (big picannins) was essential and that 'there was no other alternative'. Yet these children and juveniles worked long hours. Starting at 6 a.m., they finished 'at all hours these days' in conditions which, as we have seen, aroused bitter resentment among Africans.[50] And it was on the whole the more progressive and liberal-minded men who bothered to give evidence to the Committee; the attitude of the majority of the employers was reflected in their reactions when they were questioned on African wages by the Junior Chamber of Commerce at Bulawayo: 'They were rather shocked, I'm afraid,' said Mr. J. C. Fletcher, the Chamber's spokesman.

[49] Evidence to the Howman Committee, pp. 122, 299, 390.
[50] See above, p. 226.

'It seems to me that a lot of them had never thought of the matter at all.'[51]

This unconcern had a powerful ally in the concept of segregation. The towns were part of the white man's world. There his interests alone should be considered and his outlook should prevail. The black man's needs and security were to be provided for in the Reserves; there was the centre and focus for his life, and his periods of labour for European employers were merely brief interruptions. Mr. Robert Tredgold, Minister of Justice and Defence, vindicating the severity of the fines imposed by his Department on Africans, told the Legislative Assembly in May 1941 not to 'consider the thing on the basis that a native's wages and a white man's wages are on the same footing, because they are not. The native's wages are pocket money.' After being taken up by Eastwood, the Minister qualified this statement.[52] But that a man of such high character, and so soon to be universally respected as a foremost advocate of inter-racial harmony and justice, especially in this matter of urban wages,[53] should have thought in this way is perhaps the most vivid illustration of the extent to which segregation coloured European thought, and of the revolutionary change which was to take place in the approach of some white Rhodesians. As has been seen, a nucleus was already deeply concerned over the plight of the urban African. But the efforts of Ibbotson, Eastwood, Wilson, and Batson, and the organizations they represented, together with the evidence laid before the Howman Committee, achieved no immediate results. Their recommendations remained unimplemented until the dangers of inaction were suddenly exposed by the strikes of 1945 and 1948. In the meanwhile they also drew attention to the question of African labour efficiency and the broader problems of urban life.

[51] Evidence to the Howman Committee, pp. 308, 311, 374–6.
[52] 'I recognise there are natives in urban areas who have to find their own living, but normally those natives would draw a relatively higher rate of pay. I did not say in every case a native's money could be regarded as pocket money; I simply suggested it was a factor to be borne in mind.'
[53] See below, Part I, Chap. IV, p. 284.

2. PRODUCTIVITY

While the cost of living was the facet of industrialization most evident to the African, the European was increasingly preoccupied with the problems of African productivity. The manager and foreman joined the farmer, the miner and the housewife in what sometimes seemed a hopeless, unending search for dependable labour. Complaints of laziness and lack of stamina, of clumsiness and unadaptability, of chronic absenteeism and complete disregard of contracts, of insolence and indiscipline, were almost ubiquitous. With an African population of 18,000 in Bulawayo it was estimated that 'probably 1,000 "Master and Servant" cases were attended to by the N.C. and A.N.C. during the six months ended 31 July 1943. Over a year this means that one out of every nine Natives is concerned in some trouble and this ratio does not allow for Magistrate's court cases and admonishments by the Police who are always being called upon.'[54] The damaging effects of this constant irritant coloured many Europeans' whole conception of African character; and the question of raising African efficiency was crucial to the permanent success of industrialization in Central Africa. Satisfactory wages and the complete corpus of welfare measures needed to support an emergent urban community could ultimately be maintained only by a radical and unimpeded increase in productivity. And as observers began to study this problem it soon became evident that by no means all the obstacles to this increase were caused by African ignorance and ineptitude. The situation also demanded an immense readjustment from Europeans.

One large section of African urban employees, although separate from the main industrial labour force, occupied a prominent place in inter-racial relations. In 1946 nearly one-third of the Africans employed in Bulawayo and Salisbury were working in domestic service, and the vast majority of domestic servants were male: 92·5 per cent. in 1946, and 88·8 per cent. in 1951. This serious waste of potential productive labour was a source of complaint among thoughtful Africans as well as farmers

[54] Evidence to the Howman Committee, p. 56.

and other Europeans short of labour.[55] These servants, however, were reluctant to change their employment. Domestic service demanded a certain standard of English and a knowledge of European domestic arrangements and cooking. Men with these skills, slight as they often were, were naturally unwilling to venture into the wider labour market, where nearly all openings for Africans were still severely restricted to unskilled labour.[56] Their material position also compared favourably with that of industrial workers. Since they received rations, accommodation, old clothing, and a plentiful supply of food scraps, their wages were often indeed merely 'pocket money'. They were separated, as one observer noted, from the 'hurly-burly of Location life'. They experienced few of the tensions of urban life and they took little part in political organizations.[57] Their replacement by women was moreover made impracticable by the lack of provision for a stable urban family life. In the prevalent overcrowding there was little accommodation in the African urban areas for single girls, who therefore either returned to the Reserves or maintained themselves by concubinage. And concubines soon protested that scrubbing or hard manual labour was 'boy's work'. Married women, although anxious to work, had nowhere to leave their children away from home.[58] Until there were widespread openings for Africans to use their skill in industry, and until provision was made for settled urban life, the productive labour of thousands of Africans would remain a wasted asset.

But it was not only as a wasted asset but also as a source of friction that domestic servants played a prominent part in interracial relations. The worst and most damaging tensions occurred in the households of newly-arrived immigrants. 'It is an unpleasant experience', said an official of the Native Affairs Department, 'to witness the humanitarian, generous impulses of English couples change into virulent detestation of the Native under the influence of household troubles.' There were, of course, faults on both sides —'many Europeans are quite unconscious of their own rudeness

---

[55] E.g. a letter from L. C. Vambe in *The New Rhodesia*, 7 May 1948.
[56] See below, pp. 240–50.   [57] Gussman, op. cit., p. 71.
[58] *The New Rhodesia*, 7 May 1948.

to Natives which provokes retaliation'—but there was a weight of evidence to show that, in Bulawayo at least, it was 'no exaggeration to say that there is a spirit of insolence, irresponsibility, and deliberate disregard of kindliness and attempts to teach him on the part of the Native, and a spirit of helplessness, disillusion and racial bitterness on the part of the European'.[59]

These difficulties were partly caused by the arrival of the R.A.F. in Bulawayo during the war and afterwards by the increased tempo of immigration, which, by greatly increasing the demand for servants, inevitably diluted the quality of their service. More fundamentally, however, these troubles reflected the corroding influence of instability. Young peasants pitchforked temporarily into a wage-economy were casual and irresponsible. For most of them dismissal was no great hardship. On the other hand, good, steady service was seldom rewarded substantially, while a potentially loyal and capable servant was often slighted and shown distrust, which quickly led to a loss of self-respect. 'In the general chaos the good servant is not only indistinguishable but the professional thief, the truculent waster and the general riff-raff of the location are free and able to prey on the housewife and her home.'[60] This situation could be expected to improve only when a large measure of stabilization was achieved, and when a premium was set on efficiency. Meanwhile most Europeans when confronted with the daily struggle in the home forgot this sociological background and became convinced that their trials sprang from the ineradicably primitive, racial characteristics of the African.

Domestic servants were conspicuous not only in forming the European's conception of the African, but also in shaping the African's impression of European character. They were the principal source of inside information on the 'private lives' of their masters and mistresses. As groups of Africans eagerly listened to the latest purveyor of gossip, the mask of the European was stripped off and the ordinary human being revealed. For the picture, which missionary education had sometimes painted, of a firm, unbending moralist, an almost superhuman being, there was

[59] Evidence to the Howman Committee, pp. 57–8, 277.   [60] Ibid.

suddenly substituted an equally exaggerated impression of hollow hypocrisy and insincerity.

Stories of the seduction of African servants by European mistresses are bandied around and, whether true or false, create the view that the European is a very much more venal creature than the African. With the existing morality laws punishing an African for intercourse with a European woman, irrespective of where the fault lies, while a European man can seduce as many African women as he chooses, such tales emanating from domestic servants add fuel to the ever simmering fires of race relations.[61]

Stereotypes, rigid conceptions of group characteristics, inevitably distort and obstruct the relationships between individuals of different groups, even where, as in Western Europe, the groups are often physically indistinguishable. In cases where colour vividly and immediately identifies the individual the danger of rigid thinking is increased; and in Central Africa, where personal contacts are so strictly limited, the portraits formed on both sides, by the media of domestic servants, were of disastrous consequence.

In the main fields of secondary production many European employers were convinced that the African was chronically incapable of satisfying the demands of modern industry. The principal counts in the indictment were absenteeism, the rapid turnover of employees, and the low average output. In Southern Rhodesia the Commissioner of Native Labour reported in 1948 that 'the curse of the Colony as far as African labour is concerned is, without question, absenteeism. Apart from the disastrous effect it has on output as a whole, it is the principal cause of disturbed relations between European employer and African employee for it probably engenders more outright exasperation than any other form of misdemeanour.'[62] A contractor in Salisbury told the Howman Committee that he needed a 10 per cent. surplus constantly on hand to meet the fluctuating absentee shortage. A Bulawayo miller thought this was 'slightly exaggerated' but he admitted to having 'great trouble' from absenteeism on Mondays, while other industrialists reported how they maintained thirty out

---

[61] Gussman, op. cit., Part I, p. 71.
[62] *Report of the Chief Native Commissioner for 1948*, p. 48.

of 108 and twenty out of 150 men as a permanent 'surplus', a brickmaker adding: 'As a matter of fact I never know how many I have.'[63] Desertion and a constant turnover caused much inefficiency. 'Once they have learnt the work they leave me,' said the owner of a laundry and dry cleaners. 'We waste a lot of time teaching the natives.' An industrialist, after mentioning that he had a few old hands who had worked for twenty years with his firm, added: 'They are still unskilled, and they will let you down, as all Natives do, just when you want them.' And a miller in Salisbury with 250 labourers said that his experience had been 'that very few natives respond to really good treatment', not more than 5 or 10 per cent. ever becoming permanent.[64]

The low average output was variously explained. Many employers resignedly accepted it as due to the laziness ingrained by many slothful generations of kraal life; others complained of the lack of stamina, the general lassitude, and debility of their African workers. Some attributed it to sheer ineptitude: 'We have always found that 30 per cent. of the boys are stupid . . . only good for lifting sacks. . . . If I tell a boy to fill five drums you will find later he has done four or six.'[65] Others mentioned the lack of proper supervision, and many maintained that in the existing circumstances money was an insufficient incentive to harder work. When Africans were put on piece-work it was often found that they could easily increase their output and would work rapidly and efficiently in order to have longer periods of leisure. Among the numerous Africans who appeared before the Howman Committee 'only one correlated the amount of pay received with the value of the services performed',[66] and many employees considered that it was positively dangerous to reward good work with increased wages, so great was the apparent gulf between the 'native mentality' and that of Europeans.

You have to be careful because once you show a native that he is really good you get to a stage where you may as well sack him because he gets it into his head that you cannot do without him. I give my boss

---

[63] Evidence to Howman Committee, pp. 207, 289, 291.
[64] Ibid., pp. 204, 217, 288.　　　　　　[65] Ibid., p. 179.
[66] *Howman Report on Urban Conditions* . . . para. 12.

boy £1 a week, but if I were fair this boy should be getting £3 a week at least, but I dare not give that amount because that would be the end of him. In no time he would not want to work any longer and would leave.[67]

In the general irritation and bitterness engendered by these experiences many Europeans lost sight of certain of the factors which might have been expected to prevent Africans from giving of their best, and were inclined to attribute all their difficulties to ineradicable aspects, real or imagined, of the African's character. In the absence of any thorough study of industrial relations it was impossible to check accurately the incidence of labour absenteeism and turnover. A small survey in Bulawayo carried out by B. W. Gussman suggested that the overall incidence did not in fact compare too unfavourably with that found in industrial enterprises elsewhere, but it did also demonstrate that there were wide variations between individual undertakings and that in some of these the situation was serious. These variations could partly be explained by the level of supervision and the standards of working conditions in the factories. The casual attitude of many Africans towards their work was paralleled by that of several employers to their labour force. In one factory, for instance, where 73 per cent. of the African employees had been with the firm for less than six months, 'the work was dirty and washing facilities were extremely limited. No food was provided at mid-day, no protective clothing was issued, machinery lacked safety devices and the whole lay-out resembled in its drabness, its dirtiness and its lack of organization, the type of factory that existed in industrial Britain before the days of the Factory Act. Supervision was exercised by the type of person who believed that foul-mouthed invective in a native tongue was the best corrective.'[68]

There was other evidence that the rapidity of industrialization, coupled with a lack of control, was producing many instances of bad working conditions which naturally affected productivity.

[67] Evidence to the Howman Committee, p. 174. See also an admirable exposition of this point of view in 'Advice to New Settlers on the treatment of Native servants', *The New Rhodesia*, 2 January 1948.

[68] Gussman, op. cit., Part I, pp. 59–66.

The Chairman of the Industrial Development Advisory Committee told the Howman Committee that conditions in the clothing industry were, with a few honourable exceptions, 'really bad', that in several saw mills all over the country 'natives were being employed on operating circular saws under the most appalling conditions', and that one toy factory in Salisbury with 'a very satisfactory balance sheet' was 'cluttered up with machines and natives falling over each other, mostly of the juvenile type'. The owner of the brickworks, who has already been quoted on the subject of absenteeism and who also had considerable trouble from desertions, admitted that conditions were bad and conducive to pneumonia. 'Especially this last twelve or eighteen months we have been very pushed for bricks. Normally we don't look at a kiln until it is nice and cold; but we have had to go into kilns with pretty steep temperatures. Though in England a lot of womenfolk unload "continuous" kilns where you can see the white heat further down from where you are working, unless you are trained to it you cannot stick it at all.' It is not surprising that this employer found it necessary to be 'exceedingly firm' with Africans. 'If you are at all soft you haven't got a snowball's hope . . . they will take every advantage of you they can. Down there we stand no nonsense and they don't report me.' One factory manager said, 'I was astounded when I came to this country at the way the natives were treated, particularly in the building trade. Whatever happens the native is abused and insulted and often there is no justification and it must cause resentment.'[69]

Food and health had an obvious influence on African efficiency. Employers' complaints were not the only evidence of lassitude and lack of stamina. Chemists who specialized in trade with Africans found that 'tonics', 'fattening mixtures', and 'pick-me-ups' were a major line, and the *Bantu Mirror* carried expensive advertisements whose theme was 'prevent that tired feeling'.[70] The doctor in charge of recruit examinations at Nkana on the Copperbelt stated that the great majority of rejections were due to malnutrition.[71] The severe effect of inadequate wages on food

[69] Evidence to the Howman Committee, pp. 292, 370, 372, 391.
[70] Ibid., p. 55.   [71] Saffrey, op. cit., para. 142.

consumption has already been noted.[72] In addition to malnutrition, the intestinal diseases and other infestations such as bilharzia and hookworm were seriously prevalent. It was estimated that probably 70 per cent. of African workers were infected and one medical witness to the Howman Committee commented: 'Most cases of lazy Natives are due to hookworm, bilharzia or chronic malaria.'[73] Some firms readily recognized the importance of proper feeding arrangements. One employer who provided a breakfast of tea, sugar, and bread, and 'a really good meal' of meat and vegetables at mid-day, found that 'we now have about sixty boys doing the work which was previously done by about 110 boys'.[74] Other employers, however, were less heedful. One industrialist, who prided himself on his 'personal interest' in his African labour force, confessed: 'I don't know what these boys do in the lunch hour about their food. It is a mystery.' The Howman Committee was 'particularly struck by the complete ignorance and lack of interest displayed by so many employers as to the manner in which their workers feed themselves . . . and then they hold forth on "the damned lazy nigger who won't work"'.[75]

Employers were apt to overlook the effect of factory conditions, feeding, and health on African productivity; they also often ignored the damage inflicted by segregation, or the belief that the towns must be kept 'white'. In Central Africa the migrant worker had no doubt been an inevitable phenomenon during the transition from a tribal peasantry to an industrial community; in many ways it was fortunate for both employer and employee that when the worker went home to the Reserves there was a periodical escape from the tensions of this transition. But the policy of segregation and the attitudes which accompanied it refused to recognize that the worker could not always continue to be migrant. It made no provision for the African peasant to develop into a responsible member of an industrial community. Thus besides the material and physical vicissitudes which beset

[72] See above, p. 223.   [73] *Report on Urban Conditions*, para. 35.
[74] Evidence to the Howman Committee, p. 127.
[75] *Report on Urban Conditions*, para. 45.

urban Africans—the inadequate housing, the often squalid poverty, malnutrition, and debilitating diseases—they were constantly frustrated. Urban security in the shape of home-ownership and the possession of productive property was denied to them. A few with the necessary skills were able to invest in sewing-machines or carpentry and cobbling tools which could provide a means of subsistence for persons unfitted for heavy labour. A small number—about ninety in Bulawayo in 1950[76]— were able to rent premises in the Location in order to engage in small trading businesses, but with little or no training in shop-keeping their profits were rarely substantial and, when they occurred, were often appropriated by exacting relatives. Apart from the purchase of gifts for rural relatives and the acquisition of cattle in the Reserves—increasingly difficult as a result of the de-stocking policy—there were practically no means for urban Africans to provide for the future. A few of the larger industrial concerns offered rewards for exceptionally long service, but a gratuity of even fifty pounds after twenty or twenty-five years' continuous employment with one firm, although it enabled a man to return honourably to his Reserve, was completely in-adequate for those who had lost contact with their rural origins. Segregation, therefore, denied to the urban African the basic and urgent human need of roots, of a sense of belonging in the society in which he found himself. It put a premium on irresponsi-bility; apart from the dreary struggle to eke out a mean existence, the African had little incentive to raise his purchasing power. Money could do little in the way of providing substantial security or even prestige. In these circumstances it is not sur-prising that the beer-hall and the skokiaan session, like the gin palace in early industrial England, offered the commonest means of escape.

The complexity of the psychological background to African urban inefficiency was revealed in a psycho-analysis of John Chavafambira, a Manyika diviner whose home was near Umtali. Although the analysis was conducted in the years preceding the Second World War and was mainly concerned with his experi-

---

[76] Gussman, op. cit., p. 80.

ences in Johannesburg, many of the findings are applicable to post-war conditions in Rhodesia. It was found that John's tragedy, 'like that of so many Africans', was that he lacked the drive and perseverance necessary for achievement. His personality seemed to condemn him to drift through life an ineffective failure. When he was confronted with a difficulty his chosen solution was renunciation and flight, or, if this was impossible, a resigned submission to suffering. He could, for instance, never refuse a request, but preferred to make promises which he knew he could not keep. In his case this indecision and ineffectiveness were partly explicable in the purely personal terms of an Oedipus complex, but were greatly intensified by the tensions to which John, in common with other urban Africans, was subjected.

John's early training and childhood in a kraal surrounded by the forces of magic fostered a fatalistic approach to life. There was little reliance on individual reasoning and not much strengthening of the will-power of the individual. In later years this was not offset by any true and deep educative contact with the modern world. He grew up therefore with virtually no idea of scientific cause and effect, he had no developed sense of reality, and as a result he was often swept into a completely groundless optimism or a bleak void of despair. He found himself beset with fear. On the one side there was the world of his childhood and his ancestors, a world whose sanctions were still naturally most real, especially to one of his profession. Then as he moved into urban life there were new and overpowering anxieties. In all sorts of daily situations he constantly encountered what seemed to be an inexplicable and unrelieved weight of European hostility. Individuals, police, and regulations bullied, dragooned, and bewildered him. He was suddenly exposed to a host of incomprehensible dangers for which his previous experience offered him no remedy or defence. Since he was both sensitive and intelligent he was engaged in a continual attempt to reconcile the new and the traditional modes of life, an attempt which consumed an enormous amount of mental energy.[77]

[77] Wulf Sachs, *Black Hamlet: the Mind of an African Negro Revealed by Psycho-analysis* (1937), pp. 174–6.

R

It is dangerous to generalize from one instance, and against the failure of John Chavafambira must be set the astonishing success of scores of Africans who surmounted similar difficulties. Nevertheless there can be little doubt that the conflict of cultures, the constant necessity of choice and action in completely unfamiliar situations, must have imposed an enormous strain on countless urban workers, with inevitable consequences on their level of production. Europeans found Africans completely unprepared for the complexities of industrial life; they recognized this, but failed to provide the help that was surely needed if a secure urban society was to be built. Indeed, they stood in its way, yet such security was a condition of efficiency.

In the early years this failure was at least partly due to a lack of imagination and an almost complete ignorance of the conditions under which Africans lived in the towns. But it soon became clear that there was positive opposition. As the evidence accumulated and the results became manifest in explosions of unrest, the need for stabilization began to be accepted.[78] Yet segregation in its urban aspects implied not only a refusal to permit Africans to establish permanently their families and institutions in the towns; it also consisted of a determination to prevent them from advancing, with their lower rates of pay, into the jobs held by European artisans and semi-skilled workers. The colour bar acquired an increasing importance in the post-war years. It was intimately connected with the whole problem of African productivity: on the one hand experience of irresponsibility and ineptitude in the mass of Africans caused some Europeans to question the possibility of advancing even an *élite* few; and on the other hand the severely restricted opportunity for Africans to obtain and practise skills was a serious waste of potential labour and a deeply frustrating barrier to the African. It was indeed impossible to envisage a stable, contented industrial community unless this skill was rapidly developed and harnessed.

There was an effective, if somewhat disguised, colour bar in the principal industries in both the Rhodesias. In Southern Rhodesia it was entrenched, legally though indirectly, in the Industrial

[78] See below, Part II, Chap. IV.

Conciliation Act;[79] in Northern Rhodesia, although the Under-Secretary of State for the Colonies declared in the House of Commons in March 1941 that 'the Colonial Office and the Government do not stand for the colour bar in this country or in any of the Colonies',[80] the barrier was in that very year being consolidated on the Copperbelt. During the disturbances in 1940 [81] the Africans publicized their frustration at their exclusion from skilled work by challenging the Europeans to a production test, one shift to be worked by Europeans and the other by Africans. The Commission appointed to inquire into the disturbances recommended that 'the mine managements should consider with representatives of the Government and the Northern Rhodesia Mine Workers' Union to what positions, not now open to him, the African worker should be encouraged to advance'. The issue was complicated and made more urgent by the vital importance to the Allied war effort of a maximum production of copper, which it was thought would make it necessary to employ Africans in work previously undertaken by Europeans. In July 1940 the Union agreed to this dilution on condition that their members would be re-installed after the war. In fact many of the vacancies were filled by immigrant Europeans and dilution was 'negligible'.[82] The Union also pressed its claim for a 'closed-shop' agreement with the Companies, which, since Africans were debarred from Union membership, was tantamount to enforcing a rigid colour bar. This was rejected by the Companies in 1940, but the following year the Union renewed their claim and the Companies, 'being again told by the Government of the United Kingdom to allow nothing to interfere with copper production, felt obliged to concede it'. Immediately after the war the Companies were still apparently unable to reopen the question. The agreement with the Union was given further recognition. Early in 1946 the clause permitting dilution of labour was deleted and the 'closed shop' was entrenched in the following clause:

[79] See above, Part I, Chap. III, pp. 102–3.
[80] Quoted by J. Lewin, *The Colour Bar in the Copper Belt.*   [81] See above, p. 224.
[82] Government statement on the Report of the Commission appointed to inquire into the disturbances in the Copperbelt, Lusaka, 18 February 1941.

The Company agrees that work of the class or grade that is being performed, or job that is being filled, by an employee at the time of the signing of this agreement shall not be given to persons to whom the terms and conditions of this agreement do not apply.[83]

In the short space of less than ten years the European Union had thus established an apparently impregnable position. The tentative 'gentleman's agreement' of 1938[84] had been consolidated into the binding contracts of 1941 and 1946. At the same time, however, outside observers were beginning to realize that the Copperbelt might well become 'the battle-ground for the colour bar' in Southern Africa. On the one side the conflict seemed to involve not only a principle—'that of the right of a man whatever the colour of his skin, to acquire, exercise, and be paid for skill'—but also the vital need to increase the African's purchasing power and productivity, to fit him to be a successful member of the modern world.[85] On the other side there was also a vital principle: the right of European immigrants to defend their standard of living for themselves and their descendants in a country to whose spectacular development they had made so considerable a contribution. The clash of these views became more apparent in October 1947, when the Government, after an abortive conference in May, took the initiative in appointing a Commission under the chairmanship of Mr. Andrew Dalgleish to inquire into the advancement of Africans in industry in Northern Rhodesia.

Some Europeans claimed that the African was already employed to the utmost of his capacity. They maintained that 'the African would only work when he knew that he was being watched, (that) he had the mind of a child, [that] he had an utter lack of responsibility and [that] he had not the European's pride in his labour'. The Commission's report pointed out, however, that responsibility, keenness, and pride in the work were attributes

[83] *Report of the Board of Inquiry appointed to inquire into the advancement of Africans in the Copper Mining Industry in Northern Rhodesia* (Lusaka, 1954), para. 19, 21. Subsequently referred to as the Forster Report, 1954.

[84] See above, Part I, Chap. III, p. 106.

[85] E.g. W. J. Busschau, *Report on the Development of Secondary Industries in Northern Rhodesia* (Lusaka, 1945), pp. 24–7.

which would develop only when the African's opportunities expanded, and that his child-like mentality could be explained by his lack of education, both in formal schooling and in the wider field of adaptation to his new environment.

The fallacy of these objections was, moreover, underlined by the success with which Africans had undertaken skilled work in every occupation to which they had unobstructed access. Just over the border at Elisabethville in the Congo the Commission saw 'Africans doing a far larger range of semi-skilled and skilled work in the railway work-shops and with very little supervision'. In Nyasaland Africans held responsible posts on the railways, and in Northern Rhodesia itself, outside the mining industry, there were many skilled African bricklayers, carpenters, plumbers, and machine operators. Above all, the artificial nature of these objections based on the supposed inability of Africans to undertake more advanced work was demonstrated by the fact that all of the twenty-eight different kinds of job which the Commission considered Africans capable of filling immediately were 'already being done, or had in the past been done, by Africans on one mine or another but not on *all* mines'. The Commission therefore recommended that Africans should be given these jobs 'as early and as unprovocatively as possible' when vacancies occurred; they also considered that eleven categories of semi-skilled work were suitable for Africans after a short training, and nineteen others after a longer and more intensive training.[86]

Yet behind these objections voiced by Europeans there was a bitter intransigent opposition. Even in the ultra-modern conditions of the Copperbelt, mining remained a dangerous occupation; as he plunged into the broad web of galleries and moved deeper towards the pit face, a man could not but be conscious that in a crisis his life would perhaps depend on the reactions, ability, and experience of his neighbour. And although they may have had little rational cause to mistrust the ability of the African, prevalent European conceptions of the African's character must inevitably have reinforced the miners' opposition to

[86] *Report of the Commission appointed to inquire into the Advancement of Africans in Industry* (Lusaka, 1948). The Dalgleish Report.

giving Africans any responsible work underground. But the over-riding cause of their opposition was undoubtedly the belief that any dilution, any advance of the African, would merely prove to be the beginning of the expulsion of the European from Northern Rhodesia. They said that they were not seeking to maintain a colour bar; they adhered 'entirely to the principles of trade unionism . . . to the principle of equal pay for equal work'. Since this principle was not specifically included in the terms of reference, they decided to boycott the Commission, stating as an additional objection that it was composed of people from outside the territory. Later, the President of the Mine Workers' Union announced in the Legislative Council that he considered the correct approach was 'to give the African the necessary primary education, to qualify him to enter an apprenticeship on a competitive basis with the European so that he can command the pay'.[87]

Few people could take exception to this principle of thorough equality on the sole basis of individual ability as an ultimate goal; it was no solution, however, to the immediate problem. These were not highly skilled posts which required a long period of training; they would, however, provide an invaluable opportunity for a limited number of Africans to exercise a degree of responsibility and skill easily within their immediate capacities. They would at least start to fill the gap between so-called skilled and unskilled labour. And, as the Commission pointed out, no European would be discharged to make room for an African, while in the long term there could be little doubt that there would be 'ample scope in a country whose natural resources are as yet mainly untapped for the sons of those Europeans at present in industry'.[88] As Professor Clay had pointed out to the Southern Rhodesians,[89] there was no rigidly limited amount of work: the skill of the African would be complementary rather than competitive. Mr. Welensky, the leader of the European Unofficials in the Legislative Council, thought, however, that the Commission's report, if accepted, would 'lead to the elimination of the

[87] Northern Rhodesian Debates, 12 March 1948, cols. 87–90.
[88] *Dalgleish Report*, para. 256.   [89] See above, Part I, Chap. III, pp. 95–8.

European'. If Africans were to better their conditions they must do it by being able to maintain production at European standards. The way to deal with the problem was, he thought, 'not by Commissions but for us to settle down and develop this country'.[90] The Commission's recommendations remained unimplemented. The issue was later reopened at the instance of a new power, the African Mine Workers' Union,[91] but by that time African advancement was beginning to mean the advance not only of a small *élite* but also of the mass, and the problem became no easier with the passage of time.

In Southern Rhodesia Europeans took a similar stand on the principle of equal pay for equal work, and they too denied that this implied a fixed colour bar. Mr. Davies, leader of the Labour Party, said, for instance, that 'when the time comes that the native has progressed in his standards so that the considerable disparity which exists to-day between him and the white worker has been bridged, there will be no bar to his entry into the skilled trades provided he can conform with the requirements'. His warrant for making that statement was, he claimed, that already the trained artisan admitted the Coloured man of mixed blood into his ranks.[92] His optimism was, however, scarcely justified by the findings of a Commission of Inquiry which reported later the same year. They found that there was 'a very definite "colour prejudice" against the Coloured man', that it was 'virtually impossible for a Coloured youth to become apprenticed in the majority of the skilled trades because no European journeyman would undertake the task of training a Coloured youth', and that 'no matter how skilled and trustworthy a Coloured journeyman might be it would be extremely difficult for him to get employment in most skilled trades as the European journeyman would resent working side by side with a Coloured man, and if an employer insisted the probabilities again were that he would be faced with serious labour troubles with his white employees'.[93]

[90] N.R. Debates, 12 March 1948, col. 79.
[91] See below, Part II, Chap. V, p. 351.
[92] S.R. Debates, 17 January 1946, col. 3121.
[93] *Report of the Commission of Inquiry regarding the Social Welfare o the Coloured Community of Southern Rhodesia, 1946*, paras. 53–7.

The effects of the Industrial Conciliation Act were strikingly evident: in the richest section of the building industry, organized in terms of the Act and covered by an Industrial Council, there were no Coloured artisans or apprentices. In the motor industry there were eight Coloured journeymen employed at Industrial Agreement rates, but, since many of them had entered the industry before it was organized under the Act, it was felt that their position was precarious, and future apprenticeship was practically impossible.[94] Here, then, there was not merely a determination to maintain a given standard of living; there seems also to have been the fear lest contamination with the Coloured journeyman on a basis of equality at work might insidiously rob the European artisan of all the other privileges and prestige which the colour of his skin procured for him in other spheres. The experience of Coloured workmen, therefore, offered little encouragement to Africans who were completely excluded from the skilled trades, and among the more gifted Africans this barrier of frustration deadened their initiative and deeply affected their attitude to their work. The Director of an engineering firm, who took an outstanding interest in the health and welfare of his African employees, on being asked by the Howman Committee whether his 'boys' took a pride in the result of their work, replied: 'I would not like to say that because in our firm all the skilled work is European.'[95]

On the railways also there was a 'very strong' prejudice against employing Coloureds or Africans in posts in which Europeans were employed;[96] and although in 1947 the Secretary of State for the Colonies permitted the nationalization of the Rhodesia Railways only on condition that Africans would be given 'opportunities for employment in more responsible work as and when they are qualified to undertake such work', the Railway Commission took no active steps to implement this condition.[97]

In the newer, manufacturing industries, however, Africans

[94] *Report of the Commission of Inquiry regarding the Social Welfare of the Coloured Community of Southern Rhodesia, 1946,* paras. 83, 107.
[95] Evidence to Howman Committee, p. 130.
[96] *Report on Coloured Community,* para. 171.   [97] *Dalgleish Report,* para. 24.

were beginning to advance on a large scale into work which sometimes demanded a high degree of skill and ability, though not a journeyman's certificate. This process was aided by the war, which not only stimulated the growth of local secondary industries, but also produced a shortage of European labour which forced some firms to employ Africans. In 1943 the Howman Committee was told that Africans were being given 'more and more responsible work' in European stores, and in factories like the Lion Match Company and the United Tobacco Company Africans were replacing European male and female labour.[98] Factories producing primarily for the African market were anxious to employ Africans in order to keep the price of their products within the purchasing power of Africans. In 1943 it was thought that the clothing industry in Bulawayo employed about 400 Africans and that there were immediate vacancies for at least sixty African machinists; some managers in this industry were already beginning to appreciate the importance of stabilizing their experienced labour and were willing 'to pay a boy £2 a week if he knows the work'.[99]

The largest and one of the most progressive of these new factories serving the African market was the Bata Shoe Factory, started at Gwelo in March 1939. Originally the Government's Chief Industrial Inspector wanted the factory 'to exclude natives largely from industry' and to follow the precedent of South Africa, where Coloured and cheap European labour was employed at a minimum of £2 or £3 a week. The Company argued, however, that in the Union there was heavy customs protection against overseas competition and also a considerable skilled labour market. In Southern Rhodesia these conditions did not exist, and at Gwelo the Company insisted on using African labour; by 1943 they were employing 400 Africans and they already had 'ten boys who can supervise a section of work' and who were supervising other Africans. They encouraged married men, for, as the manager put it, 'there is such a lot of training involved that we can't afford to lose a native if he is good'. They were definitely of the opinion that it paid to increase

[98] Evidence to Howman Committee, pp. 190, 276, 375.   [99] Ibid., pp. 284–5.

wages; they were never short of labour, and they had very little turnover, especially in the higher-paid classes. In fact they presented so great an exception to the general run of employment that they received complaints that they were 'spoiling their natives' by paying too much.[100]

Besides this increasing use of African labour in new fields of secondary industry, the war years witnessed the beginnings of another development which also seemed likely to aid the gradual assimilation of Africans into skilled employment. The Industrial Conciliation Act of 1934 had been designed to deal with the situation when there was little secondary industrial development and when there was no established secondary industry whose basic production was intended to be carried out by Africans. Secondary industries were purely small jobbing industries, operated by skilled white tradesmen, with the African working merely as a completely unskilled labourer. In this situation the Act, as has been seen,[101] in practice effectively controlled, by a colour bar, entry into apprenticeship and employment as a tradesman. But the British and American experience of intense wartime mass production opened up new possibilities. In the armament factories much was learnt 'about the breaking down of complicated processes into simple operations that could be performed with the assistance of suitable mechanical aids and fixtures by comparatively unskilled labour'.[102]

The relevance of this technique for Central Africa was obvious and it influenced not only the newly-established processing industries but also the older industries already organized under the Industrial Conciliation Act. A gradual reclassification of the grades specified in the agreements drawn up by the various Industrial Councils was tentatively set in hand. Work of a semi-skilled nature was defined as a separate grade, so that a relatively simple repetitive operation could be detached from the reserved province of a skilled tradesman. An African, for instance, might operate a lathe which turned a component as an operation

---

[100] Evidence to Howman Committee, pp. 65–7.   [101] See above, p. 246.
[102] *First Interim Report of the Southern Rhodesian Development Co-ordinating Commission, 1948*, para. 15.

in its manufacture. The operation might require little skill, yet the turning was technically part of the general classification of a 'turner', and hence if the Council's agreement remained unmodified the unqualified worker would be officially excluded from the job, although he might undertake it under the 'supervision' of a tradesman. Once the reclassification was completed, however, he was free to carry out the operation in his own right and the job could be paid at a rate substantially higher than that commanded by unskilled labourers, while the standards of the skilled artisan were protected.

By the end of the war this process was apparent in several industries. In the motor industry, for example, where the journeyman mechanic's wages were fixed at 3s. 6d. per hour, a new classification was introduced of 'vehicle assembler' at 1s. 8d. per hour, and in the printing industry there was a semi-skilled grade known as 'printer's assistant'. In the engineering industry there was provision for three semi-skilled grades, and in subsequent years these grades were further sub-divided.[103] At first these grades were considered to be especially suitable for Coloured workmen, but gradually Africans were brought into this process of assimilation. It offered of course no immediate solution to the major problem—that of apprenticeship and employment as skilled artisans—but it did begin to introduce a measure of flexibility. The gap between white skilled artisans and black unskilled labour was diminished—a factor of considerable importance in a rapidly expanding economy, and one which might even lessen colour prejudice. The secretary of the Southern Rhodesia Section of the South African Typographical Union told the Commission on the Coloured Community:

When the Coloureds first came into the printing industry (in the semi-skilled grades) I had quite a lot of trouble with the ordinary rank and file members of the Union. I heard threats from time to time that they would refuse to work alongside the Coloureds. That prejudice, as far as the printing industry is concerned, has more or less broken down, but if there were any indication of starting a quota system amongst the

---

[103] *Report on Coloured Community*, para. 69. See also a memorandum by the National Industrial Council of the Engineering Industry, 23 February 1954.

apprentices I think we would have the bother all over again. I am afraid it must come about by natural evolution.[104]

But would there be time for an unhurried, graceful adaptation? In the crucial industries in both Rhodesias Africans remained effectively debarred from acquiring and exercising an artisan's skill. In an under-developed economy this was a waste difficult to justify: in a country where whites were rich and blacks were poor it was a grievance dangerous to ignore. And beyond this publicized problem of the advance of the African workers' *élite*, there remained the principal question of increasing the productivity of the masses. It was a question of recognizing that African inefficiency stemmed not so much from temperament as from environment; of deciding, as in the Katanga, to break the chain of ignorance, low wages, malnutrition, disease, and ininefficiency; of creating a permanent, successful, and self-reliant urban community.

[104] *Report on Coloured Community*, para. 71.

III. THE CHALLENGES OF
URBAN LIFE

I. HOUSING

The great drift of Africans to the towns demanded radical re-
adjustments, from both Africans and Europeans. To the young
rural African the town had a fearsome reputation.[1] For him it was
the new jungle—a place of violence, uninhibited fascinations,
foreigners, bitter hostilities, loud physical rowdiness, and strange
opportunities. Often he found himself alone there, an isolated
individual, with no kinsman to assist him, and with none of the
assured wisdom, guidance, and restraint of respected elders.
Would he, and increasing numbers of his fellows, be able to catch
even a faint impression of the possible benefits of a settled, intelligent, prosperous urban civilization? Or would the future generation disintegrate into 100,000 delinquents hostile to all discipline,
obsessed with material ambitions, swayed only by superficial
emotions? Inevitably the towns were the crucible of the new
Rhodesia, and for a few years the European with his decisive hold
on policy still held the major initiative. His decisions could largely
influence future developments: but at the same time these new
communities were gathering their own momentum, and the
opportunities for a decisive intervention by Europeans were
rapidly diminishing.

The shortage of housing was one of the greatest obstacles to the
creation of contented urban communities. In 1944 the Howman
Committee reported that overcrowding was met with everywhere, with the result that 'Africans squeeze into what rooms they
can find, seek out all kinds of shelters about the towns and

---

[1] See, for example, the evidence collected in Northern Rhodesia by H. Powdermaker,
'Social change through Imagery and Values of Teen-Age Africans in Northern Rhodesia', *The American Anthropologist*, October 1956.

"married" couples share rooms with bachelors'. The Committee considered that this state of affairs was due not to the war but to 'a short-sighted and unsocial view of industrial progress'; industries were encouraged and large areas were set aside for factories, but 'no thought and no provision' was made for the African labour force. The Government was prepared to make only short-term economic loans at $4\frac{1}{2}$ per cent. to the Municipalities. In Salisbury and Gwelo the Municipalities' insistence that only highly-paid European artisans should be employed considerably increased the cost of building houses for Africans.[2] Houses which cost £125 at Shabani when built with African labour cost £500 at Salisbury.[3] As urban industries expanded, the housing situation deteriorated, and in the immediate post-war years shortages of labour, building materials, and finance delayed any improvement. European immigrants, arriving in greatly increased numbers, experienced considerable inconvenience and even hardship for a time,[4] but among urban Africans the conditions were often appalling. Let us first examine in detail the situation in one important area.

By 1950 the principal accommodation provided by the Municipality in Bulawayo consisted of the Old Location, containing 1,884 rooms and 341 two-roomed cottages, and Mzilikazi village, which had been started in 1942 and contained about 1,600 cottages with one to three rooms each with a kitchen in addition. A municipal count taken in 1949 showed that on an average 4·9 persons shared each room in the Old Location. Five young adult males sharing a room of eleven feet by ten with a small kitchen built off in the rear is not an unduly alarming figure, but almost half the people were living in rooms containing more than five people. And the count did not of course reveal the full extent of illegal occupation nor the proportion of women and children in these rooms. A sample survey of seventy rooms taken later showed an average of just under one woman per room, and one of the worst cases encountered was of a room that contained five men, two women, and two adolescent girls.[5] Individuals liv-

[2] *Report on Urban Conditions*, paras. 64–71.
[3] Evidence to the Howman Committee, p. 352.
[4] The 1951 Census showed a shortage of 2,409 dwellings for European families.
[5] Gussman, op. cit., pp. 16–18.

ing under these conditions might well be expected to renounce their traditional code of behaviour and even lose all sense of cohesion and human dignity. Many undoubtedly were—and are—permanently injured; but even in the most degrading circumstances pathetic yet determined and noble attempts were made to salvage shreds of privacy and to achieve a human standard.[6]

The cottages in the Old Location were much less overcrowded; the majority of them were inhabited by married couples and the municipal count in 1949 gave a figure of 4·8 persons per cottage, which, if most of these were families, cannot be considered excessive. In the new Mzilikazi village the average was 5·2 persons per cottage.[7] This was a reasonable figure, considering the overall situation, for a family in a two- or three-roomed cottage, but in the cottages with only one room and a small kitchen it meant overcrowding.

The best conditions for Africans working in the area of Bulawayo were provided by the Government at the Native Village Settlement of Luveve, about six miles out of Bulawayo. In 1950 it contained 430 houses, the majority of them standing on an eighth of an acre and consisting of three rooms and a kitchen. Tenancy was strictly limited to Africans of good character and lasted only while they were actively employed in Bulawayo. There was virtually no overcrowding, but, as one observer commented, this was 'as much due to the inconvenience of bicycling twelve miles over an exceptionally badly corrugated road as it (was) to the efficiency of the administrative system'.[8] Here, however, was a relatively settled nucleus which, given the opportunity and encouragement, might develop into a responsible self-reliant community.

In the Old Location, the Mzilikazi village and Luveve, the Municipality and the Government provided accommodation for about 21,000 Africans. Some 10,000 domestic servants were accommodated on the private premises of their employers. The

[6] One evening in 1956 I saw some of the worst of these rooms in the Old Location. Ten or twelve men, women, and children lived together in one room whose walls were patterned by live and dead cockroaches. The dignity of the inhabitants was in extraordinary contrast to the environment.

[7] Gussman, op. cit., p. 19.   [8] Ibid., p. 22.

remaining third or half of Bulawayo's African population, which was variously estimated at between 45,000 and 60,000, were housed principally in compounds erected and controlled by public and private industrial concerns. The largest group consisted of five compounds where the Rhodesia Railways housed 4,000 African employees together with 4,500 women, children, and lodgers. In 1945 a Commission of Inquiry under the chairmanship of Mr. (later Sir Robert) Tredgold reported in the following terms on the worst of these:

In its heyday, which was back in the early years of the century, the compound could not have been a particularly attractive residential provision. For the most part it consists of ill-lit and ill-ventilated barrack-type rows of rooms. Now 2,173 African men and women are housed in accommodation which officially should house 1,450. Latrine and bathing provision is inadequate. Save in one section of the compound, there is no provision for cooking, which is done for the most part on home-made braziers in the open. Cooking in wet weather must be very difficult. Men and women are crowded in rooms without regard to hygiene or decency. For example, we found six males, three females and four children occupying one room 15 ft. × 17 ft. 9 in. × 11 ft. 6 in. high. This was by no means exceptional. In an attempt to gain a little privacy, partitions of old sacking or rags are erected which further reduce the light and ventilation. It is a miracle that no serious epidemic has originated here.[9]

The Railway compound at Salisbury and another one at Bulawayo were 'somewhat better, but still shocking'; but the Commission found that the compounds built by the Railways since 1942 were excellent, with pleasant semi-detached cottages,[10] and after the strike in 1945 and the creation of an African Affairs Department on the Railways the conditions for African employees improved very considerably.[11]

Some of the compounds erected by private firms were responsible for conditions far worse even than those reported by the Tredgold Commission. After a thorough investigation of the

[9] *Report of the Commission to investigate . . . the strike amongst the African employees of the Rhodesia Railways, 1946*, p. 12. Hereafter referred to as the Tredgold Report.
[10] Ibid., p. 11.   [11] See below, Part II, Chap. IV, p. 288.

situation in 1948 Mr. J. P. McNamee, an experienced administrator from the Union of South Africa, concluded his description
of the private compounds in Bulawayo with the following
words:

Some years ago, Sir Edgar Thornton, of the Union Department of
Public Health, described a certain area situated immediately outside the
boundaries of Port Elizabeth as 'the worst slum in the world'. He
might well have qualified that statement had he seen the conditions of
some of the shanty settlements in Bulawayo's industrial area.

One of the compounds which adjoined the Location consisted
mainly of tin shanties, was 'disgustingly filthy', and 'reeked of
liquor'. It was, McNamee thought, 'nothing short of a menace to
the health, orderliness, and welfare of the inhabitants of the
Location'. At another the conditions were 'indescribable. To be
believed they must be seen.'[12] In some cases the owners of the
compounds erected good brick houses, but these were quickly
overcrowded, and as a general rule Africans were left to put together tiny shanties of paper, sacking, and scraps of iron, wood,
and asbestos, the roofs of which invariably leaked and were often
blown away. Many firms provided no sanitation facilities whatever, and those that were provided were nearly always hopelessly
inadequate.

In 1945 the Medical Officer of Health reported serious overcrowding in the compound provided by the Municipality for its
own employees. The main compound had room for '950 single
natives according to the rather inadequate requirements of the
applicable Government Notice 573 of 1935'. In 1945 it housed
1,400 men, of whom approximately 240 were living in old back-
to-back buildings, badly lighted and insanitary. Twenty-one w.c.
pans, all situated in one part of the compound, had to serve the
needs of all the inhabitants, which worked out at about one pan
for every seventy men.[13] No action was taken on this report until
after the 1948 strike—which originated among the municipal

[12] *Report on Native Urban Administration in Bulawayo* ... by J. P. McNamee, 2
December 1948 (typescript).
[13] Quoted in Gussman, op. cit., p. 20. The standard laid down in South African law is
one pan to every twelve persons.

S

workers—when some steps were taken to reduce the overcrowding.

There remained several thousand African workers in Bulawayo for whom no provision was made either by their employers or by the Municipality. About 2,000 Africans travelled into Bulawayo every day from outlying districts where they lived either as tenants of European farmers or in native Reserves. A further 2,000 were squatters on small plots on the commonage originally leased to Coloured market-gardeners. Gussman reported that in 1949 'the majority of the huts occupied by these Africans were unfit for human occupation, sanitary arrangements were rarely available, either for latrine or washing purposes, and many of the shanties or shacks were shared with domestic animals belonging to the plot-holders'. Many other Africans, often accompanied by their wives and children, were left to find a sleeping-place in derelict or unbuilt-up areas of the city itself and most builders' labourers were permitted to sleep on the sites where they were working.[14]

The overall picture, then, that emerges of Bulawayo in the immediate post-war years is one of widespread squalid overcrowding, occasionally relieved by the more recent, roomier little cottages. In part this was doubtless due to the pace of industrial expansion. But also, more fundamentally, it was the result of the European frame of mind, which insisted that the African worker was merely a temporary participant in urban life, that his wife and children should be left in the Reserves, and that a single room was therefore a perfectly adequate provision for four adult males and was even an advance on the primitive rural conditions to which they were accustomed. The health authorities immediately concerned with the situation realized the fallacy of these assumptions, and, as we have seen, many of the cottages constructed by the Municipality and the Railways since 1942 were designed to make possible a stable family life. Officials were, however, hampered by shortages—McNamee reported that the Council's 'altogether inadequate' rate of building was further reduced in 1948 by a shortage of staff, and it was only after the 1948 strike that the urgency

[14] Gussman, op. cit., p. 27.

of the problem began to be recognized.[15] In the meantime the majority of Africans experienced few of the benefits and many of the evils of urban life.

Detailed accounts of the housing situation in other Southern Rhodesian towns in the immediate post-war years are not available, but the situation was undoubtedly serious. Salisbury was expanding even more rapidly than Bulawayo. In 1936, 20,177 Africans were employed there; by 1946 this number had risen to 45,993, and by 1951 it was 75,500.[16] In 1946 the Council provided housing for 10,025 men, 2,535 women, and 4,539 children, about 17,000 people in all, a figure which should be compared to the 18,000 provided for by the Bulawayo Municipality, where only some 30,000 Africans were employed.[17] In 1948 the Chief Native Commissioner reported that there was a waiting list of 'hundreds of applicants' for married housing in Highfield village, just outside Salisbury.[18] In other centres where expansion was on a smaller scale the pressure was less. In 1950, when the building programmes of all the Municipalities were slowly gathering momentum, it was reported that the demand for accommodation for single men had been met at Umtali and it was hoped that the shortage of housing there for married men would shortly be overcome.[19] But in the same year the Chief Native Commissioner still expressed 'grave concern' over the acute shortage of adequate African housing, and this shortage remained a major problem in Southern Rhodesia.

In Northern Rhodesia conditions varied enormously. In the compounds of the copper-mining companies the housing of African employees was much better than elsewhere in the Rhodesias. In 1947 the Dalgleish Commission reported that married men with children were given two-roomed houses, or one room and a kitchen if they were without children. Four single men generally shared one hut of 160 square feet. In most cases washing and lavatory facilities were communal, but they did at least exist. The Commission seem to have considered that conditions were

---

[15] See below, Part II, Chap. IV, p. 295.   [16] Census Reports.
[17] *First Annual Report of Director of Native Administration, Salisbury.*
[18] *Report of the Chief Native Commissioner for 1948*, p. 31.
[19] *Report of the Chief Native Commissioner for 1950*, p. 2.

better in Elisabethville, just over the frontier in the Congo, where the new houses in particular were 'a very marked improvement'. A general claim was made by African witnesses for an improved class of housing with more accommodation for adolescent children, for lighting, and for an extension of the five-acre plot system in operation at Broken Hill. But at least the bare minimum was adequately provided.[20]

Outside the Companies' compounds conditions in Northern Rhodesia were often deplorable. A Commission appointed in 1943 to inquire into the administration and finances of Native Locations in urban areas reported that in the locations visited by it there were approximately 6,729 dwellings, of which only 689 had more than one room, despite the fact that 5,305 out of the 9,407 male inhabitants were married. The single-roomed dwellings, many of them occupied by married couples with up to seven children, ranged from ancient mud huts to well-built structures with kitchens and verandas attached, but all of them fell short 'of the minimum requirements of decency and hygiene when occupied by married people'.

In addition to these Locations the Local Authorities also provided 'grass compounds', which consisted of plots of varying dimensions leased to Africans who built their own huts and houses of mud or sun-dried brick. Under firm and sympathetic administration these plots might well have been a satisfactory, if temporary, solution. Indeed, in 1955 the Dow Report on East Africa recommended the adoption of this expedient.[21] But in Northern Rhodesia in 1943 the Commission found that most of the buildings were 'thoroughly unhygienic and quite unsuited to urban conditions'. A number of locations were established on private property where the owner leased plots to Africans at a rental which was often high, considering that services were seldom if ever provided. Some commercial concerns had quarters for their employees in the trading areas and in the majority of cases the standard was 'disgracefully low'. And for the rest Africans squatted in unauthorized settlements, mainly on Crown land, where the sanitation was non-

[20] *Dalgleish Report*, pp. 32–3.
[21] *Report of East Africa Royal Commission, 1953–55* (Cmd. 9475, 1955), pp. 229–32.

existent and they were 'a constant menace to the health and well-being of the whole community'.[22]

In June 1946 the Northern Rhodesian Government set up a Department of Local Government and African Housing and one million pounds was voted for the construction of permanent housing. By that time, however, the situation was so acute that resources had to be diverted, as in Britain, to the construction of temporary housing. In the following years costs rose, materials remained scarce, and Africans continued to enter the towns. In 1943 the African urban population in Northern Rhodesia, excluding employees of the mining companies, was estimated at 54,000; by 1956 this figure had increased to 225,000. It is not surprising, therefore, that housing continued to be an increasingly urgent problem.[23]

In both Rhodesias the housing shortage affected African women most harshly. The Howman Committee referred in 1943 to the 'startling increase in the number of women flocking to the towns',[24] the Bulawayo Municipality estimated that while in the years 1944–9 the male population of the Location increased by 30 per cent., the female population increased by 101 per cent., and although this rate of increase was probably not maintained outside the Location it does seem to have been indicative of a general trend.[25]

The women came for various reasons: to escape from rural poverty and the agricultural work, which weighed far more heavily on them in the absence of the able-bodied men from the Reserves; to join the males of their age-group and to find husbands; to evade the discipline of their elders and to seek employment, independence, or gaiety. They found in the towns an extraordinary emancipation and also a confusion amounting to anarchy. As we have seen, a sample survey of the single rooms in the Old Location at Bulawayo showed an average of just under one woman per room. Only twelve of the sixty-three women found to be living in the seventy sample rooms claimed to be married to any of the men living with them.[26] In one compound in Salisbury in 1943 34 per cent. were 'temporarily married', while the Town

[22] *Report of the Commission appointed to Inquire into the Administration and Finances of Native Locations in Urban Areas* (Lusaka, 1944), paras. 52–75.
[23] Annual Reports of the Department of Local Government and African Housing.
[24] Report, para. 21.   [25] Gussman, op. cit., p. 39.   [26] Ibid., p. 18.

Clerk of Que Que, discussing with the Howman Committee the feasibility of increasing the wages of married urban Africans, remarked: 'The point is who are married and who are not; they all have a woman.'[27]

Many Europeans thought that this situation was merely the natural consequence of primitive sexual morality. They thought that in the rural areas these young women were 'purely animal'; and therefore the fact that, as a Native Commissioner put it, 'every nurse-girl in Que Que without exception is a prostitute',[28] was seen merely as an expression of the African's nature in an urban environment. It is an ironic and tragic example of mutual incomprehension that, as the more percipient of the Europeans realized, the downfall and degradation of their womenfolk were among the bitterest charges which the older generation of Africans levelled at their European rulers.[29]

Actually there seem to have been relatively few habitual professional prostitutes. Women were as anxious to obtain shelter as they were cash,[30] and it was concubinage, which sometimes developed into a semi-permanent union, that was particularly widespread. As the Native Commissioner, who was quoted above, explained: 'The only way these girls can live in Que Que is as so-called wives.'[31] Association with these young women, widely referred to as 'spares', was, however, usually temporary; labour was continually on the move and few young, unskilled workers could afford to keep a woman permanently. Openings for women in industry and employment were limited, and even when they could obtain an honest independent means of support there remained the problem of accommodation. At Umtali missionaries ran a hostel for about twenty-five girls who were generally in domestic service. Their way of life was, however, severely regimented and could have appealed, one feels, only to a minority. 'The girls', wrote the Superintendent, 'leave at 6.15 a.m. after prayers which all must attend for fifteen minutes. They must be in before dark. . . . All are required to come to the hostel on

[27] Evidence to Howman Committee, pp. 222, 229.   [28] Ibid., p. 235.
[29] E.g. C. E. Fripp, *One Aspect of the Labour Question* (Salisbury, 1941).
[30] Gussman, op. cit., p. 113.   [31] Evidence to the Howman Committee, p. 235.

Wednesday afternoons for a little religious service and interviews, if desired. They have Sunday afternoons and a check is kept of their church attendance at the church of their choice.'[32] In Bulawayo the Municipality completed a hostel for sixty women in 1945; further extensions in 1950 and 1951 provided for a total of 130 women. This was a pleasant modern building where the discipline was perhaps not as narrow as that in Umtali. Yet although by 1951 nearly 5,000 African women were employed in Bulawayo, the hostel occasionally had accommodation to spare, and while it undoubtedly performed a most valuable service for a minority, the majority preferred to live in more 'human' surroundings, squalid though they might be.

There was also a core of hardened prostitutes. In a survey of venereal diseases of the African in Southern Rhodesia undertaken in 1949 at the request of the Government by Dr. Wilcox, a London specialist, fifty-one out of 177 women V.D. patients questioned in twenty clinics 'owned to being harlots', while fifty-three could have been classified as 'spares'.[33] In Bulawayo there seems to have been little organized vice,[34] but the Salisbury 'tea-parties' were notorious as far away as Cape Town. The name was derived from the more respectable dances held by mission schools as a means of raising funds, where the organizers provided food and soft drinks and in addition charged for admission and dancing. But in Salisbury the institution to which the same name was ironically given had developed on an 'almost exclusively sexual basis', with pimps controlling assignations and long queues forming in the bush or outside the houses while 'intercourse apparently often took place within sight of the next on the line'. Early in 1949 twenty or more regular parties were held in Salisbury and its environs every Saturday night, and they were spreading to the outlying farming districts of Norton, Darwendale, and Marandellas. In May police action obtained a temporary closure, but by October they were again flourishing.[35]

It is not therefore surprising to find that venereal disease was

[32] Evidence to the Howman Committee, p. 248.
[33] R. R. Wilcox, *Report on a Venereal Disease Survey of the African in Southern Rhodesia* (Salisbury, 1949), p. 46.
[34] Gussman, op. cit., p. 114.   [35] Wilcox, op. cit., pp. 41-5.

widespread. Evidence submitted to the Howman Committee in 1943 showed that from one-quarter to one-third of the patients admitted to clinics were V.D. cases.[36] Figures collected during 1945–9 gave a suspected syphilis rate among pregnant African females in Bulawayo of 32·9 per cent. and in Salisbury of 14·1 per cent.[37] At the 'model' village of Luveve 4·5 per cent. of the school children had congenital syphilis,[38] and in a blood test 23·8 per cent. of the men showed positive results, with 12·4 per cent. doubtful.[39] Overall figures of the incidence of venereal disease in the country as a whole were impossible to obtain, but those compiled from prison records gave an incidence at a given moment of 8·4 per cent., and Wilcox thought that this was probably the most reliable indication of the state of affairs.[40]

The disease was on the whole contracted in the towns and spread from there into the kraals, and Wilcox left no doubt in his report that this was a social rather than a medical problem. He said that married men were much less prone to the disease, and until there was an adequate provision of decent married quarters and of large-scale facilities for recreation, venereal disease would continue to undermine the health of the African. It would also threaten the health of European homes. And it was not only venereal disease that was fostered by inadequate housing. The Howman Committee received much evidence 'as to the increase of tuberculosis among Africans whose resistance to this dangerous disease is not only very slight, but is weakened so much by malnutrition and deficiency diseases that few can survive its attack'. One medical witness reported that it had become 'one of the commonest diseases', and Medical Officers of Health faced with the conditions in the Locations and on private land felt that they could do nothing.[41] Here again was a disease which could spread with frightening ease into the European part of the population.

Faced with the widespread overcrowding and the consequent

---

[36] Evidence to Howman Committee, p. 203(a).

[37] Wilcox, p. 20.   [38] Ibid., p. 32.   [39] Ibid., p. 22.

[40] Ibid., p. 6. In 1954 in a paper read to the Inter-racial Society a private doctor in Bulawayo criticized Wilcox's figures as being far too low and thought that the incidence over a five-year period was probably between 70 and 80 per cent.

[41] *Howman Report*, paras. 40–43.

disappearance of respect and traditional moral standards, many married Africans were 'too dead scared to bring their women into town'.[42] Moreover, those families who did settle in the towns, and who were fortunate enough to obtain a cottage to themselves, were immediately confronted with a host of problems of a different order. Traditionally marriage was dependent on the active co-operation of a wide range of kinsfolk. Legally it was ratified when the *lobola* of cattle was deposited with the wife's relatives as a guarantee of the permanence of the union, while among the non-cattle-owning tribes a complex series of gifts and services was required. Spiritually it demanded the ritual help of specific elder relatives. Economically the extended family formed a closely integrated unit every member of which performed a vital function, and a woman was loved and valued not so much as the partner and companion of her husband, but as a mother, a sister, and an aunt. The towns destroyed her traditional dignity and position. In many cases *lobola* lost its deep social significance and became a mere monetary transaction, an excuse for exploitation on the part of avaricious parents who had sometimes made a substantial 'investment' in a daughter's education. Ritual and social ties with the rest of the family were often snapped or seriously weakened, especially as inter-tribal marriages increased. The woman's agricultural, economic value vanished as in general the man became the chief bread-winner; often, with the elder children sent to rural relatives to escape the effects of overcrowding, even her domestic duties dwindled. A few women were able to cultivate small garden plots —especially on the mines in Northern Rhodesia—and a minority began to learn new domestic arts, but with their low average standard of formal education it was inevitable that their status declined. Many of the more educated men married educated women from the High Commission territories and the Union of South Africa and found satisfaction in a new form of relationship, but for most Africans this was unattainable, and poverty and the prevalence of concubinage destroyed the stability and happiness of the family.[43]

[42] Evidence to Howman Committee, p. 232.
[43] Wilson, op. cit., Part II. Gussman, op. cit., pp. 115–39. See also a study of a Johannesburg slum yard: E. Hellmann, *Rooiyard*, Rhodes–Livingstone Papers, No. 13, 1948.

2. LOCAL COMMUNITIES

Adequate housing was obviously the first requisite for the development of a healthy and contented urban community. Yet it was by no means the sole requisite and—although this presented difficulties enough—in the long run it was perhaps the easiest to supply. Not only the wives and the young women but also the children and the aged found themselves disastrously handicapped in their new environment. In Johannesburg and other towns in South Africa similar circumstances on a much larger scale were already producing widespread lawlessness and gangsterism, and the notorious '*tsotsis*'—gangs of armed youths—were a terror to their neighbourhood—as well as being often the nearest approach to an educational influence that a young man encountered. In Rhodesia this problem was, as yet, not nearly so grave. The head of the Salisbury C.I.D. told the Howman Committee that there had not been an increase in crime proportionate to the growth of the towns. He thought that, considering the number of Africans in the towns, the amount of petty thieving was small. They were 'lucky to have a law-abiding population', but he added that he would not say that, with 'this drift of youngsters to town', the problem they had in Johannesburg would not arise.[44]

Already there were signs that the police had good cause for concern. The children sent away from the towns to stay with their rural grandparents were, it seems, about as many as those who came in without their parents. An independent census carried out in Umtali by an Inspector of Native Education gave a total of about 600 African juveniles in that relatively small community.[45] It was thought that the majority of these came from across the border of Portuguese East Africa. Many of them were employed by African bachelors and married couples as 'cooks and bottle-washers', for which they received three to five shillings a month. The Native Commissioner at Umtali thought that neither party gained much from this arrangement: 'Obviously these juveniles can't be expected to prepare meals as well as experienced women, and there is the danger that they are led into all sorts of tempta-

[44] Evidence to Howman Committee, p. 183.   [45] Ibid., p. 120.

tions, such as gambling and drinking and they have not the money to do this.'[46] Those who were employed in industry often fared little better; the concern of responsible Africans and Europeans over conditions for juveniles in factories has already been noted.[47]

It was also disturbing that the influence of the urban schools was so restricted. In Salisbury in 1943 missionaries and officials thought that only about half the children of school-going age were at school,[48] and three years earlier a careful survey gave the same proportion at Broken Hill in Northern Rhodesia.[49] Even if the schools could have provided sufficient places, poverty prevented many children from taking advantage of the facilities. Education usually demands sacrifices from parents anxious to give their children the best possible opportunities, but the very poor may not have sufficient resources for any sacrifice at all. It was not solely a question of school fees; though here perhaps one should remember that, whereas compulsory education was provided free of charge at Government schools for all European children not at private schools, Africans had to pay fees at the mission schools, which were still in 1943 the only ones available to them except at Highfield and Luveve village settlements. These fees were by no means high—at Salisbury for instance they varied between three and eight shillings per annum—but there was also the cost of books, all of which had to be purchased by the students themselves, contributions to sports and other funds, and the cost of a school uniform for girls.[50] Even for one child this outlay represented a considerable sacrifice, especially in view of the fact that the benefits of schooling were often neither obvious nor certain, and for more than one child it was a sacrifice which many parents were quite unable to make. Some Africans of course spent far larger sums in educating their children by sending them away to rural boarding schools, and even to the Union for secondary and higher education. These, however, were the fortunate few who had managed to get their heads above the crowd. They were able and willing to make the

[46] Evidence to Howman Committee, p. 114.
[47] See above, Part II, Chap. II, pp. 226–7, 236.
[48] Evidence to Howman Committee, pp. 223, 384.   [49] Wilson, p. 32.
[50] Evidence to Howman Committee, p. 223, and Gussman, op. cit., p. 156.

sacrifice, even though it had not been considered in assessing their 'cost of living'.

But over and above the immediate problem of the out-of-pocket expenses of education there was the pressure, common to most really poor communities, on every individual, however young, to become self-supporting, or at least to make an immediate contribution to the household's income. In many homes this must have been the basic force driving the child out to factory, European garden, or location bottle-washing. Often there were of course the attractions of independence, and no doubt in some cases education was not desired enthusiastically—though this seems to have been relatively rare among African parents by the time of the Second World War; but beneath all lay the ugly compulsion of poverty.

The situation might have been less serious had the schools been able to influence decisively those children of the urban areas who did attend them. But attendance was irregular and few pupils reached even Standard One. Very few indeed reached Standard Six, the end of primary education; at the schools for Africans in the Bulawayo area in 1950 over half the children were in the two sub-standards and only 4 per cent. were in Standard Six.[51] As a result Africans tended to have a ridiculously exaggerated idea of the importance of Standard Six and the positions for which it qualified them. On the other hand, Europeans, irritated by the pretensions of the Africans and exasperated at the expense of a system which produced so many apparent failures, questioned the necessity and benefits of African education as a whole and insisted that it should merely concern itself with discipline and the dignity of manual labour.[52] Yet perhaps these failures were not the fault of the curriculum or even of the staff, inadequate as this often was, but of the fact that far too many children received far too little schooling, and it was idle to blame the schools for conditions over which they had no control. The situation demanded not only a

[51] Gussman, op. cit., p. 151. In the country as a whole only 1 per cent. were in Standard VI. From the end of Standard VI, which admits to the beginning of secondary education, it takes two years to complete Standards VII and VIII.

[52] Ibid., p. 160. Some Europeans also feared the potential competition of well-educated Africans.

great increase in the number of schools and fully trained teachers, but also an equally resolute attempt to lift the burden of crushing poverty from African families and to make it possible for the youth of the towns to grow up in a stable, secure community.

The aged presented perhaps the most intractable problem of urbanization. They were almost as important to a contented community as the women and children; their wisdom and experience would enrich and mould public opinion; their presence would enormously strengthen parental authority. But few African men and women could look forward to a secure old age in the towns. The despair expressed by elderly African witnesses to the Howman Committee has already been mentioned.[53] They had managed to save nothing; turned out of their jobs and homes, they could not hope to continue to live in the towns, whilst their links with the rural areas had been broken. Relatively few African workers were sufficiently valuable to justify the provision of a pension by their employers, and a lump sum availed little in the towns.[54] They were forbidden by the Land Apportionment Act to purchase property in the European areas. The Native Purchase Areas were, in general, situated at far too great a distance from the towns to meet the needs of urban Africans, and although a few of the wealthier urban Africans did manage to purchase farms in them, they were primarily designed to encourage a class of yeomen farmers rather than absentee landowners with little farming experience.

Elderly Africans voiced their demands quite clearly. They wanted a system of house-ownership in the newer Locations, and the possibility of purchasing land on which to build their own houses in an urban suburb. 'Lack of this', said a member of the Native Welfare Society, 'makes it impossible for us to become good workers because, if I have my home in the Reserve, I have to go home and plough.' Mr. Dick Masunda, a cook at a hotel in Bulawayo and a member of the Native Council in the Location, asked the Howman Committee why the Municipal Council could not set aside a place where Africans could buy land.

I put it to you, Sir [he added] I have been working for forty years, I would be no more use to go back to the kraal. My life is not the same,

[53] See above, Part II, Chap. II, p. 226.   [54] See above, Part II, Chap. II, p. 238.

I have lost the customs of the Reserves and I could not settle down. My dress is different, and I use soap and have good food and a decent sleeping place. I would appreciate a little place to have a garden. The people in the Reserve look upon me as having spent all my life with the European. I am not going to save enough money to afford to stay in the location. I must have my own property, and I am getting old now.[55]

In two experiments in Northern Rhodesia some measure of assistance and security was given to urban Africans. At Broken Hill the mine provided 750 five-acre plots where some of its employees were able to construct two or three huts and grow maize and vegetables, and following this lead the Government also leased out similar plots for fifty shillings a year with no services provided. Already by 1940 these plots were proving to be a 'very valuable' provision for aged relatives.[56] This example was not followed in other Northern Rhodesian towns, but by 1947 five African townships were established within five to eight miles of European towns on the Copperbelt. They were primarily intended for self-employed Africans, for traders and craftsmen, and in 1951 their total population was estimated at 5,000. Africans could rent residential plots on which they could erect their own houses, and they could also rent garden plots for maize and vegetables. There was no provision for freehold ownership, and consequently Africans were still unable to raise a mortgage, but these townships were self-governing and almost self-supporting,[57] and they offered a new hope to the urban African.[58] In Southern Rhodesia, as Mr. Howman pointed out to Masunda, the policy of segregation precluded any similar development. But even if this had not been so it seems improbable that a city as large as Bulawayo could ever find sufficient land close enough at hand to provide large plots for the majority of its African workers, and this fact would seem to constitute a strong argument for decentralization. It is true that satellite towns, garden-cities for wage-earners, have only recently been built in England, but in Africa, where industrialization causes a far more tumultuous social upheaval, the need is greater.

[55] Evidence to the Howman Committee, pp. 294, 336.
[56] Wilson, op. cit., Part I, pp. 22–4, 56.   [57] See below, p. 272.
[58] Annual Report of African Affairs Department, 1947; L. D. Conyngham, 'African Towns in Northern Rhodesia', *Journal of African Administration*, 1951, pp. 113–17.

Housing, schools, and security for the aged were the basic requirement of any satisfactory family life in the towns. They were the essential complements to increased wages and greater productivity. Yet it was already apparent that one thing further was needed. Urban Africans, particularly in Southern Rhodesia, had remarkably few opportunities for developing, as a community, any corporate independence, initiative, and self-respect. In part this was due to the incessant movements of the mass of Africans, from job to job, from location to kraal, from the Protectorates to the Union. For example 49·6 per cent. of the labour force employed by the Salisbury Municipality changed employment during the year ending 30 June 1948.[59] This instability gravely handicapped all attempts at association, from the myriad little burial and self-help societies to the efforts to promote trade unionism.

In part this communal ineffectiveness may also have been due to the heterogeneous nature of African urban communities. A recent study on the Copperbelt has shown that tribal affiliations seem to be of only secondary importance in the emerging urban environment. But in the mining community, even after the development of trade unions, tribal, linguistic, and cultural differences have remained important. In addition to their domestic and social significance, they intensify divisions based on the emerging class structure.[60] Away from the mining communities the influence of tribal differences seems to have been greater; Gussman, for instance, considered that 'to the Matabele who thinks along tribal lines, Bulawayo is overwhelmingly populated by aliens'.[61] But in the post-war years Central Africa would seem to have escaped the tribal faction fights which are a feature of the South African urban scene.

In Southern Rhodesia European policy and administration constituted the final factor preventing the emergence of a vigorous and effective African public opinion in local urban affairs. Africans were constantly reminded of their conquered status by the Pass Laws—a stigma of defeat, destroying their self-confidence and

[59] *Second Annual Report of the Director of Native Administration, Salisbury.*
[60] A. L. Epstein, *Politics in an Urban African Community* (Manchester, 1958), *passim.*
[61] Op. cit., p. 36.

exposing them to the never far distant fear of interference from the police. In 1942 there were 18,000 convictions under the Pass Laws.[62]

Another aspect of this subjection to a thorough and far-reaching administration was the fact that all disputes involving urban Africans were, in Southern Rhodesia, settled by Europeans: minor cases were often decided by location and compound managers, while others were brought to the office of the Native Commissioner or the Magistrate's Court. This was in striking contrast to Northern Rhodesia, where African Urban Courts played an important part in the life of the community. They had been started in 1936, when courts in the rural areas, established as part of the policy of indirect rule, were functioning very successfully, and it was decided to appoint a panel of African Assessors, drawn from the councillors of rural courts, to assist the District Commissioners in urban areas. Originally it was feared that the Urban Courts would be quite unable by themselves to administer justice in the midst of so radical a social transformation, that they would evolve a law that was 'neither customary nor English', with no settled procedure, and that in an urban area the members of the court would be unusually open to bribery unless they were under close and constant supervision. The District Officers, however, found that they had insufficient time to sit with the African Assessors and that in fact they proved quite capable of hearing the cases by themselves. The first Urban Court was established at Mufulira in 1938, and by 1940 fully constituted courts were successfully functioning on the Copperbelt and at Lusaka, Broken Hill, and Livingstone.[63]

Traditionally, tribal courts were concerned with upholding broad moral values rather than enforcing specific points of law; they sought to discover which of the parties had conformed more closely to their ideal form of social relationships. Thus, despite the wide variety of tribal customs with which the courts were confronted in the urban areas, they could avoid a conflict of law by employing the traditional procedure of appealing to supreme

[62] Evidence to the Howman Committee, p. 362.

[63] R. L. Moffat, 'Native Courts in Northern Rhodesia', a paper read to the Institute of Administrators of Non-European Affairs, 1955.

values without referring to any particular system of tribal law. Marriage contracts, for instance, might differ greatly in form between tribes, but there was a general agreement about the moral values demanded by a marital relationship.[64] The value of such courts in giving urban Africans an opportunity of maintaining by themselves a 'positive public ethic' was recognized by far-sighted administrators in Southern Rhodesia,[65] but in 1956 there were still doubts south of the Zambezi whether Africans had sufficient integrity to preside in court and whether the litigants should not return to the rural area for the issue to be tried there. The necessity —even the educative value—of allowing urban Africans to exercise responsibility on their own was by no means generally accepted.

The problem of giving urban Africans some degree of legislative and administrative—as opposed to judicial—responsibility in their own affairs was even more complicated. In Southern Rhodesia Advisory Boards, with their members at first appointed by location superintendents and later elected by the tenants of Council rooms and houses, sometimes acted as a useful channel for grievances. The authorities were, however, by no means bound to take effective notice of their opinions, and in general the Boards gave no training in responsibility, but merely added to the frustration of the urban African. In Northern Rhodesia, in those towns which were governed by local authorities responsible to European ratepayers, conditions were very similar. Urban Advisory Councils were merely a channel for complaints. Reporting on Broken Hill and Lusaka for 1950 the Provincial Commissioner wrote: 'Earlier enthusiasm is being replaced by a sense of frustration which has expressed itself in the greater volume of grievances—genuine and illusory. This is to be expected when Council proposes and the Town Board disposes.'[66]

In contrast to those in Southern Rhodesia, these Northern Rhodesian Urban Advisory Councils had one important positive

---

[64] Epstein, op. cit., pp. 198–223.
[65] E.g. A paper read by Dr. Hugh Ashton to the Institute of Administrators of Non-European Affairs, 1954.
[66] Quoted in a Report on Local Government, by Roger Howman (cyclostyled, Salisbury, 1952–3), Part II, para. 88.

T

function: together with the Tribal Councils and Authorities they were the base of the pyramid of indirect elections by which Africans sent forward their representatives first to the Provincial Councils, then to the Protectorate Council, and finally, in 1948, to the territory's Legislative Council. This chain of representation stimulated political discussions through all levels, and not least in the Urban Councils, where there was a far greater concentration of politically-awakened Africans; it did not, however, fulfil the need for a conscious, increasing control over their own affairs at a local level. This control, together with spontaneous initiative and responsibility, was found only in those five purely African satellite townships on the Copperbelt previously referred to.[67]

Each of these townships had a Board of five to seven African members elected by a ballot of house-owners. The Boards levied rates and earned other revenue from licence fees, and from the sale of bricks, beer, and timber. They received direct grants from the Government, though these decreased as the towns became established and were able, like the European towns, to raise loans. They were served by Town Secretaries, young educated Africans, with a salary of £5 to £7. 10s. per month, on whose enthusiasm, interest, and initiative much of the success of the system depended. Responsible for all services for which there was an expressed demand—roads, buildings, lighting, schools, health, and welfare—these Boards showed that Africans were capable of providing and running modern amenities for themselves. Admittedly they only catered for small communities, minute in comparison to the great masses accumulated in the 'European' townships. But in Southern Rhodesia the Government village settlements of Luveve and Highfield presented a comparable opportunity; yet these model villages had 'never been cemented into an organic self-conscious community'. At Highfield in 1953 there was no community centre, 'not even the essential village hall'; there was an unofficial 'Advisory Council' for consultation but it had no constitution and no responsibilities.[68]

In the areas administered by European local authorities there was then, in both the Rhodesias, little opportunity for Africans to exer-

[67] See above, p. 268.　　　　[68] R. Howman, Part VII, para. 69.

cise any control and initiative. And surely if the towns were to assist in the creation of a united, industrial country it was essential that urban Africans should not be left disastrously frustrated with little chance of developing responsibility. This opportunity, this chance, might have been given to them in either of two ways. The existing urban conglomerations could have been broken down into smaller units and, especially in freshly constructed areas of family housing, given a practical autonomy with loose European control. But if this alternative were chosen there would probably be considerable difficulty over the allocation of funds and functions. Or, secondly, if the municipal investment in housing and services precluded the first alternative, there would have to be a gradual extension towards a common municipal franchise, with direct representation of the African areas in common with the rest.

In this urban situation the Christian missions had a great opportunity. They could have provided an opening for African initiative and leadership, a demonstration of inter-racial co-operation, and a source of new values adapted to the new environment. In fact they were succeeding only to a very limited extent. They were heavily committed in the rural areas with an accumulated burden of responsibilities for schools, hospitals, and pastoral work. Even had the urgent needs of the towns been fully recognized it would still have been difficult to divert personnel and financial resources. The European missionaries stationed in Bulawayo, for example, spent most of their time supervising the rural kraal schools scattered throughout Matabeleland; practically no house-to-house visiting was possible for them, they appeared but seldom in the Location, and in 1951 the only European specially allocated to attend to the pastoral needs of the 60,000 Africans of Bulawayo was one Roman Catholic priest. Other denominations had African ordained ministers residing in the Location. Often they were experienced men of considerable moral stamina and sincerity, but in general their education had ended at Standard Six, they had very little theological training, and they were burdened with rural responsibilities. Most of the church buildings were situated in Church Row in the Location. They were used as classrooms during the week, and one observer reported that, with the exception of those belonging to the Roman Catholics and Anglicans, the churches in the Location presented a general appearance of dirt, drabness, and disrepair.[69]

Tensions between African church members and European missionaries were already evident in the inter-war period;[70] they were intensified in the towns. The great work of the pioneer missionaries had created a deep fund of loyalty and gratitude among many Africans, but the days when the missionary often stood out as a unique champion of African rights had passed. Now Africans, especially in the towns, were coming to believe that their future depended on their own strength and efforts, and they were correspondingly disinclined to accept without question European rule in any sphere. They were more and more reluctant to contribute financially to an organization whose European leaders lived at a far higher standard than themselves, and few were capable of appreciating the missionaries' sacrifices. In the towns Africans realized that most Europeans were not church-goers, they were confronted with a bewildering number of denominational differences—fourteen in Bulawayo alone—and in the conditions in which they lived it is not surprising that many abandoned all interest in religion. Some of them joined Separatist Churches, while others returned to a belief, which had perhaps never been wholly abandoned, in the religion of their ancestors.[71] Often it was still the diviner who could most effectively bring comfort and relief to urban Africans, and in the dearth of professional openings for educated Africans his career was still one of the few which conferred any considerable prestige and satisfaction.[72]

We have seen, then, that the influx of Africans into the towns presented Europeans with two main problems. There were first the thousands of migrant males who had formed the bulk of the labour supply for mines and farms and who continued to arrive from the neighbouring territories and the Reserves. In the towns these men needed the help and control of a firmly paternalistic authority. They needed hygienic quarters, adequate feeding

[69] Gussman, op. cit., pp. 250–3. [70] See above, Part I, Chap. IV, pp. 144–6.

[71] Gussman, op. cit., pp. 250–73.

[72] Wulf Sachs, op. cit., pp. 101–3, and Hellmann, op. cit., p. 109.

arrangements, health inspection, good, cheap beer, football, and strict policing. All this was on the whole readily appreciated by Europeans and the difficulty in dealing with the problem was mainly one of finance.

But the development of secondary industries, with their interest in a more stable labour force, the desire of Africans themselves to settle with their families in the towns and the necessity of fostering stability and good farming practices in the rural areas, confronted Europeans with the entirely different problem of building up permanent urban African communities. This was far more complex— perhaps impossible for an alien race. Certainly the problem was not clearly visualized as a whole, and in Southern Rhodesia the belief that the European alone had a permanent stake in the towns created a host of difficulties and obstacles. The Land Apportionment Act intensified congestion and prevented Africans from being given adequate plots for allotments and aged relatives. It denied them security of tenure, making it impossible for an African to raise a mortgage, build his own house, or provide for the future. And under this Act it was the African squatter and not the European landlord or employer who was liable to prosecution.[73] Municipal financial accountancy often made the African section of the town pay more heavily for municipal services; profits from Kaffir beer were used to finance projects which were provided for other races out of general funds.[74] The barrier against the African skilled worker extended in some cases to the construction of African housing.[75] And the refusal to permit the urban African to exercise initiative and responsibility intensified the difficulties and dangers that lay ahead.

[73] Evidence to the Howman Committee, p. 68, and McNamee, op. cit.
[74] G. Ballenden, *Report on Salisbury's Native Administration* (cyclostyled, 1945).
[75] See above, p. 252.

IV. EUROPEAN AWAKENINGS

I. STABILIZATION

The 'Statement on Native Policy in Southern Rhodesia' published by Sir Godfrey Huggins on 6 November 1941 was the final official exposition of the policy of segregation as formulated in the inter-war period. Replying to overseas allegations that segregation prevented Africans from advancing, Huggins maintained that there were more than sufficient openings for the advanced African in his own areas. In the Native Reserves there was an 'urgent need' for teachers, medical orderlies, and midwives, and a start was being made on secondary education, so that ultimately Africans could provide their own doctors. Clerks were needed for the Native Councils and Courts; African townships were visualized in the Reserves 'where all the services will be provided by Africans'. Those who advocated more openings for Africans in the European area were, therefore, 'rendering a signal disservice to the Africans as a whole. . . . In the white towns—what might be described as the white reserves as opposed to the Native Reserves—the African has to conform to white requirements. It should be noted that he is not obliged to go to a white town; he can earn outside the town what for him is a good living, if he does not like the restrictions in the towns.'

The immediate policy was thus still completely unaffected by the dramatic industrial and urban developments which were already taking place. Colour classified the individual, and even for the 'advanced African' it was the major determinant of his status and opportunities. The towns, like the European farms, were sacrosanct; the communities they nourished were to be inviolably white. Eyes were closed to any other immediate possibilities; the only sure signpost to the foreseeable future pointed to segregation.

This policy of segregation was adopted in the twenties from a variety of motives.[1] Fears of miscegenation and of close contact with a strange and primitive people had made segregation seem the natural and inevitable method of confronting the threat of economic and political competition. Some people thought that this separation should be made as thorough as possible; others had hoped that economic co-operation would steadily increase. There was, however, no widespread and passionately held conviction that racial segregation was unalterably ordained by Science or the Deity. The approach of many Europeans remained to a certain extent pragmatic, and in 1941 Huggins underlined the uncertainty of the future. His 'Statement' envisaged the possibility 'of the two parallel lines in our parallel development policy coming together in some very distant future . . . you cannot plan for the unknown, to state that the lines will never meet is stating what is not and cannot be known.'[2] Huggins' freedom from doctrinaire obsession, however cautiously expressed, was of considerable significance for Southern Rhodesia; but there was as yet no appreciation of the immediate challenge of industrialization, and no sign of the complete change in his views which he saw when, fourteen years later, he looked back over his political career.[3] This, however, was soon to come.

The urgency of the urban problem was rapidly revealed to the Government. Ibbotson's report documenting the poverty and hardships of urban Africans was published in 1943, and in the same year the Howman Committee collected its evidence. Several industrialists who gave evidence maintained that since stability of labour was essential, the policy of segregation would have to be modified. The spokesman of the Junior Chamber of Commerce at Bulawayo thought that segregation was not feasible 'because you are bound to get the Native to help the European in this country'. The President of the National Industrial Council of the Building Industry did not believe in segregation because 'the Native must be educated up to take his part in industrial life'; he thought that

[1] See above, Part I, Chap. I.
[2] *Statement on Native Policy in Southern Rhodesia* (Salisbury, Government Printer), 6 November 1941.
[3] Cf. Speech at Umtali, *Rhodesia Herald*, 21 September 1955.

provision would have to be made for those whose outlook was industrial and not rural. The manager of the *Bantu Mirror*, the first newspaper for Africans in Bulawayo, who a few years previously had been 'an ardent segregationist', was now convinced that Africans had 'got to become permanent town dwellers'. Some officials supported these opinions. A town planner said: 'I have never really thought the Land Apportionment Act a really practical measure because it is too costly to put into action.' An official appointed to report on plans for social security was certain that if there was no social security for urban Africans there would be none for Europeans either, and the Director of Native Education said in reference to urban Africans: 'Despite what we may think about the segregation policy, these people are here to stay.'[4] Howman himself in the twenties had been a believer in as thorough a separation as was possible,[5] but towards the end of the Committee's sittings he told a witness: 'The Government's policy is segregation, but it seems to have gone by the board.'[6] The Committee's report was severely critical of some of the effects of segregation.

Segregation [it said] has assigned to these labourers a purely temporary, make-shift existence in the urban area; the very words 'Location' and 'Compound' are expressive of the theory which visualizes 'homes' and 'communities' as something to be associated only with the Native Reserves to which the labourer was expected to return. . . . Segregation has not only tended to suppress family life, but to place most strenuous obstacles in the way of those who have sought to set up homes in the urban areas and the consequences ramify into every field of the economic, industrial, moral and social order. Perhaps such unnatural conditions are an inevitable phase in the quick transition from a simple peasantry to an urban proletariat but the tragedy lies in the failure to appreciate the grave need to provide the fullest possible community facilities, housing and educational machinery that would make possible the growth of a natural family, community and social urban life . . . what is culpable is our failure to recognise it as a transitional phase which deserves all the social or educational machinery we can bring to bear on it. Instead our segregation policy prolongs it by en-

[4] Evidence to the Howman Committee, pp. 22, 136, 158, 201, 309, 385.
[5] See above, Part I, Chap. I, p. 17.   [6] Ibid., p. 269.

deavouring to keep the African a tribal peasant, in a peasant's home with haphazard peasant standards and attitudes, with an occasional spell in industry: a chameleon-like change to meet the régime of town life and efficiency.

The Howman Committee presented its report in January 1944. In November Huggins laid before the Legislative Assembly some tentative proposals for legislation designed to deal with the most urgent problem of housing for African workers and families. The 1930 Land Apportionment Act had enabled local authorities to set aside a scheduled Native Urban Area and assume responsibility for its administration. Since Africans continued to have a legal right to own or occupy property in the town until such an area was set aside, it had been assumed that the local authorities would hasten to implement this provision. In fact, however, although a few Africans occupied small shops and eating-houses in the meaner quarters of some towns, none had been able to acquire property and, consequently, all the local authorities had been content to bide their time. Huggins now proposed to enable the Governor to compel local authorities to set aside Native Urban Areas and to undertake specific responsibilities. They were to provide 'adequate housing' for all urban Africans except those who were housed on approved private premises. All employers of Africans in the area of a local authority would be compelled to provide free accommodation for their employees either on their own approved private premises or by hiring accommodation in the local authority's Native Urban Area. So far this merely meant the legal tightening up of what was general practice, but Huggins added one small clause which involved a dramatic departure from previous official policy. The rent payable by the employer for housing in the Native Urban Area was to be the same for a married African and his wife as for a single man. Since the rents would be used by the local authority to cover the costs of all their housing, married and single quarters alike, this clause was in essence an ingenious and efficient device which forced all urban employers to subsidize married Africans.

Huggins' proposal was the first move towards a new policy of stabilizing the African population into rural and urban sections,

of gradually recognizing that the races were daily brought together in a closer economic integration and interdependence. He
defended this departure on three main counts:

First, we have to get away from the unnatural life of masses of males
living together without their wives, and the complete absence of any
home life. Secondly, we cannot go on for ever finding more land for
natives to live on, or, rather, their family and stock to live on whilst the
male has another home in the town location. We have to realise that a
permanent urban class is arising and is bound to grow in the future
unless the people in the European towns are prepared to manage without any native assistance, and the time has passed when that might have
been possible, so we must face the facts as they are. [Thirdly there is
the new need of secondary industry for] an efficient, stable labour
force. . . . In practice the provision of decent accommodation for
married natives is essential if the native is to become more efficient and
good at his job, and unless we can improve the native worker and incidentally make him worth more, there is little future for the country.[7]

Other proposed clauses enabled local authorities to establish
employment bureaux where all Africans employed in urban areas
would be compelled to register and records would be kept in an
attempt to distinguish between good and bad workers. Local
authorities were also 'to control the entry of all natives into the
European town', and to this end they were to have the power 'to
set up their own Native Department to undertake the duties of
registrar of Natives and town pass officer appointed under the
Natives Registration Act and inspectors under the Native Urban
Location Act'. To finance this registration they would be empowered to impose a tax on all employers and to receive all fines
paid for the contravention of their by-laws. The Government
was to remain responsible for hospitals and when it could provide
sufficient facilities 'education of a suitable character' would be
made compulsory for all juveniles, none of whom would be given
permits to work in the town.[8]

In closing the debate Huggins stated that twenty years previously his proposals would have been received with derision.
During the Second World War, however, people realized that

[7] S.R. Debates, 23 November 1944, cols. 2499–2506.   [8] Ibid., cols. 2499, 2510.

they were 'fighting the herrenvolk theory' and the 'great interest which has been taken in social security' made many people think that 'we cannot have social security on a racial basis'.[9] The isolation of this outpost of Europe was diminishing and a few of the white Rhodesians were becoming readier to reconsider the future of their country and to take a serious interest in all sections of its people.

Huggins was careful, however, to emphasize that he did not consider that his proposals clashed with the policy of segregation. He criticized the Howman Report for blaming segregation for the disruption of family life. Segregation, he said, did not necessarily separate families: lack of accommodation and a sufficient wage to keep a wife in an urban area was, he thought, the cause of this disruption. 'I mention this to the House', he continued, 'because segregation is often blamed in error, and partial segregation is our policy at the present stage of development.'[10] In part this may well have been lip-service to a doctrine which was still dear to his constituents; but Huggins also showed signs of being reluctant to examine the full implications of stabilization. He mentioned the necessity for recognizing the growth of a permanent urban class, but he did not go into the question of what was to happen to those who were too old to work. He merely said that this was 'all wrapped up in social security in general': nor did he even mention the basic problem of giving Africans security of tenure and a stake in their new environment. There was little appreciation of the urgency of creating sturdy communities capable of assimilating the benefits of an urban civilization; and no public recognition of the obstacles which segregation and its assumptions placed in the way of this assimilation. Huggins' proposals amounted in fact to a policy of firm paternalism: a partial readjustment to the more obvious needs of the African worker in a European town.

The proposed legislation was, moreover, merely of an enabling nature. The local authorities could, if necessary, be compelled to take action, but the whole scheme hinged on their co-operation and on the provision of adequate married housing in their areas.

[9] S.R. Debates, 30 November 1944, col. 2802.   [10] Ibid., col. 2514.

The chief point of Huggins' accountancy device was lost if there were no houses for married Africans. In the Union of South Africa the Central Government had assisted local authorities with sub-economic loans for the erection of African housing, and some critics of Huggins' proposals thought that the Government was trying to evade its legitimate responsibilities. One of the strongest critics was Donald MacIntyre, a Bulawayo industrialist, shortly to become Mayor of Bulawayo and at that time a leading member of the Southern Rhodesian Labour Party. He considered that the Central Government, including the farming and mining interests, should share in the burden because 'most of the taxation' already came from the urban areas. He thought that the problem could be met by raising the standard of wages throughout the country, though he admitted that this would adversely affect the powerful farming interests.[11] The answer to this criticism was that the only beneficiaries of a sub-economic housing scheme were the payers of low industrial wages and that by bearing the burden directly themselves industrialists would be encouraged to increase the efficiency and output of their labour. But it remained arguable that the Government should play a much more active part in urban affairs and, as one of Huggins' supporters realized,[12] his proposals remained at the mercy of obstruction and non-co-operation by those most directly involved.

The other main line of European criticism came from those who still believed that racial separation should be implemented as thoroughly and energetically as possible. In the twenties this line of thought had been supported by many officials and other Europeans who felt that such a separation would be the only means of preserving African integrity and culture and of very gradually adapting them to the needs of the modern world. By the forties, however, it was evident that the process of disruption had proceeded too far, and the policy of total separation was now inspired almost solely by the conviction that it presented the only hope of European survival. In the Legislative Assembly this point of view was most forcibly stated by J. H. Smit, who until his resignation in 1942 had been Finance Minister in Huggins'

[11] S.R. Debates, 24 November 1944, col. 2568.   [12] Ibid., col. 2556.

Cabinet. It was evident, he said, that Huggins still had no native policy. The question should have been tackled from the foundation, and, Smit continued:

the foundation is this, that the native population of the Colony has to be developed on the family and communal life in the native reserves, that is, in their own territory. We have to prevent that drift to the towns which has been so greatly brought to our notice of late years... then we would see that the natives would not stay away from their families so long that it might do damage to the family life in the reserves.[13]

Although its practical implications were never very clearly stated or the exact ways in which it differed from Huggins' proposals made perfectly clear, this policy of total separation still commanded widespread support among the European electorate. Huggins' proposals were eventually embodied in the Native (Urban Areas) Accommodation and Registration Act of 1946; in the election which followed later that year the newly-formed Liberal Party, led by Smit, captured twelve seats as against the thirteen won by Huggins' United Party. Huggins later said that the Act was used against him during the election 'because it was novel and not done in the Union or, for that matter, in the United Kingdom',[14] and the result of the election underlined the difficulty of achieving even the modest readjustment envisaged by Huggins.

While Huggins was preparing legislation designed to deal with the housing situation, an event occurred which emphasized the urgency of the other immediate problem of urban wages. On Monday, 22 October 1945, the 2,400 Africans employed by Rhodesia Railways at Bulawayo came out on strike. They returned to work the following Monday only after the Government had intervened and promised to appoint a Commission to inquire into their grievances. In the meantime the strike had spread to other railway centres in both the Rhodesias and it was 3 November before the last of the strikers returned to work. The actual occasion of the strike was the introduction of a new rate of overtime pay, which, although an improvement for most workers,

[13] S.R. Debates, 24 November 1944, cols. 2551–2.
[14] Speech to the Native Welfare Society, 20 August 1946, reprinted from the *Bulawayo Chronicle*.

was a reduction for a minority and was in any case widely misunderstood. There had, however, previously been considerable signs of discontent among African employees: there were meetings in the Railway Compounds, and in March 1944 the 'Rhodesia Railways African Employees' Association' was formed in Bulawayo. This body continued to submit claims for an increased cost of living allowance and better working conditions, but the Railway Administration refused to grant it any recognition or to respond to its requests. Finally, in October 1945, a delegation wishing to see the General Manager with reference to the new overtime rates was informed that 'if they waited six months they would not be seen'. The strike, however, made action imperative.

The Chairman of the Commission appointed to inquire into the strikers' grievances was Sir Robert Tredgold, then a Judge of the High Court, and the Rev. Percy Ibbotson was a leading member. In their report the Commission recommended a basic wage of 30s. a month for the Railways; for industry as a whole they considered that 'immediate action' should be given to the creation of a sub-department, under the Native Affairs Department, specially charged to deal with the problems of native labour. They also recommended that the Government should consider legislation similar to the 1937 Wage Act of the Union whereby a Board appointed by the Government could fix wages in different industries and types of employment. Above all, the Commission urged that the assumption that the urban African employee could be treated as a single man was no longer valid.

It is generally overlooked [said their report] that the so-called 'bachelor' has often a wife and children or other dependants in a native area. In the past it is possible that this assumption involved no great hardship, for as a general rule these people were at least partially self-supporting. But the assumption cannot continue. A large number of Africans is becoming more or less permanently urbanised. Apart from this, the growth of population in the native areas, and their exhaustion through past neglect, is increasing the dependence upon the wage earning worker in the town.[15]

[15] *Report of the Commission to investigate the grievances which gave rise to the strike amongst the African employees of the Rhodesia Railways* (Salisbury, 1946).

Thus under the impact of the strike the recommendations of Ibbotson and the Howman Committee were at last accepted, at any rate partially, in official quarters. The contrast with Tredgold's opinions of four years previously[16] is a striking example of the way in which some thoughtful Rhodesians were prepared to re-examine their basic assumptions. The successful organization of the railway strike 'compelled' the leader of the Europeans in Northern Rhodesia, Mr. Roy Welensky, himself a railway trade unionist, to change his views on African capabilities.[17] Eyes which had previously been closed to the world around them were gradually being opened.

Huggins accepted the principal recommendations of the Commission. In 1947 the Native Labour Board Act created the machinery for dealing with wage disputes affecting Africans, and in the same year a sub-department of Native Labour was established. Its immediate impact was, however, limited by lack of staff and, as events in the following year made clear, the slow-moving machinery of the Labour Boards was an inadequate substitute for collective bargaining. The immediate effects of the Native Urban Areas Act were also disappointing. The Act was at first virtually ignored by the Bulawayo Municipality, where the old régime of divided responsibility continued and where there was in consequence no overall urgent attempt to deal with the urban problem. In Salisbury the Municipality established a Native Administration Department in March 1946 and the Act was brought into force on 10 January 1947. One of the immediate benefits was that the income from rents, now collected directly from employers, more than doubled. Plans were drawn up for further housing construction, and it was decided to provide better accommodation for married Africans, with a separate lavatory for each family. The provisions covering Registration were enforced and gradually it became possible to gain a more accurate grasp of the situation in the main township of Harare.

By 1949 it was ascertained that there were nearly 3,000 Africans, all holders of certificates of occupation, over and above the

[16] See above, Part II, Chap. II, p. 229.
[17] Cf. his speech to the Royal Empire Society, *African Affairs*, Vol. 45, p. 188.

approved capacity of the existing accommodation. Housing in the Old Compound was henceforth used for single males, and was let to ten firms on the understanding that on termination of employment the employee would be obliged to vacate the accommodation. This system of 'tied' housing was, however, applied only to what was in the main the migratory type of labour and none of the cottages for married couples was tied to a specific employer. In the rest of Harare 'a general post of inadequately housed families' was organized. Childless couples and those with one child were grouped into one section of the old township, while those with four or more children were given the new semi-detached cottages of three rooms with kitchen, shower, and w.c.[18]

Unfortunately this bringing of order out of seeming chaos often involved cases of considerable hardship and sometimes completely disrupted social bonds which had developed in however tenuous and haphazard a manner. Under the new regulations, for instance, a man could only obtain married accommodation after he had been in continuous employment in Salisbury for at least two years. Although it may well have been necessary to have some such principle as a guide in the allocation of the limited housing available, an investigation carried out by Ibbotson showed that the sudden rigid enforcement of this order caused considerable hardship and aroused much discontent. Prior to 1947 a number of 'advanced' Africans occupied rooms by themselves in Harare; under the new régime they were compelled to live four in a room and cheek by jowl with illiterate migrant workers. There was little sympathetic appreciation of the needs of these men—the natural leaders in an urban environment—and little use was made of the provision in Section 54 of the Act, whereby individuals or classes of individuals could be given exemption from the restrictions imposed by the procedure of Registration.[19]

The implementation of the Act also affected the many Africans living on private plots owned by Europeans. There were, for

[18] *Annual Reports of the Director of Native Administration, Salisbury Municipality.*
[19] Percy Ibbotson, *Report on Effect on Africans in Salisbury of the Implementation of Native Urban Areas) Accommodation and Registration Act of 1946* (cyclostyled, Feb. 1949).

example, the wives and children of domestic servants. Officials found that

> while the average employer considered his cook or other servant to be a decent citizen in favour of whose wife and children he felt the law should be relaxed, the neighbour inevitably felt that the unfortunate native together with his wife and children were certainly of the most objectionable type and could not be tolerated.

In one year 275 complaints from neighbours 'were received and dealt with. These involved the removal from private premises of 867 native women and 1,160 children found in illegal occupation of native quarters.'[20]

Many Africans had found shelter on neighbouring European farms. In some cases this had led to abuses where so-called farmers reaped a harvest of exorbitant rents from squalid little plots. More often, however, there had developed a mutually satisfactory relationship in which the Africans performed small services in return for permission to live on the farms. One example, reported by the European land-owner, was that of six Africans living on a four-acre store plot at Widdicombe Park just outside Salisbury. One was a builder, most of whose contracts for Europeans were 'in respect of virgin bits of veld' where his employers were unable to give him anywhere to live. He looked after the land-owner's store of building materials, regularly paid his 5s. per month rent, and was 'well-behaved'. Another was a painter who had painted the store and paid a rent of 12s. 6d. per month—'an excellent and hard-working type'. A factory labourer watered the fruit trees on the plot and protected it from veld fires. Two others had small carpentry and shoe-making businesses—'a boon and asset to the neighbourhood'—and a sixth, a waiter in Salisbury, looked after livestock on the plot. All these men were suddenly informed in August 1946 that they must quit the premises by the end of October; and their fate was shared by many others.[21] Throughout the Salisbury Municipal area, therefore, many Africans were finding themselves harshly affected by the Act. Its benefits were not

[20] *Annual Reports of the Director of Native Administration, Salisbury*, 1947–50.
[21] Copy of a letter by G. Taylor, 29 September 1946, circulated by the Southern Rhodesia Labour Party.

immediately apparent; it involved much disruption; and a storm of discontent with official policy was added to the burden of poverty and the discomforts of the new environment.

Only on the railways was any improvement felt at once. The Railways Administration created an African Affairs Department responsible for African labour throughout the railway system. This Department carried out a thorough survey of all housing for African staff. Between 1947 and 1950 about 2,300 new quarters were built, costing approximately a quarter of a million pounds, and in 1951–3 it was planned to spend three-quarters of a million pounds. The houses, which cost approximately £130 each, had individual sanitation, stoves, shelves, and storm-water drainage. Extensive welfare activities were undertaken and arrangements were made with the Government for the construction of schools. The Railways adopted a policy of providing for a 75 per cent. married strength 'in order to stabilise labour and obtain greater effectiveness'.[22] They were also far more ready to consider promptly the claims of African employees. Railway Township Advisory Committees were established in nearly all centres, representing the main departments and elected annually by 'popular vote' of the African employees. In August 1947, on receipt of an application from the Rhodesia Railways African Employees' Association, the Native Labour Board was instructed to consider the general conditions of service among Railway African employees. Their recommendations were published on 27 February 1948 and were accepted by the Association as 'on the whole quite satisfactory'.[23] It seemed to Africans that all this had been achieved under the stimulus of the strike of October 1945, and it was natural that Africans outside the Railways should hope to improve their lot by a similar action.

Signs of impending trouble appeared in Bulawayo towards the end of 1947. European employers were circularized with demands for an increase in wages, and in October the African employees of the Municipality held a meeting at which it was suggested that a

[22] Memorandum by Dr. E. M. B. West, Chief Officer, African Affairs Department, Rhodesia Railways, November 1950.
[23] General Secretary's report of the Rhodesia Railways African Employees' Association, October 1952.

strike should be organized if there was no satisfactory reply to
their demands. No answer was given until 22 February 1948, when
the Mayor made what he described as a 'snap offer' of a wage
increase. The employees rejected this offer and asked for the
appointment of a Labour Board to investigate their conditions.
It was, by then, six months since their demand had first been made
but, although the employees followed the procedure laid down by
the Native Labour Boards Act, they were given no answer pend-
ing a conference of employers at Salisbury on 6 April. When they
learnt that the Government had postponed the appointment of a
Labour Board at the request of certain Councillors 'they felt, and
their feeling was communicated to other Africans, that the
Government was on the side of the employers and that they could
expect no help from it'. Tension increased and mass meetings were
held in Bulawayo Location, involving 6,000 Africans on 8 April
and 13,000 five days later.[24]

On Tuesday 13 April many Europeans in Bulawayo spent 'a
tense day. Rumour was rife and uncertainty the dominant note.'[25]
At dawn the next day the storm broke.

Throughout Tuesday night Bulawayo itself was quieter than usual,
but by sunrise on Wednesday morning all hell seemed let loose. From
the location there streamed hundreds of natives armed with knob-
kerries, sticks, hatchets, lead piping, bicycle chains, etc., and they proceeded through the streets yelling, shrieking and booing and beating up
any natives who appeared to be going to work. The mob stopped cars
with natives and dragged them out. They entered private gardens and
forcibly ejected domestic servants, in some cases entering houses and
searching under beds, in cupboards, etc., and again bashing any boy
who resisted. Some women kept the mob from the house by standing
on guard with a gun. School hostels, hospitals, hotels and flats were
similarly treated and after eight o'clock armed pickets circulated
through the back streets of the business centre securing natives from
garages, shops, etc.[26]

The *Bulawayo Chronicle* reported two cases of violence involving Europeans in the centre of the city. In Main Street a European

[24] *Abridged Report of the Commission appointed to inquire into Native Disturbances, 1948.*
[25] *Bulawayo Chronicle*, 14 April 1948.   [26] *The New Rhodesia*, 23 April 1948.

motorist, 'trying to get past a horde blocking the street, was being
pulled from his car by angry natives when Europeans came to his
aid'; and in Fife Street, near the Cecil Hotel, 'a native was seen in
a vanette driven by a European. A milling mob formed up round
the vehicle, beat the van roof with sticks and dragged the native
out.' The strike, it reported, was 'more organised than most people
anticipated. As people drove into the city to start the day's work
they saw native leaders organising and directing their fellows in
pickets and gangs throughout the municipal area.'[27] The police,
however, reinforced by specially enrolled civilians and military
assistance, soon regained control in the centre of the city. 'They
made a quick job of hooligans' and from midday onwards 'scores
of thousands of natives' gathered at various meetings on the out-
skirts of the city. From an aeroplane flying over the location at
4 p.m. fourteen large gatherings were seen 'like clusters of bees,
with individuals and small parties running from one crowd to
another'.[28]

In Bulawayo the strikers soon returned to work, persuaded by
one of their leaders that the Government would review all wages.
But in the meantime the strike spread to Umtali and then Salisbury
and gradually to all the major mining and urban centres in
Southern Rhodesia. Here, however, the Europeans were fore-
warned by the experience of Bulawayo and there were far fewer
encounters with violent mobs. In Salisbury the mass of Africans
were carefully confined in Harare, and one schoolboy reported
that 'at the railway crossing and round about were cheerful looking blokes in khaki. There must be some spiritual satisfaction
derived from twirling a truncheon. At least, I so suspect, for I have
never seen so many cheerful policemen in a long day's march.'[29]
The shock to Europeans was, therefore, greatest in Bulawayo; but
even in the smaller centres the normal run of life was rudely
interrupted. At Marandellas, for example, a dangerous situation
was only narrowly averted:

The Africans attempted to march towards the town on Wednesday
and all attempts at preventing them from doing so broke down. As a

[27] *Bulawayo Chronicle*, 15 April 1948.   [28] *The New Rhodesia*, 30 April 1948.
[29] Ibid., 23 April 1948.

final resort, residents took up shot-guns, rifles and revolvers and threatened to shoot if the strikers took another step forward. The location superintendent and members of the police talked with the natives, got them to sit down, and eventually dispersed them.[30]

Throughout the country Europeans were profoundly disturbed by this sudden interruption of their normal way of life. The railway strike of October 1945 had impressed European leaders with the necessity of providing better conditions in an important industry. It had also helped a few Europeans to see more clearly the necessity of accepting some of the recommendations of Ibbotson and of the Howman Committee. But although this first example of African industrial action had surprised and alarmed many people,[31] it had soon been forgotten and could be said to have passed almost unnoticed by the majority of Europeans. The events of April 1948, however, abruptly and intimately affected every urban European. To their surprise and indignation many were suddenly confronted with the challenge and rivalry of their modern African neighbours. Their immediate reaction seems to have been one of almost bewildered anger. Public meetings protested against 'the maladministration in native policy which has resulted in the present emergency' and demanded firm action against the ringleaders and the sources of 'anti-European propaganda' which were behind them.[32] The Government and the African 'agitator' were the obvious scapegoats even if they had little to do with the actual situation. The Chairman of the Federation of African Welfare Societies reported 'a serious setback owing to the recent strike': people previously associated with Welfare Societies had 'in certain isolated cases already severed their connection with these activities'. The strike and 'hooliganism' had alienated European sympathy, had 'undoubtedly created racial tension', and 'relationships between Europeans and Africans' had been put back for several years.[33] A Rhodesian historian and

---

[30] *Bulawayo Chronicle*, 23 April 1948.

[31] E.g. McNeillie's statement, S.R. Debates, 30 June 1948, col. 1616.

[32] E.g. reports of meetings in Fort Victoria and Umtali, *Bulawayo Chronicle*, 27 April and 1 May 1945.

[33] Memorandum, *The Importance of African Welfare Societies*, issued by the Federation.

writer later gave his impressions in a novel based on his experiences
of the strike in Bulawayo:

This morning, the shops and businesses were open, but the city had
an anaemic look as if some of its blood had been drained off. The white
people made much show of going about their affairs as usual. They pre-
tended they were glad to be without the natives and even tried to make
themselves believe it by saying to each other, 'Isn't it refreshing not
having a lot of bloody kaffirs about?' And their friends would reply,
'Yes, it seems like a real white man's country at last,' as if that were
their goal and they had not freely chosen to come to a country where
the black people were in a majority.

In the bars and at street corners there were many opinions expressed,
and they all summed up to the same things. Some said, 'Arrest the
leaders and sjambok them.' Others, more orthodox, said, 'Shoot them.'
To most people, the only concern was retribution for the natives.
There were some—the unconventional few—who suggested it was just
as necessary to find out the cause of their discontent and put it right.
Such people were looked on with proper suspicion, for in their talk was
the breath of Communism. The ordinary decent citizen, with no
treasonable doubts about the correct relationship of the races, merely
looked on the native as a useless parasite and in his view it was shameful
to suggest, as so many people were doing, that the country's very
existence depended on his work. If the native were to get the idea into
his head, everybody would be at his mercy.[34]

Most Europeans demanded retribution, but some were suddenly
galvanized into a new approach to the problems of a multi-racial
society. The writer of this account was himself an example of the
reaction of some thoughtful European Rhodesians to the impact of
industrialization. Only the previous year he had published a commentary on Southern Rhodesia which advocated an extension and
an ever-increasingly thorough application of the policy of segregation and parallel development. He supported a union with the
territories north of the Zambezi so that Southern Rhodesia could
'offer her black people room to build their own civilization in
climatic conditions that fortunately suit them . . . the principle of
separate settlement areas as already established in Southern
Rhodesia could be extended throughout, and in his own area the

[34] Peter Gibbs, *Stronger than Armies* (Central News Agency, South Africa, 1951).

black man or the white man would have his own franchise, look after his own affairs and live his own life'.[35] This policy, he felt, provided the only alternative to an unending struggle for racial supremacy in which the black would either eventually dominate the white or would be held in perpetual suppression. The 'mingling of the races' would inevitably lead to miscegenation and the Cape Coloured people were 'a warning to civilization of what can and will happen to Africa if racial exclusiveness is allowed to lapse'.[36]

Eight years later these fears had receded into the background; Gibbs had accepted political integration, and had become an active supporter of the Capricorn Society's franchise proposals and of the attempts to implement a policy of partnership in the urban areas. Doubtless many factors influenced his radical change of opinions, prominent among them no doubt his realization, as Secretary of the National Industrial Council of the Engineering Industry, of the inevitability of industrial integration. But it is perhaps not wrong to see the Bulawayo strike as the shock which first started a fresh train of thought. Gibbs described how the strikers entered the garden of the principal character in his novel in search of his domestic servants:

Philip walked confidently up to the leaders and called, 'Get outside the gate!' It was only necessary to command natives firmly and they obeyed. The little native held his ground. 'We will go very soon, baas,' he said, 'but first we must take the baas's cook who is working. We will not hurt the baas or his missus—not this time. That will come one day,' he added gratuitously. This was the first expression of hostility to his race that Philip had heard in his twenty years in the country. He was to look back at that moment as the split second in time when the world he knew entered a new era.[37]

In the Legislative Assembly Huggins offered little comfort to those Europeans who demanded retribution. Instead he stood by the pledges which had been given to the strikers and urged his fellow Europeans to face the facts of the situation. 'Our experience is not unique. We are witnessing the emergence of the proletariat

---

[35] Peter Gibbs, *Landlocked Island* (Bulawayo 1947), pp. 115–16.
[36] Ibid., pp. 112–13.   [37] Gibbs, *Stronger than Armies*.

and in this country it happens to be black.' He thought they were fortunate that very little racial hatred had been displayed, and he maintained that the issue was 'purely economic'.[38] He agreed that it might be 'embarrassing' if an increase of wages was awarded, but he was certain that the only alternative was to have another strike, and he warned the House of the dangers of a 'showdown'.

I quite agree if the natives are going to continue to act in an irresponsible way . . . we will have to have a showdown. That is certain. But I want the House to realise what this is going to involve. Showdowns with the working classes in England when they were emancipated only led to a bit of blood-shed and rioting and then everybody went to work and all the rest of it with some small gain on the part of the workers on each occasion. What would happen here? We should still have a certain amount of casualties and I would like to put this to the employers in this country; what would the next thing be? Fifty-four per cent of our labour would go home, which is not in Southern Rhodesia—and you would never get it back. . . . You are going to paralyse the whole country unless you handle the thing with extreme tact and forbearance. Our natives would go back to their kraals. We should soon get them back. But the alien natives on whom we depend, if you have a showdown, would never come back, and we would not have any labour to carry on the industries of the country.[39]

These cooler counsels prevailed; the anger ebbed away; and there was an accelerated implementation of the policy of firm paternalism in industrial and urban affairs. The strike had made the Colony 'African-conscious'. It had, wrote one commentator, 'awakened in every Rhodesian a sense of indignation and disgust, coupled with an urgency to settle once and for all time just what place, and under what conditions, the African shall now be allowed to share in the life, both present and future, of this Colony's economic set-up'.[40] In September the electorate acquiesced in Huggins' approach, finding no real alternative.[41] A Native Labour Board conducted an intensive survey of conditions of African employees in urban areas. Its recommendations of a rise in basic

[38] S.R. Debates, 5 May 1948, col. 19.
[39] Ibid., 30 June 1948, cols. 1610–13. If read by Nyasaland Africans this reasoning might well increase their fears of Federal control.
[40] *The New Rhodesia*, 7 May 1948.   [41] See below, p. 308.

wages and the compulsory introduction of a system of grading throughout industry were accepted by the Government, and the Native Labour Department was strengthened in an attempt to enforce these provisions.

In Bulawayo the Native Urban Areas Act was at last implemented, and an experienced administrator and anthropologist, Dr. Hugh Ashton, was appointed by the Municipality as Director of African Affairs. Perhaps profiting from the experience of Salisbury, the Bulawayo authorities kept the disruptive and restrictive aspects of the Act to a minimum. There were, for instance, no large-scale police raids for unauthorized women in the Location; instead the powers under the Act were invoked only if an individual was proving to be a nuisance. There was a whole-hearted attempt to make a success of the system of Advisory Councils, although the unsatisfactory limits of the system were clearly recognized.[42] In an effort to counteract the brewing of illegal beer the quality of Municipal beer was raised, and attractive beer kiosks and gardens were constructed to offset the somewhat squalid atmosphere of the beer-hall. Above all, the major problem of housing for married Africans was faced with increasing urgency. In January 1950 the Government proposed a ban on the sale of industrial sites until there was sufficient Municipal accommodation for African workers, but by December the ban was withdrawn in view of the Council's efforts. An emergency scheme was approved by which the Council laid out 2,400 stands for Africans to erect their own accommodation at Hyde Park, a district some miles from the centre of Bulawayo, and at the same time plans were drawn up for very large-scale housing schemes in attractive community suburbs on 1,000 acres of the Western Commonage. But by April 1951 there were nearly 2,000 married Africans on the official waiting-list for accommodation, the waiting-list for single accommodation was growing, and little had been achieved 'in the way of clearing the black spots of the city and the unauthorised erection of shacks in the industrial area'.[43]

The reports of Ibbotson and the Howman Committee had

[42] See above, Part II, Chap. III, p. 271.
[43] Information taken from notes by Dr. Hugh Ashton.

clearly revealed the need for a radical readjustment of policy. With the Native Urban Areas Act, Huggins had provided the legislative basis for a fresh approach to the problem of housing, but no heed had been taken of the repeated recommendations in favour of official wage determination. Practical results were obtained only under the stimulus of the strikes of 1945 and 1948, and even then there was little sign of a fundamental readjustment of outlook. Gradually the emphasis was shifting from 'segregation'—which might or might not mean 'segregation in the African's own interest'—to the choice between 'white leadership for the foreseeable future' and some form of integration. And there were not yet many Europeans who realized that the 'foreseeable future' was a vista that was becoming rapidly shorter; still fewer were aware of the implication in the phrase that when the end of the vista was reached, something was likely to happen. The necessity for permanent African urbanization was slowly becoming accepted, but the full implications were as yet scarcely considered. Indeed, from the point of view of the Africans the results achieved by the 1948 strike were disappointingly meagre. The majority of urban Africans continued to live on the verge of abject poverty and the more able of them still found themselves confined and prevented from advancing to the full extent of their capacities. The hopes of a new order disappeared and their resignation became more bitter.[44]

The incipient policy of urban stabilization had a rural counterpart. Indeed, when Huggins introduced his proposals for the first steps towards this policy he stressed the influence that rural factors had had on their formulation[45] and, speaking later to the Native Welfare Society, he admitted that to his mind the question of permanent urbanization was settled inevitably by the fact that 'as time passes there will be no available land to go back to'.[46] The Natural Resources Committee of 1939 had focused attention on the destruction of the Native Reserves, due to overpopulation and primitive farming methods. Soil erosion was recognized as a pro-

---

[44] See below, Part II, Chap. V, pp. 326–7.   [45] See above, p. 280.
[46] Speech to Native Welfare Society, 20 August 1946, reported in the *Bulawayo Chronicle*.

blem of national importance, and successive Chief Native Commissioners urged the necessity of introducing legislation to restrict the overpopulation of the Reserves and to enforce better farming methods. A settled peasantry enjoying security of tenure, encouraged, and if necessary compelled, to be responsible for such measures as contour-ridging and crop-rotation, was as essential for the rural areas as intelligently trained, permanently urbanized, semi-skilled operatives were for secondary industry.

To meet this need the Native Land Husbandry Bill was introduced in the Legislative Assembly in April 1951. The Bill gave the Government powers to divide up the land in the Native Reserves and to allocate it in equal lots to every individual who had rights in the Reserves. This meant that in some Reserves the lot would amount to sixty acres per head, but in those which were overpopulated, as for example some near Umtali, there would be only one and a half acres per head. These lots would be held by the individual together with a grazing right for as much stock as it was considered possible for the land to maintain. The farming and grazing rights were to be negotiable but indivisible, so that in the course of time it was expected that the holdings would be combined and increase to larger units, while those who were dispossessed would have to find a permanent livelihood in the European areas. Individual plot-holders could be forced to co-operate in measures designed to preserve and increase the fertility of the land. The Bill was an extraordinary effort to carry an entire African population through an agricultural revolution in the space of a very few years. It was unique in Africa and was only possible because the foundations had been patiently laid by the Native Agricultural Department in its successful experiments with Master Farmers and co-operators.[47]

The Bill, however, deprived the African of his rights to the land as enshrined in the Constitution and as envisaged by the Land Apportionment Act; a new generation would grow up cut off for ever from the possibility of owning land in their Reserves. It profoundly affected the whole structure of tribal life. 'Every African', said the *Bantu Mirror*, 'feels an inexplicable pride when he enters

[47] See above, Part I, Chap. II.

a Reserve in which his tribe has lived for many years. . . . To him
it is a sanctuary. This idea of common ownership of the land
cemented tribal bonds and loyalty.' All this would be lost, and
with it much of the status and influence of the chiefs in whom the
land was previously vested.[48] The traditional authorities were
therefore hostile to the Bill, and educated Africans resented the
fact that decisive powers were vested in the Native Commissioners
instead of the Bill being used as an opportunity of giving responsibility to the Native Councils. It was feared also that the myriads of
small holdings into which the Reserves were to be divided would
condemn the African farmer to the perpetual status of a peasant,
while the problem of urban security would become even more
urgent when the dispossessed were cast on to the mercy of the
towns.

These fears and criticisms were voiced in the Legislative
Assembly by Mr. R. S. Garfield Todd. A Protestant missionary
from New Zealand, who had spent some seventeen years living on
a mission station in the midst of a Native Reserve, Todd had
caught Huggins' attention during an electoral campaign and had
been invited to join the United Party. He was returned to the
Legislative Assembly in the 1948 elections, and his forceful personality came to the fore in this debate on the Native Land
Husbandry Bill. He shook the complacency and aroused the indignation of his fellow European Members by declaring that the
Africans' resentment was 'reaching dangerous proportions', that
over the past few years there had been 'a very great deterioration'
in their attitude towards the Europeans, and that to some extent
there had been 'definite reason on their side'. He roundly criticized
the assumptions of some of the more senior Members of his party.
When introducing the Bill Mr. P. B. Fletcher, the Minister of
Native Affairs, had maintained that the African should continue to
have all his institutions in the native areas. 'If we are talking like
that,' replied Todd, 'let us have apartheid and do our own work in
the European areas, but we are not going to.' He thought the
Government had shown that it was 'all out for a system of small
peasant farming which will give the native nothing more than a

[48] *Bantu Mirror*, 15 August 1955.

subsistence however good his ideas'. His own view was that: 'We do not want native peasants. We want the bulk of them working in the mines and farms and in the European areas and we could absorb them and their families.' He envisaged giving Africans security of tenure in the European area—ninety-nine-year leases on 'a decent section ten or fifteen miles from Bulawayo' with rapid, low-cost transport supplied. 'That sounds like blasphemy,' he added, 'but I think that it is the only solution.' Then if 100,000 families moved from the Reserves, 'we can begin to cope with what is left . . . and give each family 150 or 200 acres on a ninety-nine-year lease.'[49]

This attack and this somewhat nebulous blue-print were coldly received. Todd was said by one Member, to the approbation of others, to have 'given an opportunity to create discontent where discontent may not have been before'. According to another Member of his party, he made 'a most excellent missionary speech. . . . He did not attack the Bill. What he attacked was the fundamental native policy of this country, the Land Apportionment Act. He would smash it all up to-morrow by his wonderful mass transference.'[50] Yet largely as a result of his intervention the Government agreed to set up a Select Committee to investigate the question further.

The sessions of the Select Committee on the Native Land Husbandry Bill revealed a further basic cause of African resentment. Many of the African individuals and organizations who gave evidence before the Committee bitterly complained that the Government seemed to be ready to enforce severe restrictions and sacrifices on the African section of the community alone. The Government gave Africans the impression, said Mr. M. Hove, Editor of the *Bantu Mirror*, that 'it is not interested in the mistakes of us all, but in the mistakes of a section of the population'. European speculators—said the Africans—should be taxed for undeveloped land; but a Government proposal to institute a Tobacco Tax had been withdrawn after European protest. 'As long as there are large tracts of unused land in the European area, there will be resentment by Africans of legislation such as that proposed,' wrote

[49] S.R. Debates, 11 April 1951, cols. 42-9. [50] Ibid., 12 April 1951, cols. 92-4, 105.

the Provincial Native Commissioner of the Midlands Area. In the
Selukwe District, for instance, where there was only one small,
badly overpopulated Reserve, African tenants on large estates were
about to lose their rent holdings, although much of the land would
be left 'quite unused and unoccupied'. Another Native Commissioner in a neighbouring district confessed that he found it embarrassing to try to defend Government policy since he had
recently known that 'a personal friend had been granted over
10,000 morgen *additional* land for his already large ranch'.

A group of Anglicans, led by Bishop Paget, questioned the
finality of the Land Apportionment Act, and Mr. Guy Clutton-
Brock, who was developing a successful co-operative farming
scheme on Anglican mission land, urged the Government to consider some form of controlled tenancy on large estates. Without
access to more land it was impossible for a stable peasantry to
emerge.[51]

Faced with these radical criticisms and suggestions the members
of the Select Committee, to which Todd had been appointed,
closed their ranks. Not unreasonably they pointed out that merely
to provide further land for Africans would in no way solve the
problem of protecting natural resources. 'If we opened up the
whole country,' said Todd, 'we would put off this day for twenty
years perhaps.' Sooner or later good farming practice would have
to be enforced, and there was everything to be said for making a
firm start immediately. But this line of argument hardly met the
criticisms of those who demanded that European land should be
developed rationally with some form of controlled African
tenancy, to relieve the population pressure in the Reserves and
enable larger and more progressive holdings to spread throughout
the country. As had been said, Todd himself thought that this
pressure could only be relieved by wide-scale industrialization
accompanied by security of tenure for urban Africans. He remained
unmoved by Hove's demand for an extension of rural opportunities. 'We are not going to allow the Africans to go into the European area, no matter how desirable it may seem to the African.

[51] Compare also the exactly similar plea by an Anglican priest to the 1925 Morris
Carter Commission. See above Part I, Chap. I, p. 30.

... It is not practical politics.' And the basic line of European thought was revealed by the way in which Smit, the leader of the Opposition, met Clutton-Brock's plea. The undeveloped European land was, he said, 'merely being held in trust for our future population, because surely we all desire to see as big a European population in this country as there is an African population'.[52]

With a few minor modifications the Native Land Husbandry Bill was passed into law. The three major problems, of enlisting the co-operation of Native Councils and of providing wider rural opportunities and adequate urban security, which had to be solved if there was to be any decisive advance towards a permanent racial co-operation, were ignored. But as regards the limited—yet difficult—problem of farming in the Reserves the Act was a determined effort to raise the standards of living of a largely illiterate peasantry at a rate which was startling for Africa and it has justly been watched with much interest.

Under Huggins' guidance, then, Southern Rhodesia in the post-war years was moving slowly towards a policy of stabilizing its African population in rural or urban areas. Ultimately—as a few Europeans were already proclaiming—this policy would challenge many of the basic assumptions of the previous policy of segregation, although the majority of Huggins' supporters seem to have been unwilling as yet to recognize this. Most back-benchers came to realize that some action must be taken to deal with the obvious and urgent problems of soil erosion, overcrowding and urban poverty. But the no less vital needs of a contented community—security of tenure, education, and apprenticeship, the chance to acquire a pride in one's work and a real opportunity of exercising a measure of self-government—were virtually overlooked.

Yet Huggins' response was at least in significant contrast to the trend of events south of the Limpopo. In the Union of South Africa during the war the Smuts Government took the first steps in leading the country towards a recognition of the permanence of African urbanization. The Pass Laws were relaxed by departmental action, Smuts told the South African Institute of Race Relations

---

[52] Evidence to the Select Committee on the Native Land Husbandry Bill, in the Library of the Legislative Assembly, Salisbury.

that segregation had not stopped 'in the least' the movement from town and country—'You might as well try to sweep the ocean back with a broom'—and Hofmeyr, who in this respect probably took the initiative, openly said that the Government regarded segregation as a failure: the African must now be regarded as 'living side by side with the Europeans as citizens of a common country'.[53] In 1946 Smuts appointed a strong Commission under a liberal Afrikaner judge, Henry Fagan, to undertake a thorough review of the position of the Bantu in industry and the urban areas. The Report of the Commission recommended far-reaching changes, but before it was presented Smuts had fallen from office as a result of the general election of May 1948 and any hope of its recommendations being implemented had to be abandoned. Perhaps for the first time a significant difference had appeared between the policies of Southern Rhodesia and its greater neighbour.

2. THE FRANCHISE

In addition to these immediate practical problems of readjustment to industrial and agrarian changes, the political future of the African began to thrust itself on the attention of the Europeans. The emergence of this issue was in itself the sign of a new era. In the inter-war years European politicians were relatively confident that racial rivalry had been contained by their policy of territorial segregation and they thought that the common roll could survive innocuously.[54] But now this peaceful complacency disappeared. The question of political power could no longer be left comfortably in abeyance. The dilemma of democratic ideals in a community divided by race and history but united by economic developments was becoming plainly apparent.

The problem was first acutely felt in the ranks of Huggins' opponents. In the 1939 election Huggins' United Party won twenty-three seats with 11,161 votes, but the Labour Party captured the remaining seven seats and with 7,353 votes it provided a by no means inconsiderable opposition. Its unity was impaired

[53] Quoted by Saffery, paras. 509-16.   [54] See above, Part I, Chap. V, pp. 157-8.

by the decision of two of its leaders, Davies and Keller, to accept seats in Huggins' war-time Cabinet, but during the war its influence with the electorate was increased by the widespread interest in the problems of social security and, possibly, by the Russian stand against Hitler which won support for the left-wing organization, the Friends of Soviet Russia. The Labour Party's main strength was in the railway towns among European artisans, but it also included people of strong Socialist convictions such as Mrs. Gladys Maasdorp, a Mayor of Salisbury, and Colonel Walker, who had experience of Socialism in New Zealand.

In the early years of the war the party took a keen interest in the welfare of Africans in industry. The annual congress in May 1940 carried a resolution demanding a minimum wage and maximum working week for all employees, and Walker declared that it was the duty of the Labour Party and trade unions 'to foster and guide the industrial organization of the natives'.[55] While welcoming Huggins' statement on native policy in 1941 'as showing a great advance in the outlook of the Prime Minister since the days when he talked about "rough justice" and said that what was unfair for one race might not be unfair for another', the Labour Party's journal criticized the Prime Minister for ignoring the question of the urbanized African.[56] Yet although the party advocated better conditions for the African, it did not go so far as to envisage any challenge to the supremacy of the European, and this paternalistic concern did not adversely affect any of the immediate vital interests of its members. The bitter controversy over the party's native policy only began when its European members were confronted with the possibility of accepting Africans as equals, sharing in their political influence and power.

On 10 September 1941 the National Executive Committee of the Rhodesia Labour Party, at the request of a group of African voters led by Mr. Charles Mzingeli—who a few years previously had vainly organized the Salisbury branch of the Industrial and Commercial Workers' Union[57]—agreed to register an African Headquarters Branch, to membership of which all Africans would

---

[55] *Rhodesia Herald*, 5 May 1940.   [56] *The Bulletin*, January 1942.
[57] See above, Part I, Chap. V, p. 166.

be eligible throughout the country on the same basis as Europeans.[58] It was a moment of great significance in the development of race relations. Africans in Southern Rhodesia were still mainly un-organized and uncertain in their response to the presence of the Europeans; they were still eager to find acceptance in the white man's world, still relatively unembittered, but they were begin-ning already to demand a remedy for the hardships of industriali-zation. For a brief moment it seemed possible that their hopes and grievances might be supported by an influential section of the Europeans.

In the Labour Party's informal congress of October 1941 African members took a considerable part in the discussions. In February 1944 the African branch held a two-day conference in Harare to which Europeans were invited in order, as Mzingeli said, 'that they might become acquainted with the problems of Africans in Southern Rhodesia', and leading members of various African organizations were asked 'so that they might find out for themselves the policy of the Labour Party'. Although the Africans present were warned that there might be opposition from Euro-pean trade unionists if Africans attempted to join existing unions, they were urged to organize themselves. A European spokesman assured the Africans that they would be accepted by the Trades and Labour Council, who would advise the Government to grant them recognition. 'The sympathies of the European Trade Unionists', he said, 'are with the Africans, not only for the sake of the Africans, but for their own sakes, because as long as there are large sections of the workers of the country unorganized, it is a menace to the interests of the organised sections.'[59]

The African branch, however, soon came under criticism. The decision to register it had been taken by the executive committee at a time when the party was already split by Davies' and Keller's co-operation with Huggins,[60] and the committee had never ob-tained the positive support of the trade unionists for this far-reaching innovation. The meeting in Harare precipitated a crisis.

[58] Letter to W. D. Ntuli, 18 December 1943, in the files of the Southern Rhodesia Labour Party.
[59] Minutes of Congress of African Branch of the Labour Party, 12 February 1944.
[60] E.g. *The Bulletin*, November 1941, letter by Walker defending the committee.

Immediately afterwards, in April 1944, H. H. Davies, who had resigned from the Cabinet and was attempting to rebuild party unity, demanded that the question of African membership should be reconsidered. 'It is very evident,' he wrote in an open letter, 'that any other action . . . will be followed by a very considerable lessening of the power of the Party, and, ultimately, this will be detrimental to the Africans themselves.'[61] In December 1945, on the eve of a general election, a conference was held at Gwelo to decide the issue. One group led by Davies demanded that Africans should be excluded from membership of the party, and that a liaison committee should be formed to deal with African representatives—'the Africans could form a body for that purpose to be called anything they liked'—but no longer to be an integral part of the party. Davies' supporters thought that it was premature to include the African in party politics—'the average native is not a fit person to drag into party politics'—and they feared the reactions of the electorate—'we would be a laughing stock in the country if these negotiations (for unity) fell through because it is insisted that the Africans form a branch'. The other group, however, adamantly insisted that a basic principle was at stake; registered native voters of the party had asked for 'permission to discuss their own political affairs in contact with Europeans who are in organisations which they recognise. How can we deny them the request either democratically or according to the constitution of the colony?' If the Africans were deprived of party membership it would, thought Mrs. Maasdorp, 'take them years to recover—it would be a death-blow to the relationship between the races'.[62] On this issue, then, the Labour movement remained divided.[63] It fought the 1946 general election in two opposed parties, and in a few years it lost virtually all its influence in the country. The early chances of a successful political integration between the races were shattered; the specifically Socialist voice in Rhodesia became

[61] H. H. Davies to Mrs. Maasdorp, 18 April 1944, in the files of the S.R.L.P.

[62] Minutes of Special Congress and conference in Gwelo, 8–9 December 1945.

[63] 'The failure of the unity effort, therefore, appears to have occurred on the question of the continuance or otherwise of the native branch of the S.R.L.P. That undoubtedly is a question of principle, but whether at the present stage of native political development it is important enough to split the Labour movement in twain on the eve of a general election, is not for us to say.' *Rhodesia Herald*, 13 December 1945.

muted, and the field of politics was left to the Centre and the Right.

The problem of African membership of the Labour Party had wide repercussions; it was one of the factors which convinced Huggins that the whole question of African political power had to be settled as quickly as possible. 'I realised at once then what the danger was going to be.'[64] The Prime Minister's first reaction, in 1947, was to put forward proposals embodying the example of the South African 1936 Representation of Natives Act. He suggested that Africans should be barred from the common roll for twenty years and be compensated by the appointment of two Europeans to represent African interests in the Legislative Assembly. At the same time Native District and Provincial Councils would be developed so that the African 'could prove his ability to make the Westminster system work'.[65]

These proposals were put before the electorate in the general election of September 1948. The strike in April had suddenly awakened European apprehensions on an unprecedented scale; in the Union Dr. Malan's Nationalist Party, in alliance with the Afrikaner Party, had swept Smuts out of office in May and begun to implement its proclaimed policy of apartheid. It was not surprising therefore that although in Southern Rhodesia native policy had generally been dealt with largely on non-party lines it now became, as the *Rhodesia Herald* observed, 'one of the main issues between the parties'.[66] The dilemma could no longer be disposed of by a facile solution or relegated to the shades of the unconscious: it was emerging into the open. Yet although there was much discussion, and large alarming advertisements were placed in the national press by Huggins' right-wing opponents accusing him of dangerously progressive views,[67] 'the bulk of the electorate' was thought to be 'excusably hazy on what these issues are, for the policies of all parties are largely the same'.[68] The independent *New*

[64] S.R. Debates, 8 February 1951, col. 3290.
[65] *Rhodesia Herald*, 8 February 1947, report of a meeting between Huggins and a deputation from the Fabian Colonial Bureau.
[66] *Rhodesia Herald*, 10 September 1948.
[67] E.g. *Rhodesia Herald*, 1 September 1948.
[68] *Rhodesia Herald*, 10 September 1948.

Rhodesia, often critical of the Huggins administration, also considered that there was little practical difference between the
various native policies offered by the parties; it was largely a
question of presentation, of manipulating fears and convictions.
A given native policy could be put over in such a way as both to
reassure the reactionaries and at the same time encourage the progressives: 'in other words it satisfies the one opinion that the
natives will be kept protected, and at the same time promises
measures of education, agricultural uplift, etc., that satisfy the
other opinion that the native will advance considerably.' On
the other hand, an almost identical policy could, according to
The New Rhodesia, antagonize voters from both wings, alarming
reactionaries into fears of liberalism and progressives into apprehensions about its reactionary qualities. An astute and competent
manipulation would capture several marginal seats and might well
decide the election.[69]

With the electorate virtually restricted to Europeans—on 31
March 1948 there were 258 Africans registered as voters out of a
total electorate of some 47,000[70]—it was perhaps inevitable that
the debate should be confined within narrow limits. The Southern
Rhodesia Labour Party—the left-wing section of the old Labour
Party—was the only political party to uphold the common roll
and to maintain that Africans were 'entitled to take part in the
political life of the Colony'.[71] But it took no effective part in the
1948 election.

The Liberal Party was the chief challenger to Huggins. Led by
J. H. Smit, an able and experienced politician, it had captured
eleven seats in 1946. In 1948 its propaganda was directed to arous-
ing the fears of the more reactionary section of the electorate. It
proclaimed an 'unalterable opposition' to the use of Africans as
combatant troops and demanded that the Rhodesian Rifles, formed
by Huggins' war-time administration, should be disbanded. Apart
from this, however, the only 'distinct difference' noted by the
Rhodesia Herald between the United and Liberal Parties concerned

[69] *The New Rhodesia*, 20 August 1948.
[70] S.R. Debates, 26 May 1948, col. 322. *Rhodesia Herald*, 17 September 1948.
[71] *The New Rhodesia*, 31 October 1947.

the political development of the African. Both parties agreed 'that with few exceptions it will be a long time before he will understand political action on European lines'. Both wanted to develop the system of Native Councils as an immediate alternative to the common roll, but whereas the Liberal Party envisaged that this would lead ultimately to a 'native Parliament administering what would be a native State' the United Party rejected this goal as impracticable and left the ultimate future undecided.[72]

The electorate, swollen in two years from 37,142 to 47,840 by the first waves of the post-war immigration, gave Huggins a decisive victory: the United Party, with 56·3 per cent. of the votes cast, won twenty-four seats against the Liberal Party's five and the single seat won by the former right-wing section of the Rhodesia Labour Party.[73] It was a vote of confidence in Huggins' long experience and his cautious, pragmatic approach to race relations. It also showed the reaction of the predominantly English-speaking Colony against the Afrikaner victory in the Union; although the overwhelming majority of Europeans throughout Southern Africa shared a determination to maintain their racial supremacy, a policy which advocated an ultimate form of apartheid would, it seemed, henceforth receive a dubious reception north of the Limpopo.

Huggins' victory gave him the opportunity to turn his attention to wider problems. On the day after the election he affirmed his belief that 'there is going to be a United States of Africa, as sure as the sun comes up'. First the two Rhodesias would be linked up; then Nyasaland would join to form 'the great Middle Dominion of Africa': next would come a partnership with the Union of South Africa, and finally 'a federation of every African territory into one United States'.[74] Two weeks later Huggins left for the Commonwealth Prime Ministers' Conference in London, and henceforth, in collaboration with Welensky from Northern Rhodesia, he was to set the pace towards the Central African Federation.

This concern with the wider setting of Southern Rhodesia,

[72] *Rhodesia Herald*, 10 September 1948.   [73] Ibid., 17 September 1948.
[74] Ibid., 18 September 1948.

however, compelled Huggins to reconsider his approach to the problem of the political future of the African within the Colony. Previously, in February 1947, he had been warned by the Fabian Colonial Bureau, in the presence of Lord Addison, Labour Secretary of State for the Dominions, that there would be 'considerable resistance' in the United Kingdom to his proposed closure of the common roll to Africans. In July 1947 two Labour Members of Parliament tabled a motion urging their Government to exercise its right to veto 'with respect to any change in the Southern Rhodesian Electoral Law which would deprive Africans of their present right to be admitted under certain conditions to the Common Voters' Roll', and *The Economist*, supporting this opposition, asked: 'Cannot Southern Rhodesians learn from the deteriorating race relations in the Union . . . that to limit the franchise would solve nothing?'[75]

Huggins had pledged his party, and had been given a mandate in the 1948 Southern Rhodesian general election to close the common roll to Africans for the foreseeable future. Nevertheless he decided to reconsider his proposals, because, as he later explained to a United Party congress, 'our action would be misunderstood in the United Kingdom and the United States of America. Although it might be possible for larger countries with more economic strength to flout world opinion, we certainly cannot afford to do so.'[76] Instead the 1951 Electoral Act raised both the means and educational qualifications for the vote. Huggins said that in fact this did 'almost as much as closing the Roll for fifteen years'; it satisfactorily preserved 'what we call civilised government which is the only important thing'. On second thoughts he was sure that it was 'a far better way of dealing with it than creating the frustration it would create if the native was to be told that he was to have no say at any time in any part of the government of this Colony'.[77]

These second thoughts, this attention to the immediate practical implications of policy and relative unconcern with the ultimate future or with basic, theoretical principles, were typical of the way

---

[75] *Rhodesia Herald*, 8 February 1947, 19, 20 July 1947.   [76] Ibid., 5 August 1952.
[77] S.R. Debates, 8 February 1951, cols. 3290–1.

in which Huggins managed the Europeans as they awoke to their new, post-war situation. Yet the two hard facts remain that the only positive attempt to co-operate politically with educated Africans—that of the Labour Party—ended in complete failure and the principle of a colour-free franchise survived mainly through fear of external repercussions. It was a moment when a policy of drift might let a unique opportunity slip by. An appeal to basic principles could not be postponed indefinitely. Here again a new and more definite approach came from Garfield Todd. At the 1946 Southern Rhodesian Missionary Conference, a biennial conference of representatives from all the major Protestant missionary societies, Todd moved that the assembly should 'strongly urge' the Government that 'no racial discrimination should be introduced' into the franchise. In 1948, when he first stood as a United Party candidate, he made it clear to his constituents that in this particular matter he differed from his party. He believed that it was 'fundamentally unsound to demand, as a qualification for the vote, a state which cannot be obtained but (which one) must be born into', and in the debate on the Electoral Bill he warned the House against the danger of frustrating 'the leading and better-class Africans'.[78] But as the debate on the future became more intense, as the principles involved became more apparent, the fears and convictions of some Europeans were stated more fiercely.

The most extreme European reaction was voiced by the White Rhodesia Council, founded in 1949 'to maintain the principle of White Supremacy in the Governing of the Colony of Southern Rhodesia'. Its leading spirit was Mr. Charles Olley, a Salisbury businessman who had taken a keen interest in the welfare and working conditions of European shop assistants. He had been Mayor of Salisbury, 1943–5, and he was still a prominent figure on the Municipal Council. The White Rhodesia Council wanted to create a separate voters' roll, so that Africans could elect two or more European representatives to Parliament, and it aimed at establishing 'the principle that only Europeans shall be elected to Parliament and on the Municipal Councils or other Local Authorities'. It wanted to intensify, maintain, and enforce territorial segre-

[78] S.R. Debates, 8 February 1951, col. 3280.

gation, particularly in the urban areas. 'The number of natives in the areas under Local Authority jurisdiction' should be limited 'as far as possible by regulations', and pressure should be brought to bear 'to ensure that the natives are not roaming the streets of any Local Authority—except they are (*sic*) on the specific work of their employers'. The Council demanded Dominion Status for Southern Rhodesia and wanted to postpone any federation with the north 'for another ten years by which time the general political outlook of Africa may have improved favourably to European settlement'.[79]

Thousands of circulars were posted throughout the country by the White Rhodesia Council on such subjects as 'natives driving buses', or the Railway Act which, in response to the susceptibilities of Westminster, made provision for an African Trade Union and, in theory, for Africans to advance into more responsible jobs. At one time Olley thought that 'the cheek and insolence of the natives' was largely due to 'the propaganda—the talk and general treatment of certain members' of the Southern Rhodesia Labour Party,[80] but at other times he attributed it to different influences:

A subject that was taken up with the Minister for Internal Affairs, but without much success, is that of natives collecting certain types of magazines and weeklies depicting white women virtually in the nude. There are several magazines which contain beautiful works of art; but unfortunately the natives do not see such photographs with the same artistic mind as Europeans . . . much of the insolence and arrogance on the part of the natives comes through this form of familiarity.[81]

This demand for the Native to be kept in his place while white supremacy was maintained was supported by hopes of European immigration on a gigantic scale. The vast undeveloped acreages in the European areas were being held in trust for future arrivals,[82] and it was felt that in farming and industry a far greater use could be made of European labour. On 21 November 1950 representatives from the various municipalities, chambers of commerce and industry, native affairs departments, and various societies gathered in the Council Chamber at Salisbury to consider the shortage of

[79] From a manifesto issued in November 1949.   [80] *The New Rhodesia*, 2 April 1948.
[81] White Rhodesia Council circular, 26 January 1951.   [82] See above, p. 301.

African labour. Olley took a prominent part in the proceedings and stressed the need for a White Rhodesia. He upbraided industrialists for continuing to employ 'the most expensive labour in the world, namely, native labour'. Africans, he said, were entering into all spheres of employment; they were ousting Europeans as clerks and artisans despite the fact that their output was less. Mr. Winston Field, a Marandellas farmer who on his own account was experimenting with Italian peasant farmers as tenants on his lands, and who a few years later was to enter politics as the successful leader of the Dominion Party, 'agreed with the remarks expressed by Alderman Olley that Europeans should replace Africans as far as possible in all spheres of employment'. He pointed out that in Canada Europeans were employed in the tobacco industry on work similar to that done by Africans in Southern Rhodesia, and he thought that with increased mechanization the dependence on African labour could be reduced. When, however, one Councillor inquired what would happen 'to the 376,000 natives at present employed', Field assured him that it was not suggested that in the White Rhodesia 'any steps should be taken that would do away with the native as a labourer'. The substructure would, it seems, remain black, and in this connexion Olley 'expressed the view that efficiency can only be obtained by economic pressure being exerted on the native'. He favoured a slightly higher minimum wage with no allowance for food and accommodation, and he instanced 'the position in the U.S.A., where the Negroes were either forced to work or starve'.[83]

Morally this outlook was defended mainly by an attack on its opponents' position. The Southern Rhodesia Labour Party was dismissed as 'very definitely communistic and, in fact, a menace to this Colony'.[84] Other opponents were said to be unrealistic idealists:

[83] Notes of the Conference held in the Council Chamber, Municipal Offices, Salisbury, 21 November 1950.

[84] Letter by Olley to *The New Rhodesia*, 2 April 1948. It is perhaps worth stating that Mrs. Maasdorp, acknowledged by Olley as being 'the leading light of the S.R.L.P.', had strongly attacked the Communist Party 'which forces its way regardless of the wishes of the people'. It was, she said, gaining ground in South Africa 'for one reason only—and that was that the S.A. Labour Party did not work with the African, whereas the members of the Communist Party do'. Minutes of special congress of S.R.L.P., Gwelo, 29–30 March 1947.

For some reason or other, it seems to be the nice thing to be on the side of bishops and parsons and those who are obsessed with the view that they have a duty to Providence in lifting barbarians to equality with the white people. On this subject of the advancement of the natives, there is far too much hypocrisy prevailing—which comes about through the influence of certain Church leaders. The White Rhodesia Council does not ask anybody to forsake their religious teaching; but to face the hard realities of life and acknowledge the dangers looming in front of the white people of the world.

Was it possible, asked Olley, that the Great Architect had set out to make all mankind equal and had so lamentably failed? In Africa for over 4,000 years the Negroes had been in direct contact with Babylonians, Egyptians, Portuguese, and Greeks, and yet they had not assimilated the knowledge and refinement of these people. 'In plain words: the Negro is still a Negro!' It was true that a few had been educated, but almost invariably they had 'failed to stay with their people and lift them as the Europeans lifted them'. Instead they were ruined, became purely selfish, and finally when they had obtained the franchise and the right 'to roam the white towns' they would claim: 'This is our country, so quit.'

Actually it is not their country, in fact, less so than that of Europeans from the point of view of conquered territory, of peaceful penetration and development. The present-day tribes cannot lay claim to long-standing rights to the two Rhodesias. Africa has always been a continent in which tribe raided tribe. It is still done in parts of the Continent. . . .

The policy of the White Rhodesia Council is not to oppress the natives; but to permit them to advance at a speed in conformance with their particular stage of 'soul evolvement'. As the natives are so far behind, it means that it is imperative there shall be white supremacy for hundreds of years.[85]

The 1948 election had at least demonstrated that these opinions were not those of a majority of the European electorate, and some Rhodesians were inclined to dismiss Olley as an extravagant eccentric. But the fears which he voiced were for many inescapable, and for most Europeans they still formed the hard bed-rock of reality

[85] 'The Case of the White Rhodesian Council', *Rhodesian Monthly Review*, November 1951.

on which they lived and reared their children. In the face of these
fears any fundamental readjustment to the industrial, urban, and
political problems posed by race relations in the post-war years
was unlikely, if not impossible. It was Huggins' peculiar achievement to carry a majority of the Europeans along with him towards
the beginnings of a new approach, towards a hesitant and incomplete reappraisal. Gradually the policy of stabilization was taking
shape, and as a corollary some Europeans were beginning to regard
educated Africans for the first time as possible allies. For Todd and
Huggins they were no longer merely awkward rivals to be sent
back to find an opening in the Reserves; they were beginning to
be seen as a possible insurance against the mass of Africans, as
leaders who had to some extent to be taken into account. Otherwise, as bitter, frustrated agitators, Todd thought they could be
'dangerous to us, to our whole order in this country'.[86] And when
during the 1948 strike Huggins witnessed the emergence of the
proletariat he was soon led to think that 'we shall never do much
with these people until we have established a native middle class'.[87]

It seemed perhaps that given time this gradual, ordered readjustment might successfully surmount all difficulties. But time, in this
post-war world, was the scarcest of commodities. Already the
Europeans in Southern Rhodesia were of their own volition
stretching out their hands to assume vast new responsibilities in
Central Africa. Already the trials and tempo of urban life were
creating a new generation of Africans, awake to a wider world and
bitter at the limitations of their own small lot. Gone was the time
when the African reaction could safely be ignored.

[86] S.R. Debates, 8 February 1951.
[87] 'Human Relations in Africa', an address to the Oxford Union by Sir Godfrey
Huggins, printed in *South Africa*, 27 January 1951.

V. AFRICAN AWAKENINGS

I. SOUTH OF THE ZAMBEZI

Huggins' policy of stabilization, with the irrevocable division of the African population into town and country dwellers, was the most significant aspect of the Europeans' reaction to the growth of urban industries. The permanent presence of the black man—with his wife, children, and aged dependants—in the white man's citadel challenged the basic assumptions of the inter-war period. After the strikes of 1945 and 1948 the more obvious and urgent urban needs —housing and wages—were given serious attention; the larger implications, however, continued to be shirked and with the Electoral Act of 1951 a reconsideration of the African's political future was postponed. Yet some Europeans began to realize that the permanent integration of Africans into urban life would eventually affect every aspect of race relations. Where previously there had been complacency, rigidity, and an unawareness, compounded of both ignorance and a reluctance to face facts, now, in some minds in these post-war years, there was dawning a realization that changes—at least one day—would have to be faced.

The African break with the past was more definite. In the inter-war period the Bantu Congress of Southern Rhodesia, the representative organization of the few educated Africans—ordained ministers, teachers, clerks, and independent farmers in the Native Purchase Areas—had a restricted outlook. Its members had been concerned with legislation which adversely affected their individual interests, with the problem of gaining recognition of their status as advanced or civilized individuals, and with the need for increasing the provision of education.[1] Only the short-lived Industrial and Commercial Workers' Union had sought to appeal

---

[1] See above, Part I, Chap. V, pp. 162–65.

to the masses and had concerned itself with so mundane a matter as the basic wage rate for labourers. Other educated Africans seem to have been primarily anxious to emphasize the differences which distinguished them from their fellow Africans and to be recognized by Europeans as fellow civilized beings, potential allies against the primitive proletariat. This was surely an opportunity which, on a reasonable calculation of self-interest, the Europeans ought to have seized—but they did not. Their eyes were closed.

By the end of the Second World War the atmosphere had changed almost completely and the Europeans' chance of securing the co-operation of these allies was fast disappearing. The experiences of urban poverty and frustration were creating a new unity in which class became conterminous with colour, and at the same time the African initiative was passing to those leaders who made articulate the new demands and awareness of African labourers and their wives. The Bantu Congress itself, now known as the Southern Rhodesia African National Congress but still representative mainly of educated Africans and the elder generation of African leaders, began to take a keen interest in the problems of industrial workers. Its annual congress in 1946, presided over by the Rev. T. D. Samkange, a leading African minister of the Methodist Church, was attended by 120 delegates from all parts of the country, including many chiefs. They demanded that African trade unions, 'whose sole object was to maintain and improve conditions of African wage-earners', should be recognized by the Government, since they considered that the Government's Native Labour Board 'could not take the place of African trade unions'.[2] But even more significant than the widened interest of the elder generation of African leaders was the fact that their influence and importance had been superseded by new organizations representing not only the emergent few but also the labouring masses.

The first and in many ways the most successful of these new organizations was the Rhodesia Railways African Employees' Association. It grew out of the Bantu Benefit Society, one of many similar bodies formed by small groups of African workers to provide help in cases of financial difficulty. The first effective African

[2] *Bulawayo Chronicle*, 12 July 1946.

trade union in Central Africa was not therefore, as some Europeans imagined, an ill-prepared attempt to adopt a form of organization quite unsuited to 'African mentality and experience'. It was a natural response to the industrial situation, and, as the Tredgold Report implied, had it not in its early days been discouraged and ignored by the European management, it might well have quickly developed a 'responsible and co-operative' attitude.

At the time of the railway strike of October 1945[3] the Association had a mere 200 members, drawn mainly from the goods-sheds at Bulawayo, but its influence was far wider than its actual membership, and the success of the strike was almost entirely due to the firm leadership it exercised over the mass of railway workers. On the Sunday before the strike began the strikers were in 'a sullen mood and many were drunk', and the Native Commissioner was unable to obtain a hearing in the compound. But while they were on strike their behaviour was reported to have been 'singularly good'. The leaders maintained a 'most rigid discipline', beer in the compounds was destroyed, railway property was protected, and as a result the Government had to treat their delegations with respect.[4]

The Association's strength was further demonstrated in 1947, when it collected over £1,000 to pay for legal representation before the National Native Labour Board, and in Government Notice No. 155, dated 27 February 1948, the Association, on the recommendation of the Board, was recognized as 'a body representing a section of Railway African employees'. Through its determined control of the strike and its continued, marshalled strength, the Association had thus won for itself an established position, and largely as a result of the response of management to its intervention the wages and living conditions of the mass of railway employees were considerably improved.[5] This growth continued. In October 1952 the Association had twenty-two branches with over 2,600 members, and in the previous month a Joint Industrial Committee for Railway African Workers, consisting of representatives of the Railway Administration, the

---

[3] See above, Part II, Chap. IV, p. 283.   [4] *Tredgold Report*, paras. 21–5.
[5] See above, Part II, Chap. IV, p. 288.

Association, and the African Railway Trade Union, a body formed in Northern Rhodesia in June 1950, was established.

As their grievances had been satisfactorily dealt with, at least for the time being, the railway workers were the only section of Africans to remain at work during the general strike of April 1948. But this did not imply that they remained aloof from other African workers. The Association contributed to the funds of the strikers, and it was well aware of its strategic position in industrial relations. In 1951 it appointed a full-time General Secretary, Mr. Joshua Nkomo, a young Ndebele who had graduated in South Africa and worked as a Social Welfare Officer on the railways. At the annual conference of 1952, Nkomo urged members to remember that 'the future failure or success of African Trade Unions in Southern Rhodesia is a responsibility of the Railway Africans'. They alone, under the 1949 Railway Act, had the opportunity of qualifying for registration and, he might have added, they alone had the advantage of working together in a centrally organized and highly vulnerable industry. This concern with their wider responsibilities was not, as yet, coupled with a narrow racialism. Although he complained of the difficulties 'placed before them by both employers and European workers', Nkomo could still assert that 'it will be found in the long run that the interest of workers, be they black or white, is inseparable'.[6] Perhaps one of the major questions facing Southern Rhodesia was whether this sense of a common interest between European and African workers could be nurtured and intensified. Politically, in the Labour Party, the alliance was a failure; there seemed little ground for believing that industrially it would succeed, but on both sides a few thoughtful individuals sustained the hope.

The railway strike of 1945 evoked an immediate and far-reaching response from other urban Africans. In Bulawayo leaders of the Bantu Congress and the African Welfare Society raised twenty pounds to buy food for the strikers, and in an open public meeting at Stanley Hall in the Location it was decided to unite all workers in the newly-formed 'African Workers' Trade Unions'. In his address to a crowd of about 5,000 people, Mr. Jasper Savanhu,

[6] General Secretary's Report of R.R.A.E.A., October 1952.

then a leading African journalist and secretary of the Bantu Congress, was reported to have said:

The Railway strike has proved that Africans have been born. The old African of tribalism and selfishness has died away. Africans realise as never before that united they stand and divided they fall. The reason is not far to seek. We have found ourselves faced by a ruthless foe— exploitation and legalised oppression by the white man for his and his children's luxury. (Applause.) The days when a white man could exploit us at will are gone and gone for ever. The employer who ill-treats one of the least of African workers does it to all of us. We must not fail in our duty to suffer with him. (Cheers.)[7]

In Salisbury the response was more restrained. After the meeting held by the Labour Party in Harare in February 1944 the City Council had banned all political meetings in the Location, and Africans in Salisbury, reading reports of 5,000 Africans meeting in Bulawayo, reflected that they knew 'quite well what would have happened' had they addressed such meetings and made similar statements.[8] Instead, on the night of 15 January 1946, in heavy rain, a small group of the leaders of African associations in Salisbury met privately outside the Location 'to find ways and means of organising industry and commercial workers in Salisbury'. They were a varied group representing waiters, drivers, industrial and railway workers, the African Headquarters' Branch of the Labour Party, an 'African Burial Society', and the Mount Darwin group, 'a tribal association'. At the insistence of the leader of the Waiters' Association, who had made several approaches to Mzingeli 'even during the railway strike', they decided to invite Savanhu to speak to a small public meeting the following month. So on 10 February 1946 just over sixty Africans gathered at the Ndaba tree, opposite the native Dutch Reformed Church outside the Location. They listened to speeches from Mr. Shato of the Waiters' Association, from Mzingeli, and from Savanhu. The latter gave a résumé of British trade union history and asserted that the 'trade union was

[7] Quoted from a report supplied by Savanhu to Mzingeli in a letter to the Secretary of the S.R. Labour Party, 5 November 1945.

[8] Mzingeli to the Secretary of the S.R.L.P., 5 November 1945, S.R.L.P. to Ntuli, 23 April 1946.

Y

the only weapon for securing betterment for the workers'. The solidarity of the railway workers had, he said, 'proved to the world that the Africans have reached the stage where they should organise themselves into trade unions on the same basis as those of Europeans'. At the end of the meeting they decided to form a Reformed Industrial and Commercial Workers' Union (known as the R.I.C.U.) under the leadership of Mzingeli.[9]

Neither in Salisbury nor in Bulawayo did these groups succeed in organizing the mass of general industrial workers into coherent trade unions. The lack of continuity due to the high percentage of migrant workers was perhaps the most serious obstacle. Most labourers were also illiterate and few could be expected to appreciate immediately the principles of sustained collective bargaining. Few also, in the general poverty, could readily afford the monthly subscriptions needed to pay for legal assistance or full-time secretaries. Even on the railways Nkomo, with 2,000 members out of a potential 12,000, was forced to admit that he had found it 'most difficult and at times impossible to organise this type of labour',[10] and outside the railways where workers were scattered through a hundred firms and factories the task was even harder. Finally, successful union organization was made well-nigh impossible by European policy. Legally there was nothing in Southern Rhodesia to prevent Africans from forming workers' associations: there were no Combination Laws, as in early nineteenth-century England. But Africans were completely excluded from the machinery of the Industrial Conciliation Act, they had no rights of constitutional arbitration, and strikes together with breaches of contract could be penalized under the Masters and Servants Act. The essential weapons of a trade unionist were denied to them.

These new groups did not therefore develop into influential industrial organizations; instead they became focal points for a new range of African political and economic discontent. In Salisbury Mzingeli was for several years the unofficial mayor of Harare, and the R.I.C.U. led the opposition to the authorities. At first this

[9] Reports by Mzingeli, 21 January 1946 and 10 February 1946, in the records of the S.R.L.P.
[10] General Secretary's Report of R.R.A.E.A., October 1952.

opposition was principally concerned with the 1946 Native Urban Areas Act. The sudden, somewhat rigid implementation of this Act in Salisbury caused considerable hardship among certain classes of Africans[11] and even the Municipal Director of Native Administration reported that it was received 'by the native population with open hostility and suspicion'.[12] The Native Advisory Board provided the only recognized channel for ventilating these complaints, and the first elections for this Board were held in October 1947. All the candidates put up by the R.I.C.U. were elected, and the poll was headed by Mr. Pazarangu, a prominent member of the Union. The poll was small, but in successive years the R.I.C.U. maintained its ascendancy, and in 1953 Mzingeli won 608 votes, 400 more than his nearest opponent.[13] And the support for Mzingeli was even more widely based. Individuals with grievances against the Municipal administration or against their employers brought their cases to him, and the monthly meetings of the R.I.C.U., often attended by several hundred people,[14] became a forum for the discontented.

In particular the R.I.C.U. adopted the cause of the women of Harare, who, under the 1946 Act, sometimes found themselves exposed to considerable hardships. Not all single women were prostitutes and concubines: some were widows or deserted married women, who had perhaps lost contact with the rural areas and who, together with other single women, were attempting to maintain themselves in an honest manner. Now suddenly, under the new regulations, these women found themselves without accommodation, and, owing to the shortage of married accommodation, wives were prohibited from living in Harare until their husbands had completed two years' steady employment. Large-scale police raids 'to clean up the location' became a common occurrence and abuses were almost inevitable. One woman who had been thirty years in Harare told an R.I.C.U. meeting how she had seen many old

[11] See above, Part II, Chap. IV, pp. 286–7.
[12] *Second Annual Report*, July 1947–June 1948.
[13] *Eighth Annual Report of the Director of Native Administration, Salisbury*, July 1953–June 1954.
[14] See for example a report of an attendance of seven hundred in the *African Weekly*, 4 July 1951.

women being arrested for having no permit to live in Harare. She herself was doing laundry work and many times, she said, she had been threatened that she would lose her permit if she was not prepared 'to put herself on good terms with one police or another'.[15] In August 1951 the *African Weekly* reported that 'the womenfolk of Harare have rallied behind the R.I.C.U.', that the large attendance of women at its meetings 'would have been impossible a year ago', and that some of the women spoke 'with the same courage and wisdom as the men'.[16] As a result of these protests the raids and arrests became less frequent, but more significant than any immediate improvements was the fact that a fresh dimension of social and political action was being opened up to a new section of the African community.

In Bulawayo, where the Urban Areas Act remained unimplemented until 1949, African leaders were primarily concerned with demands for a rise in wages. Although no strong trade unions were established in industry outside the railways, Savanhu's organization, the 'African Workers' Trade Unions', did succeed in giving support to workers in various industries. In March 1946, when there was considerable unrest among African workers in the milling industry, the A.W.T.U., with the help of Ibbotson and officials of the Native Affairs Department, successfully negotiated improved conditions of service. During the rest of the year various isolated strikes occurred which, according to an official report, were 'settled peaceably', and in September 1947 the 'Federation of Bulawayo African Workers' Unions', which had developed out of the A.W.T.U., issued a circular to all employers in Bulawayo demanding a wage rise for all African employees.[17] This circular and a large meeting of Municipal employees in October were the first steps which led to the mass strike and disturbances in April 1948. By this date, however, the leadership of Bulawayo Africans was shared by the Federation and the 'African Workers' Voice Association', an organization founded earlier in 1947 by Mr. Benjamin Burombo.

---

[15] R.I.C.U. Newsletter, 3 June 1951.   [16] *African Weekly*, 8 August 1951.
[17] *Report of Commission on Native Disturbances, 1948* (and see above, Part II, Chap. IV, p. 288).

Burombo had had a varied career, representative of many Africans in its mobility. Born at Selukwe about 1907, he was educated up to Standard V, and on leaving school he worked as a salesman of religious books for the Seventh Day Adventists. In 1934 he left for Johannesburg, where he worked as an assistant chef at the Carlton Hotel, returning to Rhodesia two years later to become a cattle-dealer in Selukwe District. In 1941 he paid a brief visit to Johannesburg 'to collect his belongings', and he then settled in Bulawayo as the agent and canvasser for several insurance societies.[18] In 1945 the lease of a grocery store in the Location gave him, as it had given to Charles Mzingeli, a modest degree of economic independence and, what was perhaps as valuable, a wide circle of acquaintances. This varied experience was reflected in his interest in rural as well as urban problems, while his powerful oratory, supported by his stature and innate shrewdness, enabled him to mobilize protest on a wide scale.

If, on the one hand, the leading members of the Federation of Workers' Unions had greater organizing abilities and a clearer idea of industrial bargaining, Burombo had the power to rouse the masses. It was he who made their economic grievances and their racial resentment articulate. Militant posters appealed 'to all African workers' to attend the mass meetings of the Voice Association. On 3 July 1947 workers were exhorted to come and hear about 'the African Wages question up to date' and the agenda was announced as follows:

1. Freedom and Liberty.
2. Democracy and Freedom from Fear.
3. Southern Rhodesia's Undemocratic Native Policy.

Four months later another meeting was billed:

to discuss about African wages and the discrimination of the Colour question up to date, and join for your own benefit and the benefit of your children and grandchildren.
THE FREEDOM IS FOUGHT FOR, OPPORTUNITY COMES ONCE AS YOU KNOW, CHANCE DOES NOT REPEAT. WE MUST HAVE PEOPLE BEHIND US TO CARRY THIS CAMPAIGN TO THE END.[19]

[18] Report from Location Superintendent, 23 December 1952.
[19] Copies of posters in Mr. Burombo's possession.

There was considerable rivalry between the leaders of these two organizations in Bulawayo, and the Commission which reported on the strike of April 1948 considered that 'in their efforts to obtain further support the leaders at times vied with each other in exciting the feelings of those who attended their meetings'.[20] The strike, however, was not solely the result of mob oratory and still less of the secret schemes of a discontented clique. It was, as the Commission's report made clear, primarily due to the inactivity of employers, the Municipality and the Government, faced with the undoubtedly genuine grievances of urban Africans. In fact, far from being mere pawns 'in some political or quasi-political scheme', as many Europeans believed,[21] the African mob seized the initiative. As tension mounted on Sunday 2 April, thirty delegates from the main African organizations in the larger centres of the Colony attended a meeting in the Location at Bulawayo. According to a report in the *Bulawayo Chronicle*, they unanimously agreed that it would be wiser 'to seek satisfaction by constitutional methods' before striking, and risking failure in their unprepared state. But when the leaders attempted to put across this cautious policy to the 'vast crowd' at a mass meeting in Bulawayo on the Tuesday evening, they had 'great difficulty in making themselves heard'. The meeting broke up in disorder, and at dawn the strike began.[22]

More than any other incident this outburst of popular feeling and action revealed the gulf of misunderstanding and ignorance which separated Europeans and Africans. Seeing little further than the respect and servility of their employees or the habitual laughter and good temper of the normal run of Africans, most Europeans believed that the African masses were quietly acquiescent and that all active discontent was created by agitators where it had not before existed. But the conviction that a small conspiratorial coterie had engineered the strike and foisted it on to an apathetic mass of Africans was a complete misconception. Far from manufacturing grievances and fomenting trouble in a contented community, the leaders had found themselves swept along by the passions of the

[20] *Report of Native Disturbances Commission*, 1948.
[21] E.g. *The New Rhodesia*, 30 April 1948.   [22] *Bulawayo Chronicle*, 12–14 April 1948.

mob, and their denunciation of the common hardships had to a certain extent safeguarded Europeans against an even more violent and unpredictable explosion.

Blindfolded by the lack of accurate information, which was partly one of the by-products of the colour bar, Europeans fell into another false assumption. In the previous inter-war period emergent Africans were virtually ignored by European politicians. In theory they were restricted to the openings in the Reserves; they were to play no part in the white man's world. Now, under the impetus of the strike, Huggins, Todd, and other thoughtful Europeans began to revise their ideas. They began to think of effecting an alliance with the African *élite*, of enlisting them in support of the established order. And these European leaders took it for granted that there was in fact, or at least that it would be possible to create, a contented, dependable 'native middle class' ready to act as a protection against the demands of the proletariat.[23] But was this still the case? Before the Second World War the Bantu Congress had been anxious to fill this role, but now these moderate leaders were less willing and able to act as humble allies. They were becoming more conscious of their unity with the masses, more concerned with the problems of industrial labourers, and ready to give financial assistance in a crisis.[24] Almost inevitably the incipient middle class remained far more closely identified with their fellow Africans than with the ruling race. They had practically no opportunities to develop the cultural and material interests which might have distinguished them from the mass. Opportunities to perform skilled and professional work were severely limited; few Africans were able to own property; the outlets for investment were scanty, and the system of kinship obligations often hindered the individual accumulation of wealth. And although many educated Africans appreciated European values and sought to identify themselves with the European way of life, few received much encouragement. In a crisis, colour came increasingly to be seen as the only valid criterion.

Even if the moderate leaders had still been anxious to act as allies, their alliance was now, in the post-war years, much less

[23] See above, Part II, Chap. IV, p. 314.   [24] See above, p. 319.

valuable, for their influence was restricted and they were being superseded by a more vigorous leadership. The process has been illustrated by the post-war career of Mzingeli. Disillusioned by the failure to co-operate with Europeans in the Labour Party, Mzingeli had committed himself once more to a purely African organization. He found himself supported not only by the *élite* of the politically conscious men, who voted in the elections for the Advisory Board, but also by the large numbers of illiterate men and women, who attended his meetings and looked to him for leadership. Increasingly he represented not the ambitions of a middle class but the grievances of urban Africans as a whole. And in Bulawayo the Secretary of the Bantu Congress took a leading part in fostering the trade union movement. Henceforth if any co-operation between the races was to succeed it would have to take into account a new force, the awakening mass of Africans and not merely an emergent *élite*.

For Africans the 1948 strike was an event of profound importance. Their hopes, like those of the Chartists in Victorian England, had been high, but vague and ill-defined; they had pictured a new heaven and a new earth without being very clear what they would be like or how to get there. But their hopes, like the Chartists', disappeared in bitter disillusionment. The wild exhilaration of the first mass protest for more than fifty years collapsed with the re-imposition of law and order. The daily discipline was re-established; some Africans lost their jobs and others were sentenced under the Masters and Servants Act to various terms of imprisonment with hard labour.[25] For many the disillusionment was intensified, since, in Bulawayo, the return to work was based on a misunderstanding: when Burombo persuaded the masses to return to work he gave them an assurance from the Government that their claims would be considered, and at the same time added that 'according to the surveys[26] made as to what amounts Africans should receive, it had been stated that single Africans should get £5 and married Africans £7. 10s. a month'. When many African

[25] Mnyanda, op. cit., p. 28. On 17 April the *Bulawayo Chronicle* reported that 'fewer than two hundred' summary dismissals had already been dealt with by the Native Department.
[26] See above, Part II, Chap. II, pp. 214–15.

workers jumped to conclusions and triumphantly informed their employers of their 'new rates of pay', Burombo was hastily summoned to dispel this delusion.[27] The National Native Labour Board had to collect evidence throughout the country and it was nearly a year before its recommendations were implemented. The introduction of a new compulsory minimum scale of pay for all urban employees has considerable significance when placed in the context of the whole process of industrialization in Southern Rhodesia: it marked the extension of State intervention over the whole field of urban industry. But the amount—the new minimum basic wage was 35s. a month, together with fuel and rations to the value of 25s.—fell far short of African expectations; it could not radically relieve the pressure of poverty. Most Africans seem to have concluded that their spurt of rebellion had accomplished virtually nothing. In subsequent years the experiment of a mass general strike was not repeated, and for the moment Africans had little alternative but to resign themselves to their lot.

After the strike, Burombo and the Voice Association turned their attention to the rural areas, where, following the delayed implementation of the Land Apportionment Act, the resettlement of Africans from land in the European Area provided another difficult situation. In 1949 land was allocated in the Unassigned Area for those Africans who had to move, 'generous sums' were voted for water development, and the new areas were provided with roads, dip tanks, and medical facilities. But many Africans, 'led by a factious and plausible orator' (Burombo), refused to move from land occupied by their tribe for many generations, and the lorries provided by the Government were able to move only 1,569 families instead of the 4,482 that had been planned. Legal action was taken against this passive resistance but, owing to defects in the law, it was impossible to obtain convictions in many cases and Burombo's prestige soared. The law, however, was quickly amended, and in 1952 the resettlement resumed its inexorable course. The resistance was seen to have been in vain, and the many cattle, contributed by peasant families to meet legal and other

[27] *Bulawayo Chronicle*, 17 April 1948.

expenses, wasted; eventually these events served only to increase the African's resignation and sense of helplessness.[28]

After 1948 the other urban leaders returned to the more prosaic tasks of strengthening their organizations and of exercising what influence they could within the structure of local government and industrial conciliation established by the State. Both the Reformed Industrial and Commercial Workers' Union and the Federation of African Workers' Unions were increasingly occupied in submitting evidence to the Native Labour Boards appointed to investigate conditions in various industries. They were also able to take up individual grievances with the newly-formed sub-Department of Native Labour and a closer co-operation and confidence developed between them and at least this branch of Authority. In November 1949 the conference at Bulawayo of delegates from the fourteen unions affiliated to the Federation was opened by Mr. A. J. Huxtable, the first Commissioner for Native Labour. Welcoming the delegates as 'the leaders of the people of Bulawayo', he affirmed that whatever they did or said would be followed by the people, and he urged them to combat absenteeism and irresponsibility.[29] Like the R.I.C.U. in Salisbury, leaders of the Federation took a prominent part in presenting grievances to the local government: in 1952 six out of the twelve members of the Bulawayo African Township Advisory Board were officials or members of the Federation.[30] But the Advisory Boards gave little opportunity for the effective development of African initiative and responsibility, and the Native Labour Boards, composed entirely of Europeans, were no substitute for collective bargaining. The participation of Africans at an executive and policy-making level could alone dispel their frustration and bitter suspicion of white authority, and could alone create among them a civic and industrial pride. Without it they would remain merely a mob, crushed, ineffective, but capable of sudden, desperate, unpredictable violence.

At a national level in Southern Rhodesia there was no persistent, united African voice and perhaps, therefore, Europeans found it

[28] *Annual Report of Chief Native Commissioner, Salisbury,* 1951, 1952.
[29] *Bantu Mirror,* 5 November 1949.
[30] *Native Administration Department Reports,* 23 December 1952.

harder to appreciate the urgent necessity of incorporating Africans into the machinery of government. In the local urban spheres virile organizations were establishing a contact, however tenuous, with the mass of Africans, and, although often unheeded by the authorities, they were capable of expressing the African's response to the immediate problems of industrial poverty and urban life. But there was no powerful, well-organized, nation-wide Congress, claiming that authority which stems from 'the Will of the People'. There was no concerted demand for political rights at the national level, no passionate movement for African 'emancipation'. When, for example, Europeans were discussing so fundamental an issue as the franchise,[31] there was no rallying of African public opinion, no mass petitions, no clear demonstration of widespread African concern.

The emergence of a continuous political protest on a national scale was prevented by a variety of factors. Many of the educated men who might have played a leading part in such a movement were handicapped by, as Mzingeli put it, their 'delicate economic position'. Teachers, head-messengers, and clerks, in Government or mission employment, were afraid that their jobs would be jeopardized by political activities.[32] And in Southern Rhodesia, where alternative openings for educated men were almost non-existent, this was no small consideration.

There was no African-controlled newspaper to act as a focus and open forum for the expression of valid, if unorthodox, African opinions. The *Bantu Mirror* and the *African Weekly* performed a most valuable educational and social function in providing reading material in English and the principal vernaculars, with general news items, reports on sport, and articles of interest to African readers. As a by-product they also provided valuable journalistic and general experience for their African editors: the first Africans from Southern Rhodesia to be elected in 1953 to the Federal Parliament had both been on the staff of these newspapers. But neither paper had a vital, active, political significance. They did

---

[31] See above, Part II, Chap. IV, pp. 306–10.
[32] *Sunday Mail*, 20 January 1952. Mzingeli instanced a pamphlet issued by 'a certain mission' headed *Instructions to African Pastors, Evangelists and Teachers*.

not provide an authentic, uncensored medium, since their African staff was subject to the over-riding guidance of their European proprietors.[33] It was an avowed object of the proprietors to give their editors freedom and in the day-to-day running of the papers they had considerable discretion. But their freedom lay within certain clear limits; they could not initiate policy nor indulge in the astringent criticism which is the mark of a free Press.

In April 1953 the first issue appeared of the *Bulawayo African Weekly News*, which later developed into the *African Home News*, a duplicated independent news-sheet, published every Saturday, price sixpence. Its editor, Mr. Charlton Ngcebetsha, was on the Executive of the Federation of African Workers' Unions and a prominent, outspoken member of the Bulawayo African Township Advisory Board; in its mixture of parochial and wider issues, and in the fact that its language was sometimes exaggerated and irresponsible, the news-sheet genuinely reflected his opinions and probably those of many urban Africans. But its circulation was limited and it was hardly comparable to the Press of Uganda or West Africa.

Little political initiative could be expected from the rural areas. The Native Reserves were isolated and scattered throughout the country; there were few large concentrations of vigorous successful peasants as in Nyasaland. In the Reserves the master farmers were generally careful to keep out of any politics distasteful to the Native Commissioner, and many of the Africans who showed initiative as farmers had moved out of the tribal Reserves into the Native Purchase Areas. Under the leadership of Mr. Aaron Jacha[34] these men united to form an African Farmers' Union, which won recognition from the Government with the appointment of Jacha to the Native Land Board in 1952—the first, and within the period under review the only, appointment of an African in Southern Rhodesia to an official body charged with the initiation and control of policy. The 'very active and constructive' union was praised by the Chief Native Commissioner for the high

---

[33] A former editor of the *African Weekly* writes, with a certain amount of exaggeration: 'Mr. Paver is, in effect, the editor-in-chief. The others are merely copy writers . . .'— Mnyanda, p. 120.

[34] See above, Part I, Chap. V, p. 162.

level of debate at its annual conferences.[35] The union also enjoyed a fruitful co-operation with the Natural Resources Board, for here racial rivalry was subordinated to the common interest in preventing soil erosion. But the members of the union, primarily concerned with the Purchase Areas, had little contact with the mass of rural Africans, and their absence from the Native Reserves deprived the rural peasantry of potential leadership.

The traditional leaders, 'shorn of most of their early power . . . paid a mere pittance of an allowance',[36] played a mainly passive role. A younger, vigorous, progressive man like Chief Mangwende was a rare exception and his direct influence was limited to the narrow confines of his own Reserve. In 1951 the Government took steps to 'weed out' the minor chiefs, increased the allowance of the major chiefs, and instituted a system of Provincial Assemblies of Chiefs where the Provincial Commissioners would be able to 'explain any proposed legislation affecting the African population and invite comment'.[37] It was hoped that 'by careful tuition and handling' the chiefs could become 'an essential cog in the machinery of administration',[38] but there was little prospect of their being able to foster, or even co-operate with, a nation-wide political movement.

Only in the towns, therefore, could such a movement originate. But urban Africans were by no means united. It was nearly 300 miles from Bulawayo to Salisbury and a further 160 to Umtali. Distance was a barrier to the African even more than to the European: practically no Africans were car-owners or could afford air travel, and even the fare for the long rail journeys was more than most could afford at all frequently. It was the unskilled migrant worker, rather than the educated man with a more settled position, who moved from town to town by foot, lorry, or rail. Even among Europeans there was strong rivalry and at times tension between Salisbury and Bulawayo, as was shown for example by the debate after 1953 on the location of the territorial capital. This conflict was reproduced among Africans and intensified by the traditional enmity of Mashona and Matabele—although the leaders were perhaps divided by personal rather than

---

[35] *Annual Report of the Chief Native Commissioner, 1951.*
[36] Ibid.   [37] Ibid.   [38] Ibid., 1952.

tribal rivalries. Within the towns Africans were divided by their
diverse origins: in 1946 only 36 per cent. of the Africans employed
in Salisbury came from Southern Rhodesia, while 34 per cent.
came from Nyasaland and 24 per cent. from Portuguese East
Africa.[39] The constant flow of migratory labour seriously hindered
the development of any continuous mass political movement, and
the lack of a common language checked communication.[40]

But the lack of political initiative and the relative absence of
fierce militant action stemmed also from a psychological condition
more fundamental than all these various factors. Africans in
Southern Rhodesia could seldom forget that theirs was a conquered
country, and consciousness of this fact still largely conditioned
their political ideas and activities. The Government maintained a
remarkable control over the country, despite its size and the great
numerical preponderance of Africans. The police force was considerably larger than those of the Colonial Office territories to the
north of the Zambezi. In 1948, a difficult year for Southern
Rhodesia, the British South Africa Police Force consisted of 725
Europeans and 1,653 Africans, with 776 Europeans in reserve. In
the same year in Northern Rhodesia there were 132 Europeans and
981 Africans in the police, with no organized reserve force. Half
of the European police force was concentrated on the Copperbelt,
and the Colonial Office annual report stated that in 'vast areas'
of the territory a policeman was 'hardly ever seen'. In Nyasaland
patrols were reported to visit all parts of the territory, but since the
police force consisted of twenty-seven Europeans, three Asians,
and 541 Africans the degree of European supervision must have
been relatively slight.[41]

In the countryside of Southern Rhodesia, on European farms or
isolated mines, the police were generally readily at hand and in the
Reserves they maintained a thorough, paternal surveillance of a
high standard through their scattered posts and frequent tours of

[39] 1946 Census Report.
[40] The R.I.C.U., for instance, could not introduce the several vernaculars used in Salisbury into its Newsletter despite many requests from its less educated members. *R.I.C.U.
Newsletter*, August 1951.
[41] *Report of the Commissioner, B.S.A. Police* (C.S.R. 16, 1949). Northern Rhodesia and
Nyasaland *Annual Reports*, 1948.

inspection. In the towns a member of the C.I.D. was present taking notes at most meetings of the R.I.C.U. and, according to the woman quoted earlier, it often required considerable courage to speak out at a meeting, for repercussions—particularly from African members of the police—could be serious.[42] In the towns also the Pass Laws were a constant reminder to the African of his subject status.[43]

If the Africans found a loop-hole in the law it was quickly amended, as in the case of the resistance to the implementation of the Land Apportionment Act led by Burombo.[44] The corpus of deterrent legislation was also steadily extended. The Commission appointed after the 1948 strike drew attention to the lack of legislation covering 'the prohibition of meetings which may endanger the public peace' and 'the dispersal of riotous assemblies'. It recommended that the Government should introduce legislation similar to the Union of South Africa's Riotous Assemblies Act of 1914, and in 1950, with the Subversive Activities Act, the Government implemented this recommendation. Henceforth Magistrates could ban public meetings if they considered that the public peace would be seriously endangered, and the police were given the right, subject to certain conditions, to use firearms in dispersing persons assembled at any prohibited gathering. Under these provisions Burombo's Voice Association was temporarily prohibited in May 1951 from holding public meetings in Bulawayo.[45] This part of the Act was modelled on the South African Riotous Assemblies Act of 1914, but in addition the Southern Rhodesian legislature now empowered the Minister of Justice to restrain or control the movements of individuals who, in his opinion, were either spreading subversive propaganda or promoting feelings of hostility between one or more sections of the community. The wide terms of this Act alarmed European trade unionists, but in debate the Minister of Justice assured them that in no respect would it interfere with the legitimate activities of trade unions as provided by the Industrial Conciliation Act—from

[42] See above, pp. 321–2.   [43] See above, Part II, Chap. VIII, pp. 269–70.
[44] See above, p. 327.
[45] *Rhodesia Herald*, 11 May 1951, quoted by Mnyanda, op. cit., p. 146.

which Africans were by definition excluded—and he did not repudiate Mr. Keller, who remarked that it was therefore apparently differential legislation directed against the native.[46]

In the short term this thorough control brought the benefit of peace and order: Europeans remarked with pride that in Southern Rhodesia, in contrast to some colonial territories, no African had been fatally injured by the police since the suppression of the rebellion in 1896. But it also prevented the growth of any effective, deeply based, inter-racial co-operation. At almost every encounter with a European an African was reminded of his subordinate position. Most Africans therefore remained in a state of sullen apathy. Even if legislation was introduced with beneficent intentions, it was met with hostile suspicion. The Native Land Husbandry Bill was accepted, according to the Native Commissioner from Umvuma, 'in the same way as so much is accepted, an evil that has to be endured whether they like it or not'; and at Shamva the Native Commissioner thought that 'the natives feel this is but another measure to subjugate them and they are receiving it philosophically'.[47]

But this abject acquiescence was no longer unanimous. The Mangwende Reserve Native Council representing 42,000 Africans offered '100 per cent. opposition to the Bill'. Led by Chief Mangwende, 'all of the Councillors tried to make out that the Councils should be given the opportunity of passing such laws', and the Native Commissioner had to admit that he thought that not a single African in the district was in favour of the measure.[48] In the towns also this defeatism was being challenged. A small but significant instance was the heated discussion which took place at a meeting of the R.I.C.U. branch in Bulawayo. A certain Kumalo, an elderly man, maintained that people should not ask for higher wages.

Many speakers angrily refuted Kumalo saying that they wanted an increase of their wages. Kumalo replied that they could not get higher

---

[46] S.R. Debates, 2 June 1950, col. 1902, 20 June 1950, cols. 2361, 2366–7.
[47] Evidence to the Select Committee on the Native Land Husbandry Bill, in the Library of the Legislative Assembly, Salisbury.
[48] Ibid.

wages *because their forefathers fought the Europeans when they entered this country*. There were shouts about this until Kumalo left the meeting and the demand for an increase in wages was passed.[49]

In town and country a new response was finding expression. Slowly a new sense of unity was spreading among Africans. There was as yet little consideration of the political or racial situation of the country as a whole; the issues felt most keenly were immediate and parochial. But occasionally a more intense racial feeling was invoked. Discussing the Native Urban Areas Act at a large three-day conference of the African Voice Association at Bulawayo, Burombo proclaimed a basic tenet of African nationalism:

If we go to the reserves we are sent back to the towns, and in town we are given only 14 days to look for work. Sometimes we have no food or sleeping place. So if God does not kill us after 14 days, what are we to do? People should be allowed to build homes for themselves.

A Chinaman can return to China, a European if he wishes can go back to Europe, an Indian can return to India, but Africa is the only place for Africans.[50]

Another young man, Mr. George Nyandoro, who was becoming a prominent exponent of militant racial feelings, took part in the same conference. He drew attention to the racial conflict in the rural areas: 'Land in plenty is given to a small number of European farmers, while the Africans are packed close together.' And the following year at a public meeting of the R.I.C.U. in Salisbury he again emphasized the racial contrast: 'At present a man is paid according to the colour of his skin, and not the nature of the work in so far as the Africans are concerned.'[51]

It was becoming clear that, if this spirit developed, Europeans in Southern Rhodesia would eventually be confronted with an intransigent mass movement, and the opportunity for compromise and co-operation would be lost. But for the moment, in these

[49] Minutes of General Meeting, R.I.C.U., Bulawayo, 17 July 1955. My italics.

[50] *Bulawayo Chronicle*, 2 April 1951. It was shortly after this conference that the Voice Association was banned, see above, p. 333.

[51] R.I.C.U. public meeting, 7 September 1952. Later Nyandoro was imprisoned as the result of a conviction in a case of gold robbery, but he re-emerged on the political scene in 1956 as a leading member of the vigorous and reconstituted Southern Rhodesian African Congress.

Z

immediate post-war years, African industrial and political protest in Southern Rhodesia remained sporadic, divided and uncertain of its ultimate aims. Although African leaders were beginning to unite their people within the frontier of poverty and colour, they found it far harder to define their objectives than those Africans north of the Zambezi who, aiming at ultimate independence, could appeal not only to racial sentiment and economic grievances but also to a developing sense of territorial unity and 'national' loyalty. South of the Zambezi Europeans were so well entrenched by conquest and subsequent control, and the economic structure of the country was so patently dependent on their continued presence, that the only obvious hope for Africans still lay in striving for greater co-operation and equality; as yet few Africans in Southern Rhodesia envisaged the desperate alternative of a total uncompromising fight for racial supremacy.

2. NORTH OF THE ZAMBEZI

North of the Zambezi Africans were becoming well organized politically and industrially. The factors from which Nyasaland nationalism developed were already apparent in the inter-war period. African self-confidence, founded on the Protectorate's history and fostered by the independent, and in part relatively prosperous, peasant economy, was encouraged by the Government's land policy and indirect rule. It developed into a strong national consciousness, in which there can be little doubt that the migration of labour, despite the economic and social evils which accompanied it, played a unifying and stimulating part. The evidence submitted to the Bledisloe Commission demonstrated incontrovertibly that already, in 1938, both traditional and educated African leaders possessed a clear sense of the unity and independence of Nyasaland and a passionate desire to preserve its distinctive destiny. And the opinions of these leaders were shared by many other Africans; the contrast with the territories south of the Zambezi was not theoretical but a reality sharply apprehended by even the most illiterate migrant.[52] But before the Second World

[52] See above, Part I, Chap. V.

War there was inside Nyasaland hardly a hint of immediate protest against the country's colonial status, no demand for 'freedom',
no nation-wide organization mobilizing the country in a crusade
for accelerated self-government. European administrators and
missionaries were obeyed with apparent respect, and they saw no
reason to suspect that the policy of calm, slow development towards an ultimate goal of self-government would not continue for
many future decades.

Suddenly the whole atmosphere of Nyasaland politics changed.
On 1 October 1943 James Sangala, a former member of the
Zomba Province Native Association,[53] published a circular letter
addressed to 'All Africans Resident in Nyasaland Protectorate'.
The letter stated that in the previous months 'the community of
both Blantyre and Limbe Townships' had met together to discuss
the formation of an Association which was to be 'representative of
all the Africans resident in Nyasaland'. It went on to urge Africans
to fight for their freedom, 'to strive for unity so as to obtain the
greater development of the peoples and country of Nyasaland'.
In response to official inquiries, Sangala informed the District
Commissioner that the phrase 'to fight for their freedom' was not
meant 'to convey the meaning that Africans should enter into
armed conflict against the Europeans for the sake of obtaining self-
government, but that as self-government eventually must come if
the Nyasaland Natives were to be free in the fullest sense, the
sooner they started to do something for themselves the better'.
Yet despite this cautious gloss, the new, militant spirit was apparent even at this official encounter. Sangala went on to explain
to the District Commissioner that the lack of African representation on the Legislative Council and other official and non-official
bodies, together with other restrictions, showed that 'the Nyasaland Natives are a subordinate race', and, he thought, 'they will
remain so, so long as they do nothing themselves to improve their
lot'.[54]

This language soon found a wider audience. In January 1944 the

---

[53] See above, Part I, Chap. V, pp. 175–6.
[54] Central African Archives, Zomba, NAT 34/1, D.C. Blantyre to P.C., 8 October
1943.

Anglican Bishop of Nyasaland asked Sangala to arrange an informal meeting to discuss the Bishop's work in the Legislative Council as the representative of 'Missions and, as far as a European can, African Interests'. The meeting took place on 28 January in the presence of the Provincial Commissioner, the D.C., Sir William Tait-Bowie and Mr. R. C. Bucquet, leaders of the European Unofficials, and more than seventy Africans. A week previously Sangala had called together the select committee of the Nyasaland African Association, as the group was then called, and, after a long discussion unrelievedly hostile to various aspects of missionary activity, it was decided that Matinga[55] should prepare a statement.[56]

Matinga began his statement by deploring the fact that although the Government had appointed Africans to recognized bodies, such as the Education Advisory Board, 'not a single Mission in the country' had followed its example. 'Instead everything they do is secret to the Africans.' There were no Africans in any mission council and, he said, 'to suggest that missionaries can represent the interests of Africans is but to retard again their progress'. Africans now demanded 'majority representation in Legislative Council, Township managements, Land Boards . . . and all such boards that affect our welfare in the country'. They also wanted the right to organize trade unions. Matinga then went on to describe his people's principal demands and grievances. 'Lands taken from us and still remaining undeveloped must be restored . . . when we starve it is not because we are lazy but we have no good places to produce enough food and we have to pay higher rents when we want to stay on good land.' Africans, he said, were forced to migrate, wandering 'from territory to territory', because of the 'lack of sympathy and economic facilities in their own country'. The Government should introduce new industries and 'collective farming in the villages'. The missions 'have never tried to propose any scheme to relieve us from poverty and diseases'. Instead missionaries lost no time in complaining that the Government

[55] See above, Part I, Chap. V, p. 176.
[56] Central African Archives, Zomba, NAT 34/1, Bishop of Nyasaland to Sangala, 8 January 1944, Minutes of Select Committee of Nyasaland African Association, 21 January 1944.

wage for labourers of 8s. was too high, since they paid their own
teachers only 4s. and upwards a month. The possibility of taking
advantage of higher educational facilities abroad was denied to
Africans 'because of the fear of making us better and well educated
people, able to speak for ourselves'. In fact, concluded Matinga,
'anything that makes a race progress has been denied to us and
what has been done is to tell us to look for things that are in store
in the next world while others so privileged because of their fair
colour are making use of all and everything in this world. . . . If
there are things that are good for Europeans, Indians or Half-
Castes, we also want them.'[57]

This sudden broadside of bitter, racial criticism astonished Europeans. Various explanations were put forward. A senior official
in the Secretariat, who knew Sangala, reported that 'the whole
tone' of the protest was 'quite different' from his 'knowledge of
the Blantyre intelligentsia just before the war'. He did not believe
that it came 'entirely from their own ideas and aspirations', and he
thought that some European was perhaps inspiring it. 'They take a
long time to think about anything and do not start thinking until
someone else has produced the idea.' W. H. Timcke, a European
of progressive views who had been a member of the 1935 Committee appointed by the Governor to inquire into emigrant labour,
was suspected. He was known to have advised Sangala to contact
Mr. Creech Jones as a sympathetic helper in the House of Commons; he helped him with the draft of a letter to W. G. Ballinger
and the Friends of Africa in Johannesburg; three weeks before the
meeting with the Bishop he forwarded to Sangala a report from
the *Nyasaland Times* concerning the elections of European Unofficial Representatives to the Legislative Council and suggested
that Sangala's group should demand not less than three African
Representatives.[58] But all this was after the publication of Sangala's
circular letter, and this fairly innocuous advice hardly explains
the coherent volume of demands and grievances so suddenly
unleashed.

[57] Central African Archives, Zomba, NAT 34/1, report of meeting with Bishop by
C. J. Matinga.
[58] Ibid., letters and minutes dated 4 November 1943, 9 January 1944, 3 March 1944.

Contacts with Dr. Hastings Banda in London may well have been more important. As a boy Banda left Nyasaland for South Africa, where, like Kadalie, he 'learnt his politics'. For several years he studied in the United States, and then came to Britain, where he qualified as a doctor and established a medical practice. In 1938 he submitted a memorandum to the Bledisloe Commission in London[59] and he became an early member of the Fabian Colonial Bureau. He was particularly interested by developments in the Gold Coast, where Africans were already taking part in the Legislative Council, and throughout these early years of the Congress he is said to have been in correspondence with Sangala and Levi Mumba, the first President of the Congress.[60] Doubtless these contacts with Timcke and Banda were important for the African leaders in Nyasaland. They may even have been responsible to some extent for the form and language of the new movement; but the idea that this sudden outburst of criticism was primarily the result of external inspiration ignored the other hard foundations of African opinion. The refusal to believe that this could be a spontaneous movement reflecting widely-shared experiences and fears showed a dangerous divorce from African realities and an ignorance of the Africans' deepest motives.

Experience of the white man's world south of the Zambezi was undoubtedly the greatest formative influence behind this outburst. Charles Matinga himself was deeply influenced by this experience. In 1941, encouraged by Sangala and other African friends who subsequently became leading members of the Congress, Matinga visited Rhodesia and the Union for the first time in his life. Armed with introductions from European missionaries and the Senior Provincial Commissioner, he was able to see more than many migrant workers could. On the one hand he was greatly stimulated. Taken to Domboshawa and the neighbouring Reserves by the Director of Native Education in Southern Rhodesia, he was told that some master farmers were doing better than some European farmers, and he was impressed with the possibilities of agricultural development in the villages which had been centralized. He was impressed also by the general level of women's

[59] *Bledisloe Report*, p. 274.   [60] Information supplied by Dr. Banda.

education, particularly in Johannesburg, and at the Wilberforce Institute, founded by the African Methodist Episcopal Church and 'run by Africans for Africans', he again realized 'that Africans given equal facilities as are given to other races could do things in the same way as others do'. He returned therefore to Nyasaland impatient, enthusiastic, with a new vision of the potentialities of an active policy of development.

But Matinga also returned with a greater antipathy to Rhodesian racial policy and an enhanced attachment to the 'liberal policy' of Nyasaland. 'We are fortunate', he told his fellow-countrymen on his return, 'that there is no colour bar.' Despite the better standard of education in Southern Rhodesia, he noticed that there was no Native Civil Service there. Africans in Salisbury were surprised to hear 'that we can do any skilled work or that even the trains can be driven by Africans in Nyasaland'. Despite the master-farmers scheme and the comparative wealth of the Rhodesian economy, he thought that the general level of development in the Reserves could not be 'compared with what has taken place in Nyasaland . . . I hardly saw houses which could match with ours'. He sensed the vital significance which the countries north of the Zambezi had for the Africans in Southern Africa: at Wilberforce Institute an African Minister told him how on 'his first trip to Northern Rhodesia he felt he was entering to a sacred land where the people have not lost everything they had because of civilisation'.[61]

In a more haphazard and fragmentary fashion, though with more immediacy and perhaps more pain, thousands of Matinga's countrymen were sharing annually in a similar experience. They seized even unlikely occasions to propagate a new sense of national unity. In June 1941, for instance, after a football match at the Ndirande Welfare Club, a Mr. Mlenga, freshly returned from Southern Rhodesia and the Union 'where he had been Captain of Football teams', told the schoolboys and others present that 'the most interesting thing there was not the Tea and Scones they ate but that they met together as one people of one nation. What really the country needs is co-operation. Unite and do things

[61] Central African Archives, NAT 17, Address by Matinga at Blantyre Mission, 29 November 1941.

together. This place should be called a field where you would build up a greater Nyasaland.'[62]

It was therefore hardly surprising that in the years following the Bledisloe Commission, Africans in Nyasaland continued to voice their persistent opposition to any possibility of amalgamation with Southern Rhodesia. For example, at a meeting of the Mlanje Native Association in April 1942 all the Mlanje Native Authorities, together with 'the people who are reading newspapers', declared that they were 'always alarmed to hear about the proposed amalgamation question'. Nyasa Africans, they said, 'do not at all dream of this question because at the meeting with the Royal Commission they gave the greatest and important reasons which all were against it which are even now filed in the Colonial Office'. The Association unanimously resolved, therefore, to request the Governor that whenever *barazas* were held in the districts the question should be mentioned and that 'if required additional notes and proofs' should be transmitted to the Colonial Office.[63]

This same theme was given prominence in the meeting with the Bishop. Matinga congratulated him for 'advising the Governor about amalgamation' and declared that Nyasaland Africans totally refused 'the amalgamation or federation either with Rhodesias or the North[64] until we have been given at least 99 per cent. of the rights we are entitled to enjoy in the administration of our own country'. A few months later, in May 1944, the Introductory General Meeting of the Nyasaland African Congress requested the Governor to send a cable to the Secretary of State expressing the Africans' fears on the subject, and at the first Annual General Conference of the Congress, 21 October 1944, the President stated that 'one of the points which influenced us to organise is the question of amalgamation of the Rhodesias with our small country'.[65]

One other series of events in these years quickened the sense of nationalism and instilled militant, impatient ideas into the minds

---

[62] Central African Archives, NAT 17, Blantyre D.C., Misc. Minutes of Ndirande Welfare Club, 15 June 1941.

[63] Ibid., NAT 12/38, extract from Minutes of the Mlanje Native Association, 25 April 1942.

[64] I.e. the East African territories.   [65] Central African Archives, NAT 34/1.

of the 'intelligentsia' and even into those of the masses. The newspapers carried reports of the Atlantic Charter, of the fight for
freedom, of the threat of Nazi racialism, and of the successes of
Japan. Nearly a third of the fit African male population was on
active service; nine battalions saw service in Abyssinia, Madagascar,
India, and Burma, while a few Africans from Nyasaland were
taken prisoner at Tobruk and thus saw Italy and Germany. In
varying degrees these men understood the ideals for which they
were fighting, underwent a wide range of new experiences, and at
the same time maintained a fairly close contact with those who
had remained at home. At the first Annual General Conference of
the Congress, the President referred to the support received 'from
all people including our soldiers who are fighting for the cause of
liberty'. And in 1946 the Colonial Office annual report stated that
one effect of the war had been to make the serviceman, 'European,
Yao, Ngoni, Nyanja, or Nguru, think of himself as a "Nyasa". By
that name he was known to his comrades from the rest of the
Empire.'[66]

The new militancy, vehemence, and bitterness of the Blantyre
'intelligentsia' seem, then, to have grown from their heightened
fears of amalgamation and their participation, however remote for
most of them, in the conflict of the Second World War. Perhaps
they even had already some inkling of the fact that Africa would
never be quite the same again, that the days of undisputed European control were drawing to a close. And the fact that most
Nyasaland Africans had experienced personally, as migrant
labourers, the contrast between their country and those south of
the Zambezi, together with the experiences of those on active
service, meant that these new demands and attitudes were not
confined merely to the intelligentsia. A new nation was beginning
to awake.

On 20 May 1944 a meeting attended by more than 100 people
was held to introduce the Nyasaland African Congress to the
'Native Authorities and people of Blantyre and Chiradzulu districts'. All the Native Authorities of Chiradzulu district attended
and leading chiefs assured the Congress leaders of their support and

[66] *Annual Report on Nyasaland for the Year 1946* (Colonial Office, London).

financial aid. They welcomed the opportunity for united action: 'I trust', said Chief Kadewere, 'if we make our representations from one body such as this, Government will listen to us,' and it was he who seconded the meeting's resolution on the amalgamation issue.[67] The Chiradzulu Native Authorities were also represented at the first Annual Conference of the Congress held in the Chiefs' Council Chamber at Blantyre on 21 October 1944. But Chiradzulu district, situated in the midst of European estates, had a tradition of protest stretching back to the beginning of the century, to the early days of the Providence Industrial Mission and John Chilembwe's rising in 1915, and apart from this troubled district the Native Authorities of the Protectorate were unrepresented at the first Annual Conference. Instead there were representatives from branches of the Congress which had been founded throughout the country in the year which had elapsed since Sangala's original circular letter. In the Southern Province the greatest strength came from the branches of Blantyre and Limbe, but there were also representatives from branches in Mlanje, Cholo, Zomba, and Fort Johnston. In the other Provinces there were branches at Lilongwe, Malimba, Dowa, Dedza, Kota-Kota, Mzimba, and Karonga. In many areas these branches had developed from the remnants of the Native Associations which had been active in the inter-war period. Levi Mumba and Charles Matinga, President and Vice-President of the Congress, had both been leading members of Native Associations;[68] and at this first Annual Conference of the Congress there were representatives of the Native Associations which were still active at Livingstonia, Likoma Island, Port Herald, and Chiromo.

In many ways, therefore, the Congress movement was merely the logical development of this previous activity; its history stretched back to 1912, when Levi Mumba was secretary of the first Native Association in North Nyasa. Its new-found vigour was not the short-lived product of an imported exotic plant; it sprang from a natural, indigenous growth with its roots deep in the past. Many of the delegates to the first annual conference had started their careers as school-teachers and had become clerks; but

[67] See above, p. 342.   [68] See above, Part I, Chap. V, pp. 174–7.

among them there was also a sprinkling of Village Headmen and of the more prosperous peasant farmers. There were representatives from the 'Mlanje Native Foodstuffs Growers' Association' and the 'Mombera Dairies Co-operative Society'; there was also a representative from an association of African employees on the Nyasaland Railways. It was thus already a nation-wide organization largely representative of the more educated Africans and those who were benefiting from the country's policy of fostering peasant production; it had yet to be seen whether it could gain the co-operation of the traditional authorities and the mass of the people.

High among the claims of the Congress was the demand for direct representation on the Legislative Council. 'It is not logical', Mumba declared, 'that a population of over two and a half million can always remain without direct representation.' In order to prevent the continued migration of labour they demanded that 'the State' should 'revolutionise the conditions by developing industries', and they also passed a resolution 'respectfully' asking the Government to purchase all undeveloped land and any estates which should fall vacant 'for their return to the Africans'. The Congress totally condemned the restrictions 'which reduce the African to the state of a social inferior' and humbly requested the Government to allow the African to enter cinemas, to purchase European drinks, to enter European stores 'instead of the present practice of selling to him through the window', and to be paid 'an adequate salary according to the responsibility of the work performed and not according to his colour as is the case at present'.[69]

But in these early years education was the subject of most persistent interest to the members of the Congress, as it had been to those of the Native Associations in the previous period. In 1947 Matinga led a Congress deputation to the Governor to discuss their demands for increased educational grants. Their desire for progress was, Matinga said, 'not a censure upon the Government but was the result of the natural desires which had arisen among

[69] Minutes of the first Annual General Conference of the Nyasaland African Congress, 21 October 1944.

their people, especially in the light of the war-time experience
which a large number of them had had of many other countries'.
They demanded free compulsory education and suggested that the
Government should levy a tax on labour within the Protectorate
and also upon migrant labour. The Governor, however, pointed
out that the revised post-war development plan provided for an expenditure of £5,646,000 over ten years, of which a very high proportion, £1,483,000, was to be spent on education. The Congress
demands would have necessitated a building programme of over
£1 million and an annual recurrent expenditure of £750,000.[70]
These demands disregarded the narrow economic limits of both
the Missions and the Government; but on the other hand little
progress had been made in advanced education and their note of
urgency was echoed by a Commission sent out by the Colonial
Office.[71] Dissatisfied with the Government's response, the Congress appealed to the country for funds, and in 1948 Matinga interviewed the Secretary of State in London on the question of African
education.

After this vigorous opening the impetus of the Congress seems
to have slackened. On his return from London, Matinga was
involved in a dispute with his colleagues over finance and he
gradually withdrew from participation in the affairs of the Congress, while the deaths of Levi Mumba and Isaac Lawrence,
President General and Treasurer General respectively, deprived
the Congress of experienced leaders. When concrete results were
not swiftly gained, a certain disillusionment succeeded the first
wave of enthusiasm. It is also possible that the creation of Provincial and Protectorate Councils composed of chiefs and commoners diverted energy which might otherwise have gone into
the activities of the Congress. Just as the introduction of indirect
rule and the District Councils seems to have weakened the local
Native Associations in the inter-war period,[72] so these superior
Councils with their official status provided an alternative forum
particularly for the traditional authorities. But the rivalry between

---

[70] Central African Archives, Zomba, NAT 34/11, Minutes dated 24 September 1947.
[71] *Report on the Education of Women and Girls in Nyasaland*, August and September 1947.
[72] See above, Part I, Chap. V, pp. 173–4.

the Councils and the Congress should not be stressed unduly: many members of the Congress were also members of the Provincial Councils and, as in the inter-war period, traditional and educated leaders were united on issues of national significance.

By 1950 the activities of the Congress within Nyasaland were concentrated on Lilongwe, the centre of the prosperous African cotton and tobacco farmers. Its President was also Chairman of the African Farmers' Association, and with two other members of Congress and an ex-clerk he represented the commoners of Lilongwe district on the Provincial Council. But the support, strength, and influence of the Congress were by no means restricted to Nyasaland itself. At the time of the first Annual General Conference in October 1944 there was already a branch in Johannesburg, and in January 1945 it was reported that Nyasaland labourers on the copper mines in Northern Rhodesia had begun to form local branches of the Nyasaland African Congress.[73] Soon there were also branches in Bulawayo and Salisbury, linked up with Burial Societies and associations in the other urban centres and on the chief mines in Southern Rhodesia.

These branches outside Nyasaland were, possibly even in these early years, the most important contributors to Congress funds and their leaders were some of its most active members. At the same time these branches proclaimed to Africans outside Nyasaland their gospel of militant unity and their vision of African freedom. In Salisbury, for instance, they brought a new temper into the deliberations of the R.I.C.U. Mr. Chingattie, a young well-educated Nyasalander, declared at an R.I.C.U. general meeting in January 1950 'that African people should regard any one black as his brother'. He gave them a long history of the various Nyasaland organizations which had counteracted tribalism, and ended by saying: 'Europeans regard themselves as Europeans, and yet they are of different nationalities. This alone should teach the African people of different tribes the importance of unity.' Later in the same year, at the R.I.C.U. fourth annual conference, Mr. Kwenje, 'speaking as a representative of the Nyasaland

[73] Central African Archives, Zomba, NAT 34/1, Labour Commissioner, Lusaka, to Labour Commissioner, Zomba, 15 January 1945.

African Congress', said that he thought the wording of the agenda was 'too moderate' and 'far from the red-line'. He pointed out that the Subversive Activities Bill,[74] then before the Legislative Assembly, 'would suppress freedom of discussion'. He said that it was 'unreasonable to brand those under-privileged as communist because they demanded a square deal' and expressed his surprise that 'not a single African organisation in Southern Rhodesia' had sent 'any protest or expressed any opinion' on the Bill. In many cases, he said, Africans had different names for their organizations yet all of them claimed 'one thing, i.e., elementary right'. In Nyasaland 'a communist is believed to be a man who is loyal to Stalin. . . . To Mr. Olley Church leaders were communists because they preach equality of all persons before God', but, Mr. Kwenje pointed out, 'the Soviet Union have done nothing for African people under the British Empire, therefore to call any African organisation communist was not justified'.[75]

Thus in the first few years of its existence, from 1944 to the end of 1950, the Nyasaland African Congress was beginning to provide a forum and an organization for the nascent African nationalism of Nyasalanders. It had introduced a note of urgency that was in contrast to the leisurely calm of the inter-war period. Its insistent demands referred not merely to particular grievances but also displayed the first signs of a broader strategy for social and political advance. Its activities seem to have aroused a fluctuating enthusiasm and its active membership was drawn from a tiny minority of relatively well-educated and economically independent Africans; but it was drawing its strength from a wide area—from branches scattered throughout Nyasaland and also from groups situated among the thousands of migrant labourers in Southern Africa. And on the major issues of progress towards self-government and national independence it could appeal, unhindered by those tribal jealousies which erected barriers elsewhere in Africa, to a wider audience of less educated men who had been stimulated by the experience of service overseas or of work south of the Zambezi. Fear of the white South was at least as strong in Nyasaland as fear of the black North in Southern Rhodesia. This fear was no small

[74] See above, p. 333.   [75] R.I.C.U. Newsletter, 8 January 1950, 27 May 1950.

part of the Congress' *raison d'être*, and it was shared by the chiefs and by the masses.

Yet during these years, despite increased impatience, intemperate criticism, and a few undertones of incipient racial hostility, there was still a fund of goodwill, a recognition of the vital contribution still needed from European missionaries and administrators, and a real possibility of enlisting the energy of an awakening people in an ordered advance towards the declared objectives of British colonial policy. Politically, if not economically, the future of Nyasaland presented by no means an unfavourable prospect; there were as yet no signs of a complete collapse in the confidence of African leaders in the good faith of either the local Administration or of the Colonial Office. That decisive dividing-line was approached in Nyasaland only with the publication in June 1951 of the White Paper on the 'Closer Association of the Central African Territories'.

In 1951 the Northern Rhodesia Congress had a much shorter history than its Nyasaland counterpart. The Native Welfare Associations, which in a few centres had expressed to the Bledisloe Commission in 1938 their opposition to amalgamation,[76] developed rapidly in the later years of the Second World War. On the Copperbelt in particular these Welfare Societies, as they were later called, attracted the best educated, most energetic, and progressive members of the African communities. Gradually they assumed the political and social functions which the Government had hoped would be undertaken by the Tribal Elders and the nominated Urban Advisory Councils established in 1941. Despite their completely unofficial status it was they who successfully championed local grievances, sponsored activities on social occasions, prepared addresses of welcome to visiting dignitaries, and attracted attention and prestige. Their development was so striking that by 1945 Sir Stewart Gore-Browne, the Nominated Representative of African Interests on the Legislative Council, suggested the necessity of reforming and enlarging the official Urban Advisory Councils: 'in some townships at any rate,' he said, 'a visitor desirous of sounding native opinion on any matter would

[76] See above, Part I, Chap. V, pp. 190–1.

be better advised to consult the Welfare Society than the Urban Advisory Council.'[77]

In 1946 representatives from fourteen Welfare Societies throughout Northern Rhodesia met at Lusaka and formed a Federation of Welfare Societies. Two years later, at one of the conferences of this Federation, it was decided to disband the Federation and to reconstitute it as the Northern Rhodesia Congress. Contact was established with the African National Congress in South Africa, but, as in Nyasaland, the phase of mass action, boycotts, and total suspicion of the Government's intentions only began as the debate on Federation entered its final stages. It was in June 1951 that the White Paper on Closer Association was published; it was in July, with the installation of Mr. Harry Nkumbula as President, that the Congress, henceforth known as the Northern Rhodesia African National Congress, began to be organized as a mass movement spreading throughout the territory.[78]

With the emergence of the Congress movements north of the Zambezi, Africans began to take an increasingly active part in the political development of Central Africa; simultaneously the development of well-organized African trade unions on the Copperbelt marked the beginning of African power in industry. After the strike on the Copperbelt in 1940,[79] Tribal Representatives were appointed on all the mines to work in contact with the Government Labour Officers, and in 1946 their work was supplemented by the introduction of Works Committees with representatives from each of the mine departments. These Committees were mainly concerned with minor problems; they did not usually negotiate on wages or conditions of service. Together with the Welfare Societies, however, they did provide a small number of men with training in urban and industrial leadership, and this *élite* played an important part in the formation of trade unions.

In 1947, as part of the Colonial policy of the Labour Government, a British trade unionist, Mr. W. Comrie, was sent by the

---

[77] Quoted in A. L. Epstein, *Politics in an Urban African Community* (Manchester, 1958), p. 69.
[78] Ibid., pp. 157–60. Cf. also R. Howman, *Principles and Practice in Relation to the Structure of Local Government* (duplicated Salisbury, February 1952).
[79] See above, Part II, Chap. II, pp. 224–5.

Colonial Office to help to organize African trade unions in
Northern Rhodesia. With the help of the more experienced
leaders he was gradually able to win the confidence of the mass of
workers and in February 1948 the first African miners' trade
union was formed at Nkana. Mr. Lawrence Katilungu, a prominent member of the powerful Bemba tribe who had joined the
mine in 1936 as an underground worker and had then become a
recruiting clerk, was elected chairman, and together with other
officials of the Union he toured the Copperbelt urging Africans to
follow the example of Nkana. A year later, in March 1949, unions
at each of the four copper mines and at the Broken Hill mine
amalgamated to form the African Mine Workers' Union. Thus,
in contrast to the Rhodesia Railways African Employees' Association,[80] the A.M.W.U. in Northern Rhodesia to a large extent
owed its inception to external influence and guidance; only to a
limited extent had it grown out of African initiative.[81]

The trade union leaders, however, soon consolidated their
position and proved their ability. In July 1950 the Labour Department estimated the membership of the Union at 19,000, though
the fully paid-up membership was thought to be probably half
that number, and throughout this early period—until November
1953—the Companies considerably assisted the Union by collecting Union subscriptions directly from members.[82] In 1950 the
Union demanded a general wage revision and a profit-sharing
scheme similar to that of the European employees. Protracted
negotiations took place and the Government's Labour Commissioner reported that 'throughout negotiations African union
officials conducted themselves in a responsible manner, showing
high negotiating qualities which earned them the compliments of
the General Managers and Conciliator'.[83]

In 1952, after its annual conference, the Union demanded a
general increase of 2s. 8d. per shift, which for the lowest paid
workers was a rise of 178 per cent. The dispute was laid unsuccess-
fully before a Conciliation Board appointed by the Governor, and
the Companies offered to take the matter to arbitration, but a

[80] See above, pp. 316–18.
[81] Epstein, pp. 89–93.
[82] *African Weekly*, 26 July 1950.
[83] Ibid.

secret ballot gave the Union a strong mandate and a strike was called for 20 October 1952. The strike lasted three weeks, during which production was totally halted, 'complete order was maintained and there were no disturbances or incidents'.[84] Finally both parties agreed to arbitration provided that the arbitrator was chosen from the United Kingdom, and in January 1953 the African employees were awarded a large increase in pay which raised the minimum basic pay of the lowest grade workers from 45s. to 80s. per ticket of thirty days' work. The success of the Union leaders in organizing so large a number of workers alarmed and shocked European public opinion in Northern Rhodesia. 'We learn with dismay', commented an editorial in the *Central African Post*, 'that there will be practically no mining while the Africans remain out. . . . The fact that a strike of Africans can put a stop to active mining puts them in a very strong position and the companies and the country in a very weak one.'[85]

As the Central African Territories moved towards Federation Europeans retained the major political and economic initiatives; their will, their attitudes, and their actions were still the dominant force shaping race relations in the three territories. But north of the Zambezi developments had made it certain that the day of the passive participation of the African had ended; his reactions, and his initiative, were to become steadily more and more important.

[84] Report of the Arbitrator, C. W. Guillebaud, January 1953.
[85] Quoted by Epstein, p. 97.

EPILOGUE

Between 1918 and 1953 the situation of the Europeans in Central Africa changed profoundly. Their wealth, numbers, and importance considerably increased. From a few thousand farmers and miners striving to make a living under unfavourable conditions, they had become the galvanizing force and principal beneficiaries of an industrial revolution. But at the same time their protective isolation was diminishing; they were increasingly conscious of the changing currents of world opinion, and they could hardly remain unconscious of the awakening of a continent in which they were numerically an insignificant minority. Opportunities of economic expansion had opened up triumphantly, horizons had widened, and yet the future seemed less secure. The confident assumptions of the early years had begun to be challenged.

A further volume will relate how in these post-war years a majority of the Europeans became convinced that the best hope for their future lay in creating a larger territorial unit, a new State in Central Africa, which it was hoped would follow a policy of 'partnership' avoiding the extremes of white or black domination. The decision to embark on this experiment was taken as a result of European initiative; it may perhaps prove to be the last occasion in which the British, as settlers or as trustees, acted as the sole arbiters in a part of Africa. Yet, on the evidence which we have been considering, a question must be asked; did the foundations for such a partnership in fact exist?

Some crudities in race relations were disappearing. When motor-cars were first introduced into Southern Rhodesia many owners refused to allow Africans to share their new-found comfort and symbol of prestige: native servants habitually made the long, hot journey from Salisbury to Bulawayo outside on the running board.[1] By 1953 this would have been impossible and not

[1] I owe this information to Mr. Lawrence Vambe's MS. on Mr. Charles Mzingeli.

only because running boards were no longer part of a car's design. In some respects the material contrasts between European and African had become less glaring: in the towns, for instance, the wives of European artisans complained that they could no longer buy the cheaper types of cotton dresses for these were now seen on the backs of African factory girls. And in more significant ways the gap between the fringes of the races was narrowing: the best of the new housing for better-paid Africans was by no means inferior to that in which some Europeans lived, and a handful of Africans were beginning to follow professional careers.

But political and economic power remained firmly in the hands of the Europeans and a gulf of mutual ignorance and incomprehension continued to divide the races. In Rhodesia there were still two nations, even if the Europeans' declared objective was no longer to increase and perpetuate this division. And in judging the trend of race relations it was no longer sufficient to examine the attitudes and the 'native policy' of the Europeans. Another initiative had to be taken into account.

Compared with the gradual and partial readjustment of the Europeans, the change in the reactions and attitude of Africans during these thirty-five years was revolutionary. After the First World War, on both sides of the Zambezi increasing numbers of educated Africans were leading their fellow tribesmen towards a positive acceptance of the European way of life. Primitive hostility and suspicion were abating; the first rebellions against the white man's rule had failed. The prevalent ambition of clerks, teachers, *capitaos*, and carpenters in rural Nyasaland or in small, growing towns of the Rhodesias was that they, their children, and their fellow Africans should be permitted to establish themselves firmly in the new world of wide opportunities they had glimpsed. Their great desire was that Europeans should welcome this ambition, recognize the steps they had already made, and actively assist their progress. They wanted equal rights for 'civilized' men and equal opportunities—in education and work—to become 'civilized'.

This mood persisted into the thirties, but constant disillusionment induced ever-widening doubts and resentment. Gradually the emphasis shifted to militant self-help; leaders came forward asserting that progress was dependent on the organized strength of Africans fighting to obtain an entry into the modern world, and inexorably this reasoning gave support to the cry of 'Africa for the Africans'. North of the Zambezi this process was immeasurably hastened by the threat of amalgamation with Southern Rhodesia, and the fears by no means subsided even after the Bledisloe Commission had recommended caution and delay. At the same time, on the Copperbelt and in the towns, poverty forged a new unity among Africans and the new weapons of strike and mass action came into use. By 1953 the chances of creating a co-operation between European and African leaders had become terrifyingly slender, the one concrete attempt had ended in failure, and Europeans were faced with the problem not of an emergent *élite* but of an unpredictable and increasingly hostile proletariat in the Rhodesias and a united national movement in Nyasaland. In Victorian England the existence of the two nations necessitated a leap in the dark; if, after 1953, partnership was to succeed in Central Africa, some such leap would surely be necessary, but the fence looked very high and the darkness seemed even more obscure.

BIBLIOGRAPHY

Colonial Office Library, London.
 Evidence to the Royal Commission on Rhodesia and Nyasaland, 1938.
 (Evidence to the Bledisloe Commission.)
  This is particularly valuable as it provides a record of the opinions of
 African as well as European witnesses.
Central African Archives, Salisbury. (C.A.A.)
 Files: ZAH 1/1/1-4. Evidence to the Morris Carter Land Commission, 1925.
  ,, N 3/21/1-10. Official correspondence and documents relating to Native
   Associations, 1915–1923.
Central African Archives, Zomba. (C.A.A. Zomba.)
 File Miss. 12/10. Official correspondence relating to Independent Churches.
  ,, S1/2065/19
  ,, S1/1481/19
  ,, S1/1598/29   Official correspondence relating to Native Associa-
  ,, S1/3263/23   tions.
  ,, NAT/12/3, 33, 38
  ,, NAT/17
  ,, NAT/34/1-11. Official correspondence relating to the Nyasaland
   African Congress.
Legislative Assembly Library, Salisbury.
 Evidence to the Select Committee on the Native Land Husbandry Bill, 1951.
Papers of the Anti-Slavery Society, deposited at Rhodes House, Oxford.
 There are a few letters which throw light on African organizations in
  Southern Rhodesia during the period 1918–1939.
International Missionary Council, Edinburgh House, London.
 Correspondence with the United Missions on the Copperbelt.
In private ownership:
 Evidence to the Committee Appointed to Investigate Urban Conditions in
  Southern Rhodesia, 1943. (Evidence to the Howman Committee.) The
  official record kindly lent by Mr. Roger Howman.
 Records and correspondence of the Southern Rhodesia Labour Party, kindly
  lent by Mr. N. Zelter.
 'Mzingeli: Gandhi of the Africans', an unpublished biography of Mr. Charles
  Mzingeli written in 1949 by Mr. Lawrence Vambe, kindly lent by the
  author.

PUBLISHED

A. Official Publications

Abrahams, J. C. *Report on Nyasaland Natives in the Union of South Africa and in Southern Rhodesia* (Zomba, 1937).

Administration and Finances of Native Locations in Urban Areas, Report of the Commission Appointed to Inquire into the (Lusaka, 1944).

Advancement of Africans in Industry, Report of the Commission Appointed to Inquire into the (the Dalgleish Report) (Lusaka, 1948).

Advancement of Africans in the Copper Mining Industry in Northern Rhodesia, Report of the Board of Inquiry Appointed to Inquire into the (the Forster Report) (Lusaka, 1954).

Ballenden, G. *Report on Salisbury's Native Administration* (Salisbury, 1945).

Bell, Sir Robert. *Report of the Commission Appointed to Enquire into the Financial Position and Further Development of Nyasaland* (Col. No. 152, 1938).

Burden, G. N. *Report on Nyasaland Native Labour in Southern Rhodesia* (Zomba, 1938).

—— *Report on Nyasaland Natives in the Union of South Africa* (Zomba, 1940).

Busschau, W. J. *Report on the Development of Secondary Industries in Northern Rhodesia* (Lusaka, 1945).

Census Report, Northern Rhodesia, 1921, 1931, 1946, 1951.

Census Report, Nyasaland, 1926, 1931, 1945.

Census Report, Southern Rhodesia, 1921, 1926, 1931, 1936, 1941, 1946, 1951.

Central African Territories: Geographical, Historical and Economic Survey (Cmd. 8234, 1951).

Chief Native Commissioner, Annual Reports of the (Salisbury, 1913–).

Clay, H. *Report on Industrial Relations in Southern Rhodesia* (Salisbury, C.S.R. 3–1930).

Closer Union of the Dependencies in Eastern and Central Africa, Report of the Commission on (the Hilton Young Report) (Cmd. 3234, 1929).

Coloured Community of Southern Rhodesia, Report of the Commission of Inquiry regarding the Social Welfare of the (Salisbury, 1946).

Development Co-ordinating Commission, First Interim Report of the Southern Rhodesian (Salisbury, 1948).

Development Co-ordinating Commission, Third Interim Report of the Southern Rhodesian (Salisbury, C.S.R. 10–1949).

Director of Native Administration, Salisbury Municipality, Annual Reports of (Salisbury, 1946–1953).

Disturbances in the Copperbelt, Northern Rhodesia, 1935, Report of the Commission Appointed to Inquire into the (Recommendations and Minutes of Evidence) (Lusaka, 1935).

Disturbances in the Copperbelt, Northern Rhodesia, 1940, Report of the Commission Appointed in Inquire into the (Lusaka, 1940).

East Africa Commission, Report of the (the Ormsby-Gore Report) (Cmd. 2387, 1925).

East Africa Royal Commission, 1953–55, Report of the (Cmd. 9475, 1955).

Emigrant Labour, Report of the Committee Appointed to Enquire into (Zomba, 500–7581, 1936).

Gwilliam, F. H. and Read, M. *Report on the Education of Women and Girls in Nyasaland* (Crown Agents, London, 1947).

Hammond, Brigadier-General F. D. *Report on the Railway System of Southern Rhodesia under the Railway Enquiry Act, 1924* (Salisbury, 1926).

Howman, R. *Report on African Local Government*, Parts I–VII (Salisbury, 1952–3).

Indians in Kenya (Cmd. 1922, 1923).

Jenkins, E. E. *Report of an Inquiry into the Causes of a Disturbance at Nkana on the 4th and 5th November, 1937* (Lusaka, 1937).

Land in the Nyasaland Protectorate, Report of a Commission to Enquire into and Report upon Certain Matters connected with the Occupation of (the Jackson Commission) (Zomba, 10582, 1921).

Land Commission, 1925, Report of the (the Morris Carter Report) (Salisbury, C.S.R. 3–1926).

Legislative Assembly Debates, Southern Rhodesia (Salisbury).

Legislative Council Debates, Northern Rhodesia (Lusaka).

McNamee, J. P. *Report on Native Urban Administration in Bulawayo* (Bulawayo, 1948).

Native Disturbances, Abridged Report of the Commission Appointed to Inquire into (Salisbury, 1948).

Native Education in all its Bearings in the Colony of Southern Rhodesia, Report of the Commission Appointed to Enquire into the Matter of (Salisbury, C.S.R. 20–1925).

Native Education Inquiry Commission, Report of the (Salisbury, C.S.R. 6–1952).

Native Policy in East Africa, Memorandum on (the Passfield Memorandum) (Cmd. 3573, 1930).

Native Policy in Northern Rhodesia, Correspondence with regard to (Cmd. 3731, 1930).

Native Production and Trade Commission, 1944, Report of the (Salisbury, C.S.R. 2–1945).

Native Reserves Commission in North Nyasa District, Report of the (Zomba, 1929).

Natural Resources of the Colony, Report of the Commission on the (Salisbury, C.S.R. 40–1939).

Northern Rhodesia: Order in Council Regarding Native Trust Land in Northern Rhodesia, 14 October 1947 (S.R. & O. 1947 No. 2214).

Nyasaland: Ordinance No. 15 (Natives on Private Estates) of 1928.

—— Ordinance No. 8 (Africans on Private Estates) of 1952.

Orde Browne, G. St. J. *Labour Conditions in Northern Rhodesia* (Col. No. 150, 1938).

Pim, Sir Alan. *Report of the Commission Appointed to Enquire into the Financial and Economic Position of Northern Rhodesia* (Col. No. 145, 1938).

Rhodesia and Nyasaland Royal Commission, *Report of the* (the Bledisloe Report) (Cmd. 5949, 1939).

Saffery, A. L. *A Report on Some Aspects of African Living Conditions on the Copper-belt of Northern Rhodesia* (Lusaka, 1943).

Smith, E. *A Report on the Direct Taxation of Natives in the Nyasaland Protectorate* (Crown Agents, London, 1937).

Tredgold, Sir Robert. *Report of the Commission to Investigate the Grievances which Gave Rise to the Strike amongst the African Employees of the Rhodesia Railways* (Salisbury, 1946).

What the Native Land Husbandry Act Means to the Rural African (Salisbury, 1955).

Wilcox, R. R. *Report on a Venereal Disease Survey of the African in Southern Rhodesia* (Salisbury, 1949).

B. Unofficial Publications

Batson, E. *The Poverty Line in Salisbury* (Cape Town, 1945).

Brookes, E. H. *Colour Problems of South Africa.* Phelps-Stokes Lectures, 1933 (London, 1934).

Davidson, J. W. *The Northern Rhodesian Legislative Council* (London, 1948).

Davis, J. Merle (ed.) *Modern Industry and the African* (London, 1933).

Epstein, A. L. *Politics in an Urban African Community* (Manchester, 1958).

Federation of Rhodesian Industries. *Survey of Rhodesian Industry. First Interim Report* (Salisbury, 1954).

Federation of Women's Institutes of Southern Rhodesia. *Report of the Standing Committee on Domestic Service* (Salisbury, 1930).

Gann, L. H. *The Birth of a Plural Society: the Development of Northern Rhodesia under the British South Africa Company, 1894–1914* (Manchester, 1958).

Gelfand, M. *Medicine and Magic of the Mashona* (Cape Town, 1956).

Gibbs, Peter. *Land-locked Island: a Commentary on Southern Rhodesia* (Bulawayo, 1947).

—— *Stronger than Armies* (Central News Agency, South Africa, 1951).

Grévisse, F. *Le Centre Extra-Coutumier d'Elisabethville* (Brussels, 1951).

Grimston, B. *Survey of Native Educational Development* (Salisbury, 1937).

Gussman, B. W. *African Life in an Urban Area.* 2 vols. (Bulawayo, 1952–3).

Hailey, Lord. *An African Survey: a Study of Problems Arising in Africa South of the Sahara.* Revised edition (London, 1956).

Hancock, W. K. *Survey of British Commonwealth Affairs,* vol. ii, part 2 (London, 1942).

Hellmann, E. *Rooiyard. A Sociological Survey of an Urban Native Slum Yard.* Rhodes–Livingstone Paper, No. 13 (Livingstone, 1948).

Hinden, Rita. *Common Sense and Colonial Development* (London, 1949).

—— *Plan for Africa* (London, 1941).

A A

Ibbotson, Percy. *Report on a Survey of Urban African conditions in Southern Rhodesia* (Bulawayo, 1943).

Jones, T. J. (ed.) *Education in Africa* (Phelps-Stokes Report) (New York, 1922).

—— *Education in East Africa* (Phelps-Stokes Report) (New York, 1924).

Lewin, J. *The Colour Bar in the Copper Belt* (Johannesburg, 1941).

Mnyanda, B. J. *In Search of Truth: a Commentary on Certain Aspects of Southern Rhodesia's Native Policy* (Bombay, 1954).

Murray, A. V. *The School in the Bush* (London, 1928).

Norman, L. S. *Nyasaland without Prejudice* (London, 1934).

Oliver, Roland. *Sir Harry Johnston and the Scramble for Africa* (London, 1957).

—— *The Missionary Factor in East Africa* (London, 1952).

Padmore, George. *Pan-Africanism or Communism: the Coming Struggle for Africa* (London, 1956).

Roux, E. *Time Longer Than Rope* (London, 1948).

Sachs, Wulf. *Black Hamlet: the Mind of an African Negro Revealed by Psycho-analysis* (London, 1937).

Smith, Edwin W. *The Way of the White Fields in Rhodesia* (London, 1928).

Smuts, J. C. *Africa and Some World Problems* (Oxford, 1930).

Southern Rhodesia and its Living Conditions (Salisbury, 1932).

Sundkler, B. *Bantu Prophets in South Africa* (London, 1948).

Tawse-Jollie, E. *The Real Rhodesia* (London, 1926).

Thompson, C. H. and Woodruff, H. W. *Economic Development in Rhodesia and Nyasaland* (London, 1954).

Village Education in Africa, a Report of the Inter-territorial 'Jeanes' Conference Held in Salisbury, Southern Rhodesia, on 27th May to 6th June 1935 (Lovedale, South Africa, 1936).

Wilson, Godfrey. *An Essay on the Economics of Detribalization in Northern Rhodesia.* Parts i and ii. Rhodes–Livingstone Paper, No. 5–6 (Livingstone, 1941–2).

Woodward, C. Vann. *The Strange Career of Jim Crow* (New York, 1955).

C. Articles

Gann, L. H. 'The Northern Rhodesian Copper Industry and the World of Copper: 1932–1952', *Rhodes–Livingstone Journal*, vol. xviii (1955).

Jennings, A. C. 'Land Apportionment in Southern Rhodesia', *Journal of Royal African Society*, vol. xxxiv (July 1935).

Laws, Robert. 'Native Education in Nyasaland', *Journal of Royal African Society*, vol. xxviii (1929).

Mokwile, J. S. 'Native Ideals', *Nada* (1924).

Moore, R. J. B. 'Native Wages and Standard of Living in Northern Rhodesia', *African Studies*, vol. i (1942).

Powdermaker, H. 'Social change through Imagery and Values of Teen-Age Africans in Northern Rhodesia', *American Anthropologist* (1956).

Spearpoint, F. 'The African Native and the Rhodesian Copper Mines', *Journal of Royal African Society*, vol. xxxvi (1937) (supplement).

'Report on Urban Conditions in Southern Rhodesia' (the Howman Committee Report), *African Studies*, vol. iv (1945).

Wilson, G. H. 'The Labour Problem in Nyasaland', *The East and the West*, vol. xix (1921).

Wilson, N. H. 'Native Political Movements in Southern Rhodesia', *Nada* (1923).

INDEX

*Printed in Great Britain
by Richard Clay and Company, Ltd.,
Bungay, Suffolk*